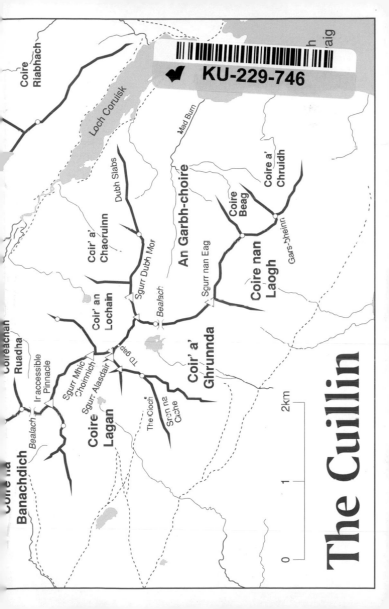

The Cuillin

Coire Riabhach

Loch Coruisk

Mad Burn

Coire a' Chruidh

Coir' a' Chaoruinn

Dubh Slabs

An Garbh-choire

Coire Beag

Sgurr Dubh Mor

Sgurr nan Eag

Coire nan Laogh

Gars-bheinn

Coir' an Lochain

Bealach

Coireachan Ruadha

Inaccessible Pinnacle

Bealach

TD gap

Sgurr Mhic Choinnich

Sgurr Alasdair

Coire Lagan

Coir' a' Ghrunnda

The Cioch

Sron na Ciche

Coire na Banachdich

0   1   2km

ed in Great Britain by the Scottish Mountaineering Trust,

ht © The Scottish Mountaineering Club

h Library Cataloguing in Publication Data
0 907521 55 X

alogue record of this book is available from the British Library

g diagrams by Mark Hudson
ial views by David Mason
dlife diagrams by Jean Thomas
er diagrams and maps by Colin Ballantyne, Douglas Benn and
Noel Williams
oduction by Scottish Mountaineering Trust (Publications) Ltd
peset by Noel Williams
inted by St Edmundsbury Press, Bury St Edmunds and
GNP Booth Ltd, Yoker, Glasgow
ound by Hunter and Foulis, Edinburgh

istributed by Cordee, 3a DeMontfort Street, Leicester LE1 7HD

Publish
2000
Copyri

Skye Scram

Noel Williams

Britis
ISBN

A ca

Walks, Scrambles and Easy C
on the Isle of Skye

SCOTTISH MOUNTAINEERING CLU

Contents

List of Illustrations

Uncredited illustrations by the author

List of Diagrams and Maps

Mountaineers and the Mountain Environment

With increasing numbers of walkers, scramblers and climbers going to the Scottish hills, it is important that all of us who do so should recognise our responsibilities to the mountain environment in which we find our pleasure and recreation, to our fellow mountaineers, and to those who live and work on the land.

The Scottish Mountaineering Club and Trust, who jointly produce this and other guidebooks, wish to impress on all who avail themselves of the information in these books that it is in everyone's interest that good relations are maintained between visitors and landowners, particularly when there might be conflicts of interest, for example during the stalking season. The description of a walking, scrambling, climbing, or skiing route in any of these books does not imply that a right of way exists, and it is the responsibility of all mountaineers to ascertain the position before setting out. In cases of doubt it is best to enquire locally.

During stalking and shooting seasons in particular, much harm can be done in deer forests and on grouse moors by people walking through them. Normally the deer stalking season is from 1st July to 20th October, when stag shooting ends. Hinds may continue to be culled until 15th February. The grouse shooting season is from 12th August until 10th December. These activities are important for the economy of many Highland estates. During these seasons, therefore, especial care should be taken to consult the local landowner, factor or keeper before taking to the hills.

Mountaineers are recommended to consult *Heading For The Scottish Hills*, which is published by the Scottish Mountaineering Trust on behalf of the Mountaineering Council of Scotland and the Scottish Landowners Federation. This book gives the names and addresses of factors and keepers who may be contacted for information regarding access to the hills.

It is important not to disturb sheep, particularly during the lambing season between March and May. Dogs should not be taken onto the hills at this time, and at all times should be kept under close control. Always try to follow a path or track through cultivated land and forests, and avoid causing damage to fences, dykes and gates by climbing over them carelessly. Do not leave litter anywhere, but take it down from the hill in your rucksack.

The number of walkers, scramblers and climbers on the hills is leading to increased, and in some cases very unsightly erosion of footpaths and hillsides. Some of the revenue from the sale of this and other SMC guidebooks is used by the Trust to assist financially the work being carried out to repair and maintain hill paths in Scotland. However, it is important for all of us to recognise our responsibility to minimise the erosive effect of our passage over the hills so that the enjoyment of future mountaineers shall not be spoiled by damage caused by ourselves.

As a general rule, where a path exists walkers should follow it and even where it is wet and muddy should avoid walking along its edges, the effect of which is to extend erosion sideways. Do not take short-cuts at the corners of zigzag paths. Remember that the worst effects of erosion are likely to be caused during or soon after prolonged wet weather when the ground is soft and waterlogged. A route on a stony or rocky hillside is likely to cause less erosion than on a grassy one at such times.

Although the use of bicycles can often be very helpful for reaching remote crags and hills, the erosion damage that can be caused by them when used 'off road' on soft footpaths and open hillsides is such that their use on such terrain must cause concern. It is the editorial policy of the Scottish Mountaineering Club that the use of bicycles in hill country may be recommended on hard tracks such as forest roads or private roads following rights of way, but it is not recommended on footpaths or open hillsides where the environmental damage that they cause may be considerable. Readers are asked to bear these points in mind, particularly when the ground is wet and soft after rain.

The proliferation of cairns on hills detracts from the feeling of wildness, and may be confusing rather than helpful as regards route-finding. The indiscriminate building of cairns on the hills is therefore to be discouraged.

Mountaineers are reminded that they should not drive along private estate roads without permission, and when parking their cars should avoid blocking access to private roads and land, and should avoid causing any hazard to other road users.

Almost all birds, their eggs and nests, are protected by the Wildlife and Countryside Act of 1981. Certain rarer or more endangered species are further protected by increased penalties under the 1981 Act, and must not be intentionally disturbed when nesting. These are referred to as Schedule 1 species. Where a species is of international importance, is a scarce breeder, is declining in breeding numbers, is restricted in distribution, is vulnerable or of special concern, it is further classified in the Red Data Books. Golden eagles, sea eagles, and peregrine falcons, for example, fall into both these categories.

Some of the crags described in this guide are the home of various birds of prey. They include species protected by Schedule 1 and Red Data Book classifications. Large fines are imposed on those convicted of deliberate disturbance. Many sensitive sites are monitored throughout the nesting season by Raptor Study Groups (licensed by Scottish Natural Heritage) to ensure they are not disturbed.

Eagles are particularly prone to disturbance, and where they are nesting an entire crag area should be avoided. The general period when nesting restrictions may apply are between 1st February and the end of July. Some species vary their nesting site from year to year, so restrictions may alter accordingly.

The Mountaineering Council of Scotland is the representative body for mountaineers in Scotland. One of its primary concerns is the continued free access to the hills and crags that we now enjoy. The MCofS urges mountaineers to contact them for advice and up to date information about bird restrictions, stalking and general access issues.

For more details and an information leaflet about bird nesting and access, contact the Mountaineering Council of Scotland at :

4a St Catherine's Road, Perth PH1 5SE.
Tel: 01738 638 227. Fax: 01738 442 950.

Finally, the Scottish Mountaineering Club and the Scottish Mountaineering Trust can accept no liability for damage to property nor for personal injury resulting from the use of their publications.

Acknowledgements

The scrambles and climbs described in this guide are largely the work of the pioneers who explored the Cuillin a century or more ago. Most of their exploits were originally chronicled in the climbing logbooks kept at the Sligachan Hotel, and in various club journals. Much of this information was collated by William Douglas in the first mountaineering guidebook to Skye, which was published as a special edition of the SMC Journal in 1907. A greatly enhanced version, *The Island of Skye*, edited by Steeple, Barlow et al, was produced as a separate guide in 1923.

Ashley Abraham published his *Rock Climbing in Skye* in 1908. This excellent book conveys well the excitement of this early phase of exploration. An important later work, *The Cuillin of Skye* by Ben Humble (1952), also gives a very readable account of early adventures in the Cuillin. It is impossible to read these works without admiring the energy and enthusiasm of the early explorers. They have left us a wonderful legacy of routes to enjoy.

However, many scrambles and easy climbs have been omitted, or only poorly described, in climbing guides since the 1950s. Consequently, the details of many worthwhile outings were in danger of being lost. This guide has built on the previous SMC scramblers' guide to Skye (*Black Cuillin Ridge*, Shirley Bull, 1980) by collating a more comprehensive list of scrambles, and including details of some lower grade rock climbs. In order to grade these outings with some degree of consistency, I have repeated them all in the last few years.

I am particularly grateful to George Archibald, Peter Duggan, Willie Jeffrey, George Sawicki, and Ken Scoular for their company on numerous routes. Steve Abbott, Donald Fraser, Simon Fraser, Pete Hunter, Iain Hyslop, Rob Milne, Gordon Rothero, and 'Beads' also accompanied me on some of the outings. Pete and Jean Thomas have willingly shared their extensive knowledge of the island with me and suggested several scrambles. Pete suggested the adjectival alternatives to the normal numerical system of grading scrambles.

Charles Rhodes made many helpful comments on the manuscript, and readily shared his great experience of, and enthusiasm for, the mountains of Skye. I am also very grateful to my colleagues at Kinlochleven High School for their banter and constructive criticism.

I thank Deidre and Willie Ingles for very kindly allowing me the use of their cottage in Torrin.

A number of people have made helpful comments and given photographic help – including Alex Gillespie, Steve Kennedy, Alan Kimber, Mike Lates, Andy Nisbet, Tim Taylor and Mark Tennant.

Anne Macdonald kindly made available to me the visitor books and logbooks kept by her family at the old Post Office in Glen Brittle. Mary Carmichael, of the Museum Service in Portree, allowed me access to a copy of the invaluable Sligachan Hotel climbing logbooks. The fascinating content and high standard of presentation of these early records makes them a joy to read.

I am hugely indebted to three talented artists who produced illustrations especially for this guide. Mark Hudson drew all the crag diagrams, Dave Mason worked meticulously on the aerial views, and Jean Thomas created the exquisite plant and animal diagrams. My only concern is that the reproduction process may not do justice to their fine work. Liz Grieve also gave me much assistance with designing the logos for the different types of outing.

I owe a special thanks to Gordon Rothero for writing the wildlife section, and for opening my eyes to the flora of the island. Colin Ballantyne and Douglas Benn supplied me with information on the geology of Skye, and generously allowed me to reproduce their diagrams. Brian Bell also helped confirm boundaries within the Cuillin gabbro. Nigel Anderson, Robin Campbell, Chris Robinson and Iain Rose helped with some historical details, and Alasdair Grant assisted with some Gaelic names.

The John Muir Trust deserves special praise for the work it has done to safeguard the magnificent mountains of Skye for future generations, and also for the sensitive way in which it tries to work with local interests. We should all support its efforts.

Thanks to David Pilling for superlative support with his desktop publishing software, Ovation Pro, and to RISCOS Ltd for continuing development of their operating system.

I thank Peter Duggan for correcting my proofs so conscientiously. Tom Prentice suggested a number of improvements and gave valuable support in the final stages of production. Last but not least, Donald Bennet is responsible for the concept of this guide. I thank him for scrutinising the manuscript and for making many helpful suggestions.

Noel Williams
March 2000

A' Chioch

Introduction

The Isle of Skye is arguably the finest of the many and varied islands lying off the western seaboard of Scotland. Second only to Lewis in size, Skye boasts the most rugged group of mountains in all the British Isles – the Cuillin. This compact massif has attracted the attention of mountaineers for well over a century. Its sharp peaks, narrow ridges, and ice-scoured corries are fashioned out of rough, bare gabbro – one of the finest of all rocks for scrambling and climbing on.

Two other spectacular but contrasting kinds of scenery are displayed by the granite intrusions of the Red Hills, and the basalt lavas of Duirinish and Trotternish. The coastline of Skye is scarcely less impressive. Its remarkably convoluted outline is many hundreds of kilometres long. The Gaelic name for the island, *An t-Eilean Sgitheanach*, means 'The Winged Isle', which refers to the shape of its major promontories. The coast is peppered with countless caves, arches, geos and stacks. There are long stretches of vertical cliffs, which in places reach several hundred metres in height.

The seaward vistas are especially varied too. Numerous smaller islands, such as Raasay, Scalpay, Soay, and Wiay, lie close in to Skye, whilst among the more distant ones, Rum, Eigg and the Outer Hebrides are conspicuous. The mountains of Wester Ross and Lochaber form a prominent backdrop on the mainland.

The landscape found in the southern part of the island, although geologically more complex, is perhaps less dramatic. However, an interesting type of landform occurs in Strath, where exposures of limestone are riddled with small caves.

This guide is concerned mainly with scrambling routes in the Cuillin. Only a selection of walks and lower grade climbs is included. The Cuillin main ridge offers the longest, and most continuously absorbing, scramble in the country, and this is fully described. However, there are all sorts of interesting outings in the flanking corries and on adjoining ridges. Indeed, the Cuillin can be regarded as a scrambler's paradise. The walks described from elsewhere on the island have been chosen to give a taste of the many delights to be found there. To explore all the corners of the island properly would take a lifetime.

Geology

The landforms of Skye are strongly influenced by geology. The jagged Cuillin peaks, the rounded Red Hills, and the plateau lavas in the north all owe their dramatic and distinctive forms to the different rocks from which they are built. Not surprisingly the island attracted geologists and scientists from early in the nineteenth century. MacCulloch, Forbes, Geikie and Harker are some of the famous names associated with the first phase of discovery. Subsequent researchers have continued to unravel the fascinating story behind the island's matchless scenery.

The rocks of Skye fall into three broad age categories. The oldest ones are more than 450 million years old (Precambrian and Lower Palaeozoic), and they are mainly confined to Sleat and the south-eastern part of the island. They include ancient Lewisian gneisses, Torridonian sandstones and shales, Moine schists, and Cambro–Ordovician quartzites and limestones. They have a very complex structure, because they were caught up in the Moine Thrust zone which developed on the north-western edge of the Caledonian Mountain Belt some 430 million years ago.

The only significant hills belonging to this group are formed from Torridonian rocks, and they occur at the eastern end of the island overlooking Kylerhea. One type of Cambrian quartzite is known as 'Pipe Rock', because it contains structures believed to be fossil worm burrows. Numerous small caves have developed in the overlying limestones and dolostones of Strath and Ord. These better drained rocks tend to produce grassy rather than heathery terrain. In the neighbourhood of later granite intrusions they have been thermally metamorphosed to marble. Various quarries have been worked in the Strath district over the last two centuries to exploit this rock as a decorative stone and for agricultural purposes.

There is a 200 million year gap in the geological record of Skye until rocks belonging to the Mesozoic Era are found. Only minor exposures of Triassic age occur, but the succeeding Jurassic sandstones, limestones and shales are more widespread. They outcrop in an arcuate strip south and west of Broadford as well as on the Strathaird peninsula, and again beneath the lavas in the northern part of the island. They can be seen easily at Elgol, for example, where limy sandstones have weathered to produce an unusual honeycombed surface. The limestones and shales are particularly rich in marine fossils, such as bivalves, brachiopods, ammonites, and belemnites. Other remains found include marine reptiles (ichthyosaurs and plesiosaurs), and the vertebra and leg bones of various dinosaurs. Fossil wood fragments and dinosaur footprints suggest the presence of a nearby landmass. There is a small museum at Ellishadder, near Kilt Rock, where many local artefacts and superb fossil specimens are exhibited. It is well worth a visit.

Tertiary Igneous Rocks

Any deposits laid down in Cretaceous times were largely removed by the period of uplift and erosion which took place at the close of the Mesozoic Era. This set the stage for the third and most spectacular episode in the geological history of Skye. At the beginning of Tertiary times, forces deep inside the earth were starting to split Greenland away from north-western Europe. Two 'plates' in the earth's crust began to move apart and create the North Atlantic Ocean. Some 60 million years ago, this resulted in great outpourings of basalt lava throughout the Inner Hebrides, as well as in Northern Ireland, Greenland, Iceland and the Faroes. The lavas of Skye and Raasay today outcrop over more than 1000 square kilometres, but geophysical surveys have shown that the same group of flows extends for a further 700 square kilometres on the sea floor beyond Canna. Before they were worn down by erosion, the lavas on Skye probably exceeded 1200m in thickness.

After an initial explosive phase, which produced deposits of volcanic ash, the lavas probably erupted fairly quietly from long, deep fissures. Individual flows are about 15m thick, although some can be double that. The upper and lowermost sections of a flow are slaggy, and more easily eroded. Amygdales are common in the upper slag. These are gas holes, which have been filled at a later date with various white minerals. Some of the intervals between flows were long enough for their upper surface to break down into red soil (laterite), and also for plants to grow. These **plateau lavas** now dominate the northern and western parts of Skye. They form distinctive flat-topped hills with stepped sides – excellent examples being MacLeod's Tables in Duirinish.

The magma not only erupted at the surface, but at a later stage also forced its way sideways, between the layers of Jurassic sediments underlying the lavas, to form thick sheets or **sills** of dolerite. Some of these sills developed strong columnar jointing when they cooled, as is seen clearly at Kilt Rock near Staffin. Indeed, the name Staffin means 'place of the upright pillars'.

A major magma chamber, some 12km across, developed within the base of the lava pile in the Cuillin area. Most of the magma had a similar composition to the basalt lavas but, because it cooled much more slowly, it crystallised into a much coarser-grained rock known as **gabbro**. It was intruded as a funnel-shaped mass in a series of stages. Included within the gabbro is a band of **peridotite**. The ultrabasic magma which produced this rock is thought to have originated from deep down in the earth's mantle, and it may have been the first to crystallise. It weathers to a produce a very rough, pitted surface with a most distinctive brown–orange colour. It outcrops from An Garbh-choire (*rough corrie*) to Coireachan Ruadha (*brown/red corries*) – both these localities getting their names from the characteristics of this rock.

Numerous minor intrusions were subsequently injected into the Cuillin pluton. Magma was forced into countless narrow, vertical fissures, and cooled to produce basalt and dolerite **dykes**. The trend of the main Skye dyke swarm is in a north-west to south-east direction. It extends beyond Skye to the Outer Hebrides in one direction, and to the Great Glen in the other. A smaller subswarm with a south-west to north-east trend has been identified in Glen Brittle. Dykes are usually softer than the gabbro, and tend to weather out into chimneys and gullies. Good examples include Willink's Gully on Bla Bheinn, and Waterpipe Gully on Sgurr an Fheadain.

Another kind of intrusion produced large horizontal and inclined **sheets** of tholeiite (a type of basalt which lacks olivine). These sheets occur notably on the western side of the Cuillin, and along sections of the main ridge from Sgurr Sgumain to Sgurr na Banachdich. In many places the sheets themselves were originally vesicular (i.e. full of gas holes), and the surrounding gabbro, into which they were injected, was broken up to form volcanic breccia.

The whole gabbro mass was also permeated by funnel-shaped intrusions of dolerite known as **cone-sheets**. These are generally less than one metre thick, and run parallel to the layered structures in the gabbro. The cone-sheets all dip towards a focal point below Meall Dearg. (They can be seen clearly on the south-west face of Sgurr an Fheadain in the colour plate between pages 130 and 131.)

The orientation of dykes and cone-sheets has an important influence on how easy it is to traverse along a ridge in the Cuillin. Where dykes cut across a ridge they tend to form deep gaps, such as on the Pinnacle Ridge of Sgurr nan Gillean. Some dykes, though, seem to be more resistant to erosion. Generally, only the later dykes,

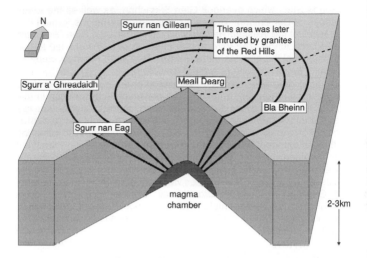

N

Sgurr nan Gillean

This area was later intruded by granites of the Red Hills

Sgurr a' Ghreadaidh

Meall Dearg

Bla Bheinn

Sgurr nan Eag

magma chamber

2-3km

The Cuillin Cone-sheets

which cut the cone-sheets, give rise to conspicuous gullies. Where dykes run parallel to the ridge they may form steep faces such as on the sides of the Inaccessible Pinnacle. Where cone-sheets dip in towards the ridge crest they weather to form convenient ledges, but where they dip away from the crest they form exposed slabs.

Both dykes and sheets, because they are fine-grained and usually well-jointed, tend to be rather brittle. They are also notoriously slippery when wet, so they generally have to be treated with much more care than the gabbro.

The Cuillin complex is also penetrated by a large number of pipe-like structures filled with a jumble of rock fragments of various types, ranging in size from fine dust particles to huge blocks. These structures are thought to represent **volcanic vents** from which a froth of lava and broken rocks was erupted. A good example of one of these pipes is exposed on the upper part of Sgurr nan Gillean.

A change in composition from basic to acidic magma signalled the next episode of igneous activity. It led to the formation of rocks loosely termed '**granites**'. The first granites comprise Meall Dearg, and

Ruadh Stac, which overlook Glen Sligachan, as well as the lower slopes of Bla Bheinn. The second group of intrusions formed the granites of the Western Red Hills, which lie between Glen Sligachan and Loch Ainort. The third and final group of intrusions led to the formation of the granites of the Eastern Red Hills, which are centred around Beinn na Caillich, west of Broadford.

These granite intrusions took place after the main phase of dyke injection had passed, and so dykes are much less common in the Red Hills. Where dykes do occur they tend to project slightly from the surface. Ring-dykes, composite sills and pyroclastic deposits complicate matters in some localities, but not sufficiently to influence the final rounded outlines of the Red Hills.

No further igneous activity took place in the remaining 50 million years or so of the Tertiary period. Instead, prolonged erosion deeply dissected the lavas. The granites were laid bare, though the summits of Glamaig and Beinn na Cro still have caps of the overlying lavas. The root of the Cuillin complex was also exposed. One more dramatic episode was still to provide the finishing touches to the scenery .

Glaciation

The earth has been completely free of ice for much of its history, but at widely spaced intervals it has experienced ice ages. The earth's climate began to cool midway through the Tertiary, and some 14 million years ago an ice sheet began to form on Antarctica. This was followed by the growth of the Greenland ice sheet some 3 million years ago. North America and northern Europe have experienced an oscillating pattern of glacial periods and rather shorter temperate interglacial periods for at least the last 0.75 million years. Water locked up in the ice during glacial periods caused sea levels to fall worldwide by up to 150m.

When glaciers were most extensive, Skye was probably overwhelmed by ice over 1600m thick. During the last glacial maximum, some 18,000 years ago, an ice dome centred on the Cuillin and Bla Bheinn deflected mainland ice to the north and south. Many peaks stood out as nunataks above the ice, including most of the crest of the Cuillin main ridge, Bla Bheinn, Glamaig, the Trotternish summits and Healabhal Bheag.

By 13,000 years ago glaciers had largely melted away throughout Scotland. Then a minor glacial episode, that lasted from 11,000 to 10,000 years ago, caused the regrowth of a large icefield over the centre of Skye, and the development of a dozen other ice masses on

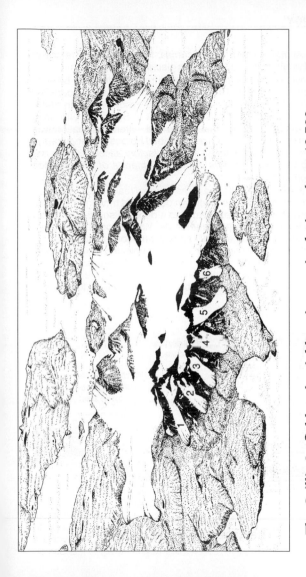

The Cuillin Icefield and neighbouring corrie glaciers about 10,500 years ago

1 Coire na Creiche
2 Coire a' Ghreadaidh

3 Coire na Banachdich
4 Coire Lagan

5 Coir' a' Ghrunnda
6 Coire nan Laogh

the island. All the western Cuillin corries, from Coire na Creiche to Coire nan Laogh, cultivated their own glaciers.

A very obvious terminal moraine dating from this time can be seen on the moor below Coir' a' Ghrunnda. This feature was first identified by the pioneering Scottish glaciologist Professor Forbes in 1845. (Forbes had made the first recorded ascent of Sgurr nan Gillean in 1836.) At that time, the idea that Britain had suffered glaciation was very contentious. Archibald Geikie described Forbes' observations in the Cuillin as *"the most detailed and satisfactory account which has yet been given of the proofs that the highlands of Britain once nourished groups of glaciers."*

Corries, arêtes and U-shaped glens are now readily recognised as being of glacial origin, as are extensive deposits of moraine. The floor of Loch Coruisk has been excavated to a depth of some 30m below present sea-level by the passage of ice. Where rocks have been scoured by ice they are generally smooth and sound. However, the peaks which remained above the ice were subjected to frost action, and hence are more broken. The upper limits of ice are marked by what are called periglacial trimlines. A superb example descends southwards from about 400m to about 250m on the west flank of Bla Bheinn.

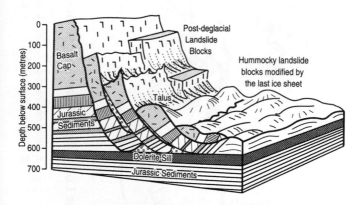

The Trotternish Landslides

Landslides

The most spectacular landslides in Britain are to be found in the northern part of Skye. All along the east side, and also around the northern end of the Trotternish escarpment there are major slipped rock masses. The two most famous areas are below The Storr and Quiraing. A subsidiary area of landslides on the south side of Glen Uig is known as the Fairy Glen.

The Trotternish escarpment is built of a thick sequence of westward dipping basalt lavas resting on relatively weak Jurassic sediments. The slides took place along curved surfaces, and as many as five successive blocks have been identified at Quiraing between the escarpment edge and the sea. In many cases the base of the slides corresponds with the presence of a dolerite sill within the Jurassic rocks. The landslides were probably initiated in Tertiary times, and the outer ones have certainly been modified by the passage of the last ice sheet over the area. The most recent ones, closest to the escarpment edge, are thought to have finished moving soon after deglaciation took place.

Melting glaciers caused sea-level to rise rapidly until some 6,000 years ago. This rise was countered by slow uplift of the land as it adjusted to the removal of ice. Postglacial raised beaches, up to 10m above present sea-level, are widespread around the coast of Skye.

Prehistory

Stone Age people started to move into northern latitudes soon after the last ice age ended some 10,000 years ago. The island of Skye has a wealth of archaeological remains, but they are poorly preserved compared with more famous examples found in Lewis, Orkney and Shetland. A **Mesolithic** (*Middle Stone Age*) shell midden recently discovered at An Corran near Staffin, and dated as 8,500 years old, is the earliest evidence of human presence in the Hebrides. These first visitors were hunter-gatherers, and they used simple implements made from antlers and stone, including pitchstone from Arran and the bloodstone of Rum. They used rudimentary boats such as dug-out canoes for some of their travels, which must have been exciting given west coast currents.

Some 6,000 years ago, **Neolithic** (*New Stone Age*) farming settlers started to travel north and introduce new skills. They sought out fertile islands, and settled in Islay, the Uists and most notably in Orkney. They reared cattle, sheep and goats, and also grew grain. No evidence of their dwellings have been found on Skye, but several stone tombs known as chambered cairns have been discovered. There is a good example of a chambered cairn at Rubh an Dunain, only a few kilometres from the camp site in Glen Brittle.

Only very poorly preserved standing stones and stone circles are found on Skye. Examples of these structures include a stone circle near Kilmarie, Strathaird, and standing stones at Borve, near Portree.

The remains of ornate pottery and stone coffins (cists), which are found in some of the chambered cairns, are assumed to have been inserted at a later date. They indicate that 'Beaker People', originally from the Rhine valley, had arrived on Skye about 2000BC. They had knowledge of metal working, and could smelt copper and tin to make **bronze**. The climate began to deteriorate from 1500BC onwards, and the colder and wetter conditions made arable farming less productive and caused peat to accumulate. The growth of peat may well have covered many of the early human remains.

During the last thousand years BC, communities began building stone fortifications to protect themselves and their livestock. This need may have arisen due to pressure from neighbours competing for land and resources, or more probably because of seaborne attacks from outsiders. A variety of structures were built, including hillforts, duns and brochs.

More than twenty **Iron Age** brochs have been identified on Skye. Most of them are badly ruined, but it is clear that at one time they must have been fairly substantial circular towers, shaped like the cooling towers in a modern power station. They had an internal diameter of some 10m, and walls about 4m thick with an internal staircase and gallery. The best example on the island, Dun Beag, is only a few minutes from the roadside near Struan, and is well worth a visit. Those travelling to Skye via the Kylerhea ferry need only make a short detour from Glenelg to examine two spectacular brochs in Gleann Beag. The larger of the two is over 10m high.

The term dun is used to describe a great variety of other structures. (Dun is the Gaelic word for 'broch', which is rather confusing.) Many of the duns were built on promontories overlooking the sea, such as at Rubh an Dunain. Interestingly, the brochs are found mainly in the north and west of Skye, whilst the promontory duns are found mainly in the south. The age of these structures is uncertain, though most of the Skye brochs are believed to date from 100BC to 100AD.

The Roman presence further south around 100AD may have reduced forays to the north, and a more peaceful period seems to have ensued. The brochs were abandoned and some of their stones re-used. Hut circles, which took the place of brochs, were mainly wooden structures built on a circular stone base. The souterrains associated with them are long, narrow stone-lined passages of uncertain purpose. They may have been used as underground shelters, or as communal food stores. The best preserved example on Skye is above the Allt na Cille about one kilometre north of Glasnakille, in Strathaird. *In Search of Prehistoric Skye*, by Ian Donaldson-Blyth, gives details of how to find this souterrain, and over forty other prehistoric sites on the island.

History

In the late third century AD, Roman writers referred to the people living north of Antonine's wall as the Pictae (*painted people*). Clach Ard, a stone slab with carved symbols, found at Tote, near Skeabost Bridge, is evidence of their presence on Skye. A finer example of a symbol stone occurs on nearby Raasay.

The Scots spread up the west coast of Scotland from Ireland around 500AD. They brought with them their Gaelic language, and the art of writing. Christianity spread to Skye a short time later. St Columba visited in 585AD, and other saints soon after. An early monastic site has been identified at Loch Chaluim Chille (now drained), near Kilmuir, in the north of Trotternish.

The relative peace of the next few centuries was shattered by the start of the Viking raids from Scandinavia. Although the Norse occupied Skye for more than four centuries, there is remarkably little tangible evidence remaining of their presence. The main signs of Norse influence that survive are the large number of Norse place names found on the island. The names of the major regions of the island – Minginish, Bracadale, Duirinish, Waternish, Trotternish, Sleat and Strath (or Strathordil) – are all of Norse origin, as are some 60% of the village or township names. The main hills were also named by the Norse. Healabhal and Storr, for example, are obviously of Norse origin, but Cuillin too is probably a derivation of the Norse word *kiolen* meaning high rocks.

Norse rule came to an end with the defeat of King Håkon of Norway in 1263 at the battle of Largs. The Sudreys (i.e. the Hebrides and the

Isle of Man) were ceded to Scotland by the treaty of Perth three years later. The clan system had evolved by the time Skye fell under the dominion of the Lord of the Isles. The inhabitants of Skye continued to regard themselves as separate from Scotland. Resistance to mainland rule continued through the fourteenth and fifteenth centuries, but feuding between clans also caused much strife. At the battle of Sligachan in 1395 a large invasion party trying to usurp the ruling MacLeods were cut to pieces. The spoils were divided at Creag an Fheannaidh (*rock of the flaying*), which some have identified as The Bloody Stone in Harta Corrie.

James IV, who came to the throne in 1488, was the last Scots king to speak Gaelic. He had some success in subduing the island chiefs, and in 1493 the Lordship of the Isles was finally forfeited to the Crown. However, clan warfare continued on Skye for another century, until a final battle in 1601. A party of MacDonalds, after raiding MacLeod properties in Bracadale and Minginish, had arranged to meet up with their spoil in Coire na Creiche (*corrie of plunder*) below the Cuillin. In the late afternoon they were set upon by a party of MacLeods, and the battle continued into the night. The MacDonalds eventually came out on top and captured the MacLeod leader and thirty of his followers. James VI, alarmed by their constant feuding, commanded the two clan chiefs to surrender themselves. They were made to settle their quarrels, by arbitration through the intermediary of other island chiefs, and the prisoners of the battle were released.

With the death of Elizabeth I in 1603, James VI of Scotland also became James I of England. He then made further efforts to tame the Western Isles. In 1609 the Hebridean Chiefs were summoned to Iona, and signed up to the Bond and Statutes of Icolmkill. The direct intention of these measures was to eradicate the Gaelic culture, and make the islanders conform more with the Lowland life-style. The importation of *aqua vitae* (whisky) was banned, eldest sons had to be sent to the Lowlands to learn English, and obedience to the reformed kirk was demanded.

Attempts to restore the Stuarts to the throne in the eighteenth century were to pose a further threat to the Gaelic way of life. Charles Edward Stuart (Bonnie Prince Charlie) landed on the Scottish mainland from France in 1745, and gained the support of sufficient Highland chiefs to launch a rebellion. His eventual defeat at Culloden the following year had great repercussions throughout the Highlands. Skye did not experience the harsh reprisals suffered elsewhere, because the MacLeods and MacDonalds of Skye had not supported the Jacobite cause. Raasay, however, was completely devastated by government forces. All property there was razed to the ground, and the livestock destroyed.

The Prince only escaped to France with his life after an extraordinary journey through Lochaber to the Outer Isles, and back again via Skye and Raasay. A young woman from South Uist, Flora MacDonald, was instrumental in the Prince's escape from the Outer Isles to Skye. Although she was captured soon after, and taken to London, she was released unharmed after a year's detention. By then she was something of a national celebrity.

As a consequence of the rebellion, Jacobite estates were forfeited, and the government banned the wearing of Highland garb, and the carrying of arms. The clan chiefs had their powers removed, and they became mere landlords. The Highlands and Islands, however, were an important source of manpower for the British army so, when the Seven Years War broke out in 1757, numerous Highland regiments were raised. By the end of the war the restrictions on dress were being relaxed, although it was a further two decades before they were repealed.

Highlanders had been emigrating to the Cape Fear district of North Carolina in small numbers since the 1730s. Some of the soldiers who fought in North America against the French now settled there too. Word spread back to Skye and, after a particularly harsh winter in 1771, hundreds of islanders tried to improve their lot by sailing off to the new world.

Flora MacDonald and her husband Allan, a local tacksman, were among those who followed in 1774, "... *as we cannot promise ourselves but poverty and oppression.*" These early emigrants had the resources to pay their own way and left voluntarily. Many of them became embroiled in the American War of Independence. Allan MacDonald and his sons fought as loyalists, and were captured and held prisoners by the colonists.

The population of Skye doubled in size between 1755 and 1831. This is remarkable considering the numbers that emigrated during that time, and also the repeated draining of men to the army. An important factor in this population explosion was the introduction of inoculation against smallpox, which was practised on Skye by the early 1760s. The preservation of life was further improved with the introduction of vaccination, which began on the island in 1800. The potato had been introduced shortly after 1750, and by 1770 it had become the staple diet of the people. The runrig system of allocating land to a different tenant every few years still prevailed. The trade in black cattle was lucrative throughout the second half of the eighteenth century, and some 4000 head a year followed the droving route from Skye to the southern markets.

During the Napoleonic wars there was a period of relative prosperity. Men found employment in soldiering, and, due to the disruption of imports, the kelp industry and cattle rearing thrived. Herring shoals were frequent visitors to the sea-lochs and fishing was successful. Land was divided into crofts, and the tenants could sub-divide their holdings among their relatives. Cottars held no land or grazing rights, but could live in cheap rented property.

After the peace of 1815 these various livelihoods went into sharp decline and great hardship ensued. The potato crop was ruined by blight in 1835. By 1837 half the people of Skye were destitute. In 1845 and during the three succeeding summers the blight returned and distress became even more acute. Landlords found their incomes falling, and sheep farms became an attractive alternative. It was found that the Cheviot breed of sheep could withstand the rigours of a Highland winter. The more fertile land was in great demand for sheep grazing, and people were moved onto the poorer ground. Several wealthy farmers from the mainland took possession of tacks on Skye. So began the clearances. Crofters were evicted from Duirinish, Trotternish, Bracadale, Minginish and Strath. In 1852 two whole communities were forcibly cleared from Boreraig and Suisnish, and their dwellings razed to the ground. This kind of brutality was perhaps exceptional, but it is estimated that 3500 were dispossessed of land and home on the whole island. The evicted were in some cases pushed onto poorer quality crofting areas near the shore, and great overcrowding took place. Multitudes had little alternative but to emigrate. Some idea of the heartbreak they suffered can be imagined from this contemporary account of a scene on board a ship as it sailed south with emigrants bound for Adelaide, Australia:

> *"The Collen (Cuillin) mountains were in sight for several hours of our passage; but when we rounded Ardnamurchan Point, the emigrants saw the sun for the last time glitter upon their splintered peaks, and one prolonged and dismal wail rose from all parts of the vessel; the fathers and mothers held up their infant children to take a last view of the mountains of their Fatherland which in a few minutes faded from their view forever."*

On the mainland genuine concern was shown for the starving and dispossessed people of the island. Schemes were devised to give employment in building roads, constructing piers and draining land. Much money was raised to assist emigration, and the bulk of the emigrants had their fares paid by the state, or by their landlords. Norman, Chief of MacLeod, was a notable philanthropist who, it is said, spent about £200 a week to alleviate the suffering. When he was warned of impending financial disaster, he said *"ruin must be faced rather than let the people die".*

Great hardship was suffered on the voyages to North America and Australia. Many died through sickness either at sea or during the early months after arrival at their destinations. Many vessels were shipwrecked with hundreds of lives lost.

The main wave of clearances had finished on Skye by the late 1870s but, when the economics of sheep farming deteriorated, landlords were squeezed to survive. Crofters then began to resist the poor treatment they received. Skyemen became leading agitators for reform in the 1880s. There were major disputes over grazing land, notably at Braes and Glendale, to which police, marines and gunboats from the mainland were called in. All this unrest resulted in the Napier Commission being set up to investigate the crofters'

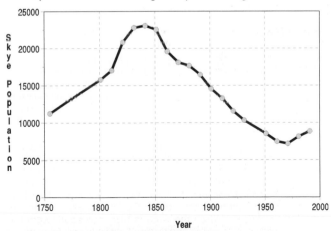

The changing population of Skye

grievances. One of the commissioners was Alexander Nicolson, the early Cuillin explorer. The resulting Crofters Act, which was passed in 1886, gave important rights to crofters: security of tenure, the right to pass on land to descendants, the right to compensation for improvements should land be sold, and a new body, the Crofters' Commission, able to fix fair rents. Despite this landmark victory, there were still grievances, and land raids took place as late as 1920.

The population of Skye continued to fall for most of the twentieth century. Two world wars took their toll, as the war memorials on the island starkly testify. The decline appears to have halted, however, and resident numbers may soon return to their level of 250 years ago. Land ownership is still a contentious issue, although crofters have been entitled to purchase their land since 1976, and a new and influential Scottish Crofters Union was formed in 1985. An important development took place in 1997 when Orbost farm estate was bought outright with public funds. The long term intention is to encourage resettlement and pass title to locally based community interests.

Tourism continues to play a big part in Skye's economy. The dramatic scenery and the superb opportunities for all aspects of mountaineering on the island are certain to remain big attractions for visitors.

Weather

The name 'Skye' is thought to be derived from the norse word *ski* meaning 'cloud' and *ey* meaning 'island'. The island is also known as *Eilean à Cheo* (Isle of Mist). These associations with cloudiness are probably related to the tendency for the high ground of the Cuillin to attract a capping of cloud, rather than implying that the island generally has a misty character. Indeed, the island has a better sunshine record than the neighbouring mainland.

Skye has a typical maritime climate, which means that its weather is greatly influenced by the sea. It has relatively mild, wet winters, whereas maximum temperatures in summer tend to be tempered by cool sea-breezes. Otherwise, Skye's weather is difficult to make simple rules about. It can vary dramatically from one end of the island to another. Even opposite ends of the Cuillin can experience very different conditions. When the wind is from the south-west the southern Cuillin can be enveloped by cloud, while the northern peaks bask in sunshine. Just the opposite can be the case when the wind is from the north. It often pays to have flexible plans. Pouring rain in the Cuillin can contrast with bright sunshine at Neist. It can be hailing in Portree when there are clear skies over Quiraing. A dreich morning can be followed by a brilliant afternoon. When only the highest peaks protrude above the clouds, a dull ascent can be rewarded with the sight of spectacular Brocken spectres. On the other hand, the whole island can be blasted by wind and rain, or, conversely, bathed in sunshine, for weeks on end.

The north has a general tendency to be drier than the south. Broadford, in the lee of the big hills, has about twice as much rainfall as Staffin in the north. In the summer, the eastern side of the island tends to be slightly warmer than the west coast.

When a long term view is taken, May seems to be the driest and sunniest month, with April and June not far behind. The main summer months of July and August are warmer, but wetter. This may not be true in any one year, and variations from the average are considerable. Sconser, which lies north-east of the Cuillin, had only 32mm of rain in December 1995, but it recorded 240mm of rain in May 1996. Only 93mm fell there in the following August, but a phenomenal 970mm of rain fell in February 1997, with a further 98mm falling in 24 hours on 1st March 1997. (Data collected at Sconser by Dr Hartley.)

Snow rarely lies long at sea-level, but in some years significant quantities can build up in the Cuillin corries, and persist until late spring. Remnant snow patches can sometimes be a welcome source of moisture on a traverse of the main ridge in early July. Cold spells of a week or more are unknown after March.

One of the early Cuillin pioneers, Charles Pilkington, had a very favourable impression of Skye weather in the 1880s:

> *"My personal experience of Skye weather is that it is the driest place in the British Isles, for I have been there three times, spending at least ten days on each occasion, and have only had four hours' rain in the three visits."*

Wildlife on Skye

The plants

This short account has been written with scramblers in mind and consequently it emphasises those plants which grow in the more rocky hills. However, on Skye, as throughout north-west Scotland, many plants that are normally associated with a mountain habitat are found right down to sea-level. Indeed, the plants that you can expect to see when walking and scrambling on Skye, particularly the more interesting ones, are often determined more by the geology than the altitude. The marked differences between the plant communities on the major hill groups are due largely to the varied nature of the underlying rocks, such as Torridonian sandstone above Kyleakin, gabbro in the Cuillin, or basalt in Trotternish. However, there are also some plants that are common over much of the island and these warrant a brief mention first.

It will probably not have escaped your notice that it rains a lot on Skye, and this excess of precipitation over thousands of years has led to the formation of extensive areas of peat, particularly on lower and flatter ground. The dominant plants growing on the peat may vary but the commonest species tend to be ubiquitous and will be familiar to most hill-goers. Heather (*Calluna vulgaris*), deer-grass (*Trichophorum cespitosum*), cotton grasses (*Eriophorum* species), cross-leaved heath (*Erica tetralix*), bell heather (*Erica cinerea*), purple moor grass (*Molinia caerulea*), bog myrtle (*Myrica gale*) and bog-mosses (*Sphagnum*) are more or less abundant everywhere on the peat. In the wettest areas the bog-mosses form large lawns and hummocks of green, ochre and red. Skye can even boast its own endemic species in *Sphagnum skyense* which is only known from Strath Suardal. A closer look at the bogs will reveal other plants of interest. These include all three British species of the insectiverous sundew family (*Drosera* species), the starry yellow flowers of bog asphodel (*Narthecium ossifragum*) and, in bog-pools, the three-lobed leaves and the pink flowerheads of the bogbean (*Menyanthes trifoliata*).

In the bogs and also in most areas of hill grassland the small, yellow four-petalled flower of the tormentil (*Potentilla erecta*) is common and enlivens the scene from early summer to late in the autumn. Another common plant on boggy ground, which can also be abundant in a number of other habitats, is devilsbit scabious (*Succisa*

A   Devilsbit Scabious
B   Mountain Everlasting
C   Mountain Avens

pratensis), a tall plant with dark green lanceolate leaves and a rounded head of small, blue-purple flowers. The heath spotted orchid (*Dactylorhiza maculata*) is also very common on the peatlands and damp grassland, its spikes of flowers varying in hue from white through pink to pale purple.

In drier grassland, thyme (*Thymus polytrichus*) is often so abundant that the distinctive aroma of its leaves accompanies each footstep. On better drained ground there are areas of heather moorland usually with abundant bell heather, but much of this has been converted over the years by burning and grazing into grassland with the common grasses being fescues (*Festuca* species) and bents (*Agrostis* species).

The richest woodland on Skye is in the Sleat peninsula. Over the poorest soils the dominant trees tend to be birch (*Betula pubescens*), oak (*Quercus petraea*) and rowan (*Sorbus aucuparia*) with scattered hollies (*Ilex aquifolium*). Alder (*Alnus glutinosus*) is generally common on the wetter soils. Over the richer soils, and particularly over the limestone at Ord and Tokavaig, hazel (*Corylus avellana*) can be abundant – often with ash trees (*Fraxinus excelsior*) and, more rarely, gean (*Prunus padus*).

The more interesting flowers occur on the limestone where spring produces an abundance of primroses (*Primula vulgaris*), wood anemone (*Anemone nemorosa*) and bluebells (*Hyacythoides non-scripta*) and, more locally, ramsons or wild garlic (*Allium ursinum*). Later in the season, flowers of meadow-sweet (*Filipendula ulmaria*), marsh hawksbeard (*Crepis paludosa*) and, on ledges, globeflower (*Trollius europaeus*) appear. Rarities here include herb paris (*Paris quadrifolia*) and long-leaved helleborine (*Cephalanthera longifolia*), a large, beautiful, white orchid.

The rocky nature of the woodland, in conjunction with the oceanic climate (wet cool winters and wet cool summers!) and freedom from pollution, has led to the development of beautiful carpets of mosses, lichens and liverworts on both rocks and trees. Not only are these plant communities very attractive to look at, but they are also extremely rare in global terms and some species are close to their northern-most limits in the world on Skye. More easily identifiable as separate plants are the flat fronds of the Tunbridge filmy-fern (*Hymenophyllum tunbrigense*) growing amongst the mosses, the most northerly colonies of this plant in Britain.

There are also large areas of limestone through Strath Suardal and down to Loch Slapin at Torrin. These are pleasant to wander over and have much botanical interest. Mountain avens (*Dryas octopetala*) is locally abundant, growing right down to sea level at Camas Malag, the large white flowers and neat, dark green leaves providing a wonderful display in early summer.

The grassland over the limestone is fertile and has an abundance of common flowers like thyme, fairy flax (*Linum catharticum*), bird's-foot trefoil (*Lotus corniculatus*), selfheal (*Prunella vulgaris*) and devilsbit scabious and some less common plants like northern bedstraw (*Galium boreale*), grass of Parnassus (*Parnassia palustris*), alpine bistort (*Persicaria vivipara*), field gentian (*Gentianella campestris*) and twayblade (*Listera ovata*).

In the crevices of the limestone, protected from grazing, there are many ferns and flowers like primrose, sanicle (*Sanicula europaea*), wild angelica (*Angelica sylvestris*), enchanter's nightshade (*Circaea* species) and rarer plants like herb paris and the beautiful dark red helleborine (*Epipactis atrorubens*).

The Red Hills are built of granite and have rounded, exposed ridges but also crags and areas of block scree. These hills are not botanically rich but they do support a few of the more common montane species. In rocky places the dominant plant is often the conspicuous woolly hair-moss (*Racomitrium lanuginosum*), growing with stiff sedge (*Carex bigelowii*), blaeberry (*Vaccinium myrtillus*), least willow (*Salix herbacea*) and mountain everlasting (*Antennaria dioica*). Other frequent species include heath bedstraw (*Galium saxatile*), common in all hill grassland, alpine lady's mantle (*Alchemilla alpina*), crowberry (*Empetrum* species) and, more rarely, alpine cudweed (*Gnaphalium supinum*). On the wind-blasted ridges and bealachs there are prostrate plants of juniper (*Juniperus communis alpina*) growing with other low shrubs in an attractive, open vegetation. The faces of the larger boulders in the screes are a good place to look for Wilson's filmy-fern (*Hymenophyllum wilsonii*) and, where mounds of bog-moss occur under the heather, the lesser twayblade (*Listera cordata*), a tiny orchid, can be abundant.

Scrambles in the Cuillin form a major part of this guide but climbing and plants often do not mix, and the vast expanses of bare rock which are such a feature of the Cuillin bear witness to this. The gabbro which delights climbers is a very solid rock, slow to weather and produce the soil that plants need; it is also a basic rock and the minerals that it does release into the soil are not to the liking of all plants. One plant that thrives in these conditions is the northern rockcress (*Arabis petraea*), an uncommon arctic-alpine plant that is more abundant in the Cuillin than anywhere else in Britain. Its purple-tinged white flowers and its wild habitat more than make up for its rather close resemblance to certain garden weeds. A close relative and even more rare, is the alpine rockcress (*Arabis alpina*), common in the Alps but having its only British site in the recesses of the Cuillin corries. It was first reported by H.C. Hart, the Irish mountaineer and botanist, in 1887.

The ledges on crags in corries are more productive than exposed ridges and slabs but even relatively sheltered ledges may have little more than woolly hair-moss, crowberry, alpine lady's mantle and goldenrod (*Solidago virgaurea*). Alpine lady's mantle can be abundant – its deeply divided leaves with their silvery lower surface being unmistakable. The spikes of yellow flowers of goldenrod here seem larger and more attractive than the lowland plant.

Broken crags with damp ledges, and the wet areas at the base of larger crags are more interesting; here you can find plants like starry saxifrage (*Saxifraga stellaris*), roseroot (*Sedum rosea*), stone bramble (*Rubus saxatilis*), mountain sorrel (*Oxyria digyna*), moss campion (*Silene acaulis*) and, more rarely, alpine sawwort (*Saussurea alpina*), arctic mouse-ear (*Cerastium arcticum*) and purple saxifrage (*Saxifraga oppositifolia*). More sheltered sites can also harbour a few small trees, usually rowans, sometimes growing at an altitude of over 600m.

Glen Sligachan has numerous dubh-lochans and mire areas where the pale-green, spiky rosettes of the pipewort (*Eriocaulon aquaticum*) form large mats on the bottom of the pools. Some of these rosettes produce very long flower-stems with a head of small blue flowers. The pipewort is an American plant with its only European sites in Skye, Ardnamurchan, Coll and similar oceanic areas of western Ireland. Bogbean often grows with the pipewort while lochs with a stony floor usually have the slender flower-stems and pale blue flower of the water lobelia (*Lobelia dortmanna*).

Wet, stony areas with black bog rush (*Schoenus nigricans*) often contain both the common butterwort (*Pinguicula vulgaris*), with its star-shaped rosette of yellow-green leaves and violet flowers, and the smaller, pale butterwort (*Pinguicula lusitanica*) which has lilac flowers. Both species supplement their nutrient uptake by trapping insects in the sticky mucous that covers their leaves.

The richest sites on Skye for mountain plants are the basalt crags and corries of the Trotternish ridge from The Storr in the south to Quiraing in the north. Almost all of the plants of the Cuillin occur here,

D Dark Red Helleborine
E Northern Rockcress
F Stone Bramble

and usually in greater abundance. The Storr is perhaps the best known site, but Quiraing and the area above Loch Cuithir are also very rich. The lush vegetation on the ledges is richer than that in the Cuillin, and in the grassland there are cushions of moss campion, covered in pink flowers in early summer and, in a few places, creeping stems of sibbaldia (*Sibbaldia procumbens*). Mossy cyphel (*Minuartia sedoides*) resembles moss campion but the cyphel produces rather dull, greenish flowers that are easily overlooked. Where there is less competition from larger plants, mountain sorrel, purple and mossy saxifrages (*Saxifraga hypnoides*), northern rockcress, hoary whitlow-grass (*Draba incana*) and moonwort (*Botrychium lunaria*) can all be locally abundant. In a few places there are scattered plants of alpine saxifrage (*Saxifraga nivalis*) with its tight cluster of dull white flowers, and also tiny mats of alpine pearlwort (*Sagina saginoides*). The plateau area of the Trotternish ridge and its associated stony springs has a special plant in the Iceland purslane (*Koenigia islandica*), the only other British site for this arctic species being in similar terrain on the island of Mull.

A number of plants find the habitat they need both on the mountains and on the coast. Common seashore plants that also occur in the hills are scurvy grass (*Cochlearia* species), kidney vetch (*Anthyllis vulneraria*), sea plantain (*Plantago maritima*), sea campion (*Silene unicolor*) and thrift (*Armeria maritima*). The latter forms carpets of pink on rocky shores and coastal grassland in early summer but looks equally at home growing in mats of woolly hair-moss on a windswept summit at 900m. Similarly, mountain plants like roseroot, purple saxifrage and moss campion also occur on ledges of the less exposed sea cliffs.

Lower down where the influence of salt spray is greater the common plants are thrift, sea plantain, English stonecrop (*Sedum anglicum*) and more occasionally sea campion. Where sea-birds nest and there is an accumulation of 'organic material' there can be large stands of red campion (*Silene dioica*) and stinging nettle (*Urtica dioica*). One northern plant that is common on some rocky coasts is Scottish lovage (*Ligusticum scoticum*), a large 'umbellifer' with an attractive shiny foliage. At the heads of some of the sea-lochs there are areas of salt-marsh with sea aster (*Aster tripolium*) and frequent large stands of yellow iris (*Iris pseudacorus*).

G   Alpine Sawwort
H   Moss Campion
I   Purple Saxifrage
J   Pipewort

The animals

In the nature of things, climbers, scramblers and, to a lesser extent, hill-walkers tend to visit those exposed and least productive areas that most animals tend to avoid. In the mountains on Skye, once embarked upon a walk or climb, most of the larger wildlife seen is likely to be airborne unless one is lucky (and quiet) enough to stumble across a fox. One animal is an unfortunate exception to this rule. Most visitors to Skye in the summer months are aware of the misery that the teeming midge can cause in damp, still weather (and in many other sorts of weather too), but otherwise perfect days can also be marred by biting clegs, particularly on the lower ground.

In common with most islands, Skye is poorer in most mammals than the adjacent mainland. Though there have been records in the past, relatively common animals on the mainland like badger, squirrel and wildcat are not now thought to occur on Skye. Other species have been introduced, largely during the 19th century, with mixed results. Rabbits have spread throughout the island wherever suitable habitat occurs, and the hedgehog is now sparsely spread over the island. The mountain hare is another introduction that apparently did well at first but now seems to be restricted to Raasay and the Cuillin.

The lowland brown hare is a native species on Skye but it has a very patchy distribution which is probably linked to the pattern of cultivation. Of the smaller mammals, the most frequently seen by the hill-walker is the short-tailed vole which is found everywhere except on some of the islands, and can be particularly abundant in new forestry plantations. The field mouse is limited to the richer, wooded areas and to the better crofting land, and is a frequent visitor to houses in the winter months. The bank vole is limited to the islands of Raasay and Scalpay where it has been isolated long enough to have evolved as a distinct race, being slightly larger and darker than those on the mainland.

Our two native species of deer occur on the island but again populations are much smaller than on the mainland. The roe deer is a shy and quiet animal of woodland and is thus difficult to see but it is present in much of Sleat, in Glen Varragill between Sligachan and Portree, and is reported from Raasay. Much of the red deer population is again in Sleat, close to the mainland, but smaller herds occur further north and numbers are apparently increasing. Some can even be seen in the quieter Cuillin corries such as Coire nan Laogh and Harta Corrie.

Of the predatory mammals on Skye, the stoat and weasel are present in small numbers with perhaps the stoat, larger and with a black tip to the tail, being the more numerous of the two. The most successful predator without doubt is the fox, which is present in greater or lesser numbers all over Skye but is apparently absent from Raasay. The efforts of crofters and keepers to control the numbers of foxes have been thwarted, probably by the abundance of both carrion for food, and of rough and rocky terrain for cover.

One mammal with a Skye population density probably exceeding that of the adjacent mainland is the otter. Otters, or otter signs such as spraints, have been seen over the whole of the island but virtually all sightings are coastal. Recent surveys suggest that the first glimpse a climber is likely to have of an otter is as a casualty on the faster stretches of road between Kyleakin and Luib where currently eight a year are found dead. This rate of mortality, albeit regrettable, presumably reflects a very healthy total population. The Vincent Wildlife Trust in conjunction with Forest Enterprise run a popular otter-viewing hide near Kylerhea.

The coastal waters around Skye offer the possibility of seeing a number of other mammals. Seals are the most conspicuous, both swimming and in haul-out colonies. They can be seen round most of the Skye coast with the common seal being much more numerous than the Atlantic grey seal. Harbour porpoises are fairly common around the coast, and other species which can be seen include white-beaked and Risso's dolphins, minke whales and the basking shark, the latter particularly off the Elgol coast. A pair of bottlenosed whales aroused great interest when they spent several weeks in Broadford Bay in the summer of 1998. You are much more likely to see all these species, and possibly killer whales too, from a boat when sailing around the island.

The birds with which climbers become most involved tend to be those that are interested in the remains of your lunch. It is remarkable how quickly a herring gull appears once the sandwiches are in evidence, but other birds like hooded crows and even the magnificent raven are all attracted to favourite lunch spots. Golden eagles are more stand-offish but Skye does have a good population and, though they may be difficult to see in the more popular mountain areas, visits to the less frequented parts of the hills and coast can often result in a sighting. The re-introduction of the sea-eagle on Rum has meant that sightings on Skye are now quite frequent. Buzzards – the tourist's eagle – are much more common, and there will be few days when these adaptable birds are not seen or heard, particularly on lower ground. The peregrine has undergone a steady recovery in Scotland in recent years and, though still rare on Skye, its noisy alarm call may accompany a walk past a big crag or coastal cliff.

The meadow pipit is ubiquitous in grassland on the hills and its descending trill and 'parachuting' flight are redolent of fine days in the early summer. The wheatear is also common on open stony ground, the white flash of its rump and the distinctive call, like stones being knocked together, attracting attention. Other less common birds include the ptarmigan and ring ouzel, the former preferring open ridges and boulder fields, and the latter bouldery and craggy ground in the more sheltered corries. The wild call and 'head down' flight advertises the presence of nesting pairs of red-throated divers on a number of the more remote dubh lochans.

The remarkable sea-bird colonies of the islands out in the Minch are largely absent from Skye. However, out to sea from the larger headlands, rafts of guillemots, razorbills, puffins and shearwaters can sometimes be seen, going to and from the huge colonies on the Shiants and other islands. Black guillemots nest all around the coast, particularly the more remote north and west, but nesting guillemots and razorbills are limited to a few sites in the north, often accompanied by fulmars and kittiwakes. Herring gulls are common round most of the coast and common gulls, lesser and greater black-backed gulls also have scattered breeding colonies. Flotillas of eider duck are a common sight off most of the coasts and noisy oystercatchers attract attention on the flatter coasts and offshore skerries, but the large flocks of wading birds, characteristic of the Scottish east coast, are absent from Skye.

Mountaineering History

Legend has it that the remains of a Norse princess are buried beneath the massive cairn on the summit of Beinn na Caillich above Broadford. If true this must be one of the most impressive early mountaineering feats on the island.

Some of the clan battles are reputed to have been fought at the base of the Cuillin, the last one being in Coire na Creiche in 1601. It is probable that clansmen or shepherds visited many of the Cuillin corries, but it is unlikely that they ventured onto any of the major summits of such a barren range.

The Romantics

1746 Bonnie Prince Charlie and his cohort, Captain Malcolm, walked at night from Portree to Elgol. They skirted to the west of Sligachan to avoid government troops, and probably passed through the hills to the east of Marsco, down to Loch Ainort and along Srath Mor. This was a distance of well over 40km, and they both fell into deep bogs on the way. The Prince then took a boat back to the mainland, and from there eventually sailed for France.

1772 Thomas Pennant ascended Beinn na Caillich above Broadford, and described the prospect to the west as *"that of desolation itself; a savage series of rude mountains, discoloured, black and red, as if by the rage of fire"*.

1772 Samuel Johnson and James Boswell visited Skye on their tour of the Hebrides. Boswell described the Cuillin as *"a prodigious range of mountains, capped with rocky pinnacles in a strange variety of shapes"*. Boswell ascended Preshal More above Talisker with Donald Maclean, the young Laird of Coll.

1814 Sir Walter Scott visited Loch Coruisk (after the geologist MacCulloch had described it to him in awesome terms). The following year he published *The Lord of the Isles*:

> *For rarely human eye has known*
> *A scene so stern as that dread lake*
> *With its dark ledge of barren stone*

1816 After several years work, Dr John MacCulloch produced the first geological map of Skye. He did so without managing to reach any Cuillin summits, although he walked round Loch Coruisk and climbed part way up Sgurr na Stri.

1819 William Daniell published dramatic sketches of the Cuillin.

1831 Turner painted Loch Coruisk to illustrate Scott's poems. He nearly came to grief when he slipped trying to find a good location for his composition.

The Forester, the Scientist and his Barometer

1835 The Reverend Lesingham Smith and local forester Duncan MacIntyre visited Coruisk and returned to Sligachan by crossing the Druim nan Ramh ridge into Harta Corrie. This is the first recorded scramble in the Cuillin.

1836 Duncan MacIntyre had tried repeatedly to ascend Sgurr nan Gillean, but without success. He was then engaged by Professor James Forbes, and together they made the first ascent of the mountain by its south-east ridge. Forbes noted, *"the extreme roughness of the rocks rendering the ascent safe, where with any other formation, it might have been considerably perilous. Indeed, I have never seen a rock so adapted for clambering."*

1841 Lord Cockburn visited Coruisk. He learnt that a local fisherman had been washed away and drowned three days before, in trying to cross the Scavaig River when it was in flood.

1845 Forbes ascended Bruach na Frithe along with MacIntyre and a barometer. Then they descended into Lota Corrie and climbed to the summit of Sgurr nan Gillean by its west ridge, presumably gained from its steep southern flank. Forbes used his barometer to calculate the heights of the two peaks.

Forbes intersected the Cuillin in several directions. He also circumnavigated the range with Necker, a Swiss geologist, and found convincing evidence of glaciation.

1846 Forbes published his observations on glacial phenomena in the Cuillin, together with the first good sketch map of the range.

1857 The first recorded ascent, if not the actual first ascent, of Bla Bheinn was made by Professor John Nicol and the poet Algeron Swinburne from the Loch Slapin side.

1859 Captain Wood, a surveyor for the Admiralty, was working on a chart of the coastline of Skye using triangulation methods. He mapped the southern Cuillin peaks, and identified a 3212 feet high inaccessible peak. Charles Weld, an Alpine Club member, spoke with Wood, and also ascended Sgurr na Stri. Weld later wrote a rapturous description of the Cuillin peaks which included a mention of the unclimbed Inaccessible Pinnacle. *"Surely some bold member of the* *club will scale this Skye peak ere long and tell us that it is but a stroll before breakfast."* He did not try it himself.

The Sheriff and his Plaid

1865 Alexander Nicolson started his exploratory campaign among the Cuillin at the age of 38. He was a Skyeman, born at Husabost, and later became sheriff-substitute of Kirkcudbright. With the gamekeeper at Sligachan, Duncan MacIntyre's son, he ascended Sgurr nan Gillean, and then made the first descent of the west ridge by Nicolson's Chimney. They continued below Am Basteir and ascended Bruach na Frithe.

1866 John Mackenzie began his long and distinguished Cuillin career by ascending Sgurr nan Gillean at the age of 10. He went on to become a mountain guide, and spent more than 50 years climbing in the Cuillin, most notably with Norman Collie.

1870 Newton Tribe and John Mackenzie made the first recorded ascent of Sgurr a' Ghreadaidh. It was ascended by Professor Heddle the following year.

In September a fatality took place on Sgurr nan Gillean. A scrambler continued when his companion turned back. He left his name in a bottle at the summit, but slipped and died on the descent.

1873 Professor Knight managed to bribe a local guide, Angus Macpherson, to descend from the summit of Sgurr nan Gillean with him, and make the first ascent of Knight's Peak. (This was originally known as *Needle Rock*, but Alexander Nicolson also called it the *Little Horn*.) They returned the same way.

Alexander Nicolson and Angus Macrae, a local shepherd, ascended Sgurr na Banachdich and Sgurr Dearg. They then skirted below the Inaccessible Pinnacle *("it might be possible with ropes and grappling irons to overcome it, but the achievement seems hardly worth the trouble")*, before descending into Coire Lagan and making the first ascent of Skye's highest summit via the Great Stone Shoot. Nicolson suggested that the peak be called *Scur-a-Laghain*. It was later named Sgurr Alasdair in his honour.

The Willink brothers traversed Bla Bheinn from east to west by its two very prominent gullies. They baulked at a drop part-way down the western gully, and traversed hard right to reach an easier scree gully on the north-western end of the mountain.

1874 Nicolson made his most audacious ascent *("... the hardest adventure I have had among these hills")*. He walked with a friend from Sligachan to Coruisk, and at four in the afternoon they set off up An Garbh-choire. After sheltering from a shower of rain, they reached the summit of Sgurr Dubh Mor at 7pm. They then descended to Coir' an Lochain in the gathering gloom. From eight to half-past ten they descended in almost total darkness.

"About half-way down we came to a place where the invaluable plaid came into use. My companion, being the lighter man, stood above with his heels set in the rock, holding the plaid, by which I let myself down the chasm. Having got footing, I rested my back against the rock, down which my lighter friend let himself slide till he rested on my shoulders. This little piece of gymnastics we had to practise several times before we got to the bottom of the glen above Coruisk."

The floor of Coir'-uisg was bathed in moonlight. They then tried to find a way over Druim nan Ramh, but had to retreat right back down to Loch Coruisk. They eventually escaped over Druim Hain and reached Sligachan at 3am.

1879 Nicolson made his final contribution (aged 52) – the first ascent of his own chimney on Sgurr nan Gillean – along with the Reverend Black, David Hepburn, and Angus Macpherson as guide. Hepburn described their technique:

"We had with us a strong staff about six feet in length and a long highland plaid. The chimney when arrived at gave rise to a long consultation, but eventually we decided to attack it. By means of the crook the plaid was hitched over an overhanging point, and after considerable difficulty Angus Macpherson succeeded in drawing himself up, and reported that an advance was feasible. By means of the plaid, firmly gripped by Angus, we remaining three scaled the Chimney one by one and without much further trouble reached the summit." Nicolson found *"the rockwork a good deal abraded and softened since 1865".*

The Pilkingtons, the Alpine Club and the Rope

1880 William Naismith paid his first visit to Skye. He made the first ascent of the north top of Bidein Druim nan Ramh, although, because the map of the time was inaccurate, he thought he had ascended Sgurr a' Mhadaidh.

Charles and Lawrence Pilkington, members of the famous Lancashire glass-making family, paid their epoch-making visit to Skye. They were among the foremost mountaineers of their day. The Pinnacle Ridge of Sgurr nan Gillean repulsed them, but they reached the summit via the west ridge the next day. They then made the first ascent of the Inaccessible Pinnacle by its east ridge, having approached it from Sligachan via Coruisk and Bealach Coire na Banachdich. They had to throw down a lot of loose rock as they climbed. *"The noise was appalling; the very rock of the pinnacle itself seemed to vibrate with indignation at our rude onslaught."*

The ascent was watched by John Mackenzie, who had guided the Pilkingtons to the foot of the climb.

1881 A local shepherd (almost certainly John Mackenzie) made the second ascent of the Inaccessible Pinnacle after taking off his shoes.

1883 Lawrence Pilkington returned to Skye, and had rather poor weather, although he did manage to climb the central and highest peak of Bidein Druim nan Ramh with Eustace Hulton and Horace Walker. He also re-climbed the east ridge of the Inaccessible Pinnacle in very different circumstances. *"Not a single loose rock on the ridge; ... The cloud stretched away and away all round us, a silver sea with the tops only of the highest peaks standing out like black, rocky islands. No sound!"*

1885 The Ordnance Survey produced the first one-inch map to the Cuillin. However, the surveyors had not visited many summits, and it soon became apparent that the map had many shortcomings.

1886 W.P. Haskett Smith climbed up and down the Inaccessible Pinnacle by its east ridge in twelve minutes, which included a two minute rest on top. This was the same year that he made the first ascent of Napes Needle in the Lake District.

Stocker and Parker made the first ascent of the shorter, but steeper, western end of the Inaccessible Pinnacle. They then descended the east ridge to complete the first traverse of the peak. John Mackenzie repeated this feat shortly after with R.C. Broomfield.

Norman Collie visited Skye for the first time, and was inspired by watching Stocker and Parker make a first ascent on Knight's Peak from Coir' a' Bhasteir. He telegraphed for a rope, and then made unsuccessful attempts to climb the West and Pinnacle Ridges of Sgurr nan Gillean with his brother. After consulting John Mackenzie, he managed to follow the normal south-east ridge to the summit.

1887 Charles Pilkington returned to Skye with Horace Walker and James Heelis. They employed John Mackenzie and were blessed by excellent weather. Several first ascents were among their list of outings. Charles led the way up the north-east summit of Sgurr Alasdair by a gully leading off from the Great Stone Shoot. This peak was later named Sgurr Thearlaich *(Charles' Peak)* in his honour. The party finished off by traversing Sgurr Alasdair and Sgurr Sgumain.

The next day they traversed the Inaccessible Pinnacle before making the first ascent of a 'nameless peak' by its long north-west ridge. This peak was called Sgurr Mhic Choinnich *(Mackenzie's Peak)* after John Mackenzie.

Members of Pilkington's party were also the first to tread the summit of Clach Glas. They started their ascent by a gully on the west face. High up near the summit they discovered – to their surprise – that what appeared to be a knife edge of tremendous steepness was in fact the edge of a relatively straightforward slab. This feature has since become known as the Impostor.

To round off an impressive effort they added the first ascent of Sgurr na h-Uamha to their tally. This ascent had been suggested to them by Alfred Williams, an artist who based himself at Coruisk in the summer months. They found a way to the top by a slanting break in the rocks on the north-east face.

Later the same season John Mackenzie made some lengthy traverses with a very capable climber called H.C. Hart from Dublin. At no time did they use a rope. One outing started up Sgurr nan Gillean and continued by way of Am Basteir, Bruach na Frithe, Bidein Druim nan Ramh and Sgurr a' Mhadaidh to Sgurr a' Ghreadaidh.

Their finest effort took them from Sgurr na Banachdich, over the Inaccessible Pinnacle, Sgurr Mhic Choinnich, Sgurr Thearlaich and Sgurr Alasdair. Mackenzie's boots were unsuitable for climbing and Hart had to give him a leg-up on the Inaccessible Pinnacle. They retraced their steps from the summit of Sgurr Mhic Choinnich and reached Bealach Mhic Choinnich by traversing the western flank along a line which is commonly referred to as Collie's Ledge. It should more properly be known as Hart's Ledge.

Collie, Mackenzie and the SMC

1888 Collie teamed up with Mackenzie, and so began an extraordinary partnership. Their final outing of the year together proved to be one of the hardest of Collie's mountaineering career. They started from Sligachan and reached Bealach na Glaic Moire from Coire na Creiche. They then followed the ridge all the way from Sgurr a' Mhadaidh to the Inaccessible Pinnacle. A very strong wind made things difficult, but John took off his boots and led the steep western end. Collie admitted that he went up on the rope.

They continued to Sgurr Mhic Choinnich, and used Hart's route from the summit to reach Bealach Mhic Choinnich. They crossed Sgurr Thearlaich, but had to retreat from the Thearlaich–Dubh Gap.

So to continue their traverse they descended the south-west ridge of Sgurr Alasdair and contoured beneath the summit rocks to Bealach Coir' an Lochain. From there they descended by Coir' an Lochain to Coir'-uisg. They went up and over Druim nan Ramh to reach Harta Corrie, and eventually returned to the Sligachan Hotel at midnight.

1889 After Naismith published a letter in the Glasgow Herald at the beginning of the year, the Scottish Mountaineering Club was formally constituted on 11th March.

Collie and Mackenzie spent five hours one afternoon seeking a route to the summit of the unclimbed Bhasteir Tooth. They eventually succeeded by descending some way into Lota Corrie and following a slanting weakness on the south face of Am Basteir.

1890 The Scottish Mountaineering Club Journal was published for the first time. The second one appeared in May and contained an article by Naismith entitled 'Three Days among the Cuchullins', the first of many relating to Skye.

Charles Pilkington organised a meet for an accomplished group of Alpine Club members. They had many fine days out, with Charles starting them off on the Pinnacle Ridge of Sgurr nan Gillean. Charles' wife became the first woman to climb the Inaccessible Pinnacle, and a party of three had an unusual aquatic outing up the Basteir Gorge. However, this team also failed to cross the TD Gap.

1891 Charles Pilkington published his 'Corrected Map of the Coolins'. *"... it is probably the most correct map of these mountains obtainable."*

An important pioneer by the name of Wickham King joined Collie and Mackenzie, and between them they finally solved the problem of the TD gap by climbing up both sides. The same party had a fright on an ascent of Clach Glas. King described the incident:

"On the slabs leading to Clach Glas we were not roped. J. Mackenzie was the last man. His unsuitable shepherd's boots caused him to slip, and then he slid with face to rock for some distance. He arrested his descent himself. He needed my aid to reach a safe resting place, for he was much shaken. ... Collie soon after gave him proper climbing boots."

The sixth SMCJ was published containing the first version of Munro's Tables.

1893 Collie wrote an article for the SMCJ 'On the Height of some of the Black Cuchullins in Skye', in which he explained how he made his measurements. He established that Sgurr Alasdair is higher than the Inaccessible Pinnacle, and hence the highest Cuillin summit.

1895 Mrs Rose, guided by Mackenzie, became the first woman to negotiate the Gendarme on the west ridge of Sgurr nan Gillean.

Kelsall and Hallitt heralded the start of more difficult climbing in the Cuillin by their bold ascent of Waterpipe Gully on Sgurr an Fheadain.

Sir Archibald Geikie suggested that Alfred Harker be appointed to the Geological Survey to map the Cuillin.

1896 This was a very productive season. Sidney Williams was camped with his artist father at Scavaig. He made numerous ascents, mainly in company with John Mackenzie. These included a traverse of Sgurr Dubh Beag (avoiding the drop at its western end by a traverse on the southern side), and Sgurr Dubh Mor. He also climbed the north-east ridges of Gars-bheinn, and Sgurr a' Choire Bhig, which gave *"some excellent sport"*.

Lamond, Rennie and Douglas sailed a yacht into Loch Scavaig, and heard from Williams about his exploits. They then traversed Sgurr Dubh Beag and Sgurr Dubh Mor from east to west, but they took the drop off the former directly. They concluded, *"It gives as interesting a scramble as any in the Coolins..."* On the same day Williams and Mackenzie crossed the TD Gap without much difficulty, and on hearing of the other party's success, they too made the direct descent off Sgurr Dubh Beag the following day.

Collie and a friend, E.B. Howell, climbed one of the longest mountaineering routes on the island when they ascended Sgurr a' Ghreadaidh from the floor of Coir'-uisg. Then, along with Parker and Naismith, they climbed the north-west buttress of Sgurr a' Mhadaidh. Parker and Naismith also found a new route on the west face of Clach Glas. They then visited the summits of four pinnacles on the north-east side of the peak.

A notable event took place on 12th September, when Collie, Howell, Naismith and Mackenzie scaled the north-east face of the north top of Sgurr Coir' an Lochain, and so conquered the last unclimbed mountain summit in Britain. They completed their day by traversing the Inaccessible Pinnacle, and following the ridge to Sgurr a' Mhadaidh, before dropping down the Thuilm ridge to Glen Brittle.

1897 A detailed list of the Cuillin peaks was prepared by Douglas, and appeared as an appendix in the SMCJ. Many of the heights had been calculated from aneroid measurements taken by Collie.

The famous SMC yachting meet in April failed to set foot on Skye, because of bad weather. The summer meet fared little better. Portable huts were erected at the head of Loch Coruisk, but the weather was appalling during July and August.

"Rain! Rain! Rain! Real Skye rain and no mistake, and all the water-works of the Coolins were going at high pressure. It continued like this all day ... On our return to camp we found that the loch has raised its level by nearly three feet." Amazingly, they did manage some climbing, including the first ascent of Brown's Climb on Sgurr a' Mhadaidh. Harold Raeburn made his first appearance on Skye.

1898 The SMC reproduced the OS six-inch map of the Cuillin at a reduced scale, with additional information added by its members.

The month of August was especially fruitful. Among the many new routes completed were two sensational climbs on the main ridge. King led Douglas and Naismith straight up to the summit of Sgurr Mhic Choinnich from Hart's Ledge to produce King's Chimney. After inspecting the upper part from above with a rope, Naismith climbed his intimidating route on the Bhasteir Tooth with A.M. Mackay.

Naismith's Route gained a companion climb, when King, Gibbs and Mackenzie completed their epic ascent of Bhasteir Nick Gully, now known as King's Cave Chimney.

Harold Raeburn set out from Sligachan and soloed the north ridge of Sgurr nan Each, before traversing Clach Glas.

1899 On 10th September, a Gurka, called Havildar Harkabir Thapa, set an astonishing record by running up and down Glamaig from the Sligachan Hotel in 55 minutes in bare feet. His record stood for 90 years, although it has not yet been beaten by a barefooted runner!

Collie ascended Sgurr Alasdair with Harkabir Thapa and Major Bruce. Descending from the lochan in Coire Lagan late in the day, he noticed a strange shadow cast on the face of Sron na Ciche. It was a further seven years before Collie followed up his observation.

1900 Harker published some very informative 'Notes, Geological and Topographical, on the Cuillin Hills, Skye' in the SMCJ. Sidney Williams carried out some important explorations on the east faces of Bla Bheinn and Clach Glas.

1901 Dr and Mrs Inglis Clark had an exciting time on Clach Glas in June. They climbed a route just north of B gully. Caught in a fierce storm at the summit, they were unable to descend either the south or north ridges of the mountain. *"Conversation was impossible, while the dash of hail and roaring of the wind tended to stupefy."* They eventually found a way down the east face, reaching its base by means of Sid's Rake.

1903 The OS published the third edition of their map of the Cuillin: *"... this latest map represents a great advance upon its predecessors."*

1905 Harold Raeburn led a team up the central buttress of An Caisteal in April. He changed into 'kletterschuhe' to ascend the delicate lower slabs, but had to cope with snow and ice higher up.

The Keswick Brothers and their Camera

1906 The Keswick brothers, George and Ashley Abraham, had visited Skye a decade earlier. They took remarkable photographs of their climbs using a very cumbersome glass plate camera. Now they began to put up new climbs as well. One of their first was West Buttress, a long route on Sgurr Mhic Choinnich.

The most notable event this year, however, was the first ascent of A' Chioch. Collie had seen the shadow of this extraordinary rock feature some seven years previously. After an exploratory probe alone, Collie teamed up with Mackenzie to reach its summit. They followed a devious route up what must have felt a very intimidating face. Collie was so excited by his discovery that he led numerous other climbers to the summit over the following weeks.

1907 Collie continued where he had left off, and climbed Amphitheatre Arête up the main face of Sron na Ciche. Harland, Bartrum, Binns and Ashley Abraham between them added several important new climbs including two Severes – Cioch Direct on Sron na Ciche, and Slanting Gully on Sgurr a' Mhadaidh. They also ascended Spur and Summit Gullies on Sgurr an Fheadain.

Douglas published the first climbing guide to Skye as a special edition of the SMCJ. Most of the routes were at the northern end of the Cuillin, closest to Sligachan. The climbs were graded for difficulty using a simple (1–4) numerical system. Accompanying the guide was a reduced version of the OS six-inch map on which Harker, who was not a climber, had marked in red all the easy routes he used for getting about the Cuillin.

1908 Ashley Abraham published his inspirational book – *Rock Climbing on Skye*. It contained many superb photographs, as well as a graded list of climbs. Naismith reviewed it for the SMCJ:

"Some of the descriptions of rock climbs – the Cioch direct ascent for example – are abundantly exciting, and will be apt to cause the reader to wedge himself across his arm-chair while he gropes about for a good hitch."

Abraham's book was largely responsible for making Skye more widely popular. A burst of new route activity took place over the next few years, which was only halted by the First World War. However,

Abraham's comments about traversing the main ridge in one outing were soon to sound dated.

"I must admit that it is doubtful whether the various qualifications necessary to success will ever be possessed by any one man.

Amongst other things he would need to have exceptional physique and staying power; to be a quick, skilful, and neat rock-climber (particularly would he need to be neat, for otherwise his hands would be torn to pieces before he got half-way); to possess an intimate knowledge of the entire length of the ridge, and a familiarity with its various 'mauvais pas'. Perfect weather, a light rope to 'double' for descents, and a carefully arranged commissariat would be essential. Moreover, I think it would be advisable to start at the southern end of the ridge, because a fatigued man might find himself 'pounded' at the short side of the Tearlach–Dubh Gap.

Whether the game would be worth the candle, for the attendant risks would be considerable, and whether it is desirable that the Coolin should be treated with such disrespect, are points which each must settle for himself; but personally I think that the expressive 'Dummheit' of the Swiss guides would justly describe such a performance!"

1911 On 10th June Leslie Shadbolt and Alastair McLaren made the first continuous traverse of the main ridge. They started from Glen Brittle just after 3.30am and reached Sligachan at 8.20pm, having taken a little over 12¼ hours between Gars-bheinn and Sgurr nan Gillean. They were Cuillin campaigners of old, having pioneered a new route on the Bhasteir Tooth in 1906.

Steeple, Barlow and the Guidebook

Two English climbers, E.W. Steeple and Guy Barlow, were very active on Skye around the time that Abraham's book was published. Sometimes in company with Bowron, Buckle and Doughty, they opened up whole new climbing areas.

Their output of new climbs was so prolific that the SMC soon involved them in producing a new guidebook to the Cuillin. They camped in the high corries to carry out much of their work.

1923 The SMC published *The Island of Skye*, edited by Steeple, Barlow, MacRobert and Bell. So thorough had Steeple and Barlow been in their explorations, that only a trickle of new climbs were added in the following two decades.

The Finishing Touches

1939 Ian Charleson and Woodhurst Forde completed the first Greater Traverse, which included Bla Bheinn and Clach Glas. They took exactly 20 hours from Gars-bheinn to Bla Bheinn.

1943 The Red Hills yielded their first climb when Noel Odell carried out a geological examination of Marsco. He found the rock to be surprisingly good.

1944 Menlove Edwards, though a troubled man, completed the Greater Traverse solo in some 12½ hours. He returned to his starting point in Glen Brittle in 24 hours. Later, in squally weather, he spent eighteen hours at sea crossing to Rum and Canna, and back again, in a hired rowing boat.

1949 W.A. Poucher produced a fine book of photographs called *The Magic of Skye*. (A new edition appeared in 1980.)

1952 Ben Humble produced a fascinating book, *The Cuillin of Skye*, describing the history of climbing in the Cuillin. (A facsimile edition appeared in 1986.)

1965 The first winter traverse of the Cuillin main ridge was completed in two days by Crabb, MacInnes, Patey and Robertson.

The Glen Brittle Memorial Hut was formally opened. It was built to commemorate climbers who had died in the war.

1975 The OS published, *The Cuillin and Torridon Hills*, in their Outdoor Leisure Maps series.

1987 The Gendarme fell off the West Ridge of Sgurr nan Gillean.

1988 The Glamaig Hill Race was inaugurated – inspired by Harkabir Thapa's phenomenal performance in 1899.

1991 Robin Campbell conquered the Cuillin's last unclimbed peaklet, and named it 'Sgurr Coire an Lobhta'.

1994 Gordon Stainforth published a photographic study of the Cuillin. It included a useful description of the main ridge, which graded all the difficulties.

1995 Skye was finally linked to the mainland by a bridge.

1997 Harveys produced an excellent new style map entitled *Skye : The Cuillin*.

1999 Rob Woodall completed The Cuillin Round (i.e. a circuit of the Red Hills overlooking Glen Sligachan, the Cuillin Outliers, and all the Cuillin main ridge) in 23½ hours. He had a team of nine people to resupply him at various points.

Notes on the Use of the Guide

CLASSIFICATION OF ROUTES

There are difficulties in trying to describe a mixture of walks, scrambles and climbs in the same guide. In order to make it obvious which type of outing is involved, a logo is shown at the start of each route description. The scrambles and climbs are each further subdivided into three levels of difficulty. All the outings are graded for **DRY, SUMMER CONDITIONS**. They are likely to be much more difficult if the conditions are less than perfect.

 WALKS No attempt has been made to classify walks, although some negotiate very rough ground, and ascend to high summits. Some may also take many hours to complete, and may require considerable navigational skills. What distinguishes walks from other kinds of outings is that it should be possible to undertake them without the need to set hands on rock.

SCRAMBLES There is a widely adopted method of classifying scrambles into three levels of difficulty using a simple numerical system. The three normal numerical grades are here matched with appropriate descriptive terms.

Grade 1 : Easy Scrambles

This grade of scramble will be fairly straightforward for most experienced hillwalkers. It may be necessary to use the hands occasionally for progress, but the holds will normally be large, and the exposure will not be too daunting.

Grade 2 : Interesting Scrambles

This grade of scramble will require the hands to be used for more sustained sections. The exposure may be significant, and retreat may be quite difficult.

Grade 3 : Advanced Scrambles

This type of scramble may involve making moves on steep rock in very exposed situations. All but experienced climbers might prefer the protection of a rope in some places. Occasional moves of **Moderate** rock climbing standard may be encountered. The ability to abseil may be useful if a retreat has to be made.

CLIMBS The rock climbs described in this guide fall into the three lowest grades of the standard adjectival system (the 'Easy' grade is not recognised here). Climbs are graded for their hardest move irrespective of length. It is assumed that these routes will be climbed using normal rock climbing equipment.

Moderate
This grade of climb is slightly more difficult than a Grade 3 scramble. This may be because a route is sustained, or in a serious situation. It overlaps with the difficulty level of what is sometimes designated a Grade 3(S) scramble, where S = 'Serious'.

Difficult
Climbs of this grade will require significant rock climbing skills. There may be considerable exposure for long sections, and experience of placing protection in awkward situations may be called upon.

Very Difficult
This kind of climb will be technically harder still, usually because the holds are quite small, or difficult to use in the most effective way. Only a few climbs of this grade are described.

DIRECTIONS, DISTANCES AND HEIGHTS
The terms **left** and **right** are used when **facing** the direction being described, i.e. facing the crag for route descriptions, and facing downhill in descent. Horizontal distances in metres are shown as **metres**, and vertical heights are shown as **m**.

QUALITY
A star system has been used to indicate the overall quality of routes irrespective of difficulty. All the outings described have some merit, but only the most outstanding ones, which combine good line, fine situations, sound rock, and sustained interest, are given three stars.

APPROACH ROUTES
The double-page **aerial views** included in this guide are designed to illustrate the main approach routes to the outings described. Most of these routes follow fairly obvious paths, although some may be rather boggy. They are marked by prominent dashed lines.

CRAG DIAGRAMS

To help differentiate the types of outings on the crag diagrams,
  i) **walks and scrambles** are shown by **dashed lines**,
  ii) **rock climbs** are indicated by **dotted lines**,
  iii) relatively straightforward **descent** routes from the ridge are
     marked by the letter **D**.

ROCKFALL

Ice-scoured gabbro is extremely sound, and one of the best rocks
anywhere for scrambling and climbing on. However, the high ridges
were not covered by ice during the last glaciation, but instead
experienced strong freeze-thaw action, and so tend to be more
broken. Also, running through the gabbro, there are significant
amounts of more brittle and slippery basalt, which is less reliable.
Loose rock is one of the main causes of accidents in the Cuillin. A
helmet is worth wearing in gullies, beneath faces and on climbs.

There have been some large rockfalls in the Cuillin in recent years.
One of the most spectacular involved a massive slab of rock which
broke off the flank of Druim nan Ramh. Huge blocks fell down into
Loch Coruisk. The scar is conspicuous even from Elgol. Other
sizeable rockfalls have included the famous Gendarme on the west
ridge of Sgurr nan Gillean, and sections of crest on Am Basteir and
Sgurr Thearlaich. Another big mass fell off from near the summit of
Bla Bheinn. The lower part of the Sgumain Stone Shoot was recently
transformed by a combined rockfall and major rockslide. It has made
the approach to Collie's route on the Cioch more difficult.

NAVIGATION

The ability to navigate is an essential skill in the hills. Thick mist can
be very disorientating, especially in the Cuillin. It is quite common to
hear of climbers ending up in the wrong corrie, or on the wrong
mountain. If mist comes down, it may not be a good idea to sit down
and wait for it to clear – you might have to wait a fortnight.

The magnetic nature of the rocks in the Cuillin means that a
compass can be unreliable at times, but it can still be put to good use.
Hold the compass up high and away from any rock. If it still points in
the same general direction when you move about, the readings can
still be helpful when used in conjunction with a good map.

MAPS

1:50 000

Three OS maps are required to cover the whole of Skye:

    Sheet 23 *North Skye*

    Sheet 32 *South Skye* (not really adequate for the Cuillin)

    Sheet 33 *Loch Alsh & Glen Shiel* (includes the Kylerhea area)

1:25 000

There are two main maps of the Cuillin to choose from at this scale:

Harveys – *Skye : The Cuillin*

This map is very much aimed at the hillgoer, and includes many helpful extra details for the visitor. On the opposite side of the main map, there is an enlargement of the Cuillin at 1:12 500 scale. This shows the line of the main ridge clearly. Recommended.

Ordnance Survey – *Outdoor Leisure Map 8 :*
The Cuillin & Torridon Hills

This map does not depict the line of the main Cuillin ridge at all well, although the Red Hills and Strathaird are shown clearly.

ACCESS

By Car – The most popular route onto the island is via the toll bridge at Kyle of Lochalsh. Frequent visitors can make significant savings by purchasing books of 20 tickets. There are, however, two interesting alternative routes.

i) A small car ferry operates between Glenelg and Kylerhea from April to October. This is a very scenic route, which was much used in the days of cattle droving.

ii) A car ferry operates between Mallaig and Armadale from March to October. Booking is advisable at busy times. The roads between Fort William and Mallaig, and between Armadale and Broadford, are being upgraded, and when this work is complete an improved ferry service to Armadale is planned.

    It is worth knowing that there is a 24-hour petrol station and shop in Broadford.

Public Transport – The famous West Highland Line runs from Fort William to Mallaig. There is also a train service between Inverness and Kyle of Lochalsh. Coach services run regularly from Glasgow to Uig via Fort William, and from Inverness to Portree.

ACCOMMODATION

There is plentiful accommodation on Skye, and full details of the many 'bed and breakfast' and 'self-catering' establishments are available from the main Tourist Information Centre (01478 612137) in Portree. Additional information centres are open in Broadford, Dunvegan and Kyle of Lochalsh during the holiday season.

Camping

The two most convenient camp sites are at Sligachan opposite the hotel, and in Glen Brittle beside the beach. Other sites exist at Breakish by Broadford, and near Portree, Dunvegan, Edinbane and Staffin. Most of these sites are only open from April to October.

Youth Hostels

There is a handy Youth Hostel in Glen Brittle, as well as others at Armadale, Broadford and Uig.

Independent Backpackers Hostels

There are two very popular independent hostels quite close to the Cuillin at Portnalong. They have full facilities, and are open all year. Others exist at Kyleakin, Portree and Flodigarry.

Mountaineering Huts

The Glen Brittle Memorial Hut has sixteen places, and a resident warden between April and September. The Coruisk Memorial Hut is situated in a remote location near the outflow from the River Scavaig. It is normally locked. There are nine places.

Bookings for both these huts are normally made through club secretaries. Details can be obtained from the MCofS.

Hotels

The Sligachan Hotel has a special place in the history of climbing in the Cuillin. It remains very popular with mountaineers. Meals are available for non-residents in the commodious bar until 9pm.

MOUNTAIN RESCUE

In the event of an accident requiring the rescue services **dial 999**. Where possible give a six figure grid reference for the position of the casualty and his/her medical condition. Telephones are situated by Glen Brittle Memorial Hut, Sligachan, Elgol, Torrin and Broadford.

Strath Suardal and Strathaird

The south-eastern part of Skye, which is built mainly of Torridonian and Lewisian rocks, has its own distinctive character. It includes the large, but relatively low-lying, peninsula of Sleat, which is sometimes referred to as 'the garden of Skye'. There is pleasant walking on the hills overlooking Kylerhea, but otherwise this part of the island has limited attractions for the hillgoer.

The rocks change in character approaching Broadford, where Jurassic and Cambro–Ordovician sediments predominate. All the outings in this chapter are approached along Strath Suardal by a single track road that runs south-west from Broadford. This broad, open strath leads to the crofting township of Torrin, from where the road continues round the head of Loch Slapin and then runs across the peninsula of Strathaird to the tiny village of Elgol.

1 Suisnish and Boreraig 17km *

This is a fairly long walk if the full circuit is completed as described, although it can be shortened by some 4km if a pickup can be arranged near Loch Cill Chriosd. The outing is of interest both historically and geologically. It visits the remains of two former communities, which were 'cleared' in the middle of the nineteenth century. The route also crosses Cambro–Ordovician limestones riddled with tiny caves, and it includes a visit to a disused marble quarry. The route-finding is not always obvious, and the OS *Outdoor Leisure Map 8* is recommended.

Start

From Broadford follow the road along Strath Suardal until a little over 1km past Loch Cill Chriosd. Carry straight on where the road to Torrin forks right and continue to where the tarmac ends at a grassy area of raised beach by Camas Malag (GR 582 193).

The Route

Follow the rough track heading south. Soon after cresting a slight rise the track swings left to cross a small stream. At this point it is worth making a small diversion to examine the Camas Malag Caves. This little cave system can be found just a short distance down from the track, where the Allt na Garbhlain flows off the Beinn an Dubhaich granite intrusion and immediately sinks underground. The stream resurges about 50 metres downhill, where it is forced to cross an impervious dyke. It then plunges into a spectacular little pothole, before eventually resurging from the upper part of the nearby sea cliff, and cascading onto the shore.

Many caves also occur in the glen of the Allt nan Leac slightly further south. These include the very sporting Uamh Cinn Ghlinn – the longest cave on Skye. Details of these caves can be found in *Caves of Skye* published by Grampian Speleological Group (1995).

The track soon passes onto Jurassic shales, and continues south with fine views across Loch Slapin to Strathaird. Eventually the track leads to numerous derelict buildings that once formed the settlement of Suisnish. There can be few more poignant reminders of just how brutal some of the clearances must have been. Archibald Geikie, the geologist, described the distress of the inhabitants as they left:

"When they set off once more, a cry of grief went up to heaven; the long plaintive wail, like a funeral coronach, was resumed; and, after the last of the emigrants had disappeared behind the hill, the sound seemed to re-echo through the whole wide valley of Strath in one prolonged note of desolation. The people were on their way to be shipped to Canada."

To continue the walk pick up a narrow path which contours round the hillside to the east of the ruins. Follow this along the cliff top below the craggy south face of Carn Dearg, before eventually descending to the shore of Loch Eishort by an outcrop of peridotite. A number of dykes and waterfalls stand out on the sizeable cliffs overlooking the shore. Eventually the cliffs recede and the first ruins of Boreraig come into view. This grassy oasis must have harboured a community of a similar size to Suisnish. The area is interesting to explore, and ammonites can be found in rocks along the shore.

Look for a 'standing stone' set back some distance from the sea. It is not especially conspicuous and looks more like a slabby headstone. It helps point to the path which climbs out of Boreraig through the bracken. As the path climbs northwards, waterfalls can be seen in the Allt na Pairte to the east. Further along the path there is an outcrop of very distinctive conglomerate of Triassic age.

As the path nears its high point it becomes very boggy and difficult to follow. The scenery becomes more desolate too. Once past Loch Lonachan, however, the situation changes quite quickly, and the path soon descends to grassier terrain by the old marble quarry workings.

The marble was formed where limestone underwent thermal metamorphism along the margins of the Beinn an Dubhaich granite intrusion. A small railway was used to transport the marble to Broadford. It was removed when the quarry closed in 1912.

It is best to leave the main path at this point, and head in a westerly direction towards the prominent ruined manse at Kilchrist. There are a number of caves in the vicinity, as well as a 30 metres wide dyke, and evidence of small scale magnetite mining. These features deserve a separate visit, however, for it is only a short distance now to the road in Strath Suardal by Loch Cill Chriosd.

2 Spar Cave   Grade 1   **

This is only a short outing, but well worthwhile. It requires careful timing. The cave entrance is above high water mark, but it lies at the back of a deep cleft, which is only accessible for a short time at low tide. The cleft has been formed by the weathering out of a dyke in cross-bedded, calcareous sandstone. Limy material seeping in from the neighbouring rocks has coated the floor of the cave with deposits of spar (calcium carbonate). The best stalactite formations have not survived countless visits, but the cave is still a spectacular sight. Although the cave is quite short, a headtorch is essential.

Start

From Elgol take the road over the peninsula to the tiny community of Glasnakille. Turn right at the T-junction.

The Route

Leave the road about 150 metres after the T-junction, and descend past a stone byre. Continue down to the shore through a small depression. Turn left and clamber along the coast to the prominent cleft. If your timing is right you should be able to hop across boulders and scramble round into the cleft without much difficulty. The remains of a wall can be seen at the cave entrance.

The initial section is rather muddy. Ascend a couple of slopes with some mild scrambling up a beautiful staircase of sparkling calcium carbonate. Then descend slightly to a long pool of crystal clear water that marks the end of the cave. Scott described this in his *Lord of the Isles* :

> *Mermaid's alabaster grot,*
> *Who bathes her limbs in sunless well,*
> *Deep in Strathaird's enchanted cell.*

3 Suidhe Biorach   3km *

This clifftop walk follows a faint path out along the headland to the south of Elgol. It passes some interesting geos and promontories, where some scrambling can be included if desired.

Start

From the lower car park near the jetty in Elgol.

The Route

Pick up a path that heads south along the relatively flat clifftop. The first features of interest can be seen after 1km at Suidhe nan Eun. These include a sea stack and a depression formed by a small landslip. It is possible to scramble down from here to a natural arch much frequented by sea birds. It is a short distance then to the headland of Suidhe Biorach (*rough seat*), from where there are fine views of Rum. Numerous rock climbs have been put up on the sandstone sea cliffs here, although none are in the easier grades.

Just east of Suidhe Biorach there is a bouldery bay, which can be accessed at either end by scrambling at low tide. On the headland at the far eastern end of this bay is a cave where Bonnie Prince Charlie spent his final hours on Skye before sailing back to the mainland.

Return to Elgol by the same route.

4 Elgol to Camasunary 6km (one way) *

This route is much more enjoyable than it might appear from the map. It offers fine views of the Cuillin and leads to a pleasant sandy bay below the south ridge of Bla Bheinn. It is a fine outing in its own right, although it can also be used as part of a through route to Sligachan (Route 143) or as an approach to Coruisk (Route 144).

Start

From the higher of the two car parks in Elgol walk back up the hill for 300 metres. A signpost marks the start of the route (GR 520 139).

The Route

Follow a track past some houses, and then a path between fences to reach more open, grassy terrain. After about 700 metres the path descends leftwards for some distance. It then traverses the steeply sloping hillside below Ben Cleat, and continues under the craggy face of Carn Mor to reach flatter ground in Glen Scaladal.

Ford the Scaladal Burn, then head left and climb out of the glen by a narrow path which continues among trees, with exciting drops to the shore below at times. The angle eases after Rubha na h-Airighe Bàine, and a further kilometre of easier walking leads to Camasunary. This fine bay, more properly spelt Camas Fhionnairigh, has a big expanse of sand when the tide is out, in which case it may be easier to stay on the shore and paddle across the Abhainn nan Leac. Otherwise head for a bridge on the track from Kilmarie.

The main buildings at Camasunary are private property, but on the western side of the bay there is an open bothy. There are also plenty of opportunities for wild camping on excellent ground nearby. This makes Camasunary a good base for outings on Sgurr na Stri, Sgurr Hain, and Bla Bheinn.

5 Kilmarie to Camasunary 4½km (one way)

This is the most direct route to Camasunary, but the least interesting. It follows a vehicular track throughout. The history of this track is steeped in controversy. It was constructed by the Territorial Army in the late 1960s as part of a package of measures dreamt up by Inverness County Council and the Inverness-shire Constabulary. The justification for this work was that it would facilitate the evacuation of injured climbers from Coruisk.

Vigorous opposition from the outdoor fraternity prevented blasting of the Bad Step (see Route 144), but suspension bridges were built across the River Scavaig at Coruisk and across the Abhainn Camas Fhionnairigh. These have long since disappeared. An account of the whole sorry business is given in *The Coruisk Affair* (SMCJ 1969).

Start

Park on the east side of the Elgol road (GR 545 172) a short distance after the turning for Kilmarie.

The Route

Follow the track on the west side of the road to its high point near Am Mam (189m). From here on there are spectacular views of the Cuillin peaks. As the track swings to the north the southern flank of Bla Bheinn becomes increasingly prominent. Then start to descend quite steeply via a hairpin bend. (A faint path which leads through to Sligachan cuts off on the right a short distance before the hairpin bend – see Route 143.) The track continues descending and peters out eventually near some private buildings. An open bothy is situated at the western end of the bay – see the previous route.

Route 4 offers a longer, but more interesting, route of return if transport can be arranged at Elgol.

Spar Cave, Glasnakille, Strathaird

The Red Hills

The main road from Broadford to Sligachan skirts an impressive group of granite mountains known as the Red Hills. Although they appear more rounded and scree ridden than the Cuillin peaks, the Red Hills offer some surprisingly good walks as well as some minor scrambles. They are built from a number of separate granite intrusions. A younger group of intrusions forms the Eastern Red Hills and an older group forms the Western Red Hills.

THE EASTERN RED HILLS

The scenery west of Broadford is dominated by the Eastern Red Hills. This group extends from Beinn na Caillich in the east to Glas Bheinn Mhor which overlooks Loch Ainort in the west. Two deep glens, Srath Mor and Srath Beag, cut through the hills from north to south. The route through Srath Beag involves greater ascent, but is rather more interesting, and much drier.

6 Beinn na Caillich – The Round of Coire Reidh 11km **
Beinn na Caillich overlooks the town of Broadford and is the major mountain of the Eastern Red Hills. It is commonly ascended from Strath Suardal, but the outing described is a very worthy alternative which approaches the mountain from its northern side.

Start

Follow the main road beyond Broadford for some 5km, and park at the start of a minor track on the left side of the road opposite the island of Scalpay (GR 600 266).

The Route

Go through a gate and follow the track to Luib for some 700 metres to where it crosses the Allt Strollamus. Pick up a path on the west bank of this stream, which leads up to An Slugan – the high point on the route through Srath Beag. Follow this path as far as a stream junction, then head up the left-hand stream – the Allt na Teangaidh.

Descending the Impostor on the South Ridge of Clach Glas
(Scrambler, Willie Jeffrey)

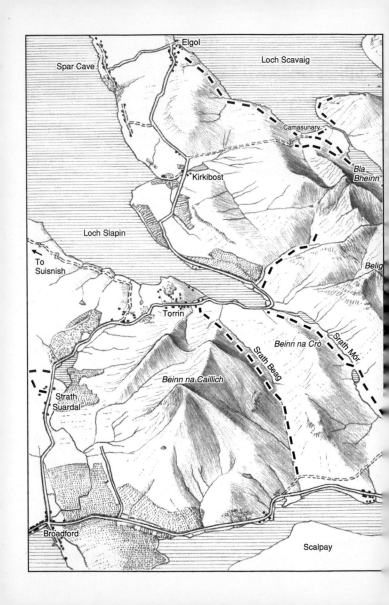

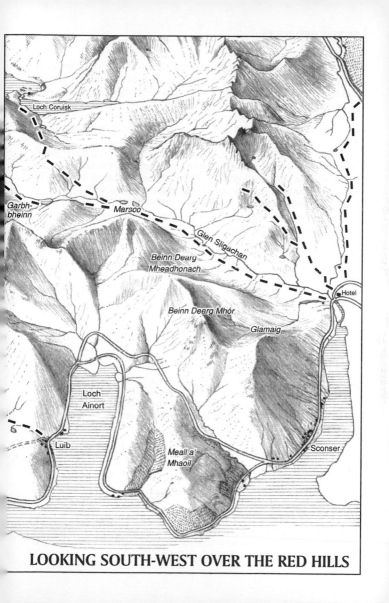

LOOKING SOUTH-WEST OVER THE RED HILLS

A prominent dark crag, Creagan Dubh, lies ahead. The aim is to reach the top of this feature. The easiest route is by a grassy runnel just to the left of the main north-east ridge. The latter can be gained by a heather terrace from the left and offers some easy (Grade 1) scrambling up slabs of baked basalt. The more adventurous may prefer to ascend a hidden gully on the right-hand side of the much steeper north face. It has a tricky exit (Grade 3).

Reach a small top (535m) above Creagan Dubh. On the slight descent from this top there is a dramatic change in the colour of the rocks as you pass onto granite. Pleasant easy walking over grass and boulders then leads to the broad summit of Beinn Dearg Mhor (709m), from where there are extensive views to the south and west.

Turn left and descend north-eastwards, and then east along a slightly narrower ridge separating Coire Reidh from Coire Gorm. Then make the final ascent to the summit of Beinn na Caillich, which is graced by a trig point and a gigantic cairn. Just past the summit there is a splendid view down Coire Fearchair to Broadford.

Now turn left and descend the north-west ridge which overlooks Coire Seamraig. Try to stay near the right-hand edge where the going is slightly easier. Eventually head west-north-west, and make a descent on slabby rocks between two streams. Return along the Allt na Teangaidh as for the approach.

THE WESTERN RED HILLS

The Western Red Hills lie between Loch Ainort and Glen Sligachan. They form a rather irregular north–south chain and can be accessed either from the roadside to the east, or from Glen Sligachan to the west. The outings are described from north to south, rather than by the natural order of their starting points.

7 Meall a' Mhaoil via the Allt Darach Gorge   Grade 3

Although this is a fairly humble hill, there is a remarkably fine panorama from its summit. This makes it a rewarding goal in its own right. The Allt Darach gorge is cut in Torridonian sandstone. The gorge approach is not recommended in wet weather.

Start

Take the old road around the coast from the head of Loch Ainort, or join it from the other end near the golf club at Sconser. Park just east of the bridge over the Allt Darach (GR 554 320).

The Route

Drop down the steep heathery bank on the south-west side of the bridge to gain the floor of the gorge. A variety of techniques have to be employed on several tiny pitches in the early section of the gorge if feet are to be kept dry. The rock is sound but rather slimy.

The difficulties soon ease and a long section of stream bed is followed before the gorge gradually gives way to gentler slopes. Eventually move onto the eastern flank of the stream and, when in sight of a lochan, head south-west to reach the summit trig point.

8 Glamaig – South-East Rib   Grade 2 or 3   *

Glamaig is the highest and most northerly of the Red Hills. The mountain boasts an annual hill race, which was set up in 1988 partly to celebrate an extraordinary feat performed in 1899 by Ghurka Harkabir Thapa, who ran to the summit and back from Sligachan in bare feet in just 55 minutes. This outing takes a more roundabout way to the summit. The scrambling is better than it looks, but can easily be avoided if necessary.

Start

The outing is best combined with one of the next two routes in the guide. The route as described starts from Bealach na Sgairde, which can be reached by descending the north-west flank of Beinn Dearg Mhor (Routes 9 or 10). Alternatively it can be approached either from Sligachan via Coire na Sgairde, or from the east along the Allt Mor Doire Mhic-uin.

The Route

The broad south-eastern flank of Glamaig can be ascended from Bealach na Sgairde without great difficulty. However, by seeking out a rocky rib a little to the right, a more interesting ascent can be made. The rock is not granite as might be expected, but basalt heaved up and much altered by the granite intrusions.

From the bealach slant up rightwards over fine dark scree to a nose feature marking the start of a blocky rib. Move round to the right and back left to gain the crest of the rib above the nose. Ascend on good rock with some awkward step-ups. From the left-hand side of the rib make a steep crucial move rightwards (Grade 3) to stay on the crest. Easier options exist on the right.

Higher up move slightly left near the top of a short scree gully and move rightwards again to regain the rib. This gives pleasant scrambling, mainly Grade 2, with much variation possible. The rock is good on the whole, although slightly brittle in places. The best section starts at a mossy nose. From its right-hand side traverse hard left to reach the crest. The rocks above if taken direct are Grade 3.

When the rock peters out higher up, continue up a pleasant grassy ridge. Towards the top traverse hard right to reach a steep rock ridge with a small gully on its left. Move round to the right of this and follow an easy grass ramp for some distance until it fades out onto easier ground. Continue on grass heading slightly left to reach flatter ground. It is a short distance then to the summit cairn. Another cairn lies a little further on, and makes a better view point. The present record to Sligachan from here is inside 13 minutes!

The route taken now will depend on your starting point, but a pleasant ridge can be followed, by the remains of an iron fence post, to the eastern top called An Coileach. If returning to the start of the next route, descend the north-east ridge as far as the 300m level, then slant south-south-east to reach the road.

9 Beinn Dearg Mhor – North-East Ridge   Grade 1
This pleasant outing has the advantage that it starts at a height of 120m. The scrambling is enjoyable but fairly short-lived.
Start
Park at the roadside just north of the highest point on the road between Broadford and Sligachan (GR 533 286).
The Route
Cross a short section of boggy ground and then ascend a heather covered slope. Short sections of fine scree lead to the start of some pleasant slabby ribs of sound granite. As the angle eases slightly the terrain changes to boulders and scree. Several sheep tracks cut across the ridge and contour around the hillside.

Higher up there is much dwarf juniper and, where the ridge narrows slightly, there are further short sections of scrambling. Turn left at the top and soon reach the rather elegant summit cairn. There are superb views down to Sligachan.

Continue down the north ridge, then zigzag down scree on the north-west flank to Bealach na Sgairde, where there is a noticeable change in rock colour. Either turn right and descend the north side of the Allt Mor Doire Mhic-uin or continue onto Glamaig (Route 8).

10 The Beinn Deargs via Druim na Ruaige   10km   *
This one of the most popular and straightforward circuits in the Red Hills. The views from the main crest are especially fine.

Start

From the old bridge at Sligachan (GR 486 298).

The Route

Follow the main path south along Glen Sligachan. Either fork left beside the Allt Daraich gorge or continue for some distance on the drier main path. Then head off towards the prominent nose at the north-western end of Sron a' Bhealain. Ascend to this small grassy top and continue along the broad ridge of Druim na Ruaige. Climb scree to the long summit ridge of Beinn Dearg Mheadhonach.

It is worth visiting the high point at the south-eastern end of the summit ridge before following the easy north ridge down to Bealach Mosgaraidh. Traverse the main summit of Beinn Dearg Mhor and zigzag down scree at its north-western end to Bealach na Sgairde. The great bulk of Glamaig looms ahead. Turn left and descend into Coire na Sgairde, then follow the Allt Daraich back to Sligachan.

MARSCO (736m)

Marsco is arguably the finest of all the Red Hills. It is set apart from its neighbours and has a particularly striking profile when viewed from Sligachan. It offers the only rock climbing in the Red Hills. The most prominent buttress situated on its western flank is called Fiaclan Dearg (*red tooth*).

11 Fiaclan Dearg – North-West Shoulder Grade 2 *

This route finds the easiest way to the summit of Fiaclan Dearg. There is some loose rock in places, but otherwise it makes an enjoyable scramble. The outing continues to the summit of Marsco.

Start

Follow the path along Glen Sligachan for some 5km. When directly below Fiaclan Dearg head up the steep heathery hillside. This takes longer than expected. The going can be made slightly easier by ascending occasional ribbons of granite slab.

The Route

From a slight bay on the left-hand side of the buttress slant leftwards up a broken rake. There is an awkward rock step fairly early on which forms the crux of the route. Continue slanting left and ascend a narrow rock ramp and a short slab to reach a grass patch. (The next route cuts right at this point.) Head left up easier ground for some distance to a grassy recess. Then traverse hard left in a slightly more

THE WEST FACE OF MARSCO

Fiaclan Dearg

2nd Terrace

1st Terrace

12

11

Allt Fiaclan Dearg

exposed position to reach the crest of the shoulder overlooking a deep gully containing the Allt Fiaclan Dearg.

Go up the shoulder to a rock band and then scramble pleasantly up rightwards by an obvious stepped weakness. Zigzag up until the angle eases and soon reach the broad summit of Fiaclan Dearg. It is best to continue to the summit of Marsco from here.

Head up the bouldery slope above. Higher up the finer scree is slightly less pleasant, but eventually the angle relents and the crest is then followed rightwards to the summit.

The best option from here is to descend the south-east ridge as far as a slight saddle and then cut down leftwards by a line of fence posts to a broad shoulder forming the eastern side of Coire nan Laogh. Find a suitable place to cross the ravine containing the stream from Coire nan Laogh, and continue more easily to Mam a' Phobuill. Descend by the north bank of the Allt na Measarroch and eventually rejoin the main path in Glen Sligachan.

12 Fiaclan Dearg – Odell's Route   Difficult   *

This route was the very first rock climb made in the Red Hills. It was pioneered by Noel Odell in 1943 when he was carrying out a geological examination of the mountain. (Odell was on Everest in 1924 and made the last sighting of Mallory and Irvine.)

Start

Approach along Glen Sligachan as for the previous route.

The Route

Slant leftwards to the grass patch as for Route 11. Then traverse hard right along a narrow foot ledge, which gradually becomes more difficult. A poor belay can be taken before climbing a damp groove and the slightly suspect rocks to its right. Then continue right more easily to reach a rising grassy ramp. Follow this right again to reach a shoulder with fine views to the south.

The rocks above look deceptively easy, but the next pitch provides the crux. Climb up steps until the rocks steepen slightly. Make a delicate move left, then continue more or less directly to reach easier ground. Ascend an alcove passing to the right of a small cavity. Trend slightly right and climb up just right of the crest. Much easier climbing and then scrambling leads to a big boulder at the top of the buttress.

Reach the summit of Marsco and return as for the previous route.

13 South-East Ridge 8km **

This is the best walking route to the summit of Marsco. There are magnificent panoramic views from the upper part of the route.

Start

The shortest approach to this ridge is from the roadside south-west of Loch Ainort. Park near a bend where the road crosses the Allt Coire nam Bruadaran within sight of a fine waterfall. (GR 534 267).

The Route

There is a path of sorts on the northern bank of the Allt Coire nam Bruadaran, but it is unpleasantly boggy after wet weather. It may be preferable to follow a broad ridge further left, heading initially towards Druim Eadar Da Choire. (A train of boulders right of this ridge marks a former medial moraine, which can be seen more clearly from the ridge later in the day.) Either route can be followed to the upper reaches of Coire nam Bruadaran. Continue south to gain a broad bouldery bealach with views across to Ruadh Stac.

Head right to reach the foot of the south-east ridge and ascend this quite steeply at first. Eventually arrive at a small top. Descend easily just beyond this to a small grassy saddle, where a line of fence posts, which has been following the ridge, now cuts off down to the right. Continue up a broader section of ridge which gradually narrows as the top is approached. There can be few finer views from a hill of such modest stature (Marsco is neither a Munro nor a Corbett).

To descend, either return to the saddle and head for Mam a' Phobuill as for Route 11, or go north from the summit and pick a way down the steeper and less straightforward north-east flank eventually traversing right into Coire nan Laogh. From near Mam a' Phobuill descend steeply at first in an easterly direction and return along the Allt Coire nam Bruadaran.

14 Ruadh Stac via the Coire na Seilg Slabs Grade 3 *

This outing combines scrambling on glaciated granite slabs with a visit to a little frequented summit, which offers unusual views of Bla Bheinn and Clach Glas.

Start

As for Route 13, at a bend where the road crosses the Allt Coire nam Bruadaran (GR 534 267) south-west of Loch Ainort.

The Route

The slabs in question are situated about 2½km from the road at GR 528 243, just below a dark crag called Creag Druim Eadar Da

Choire. Approach them by following the broad ridge leading to Druim Eadar Da Choire. This is rather hard going to start with, but persevere and it gradually improves. Move slightly left to the eastern side of the crest and, just before reaching the first granite outcrop of Druim Eadar Da Choire proper, slant leftwards off the ridge. Traverse south across the hillside to the obvious sweep of slabs. An alternative approach can be made along the Abhainn Ceann Loch Ainort.

The route takes a more or less central line up one of the cleanest and driest strips of rock. After warming up on some introductory slabs head for a point just a little to the left of a short steep wall, and to the right of some overlapping slabs. Climb steepish rock for a couple of moves before making a hard rightwards traverse for some 8 metres to get established on the main strip of slabs. Ascend this more easily (Grade 2) with the difficulties easing very gradually as height is gained. Eventually when the slabs peter out ascend easier ground rightwards to emerge at a dip below the north ridge of Garbh-bheinn.

Cross over the dip and descend only slightly, before traversing south across the flank of Garbh-bheinn. Pick up a faint path in the scree and follow this until a short descent leads down to the bealach between Garbh-bheinn and Ruadh Stac. Ascend easily onto the rounded summit plateau and continue to the highest point at its western end. This is a fine vantage point offering splendid views down the glen to Camasunary.

As you return to the bealach look out for a faint path which takes a dogleg route across the head of Am Fraoch-choire on the left. This makes a very convenient link to the broad bealach below the south-east ridge of Marsco (Route 13). From this bealach, either descend Coire nam Bruadaran and follow the very wet path along the Allt Coire nam Bruadaran, or traverse a long way right and descend the Druim Eadar Da Choire.

Incidentally, those who specialise in more esoteric outings may be interested in traversing the south flank of Ruadh Stac by an exciting animal track at about the 300m contour. It can be reached by dropping down slightly on the south side of the bealach between Ruadh Stac and Garbh-bheinn. The ground becomes more craggy and much more serious (Grade 3) towards the western end. Then a crucial line has to be found down into and out of a very deep gully. After this the going gradually eases and it becomes possible to ascend to the crest of a broad ridge north-west of the summit.

The Cuillin Outliers

The chain of hills which extends from Garbh-bheinn southwards is built from very different rocks to Marsco and the other Red Hills. The dramatic change in colour of the rocks at the northern end of Garbh-bheinn is obvious even to the untrained eye. Garbh-bheinn, Clach Glas and mighty Bla Bheinn are formed from the same gabbro intrusions as the Cuillin, and only an accident of erosion has separated them from the main Cuillin massif. For this reason this group is referred to as the Cuillin Outliers.

GARBH-BHEINN (808m)

This hill is a prominent feature looking south from the head of Loch Ainort. Three ridges radiate from its summit, and each of them offers short sections of mild scrambling. Its traverse can be made the climax of two possible circuits which include the neighbouring peak of Belig. One circuit starts from the Loch Ainort side; the other starts from Loch Slapin and includes a traverse of Sgurr nan Each.

15 North Ridge   Grade 1/2   *
Once the start of the ridge is gained, this route takes a direct and very satisfying line to the summit.
Start
From the road around Loch Ainort. Reach the dip at the foot of the ridge, either by traversing the grassy top (489m) above Druim Eadar Da Choire or by completing the scramble up the Coire na Seilg slabs (Route 14).
The Route
The initial section of ridge is fairly tame, and is marked by old fence posts, but the steeper middle section has slabby rocks with some scrambling interest. Ascend the crest where possible, thereby avoiding the worst of the scree further right. The ridge then eases slightly for some distance before a slight steepening leads to an abrupt left turn a short distance before the summit – a delightful finish.

Either descend the same way or reverse the next route, taking care at the nose at the end of the north ridge of Belig.

RUADH STAC AND THE CUILLIN OUTLIERS

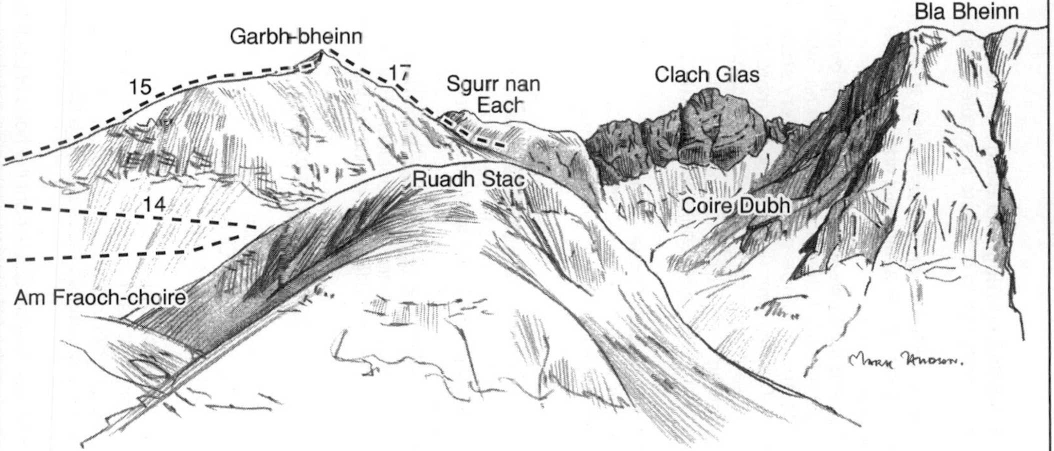

Garbh-bheinn   Sgurr nan Each   Clach Glas   Bla Bheinn

15   17   Ruadh Stac   Coire Dubh

14

Am Fraoch-choire

16 North-East Ridge via Belig Grade 1

The natural way to complete this route is as part of a circuit.

Start

The summit of Belig can be reached by its north ridge from Loch Ainort or, better, by its south-east ridge from Loch Slapin.

The Route

Descend the south-western ridge of Belig over broken rocks and scree to the broad flattening of Bealach na Beiste. Ascend a slight shoulder and continue up the bouldery slope above for some distance. The narrower upper section is more interesting, and gives some pleasant scrambling, before ending abruptly at the summit.

Depending on your approach, either descend the north ridge (Route 15) or the shorter south-east ridge (Route 17).

17 South-East Ridge Grade 1

This is the shortest of Garbh-bheinn's three ridges. An easy section of ridge links it with the western end of Sgurr nan Each.

Start

The ridge is easiest to approach from the Loch Slapin side. Either complete one of the routes on Sgurr nan Each (Route 18 or 19) or approach Choire a' Caise by the path along the Allt na Dunaiche, and ascend the right fork at the top on very steep scree.

The Route

From the western end of Sgurr nan Each descend an easy ridge in a north-westerly direction to a bealach. Follow the pleasant rocky ridge with no special difficulties directly to the summit.

SGURR NAN EACH (720m)

This top lies on a spur projecting eastwards from the ridge linking Garbh-bheinn and Clach Glas. Its traverse makes an interesting start to an ascent of either peak.

18 North Buttress Grade 2/3 **

This fine buttress is best seen from Bealach na Beiste. It was first ascended in 1898 by Harold Raeburn. He approached the route from Sligachan, and returned there via Clach Glas.

Start

The more usual approach is from the head of Loch Slapin. Follow the north bank of the Allt Aigeinn past some delightful waterfalls.

SGURR NAN EACH

North Buttress

18

Loch Slapin

The Route

Stay on the north bank until directly opposite the prominent buttress. Cross the stream and head up to the lowest tongue of rock some distance below the buttress proper. This makes a delightful starter. Climb up onto it from the right. The rock is rough and covered with holds.

Continue on more broken rocks and scree for some distance, and eventually break left up a rib and the groove on its right to reach the crest of the buttress. Zigzag up fairly easy ground to a grassy terrace below more continuous rocks. This is where the real fun starts.

Ascend the rocks on the left side of a left-slanting groove to a ledge. Continue up a steepish rib of rock with a black lichen-covered wall to the right. The rock is superb and furnished with large steps. Above a grassy ledge the rocks are less steep, until a short wall is reached. Slant right to find the easiest way up or climb a steep groove up the centre.

The angle then starts to ease slightly, and the next significant feature is a pinnacle on a narrower section of ridge. Do not follow ledges on the right-hand side, but instead made a couple of awkward step-ups on mossy ledges left of the crest. Then ascend a pleasant slab before regaining the crest on the right. The ridge pinches down to a slight neck. Outflank a small wall by its left-hand end, then continue more easily and finish on a small top (623m).

Now traverse Sgurr nan Each as for Route 19.

 19 The East–West Traverse   Grade 1/2   *
This route makes a popular start to the traverse of Clach Glas.

Start

Follow the normal approach path to Bla Bheinn along the north bank of the Allt na Dunaiche as far as a flattening at 200m.

The Route

Head right and follow a rounded ridge leading to the south-east shoulder of Sgurr nan Each. Some small outcrops high up give short sections of scrambling on a variety of different rock types. Gain the eastern end of the summit ridge, and visit the small top above North Buttress. Then descend slightly to a dip, which offers an exciting scree run down the north face.

Walk up a broad grassy ridge for some distance, and then negotiate some rockier ground to reach the main summit. A rocky eminence between here and the western top gives some pleasant

CLACH GLAS

North Ridge

Bla Bhelnn

20

25

Pinnacle Buttress

20

23

Naismith's Route

Black Cleft

20

25

Arch Gully

easy scrambling. Go round to the left of a blocky pinnacle. A prominent slab sloping down to a dip is also bypassed on the left (crux). It is easier then to the small western top. Just beyond this top, a broad slope is reached overlooking Srath na Creitheach.

The obvious options from here are to continue onto Garbh-bheinn (Route 18), or traverse Clach Glas (Route 20). However, immediately to the south, a steep scree descent can be made into Choire a' Caise.

CLACH GLAS (786m)

This spectacular and shapely peak is sometimes referred to as the 'Matterhorn of Skye'. Its summit is one of the most difficult to reach on the whole island. A traverse of the peak makes a superb outing. It is usually done from north to south, in which case strong parties will normally continue by making an ascent of Bla Bheinn.

20 North Ridge Moderate ***

This outing is mainly scrambling, with very interesting route finding, chiefly on the right side of the crest. The final tower gives the crux, where a couple of pitches may justify a rope.

Start

Approach along the path on the north bank of the Allt na Dunaiche, and head rightwards into Choire a' Caise. At the head of the corrie fork left up steep scree and boulders to gain a bealach.

The Route

Ascend a steep little wall out of the bealach, and scramble pleasantly up slabs and along a switch-back crest. Climb down steeply into a gap on the Loch Slapin side, and then scramble up a short arête. Traverse slightly easier ground along ledges below the crest, and look out for two photogenic rock lumps with remarkable holes right through them situated up left on the crest itself.

From the bed of a gully make an awkward rightwards traverse beneath steep rocks. Continue more easily, traversing beneath a large pinnacle to gain a more prominent scree gully marking the start of the major difficulties. Climb a slanting V-shaped chimney, bridging past some awkward chockstones. Part way up, a possible alternative is to climb a steep crack in the right wall to a short ridge. Turn left to tackle the summit tower. The next pitch takes a fairly direct line to the crest. It is sustained and in a sensational position. Finish along a fine ridge to gain the splendid platform forming the summit.

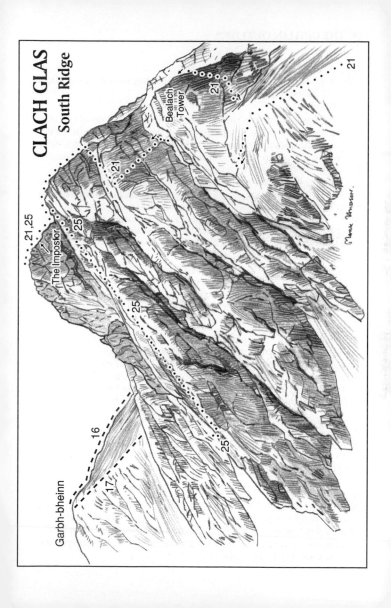

CLACH GLAS
South Ridge

21

Bealach
Tower

21

21

21,25

The Impostor

25

25

25

16

Garbh-bheinn

17

25

Mark Hudson.

21 South Ridge Moderate **

This route is described in descent – the way it is normally followed during a traverse of the mountain.

The Route

A short distance from the summit descend a shallow groove in a slab on the east side of the crest. This is the so-called Impostor. At the bottom of the slab it is necessary to face in for a couple of moves to climb down a steep and exposed rib. Reach a section of easier horizontal arête formed by a cone-sheet.

From the end of the arête descend the ridge just right of the crest until just after a tiny gap. Then descend slabs on the left-hand side of the crest and drop down to a ledge below. Follow a scree path, and then more broken rocks slanting slightly right. From a ledge, curve back left on a path to another slabby face on the Loch Slapin side. Descend this leftwards to a cleft. Climb down the cleft and then continue more easily down a sloping terrace.

Scramble down into a gap of green rock with gullies on either side. Ascend the other side more easily and then reach another gap. Make some awkward moves to escape out of this second gap, and continue towards the summit of a feature known as Bealach Tower. Immediately before the highest point cut diagonally leftwards over the crest by a narrow cleft, and descend a slab on the Slapin side. Reach a brown cone-sheet and follow this back right to another gap, with a boulder jammed across the rift on the left. Scramble out of the gap on the right-hand side and continue more easily along a ridge to a grassy hollow with large boulders known as the Putting Green.

It is possible to descend the scree slopes on the Loch Slapin side, but it is more interesting to continue onto Bla Bheinn (Route 27).

EAST FACE

The east face of Clach Glas is a striking feature seen from across Loch Slapin. It provides a couple of interesting routes with a real mountaineering feel about them.

22 Sid's Rake Grade 2 or 3 *

This is the original line on the face. It was first ascended by Sidney Williams in 1900. Dr and Mrs Inglis Clark had an epic descending this side of the mountain in a fierce storm in June 1901.

It should be borne in mind that descending from the summit will involve some Moderate climbing.

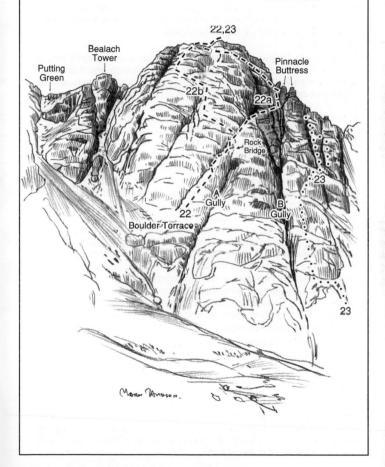

CLACH GLAS

East Face

Putting
Green

Bealach
Tower

22,23

Pinnacle
Buttress

22b

22a

Rock
Bridge

23

A
Gully

22

B
Gully

Boulder Torrace

23

Mark Anderson.

Start

Approach by the path on the north side of the Allt na Dunaiche. Gain a terrace below the left-hand half of the face, either by the scree further left or by some tricky scrambling (Grade 3) up damp slabs between the obvious lines of A and B Gullies. Traverse left across A Gully at the same level as the terrace. A gigantic boulder on this terrace offers an amusing scramble up its northern end.

The Route

Zigzag up the buttress left of A Gully on grass and rock until forced into a gully on the left. Ascend this for some distance and then climb out by its right wall to reach a sprawling juniper bush. An entertaining alternative now is to cross an amazing rock bridge onto the buttress right of A Gully, and scramble up slabby rocks before moving back left. Otherwise continue by re-entering the left-hand gully and following it to a shoulder above a gully slanting down to the right. There are two alternative routes from here.

a) **Original Route**:   Grade 2   (Grade 3 on the Impostor)   *

Ascend the grassy gully on the left, and continue to the right of a rock rib, to reach a fine col left of a small tower. Then slant right up easier ground over soil and grass – much used by sheep – heading in the same direction as a prominent slot between the two upper pinnacles of Pinnacle Buttress on the opposite side of B Gully.

Cross a tiny shoulder with orange soil left of a rock boss, before joining B Gully. Ascend loose scree in the bed of B Gully until the angle eases slightly. Continuing directly up B Gully leads to the top of the broad scree gully on the west face at the base of the summit tower (Route 20). However, it is more natural to stay on this face and follow a slanting grassy weakness leftwards well below the summit rocks, until it is possible to gain the horizontal arête just south of the Impostor. Climb a short steep rib and the slab above to the summit.

b) **'Slapin the Face' Variation**:   Grade 3   **

This is a more interesting line. Instead of continuing up the grassy gully, break left up a V-shaped groove floored with boulders. Exit up the left-bounding rib and emerge onto easier ground. Continue round leftwards and scramble up slabby rocks for some distance.

Traverse left and crawl under a huge chockstone to reach a sloping terrace. Continue leftwards, and eventually gain a broken rock rib with a gully further left. Scramble up this rib, sticking to the crest as far as possible. Continue up rocks parallel to the right fork of the gully. Rejoin the alternative line at the arête just south of the Impostor, and ascend this feature to the summit.

23 Ramp Route Moderate **

This varied route passes through some dramatic scenery. Only one pitch of Moderate grade should be encountered. Dr and Mrs Clark climbed a route in this vicinity in 1901.

Start

Approach by the path on the north side of the Allt na Dunaiche.

The Route

Ascend grass and heather right of B Gully to a grassy bay. Traverse left to reach the first reasonable rocks. Slant up leftwards at first, and then follow a delightful stretch of slabs intruded by numerous cone-sheets with good views of B Gully on the left. From a grassy terrace zigzag up a slightly steeper buttress (Grade 3), and then continue up more slabs to a second terrace.

Now slant rightwards up an obvious stony ramp. Head up and then back right to cross a steep gully, then continue diagonally rightwards up easier ground with steep rocks on the left. Ascend a short gully to reach the two main ramp features which characterise the route.

The left-hand ramp is situated at a slightly higher level below a spectacular vertical wall. It is separated from the right-hand ramp by a dyke gully. Both features offer pitches of comparable difficulty but contrasting styles. The left-hand ramp is reached by scrambling awkwardly up left. The steep initial section is climbed on small incut holds. The right-hand line is climbed by slanting right and ascending a narrow dyke. The crux is in an exposed position where the dyke thins above a steep cone-sheet. Slightly easier rocks above then allow the left-hand ramp line to be joined.

Short rock bands continue to give interest before the going gradually eases. Then start to trend up leftwards, and bridge up a short rocky gully. Traverse left along the line of a cone-sheet and enter the upper reaches of B Gully. Continue traversing left across the gully along a fairly obvious line. Slant down a short rock band to pick up a continuation of the grassy rake. Continue left for some distance, and reach the arête just south of the Impostor as for the previous route.

WEST FACE

The west face of Clach Glas has slabby rocks with two main gullies either side of the steep summit tower. The climbs here are difficult to reach, but they offer worthwhile outings in a remote setting above Coire Dubh. This corrie is also known, appropriately, as the 'Lonely Corrie'.

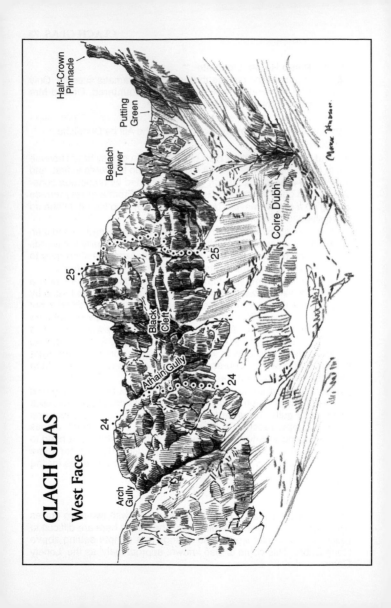

CLACH GLAS
West Face

Half-Crown Pinnacle

Putting Green

Bealach Tower

Coire Dubh

Black Cleft

Athain Gully

Arch Gully

24

24

25

25

The best approach to the west face is from the Loch Slapin side. It is much further from Sligachan or Camasunary. Ascend Choire a' Caise and take the steep right fork at its head to reach the broad slope west of Sgurr nan Each.

Descend scree fairly easily on the west flank, and curve round leftwards below the rocks north of Arch Gully, before ascending slightly to reach the floor of Coire Dubh. The prominent gully that leads up left of the summit tower is the unclimbed Black Cleft. The rocks right of this give the line of Naismith's Route (Difficult).

24 Athain Slab Route 200m Moderate **
This route was first climbed by Hamish Brown and party in 1967. Although not an obvious line, it offers enjoyable climbing. It would make an unusual way of starting the north ridge (Route 20).
Start
To the right of Arch Gully (Moderate), at a narrow slabby ramp with a steep wall to its left which is undercut lower down.
The Route
Scramble up easy slabs, then climb two pitches of slabs to a rock step. From the right-hand side of this trend back left and continue more easily to a short, wide rock step. Move up by a large lump of brown rock set in a darker matrix, and follow easier-angled slabs to the base of a steep wall. (Possible escape route up gully on left.)

Move right slightly to two boulders on an edge overlooking Athain Gully. The wall above gives the crux. Zigzag up taking care with loose rock, then pull out onto slabs and continue to the base of another steep wall. Move up and round to the right, then follow a narrow glacis across a wall for two pitches. Turn left to reach easier ground. Clamber up rocks leftwards to reach the crest of the north ridge.

25 Pilkington's Route Difficult *
This is the route climbed by Pilkington's party when they made the first ascent of Clach Glas in 1887. The climbing difficulties, which are confined to the initial section of gully, are very short-lived but sufficiently tricky to justify the grade.
Start
At the mouth of the obvious gully on the right-hand half of the face.
The Route
Enter the gully and climb rocks mainly on the left to avoid trickles of water in the gully bed. Surmount the right side of a chockstone on

damp rock (crux) to reach an easier section of the gully. When this becomes impractical, cut right along an obvious cleft to reach open slopes on the right.

Weave a way up slabs and broken rocks for some distance and eventually reach the horizontal arête just south of the Impostor. Charles Pilkington described his party's ascent. "… *we found a knife edge of tremendous steepness coming down towards us. We put on the rope and nerved ourselves for the attack; we just had a look round the edge first, and seeing a piece of slanting rock, we crossed it, and, pulling ourselves out of the neck of a little gully, walked up the impostor in a few minutes.*"

BLA BHEINN (928m)

Bla Bheinn is a magnificent mountain – the highest of the Cuillin Outliers – and a wonderful viewpoint. Surprisingly, it offers few continuous scrambles of any length.

NORTH-EAST FACE

This face rears up above the Putting Green and bars easy access to Bla Bheinn from Clach Glas. The most popular route weaves an intricate line up the face and is for climbers only. Two easier lines exist to the east and west, but both involve losing some height.

26 Dogleg Scree Gully Grade 1/2

This route is rarely used in ascent, but it offers a quick descent route into Coire Dubh after a south–north traverse of the mountain. The route is therefore described in descent.

Start

There is a small dip on the normal walking route up Bla Bheinn (Route 30), at a height of about 795m, where the ridge turns away from the north-east face and rises in a south-westerly direction. This scree gully slants down in a north-westerly direction from this dip.

The Route

Descend steep scree and loose ground until another scree gully is reached, which originates from higher up the north face. Turn right and descend this, with some scrambling down slabby rock steps, to reach easier scree slopes some 70m below the Putting Green bealach. Lower down in Coire Dubh it is best to head down into the V between two prominent streams.

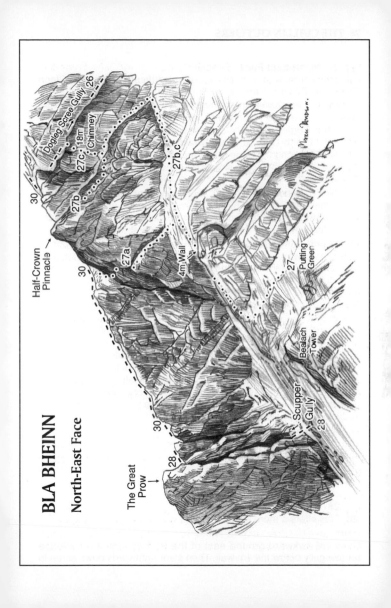

BLA BHEINN
North-East Face

Half-Crown Pinnacle

Dogleg Scree Gully

18m Chimney

26

27c

27b

30

27a

4m Wall

27b,c

27

Putting Green

Bealach Tower

Scupper Gully

28

30

The Great Prow

28

30

27 North-East Face Difficult *

This route is technically the most difficult part of the Clach Glas–Bla Bheinn traverse, although the situations (with one exception) are not as intimidating as on the final tower of Clach Glas.

Start

From the Putting Green – a grassy hollow marking the bealach between Clach Glas and Bla Bheinn. This bealach is normally approached along the ridge from Clach Glas, although it can also be reached by toilsome scree slopes on either side.

The Route

Follow a path leftwards at first, then curve back up right to a gap. Climb the steep 4m wall directly from the highest point of the gap. (The wall further left has a more awkward exit.) Then walk up an easy scree slope. There are three ways up the face above.

a) **The Left-hand Variation**: Moderate – though it seems harder.

The scariest way; not an option for the faint-hearted, or those wearing big rucksacks. Slant left up an obvious ramp formed by a cone-sheet. Turn right and crawl painfully along a ledge of sharp rock. Cross an alcove above a horrifying drop (crux), and traverse left across a slightly easier gully to join the east flank (Route 30).

The other two options are reached by slanting right up a path in the scree, and traversing right to a scree shoot. Ascend this leftwards to a sloping scree platform in a slight recess.

b) **The Gap by the Half-Crown Pinnacle**: Moderate

Continue further left and descend slightly to gain a fairly loose broad gully leading up to a gap at the back of the Half-Crown Pinnacle. Make a couple of awkward moves down big chockstones from the gap (crux), and continue down a gully until it is possible to break right and join the east flank (Route 30).

c) **The 18m Chimney**: Difficult

The classic way. Head up from the scree platform to a chimney with some jammed chockstones. Ascend this and the wall to its right. Move right at the top, then slant back left to join the east flank at the dip (795m) marking the top of the Dogleg Scree Gully.

28 Scupper Gully Grade 2

This offers a more straightforward way onto the east ridge.

Start

Descend awkward ground east of the Putting Green, or a loose narrow gully below the 4m wall. Then slant rightwards down scree to

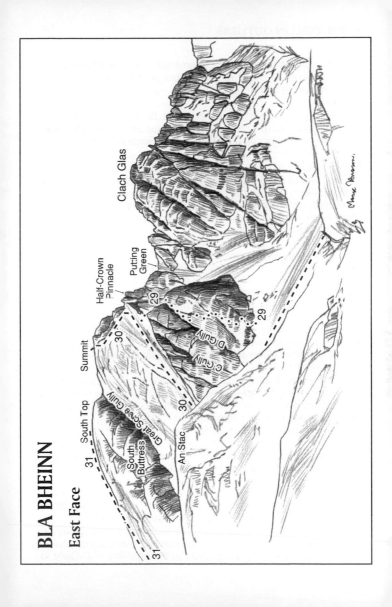

BLA BHEINN
East Face

South Top
Summit
31
Half-Crown Pinnacle
30
Puting Green
Clach Glas
South Buttress
Great Scree Gully
C'Gully
D'Gully
29
29
An Stac
31
30
31

reach the foot of a prominent gully immediately right of a soaring rock feature called the Great Prow. Do not confuse this gully with a forked gully immediately further right.

The Route

Ascend the rather loose gully easily at first. Bridge up a slightly more difficult section where it narrows. Shortly after, emerge from the gully and join the normal route up the east flank (Route 30).

EAST FACE

The east face of Bla Bheinn is the aspect seen from Loch Slapin. The normal walking route to the summit ascends the east flank, starting to the left of a complex group of buttresses forming the toe of the east ridge. Further left, the Great Scree Gully leads directly to the gap between the twin summits.

29 East Ridge   Moderate

This route takes a very devious line up the right-hand buttress and pinnacles forming the toe of the east ridge. It is not a route to be underestimated. It was first climbed in 1900 by Sidney Williams, who took three days to work out the line.

Start

Approach by the path on the north side of the Allt na Dunaiche. Slant right and zigzag up fairly grassy ground, before traversing left along a ledge with good views of the scree fan below D Gully.

The Route

The key to the ascent of the first pinnacle is a dyke chimney running up the centre. Start by interesting scrambling up rocks to the right of a right-slanting break. Then slant right before cutting back left across steep grass and rocks to reach the dyke.

Climb up the dyke, which soon develops into a chimney. About three-quarters of the way up, it is possible to exit the chimney on the right. Exciting moves in an exposed position then lead to a grass ledge. Move well left of the dyke and climb slabby rocks to gain a broad grassy terrace below a rock band.

Climb up at the left-hand end of the rock band in an exposed position level with the fork in D Gully on the left. Continue with much scrambling to the summit of the first pinnacle.

Descend behind the pinnacle towards a tricky gap. The best way to gain the gap on the far side of a rocky boss is to make a short abseil. Otherwise descend very steep grass in the right fork of D Gully to

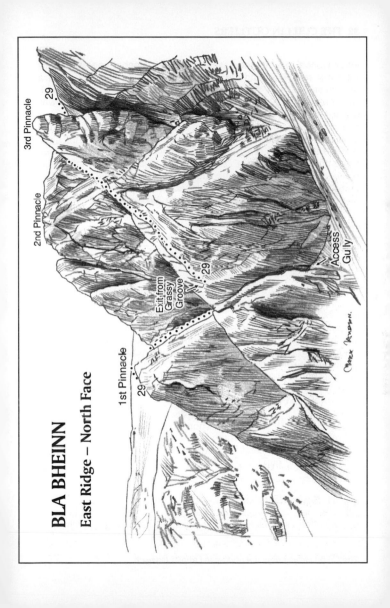

BLA BHEINN

East Ridge – North Face

1st Pinnacle

2nd Pinnacle

3rd Pinnacle

Exit from Grassy Groove

Access Gully

29

circumvent a rock rib, then ascend an even steeper vegetated gully the other side. Descend the gully on the west side of the gap for a short distance. This is the upper section of Access Gully (Difficult), which has a prominent chockstone lower down. Ascend the left wall mainly on grass to a slight recess.

The lines straight above are too difficult, so cut across right and descend a short shoot with steep drops into Access Gully on the right. Ascend an obvious grassy groove rightwards, and make a difficult move out right at the top. Easier and more enjoyable scrambling now leads up leftwards for some distance. It is possible to visit the summits of the second and third pinnacles before crossing an earthy neck to reach the east flank route (Route 30).

30 East Flank 8km *

This is the trade-route up the mountain. It is not a very inspiring line, but the upper section is rocky and offers unrivalled views.

Start

Approach by the well constructed path on the north side of the Allt na Dunaiche. Slant leftwards and ascend more steeply on the north side of a stream to reach a delightful grassy alp in Coire Uaigneich.

The Route

Turn right and ascend the steep grassy hillside, by a rather indefinite line initially, but eventually trend right on stonier ground. Higher up, the top of the Great Prow can be seen on the right, and the ridge then slants left at a tiny dip (795m). Ascend rockier ground above, with several short sections of easy scrambling if taken directly. Then follow a stony path which twists up to the summit trig point. On a fine day the views of the Cuillin are superb.

A pleasant circuit can be made by descending the south-east flank (Route 31), but this involves a short section of Grade 2 scrambling out of a gap to reach the south top. A possible, but less agreeable, alternative is to descend the Great Scree Gully (Grade 1) from the east side of the gap between the summits. Otherwise return by the same route.

31 South-East Flank Grade 2

The route is described in descent, since this is probably how it is most often used. Only a short section of scrambling is involved.

The Cuillin viewed from the north-west above Drynoch

The Route

From the main summit head off towards the south top situated 250 metres away, and descend easily into a gap. Then scramble directly up steep rock steps from the gap. Slightly easier ways can be found on the left-hand side, but they are rather looser. Continue easily to the south top (926m), which is only 2m lower than the main summit.

Continue over the summit and descend the south ridge for about 150 metres before slanting left to descend the south-east flank. Do not stray too far left where there are steep drops over South Buttress. The ground becomes loose and rather tiresome but eventually eases at a shoulder above the Abhainn nan Leac. Cut left and descend steeply into the upper reaches of Coire Uaigneich to rejoin the ascent route. There is a prominent boulder in the floor of the corrie.

32 South Ridge   Grade 2   **

This outing is mainly an exhilarating walk up a remarkably long ridge. The hardest scrambling is the short descent into the gap beyond the south top to gain the main summit. Walkers may be content to go only as far as the south top.

Start

The normal approach is from Camasunary, which is most easily reached by Route 5. Cut off the track on the descent from Am Mam just short of a hairpin bend, and follow a path across two streams – the second of which is called the Abhainn nan Leac. Continue on the path for a further 150 metres to a slight shoulder peppered with boulders. The route slants off right from here. The path, which continues across the west flank, eventually joins the main path leading from Camasunary through to Sligachan (Route 143).

The Route

Ascend grassy ground towards a rocky toe at the base of the ridge. Bypass this on the right and follow the ridge above easily at first. The ridge then becomes more interesting. In several places the crest pinches down, and it is necessary to move slightly right to avoid the heads of gullies on the west face. Several rock steps offer some scrambling opportunities.

The ground becomes much stonier higher up. After a kink to the right there is a long slog up the final section of broad ridge leading to the south top. Beyond this, descend steep rock steps with care

The Bad Step on the East Ridge of Am Basteir (Scrambler, Pete Woolnough)

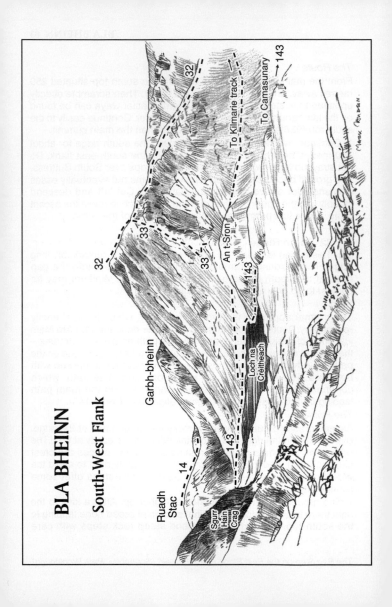

BLA BHEINN

South-West Flank

Ruadh Stac

14

Sgurr Hain Crag

143

Garbh-bheinn

32

33

33

32

Loch na Crèitheach

An t-Sròn

143

To Kilmarie track

To Camasunary

143

→ 143

directly into a gap (crux), and soon reach the main summit. There are breathtaking views to the north and west.

Various options are available from here depending on your destination. It is possible to descend into Coire Dubh (Route 26) and return to Camasunary by Loch na Creitheach. Few will wish to repeat the feat of the Willink brothers in 1873, who descended the gully on the west side of the gap between the summits. They escaped from the gully part way down and traversed right (north) to a scree shoot.

It is also possible to descend the south-west flank (Route 31) and return over the lochan strewn plateau of Slat Bheinn to the Am Mam track (Route 5).

33 South-West Buttress   Grade 3   *
This route may appeal to experienced scramblers wishing to add some spice to an ascent of the south ridge. It is at the upper limit of its grade, and requires good route-finding skills.

Start

From Camasunary as for the previous route, but continue past the south ridge to gain a picturesque bealach to the east of a small top called An t-Sron.

The Route

Head up the grassy hillside to the right of a stream, then trend left to gain a slight knoll. Descend slightly leftwards to reach an obvious sheep track. Follow this a long way left until below the lowest point of a rock outcrop. Zigzag up steepish rock on good holds, then slant right up slabby rocks. Climb a slab by a crack arising from a tiny recess, and continue right up a slabby ramp. Move up onto a higher slab and follow this rightwards to a grassy terrace with a steep wall above. Climb the wall and move left at the top onto a slab.

Head up mixed ground for some distance to a point overlooking an amphitheatre on the right. Then break back hard left across slabby rocks above a short wall, and below a bigger wall forming part of a knobble of rock above. Higher up, climb a rib right of a grassy groove, before slanting left towards a gully. Eventually climb a steep rounded rib immediately right of this gully (crux). Then continue up a broad scree slope above a chockstone in the gully.

From a slight bay left of a big wall, reach the crest of a rib on the left by cutting leftwards along a break on its right wall. Ascend the rib to a grassy ledge, then climb a short wall. Move right and climb part way up a slab before moving right to escape onto easier ground. Continue without further difficulty to the crest of the south ridge.

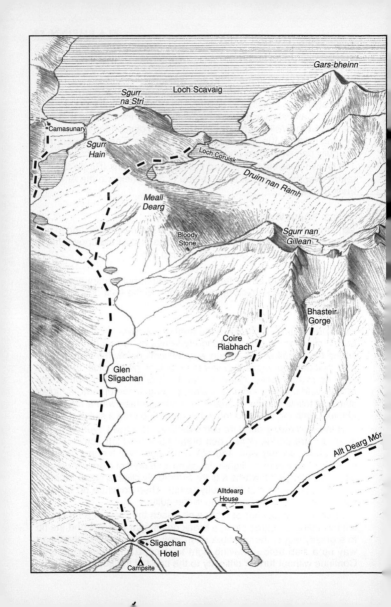

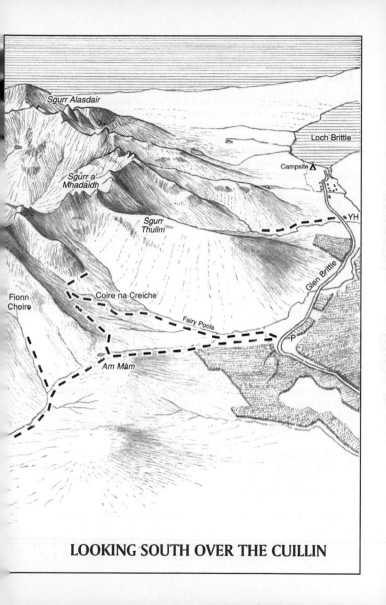

LOOKING SOUTH OVER THE CUILLIN

The Cuillin

The Cuillin massif is situated in the district of Minginish, set back slightly to the south of Glen Drynoch. In cloudy conditions the Cuillin are not as immediately apparent from the main road as the Red Hills. However, in good weather they show a very striking jagged profile, which is readily recognisable from many mainland hills.

The Cuillin peaks are arranged in a 12km long arc, which is concave towards the east. Extending on the inside of this arc is a major lateral ridge, Druim nan Ramh, with beautiful Loch Coruisk on its south-west side. More than thirty rock peaks protrude from the main spine and its subsidiary ridges, and these include eleven Munros. More than a dozen major corries flank the ridge.

The ridges and corries of the Cuillin are accessible from three main centres – **Sligachan** in the north, **Glen Brittle** in the west and **Coruisk** in the south. The outings are now described in that order, i.e. from north to south along the ridge, finishing with the routes arising from the Coruisk basin.

The main access centres are linked by three walking routes which circumvent the Cuillin:

1) Sligachan to Glen Brittle via Bealach a' Mhaim … (Route 34)
2) Glen Brittle to Coruisk via the coast   …………… (Route 141)
3) Sligachan to Coruisk via Druim Hain …………… (Route 142)

THE NORTHERN CUILLIN

The northern Cuillin group is taken to extend from Sgurr na h-Uamha to An Caisteal. It includes the shapely peak of Sgurr nan Gillean. This part of the Cuillin is most readily accessible from Sligachan and the northern end of Glen Brittle.

34 Sligachan to Glen Brittle via Bealach a' Mhaim 8km
This walking route can be used to cross from Sligachan to Glen Brittle, although it is perhaps used more frequently to gain access to the northern Cuillin peaks.
Start
By a track to Alltdearg House – 700 metres west of Sligachan Hotel.
The Route
After skirting Alltdearg House the path follows the north bank of the Allt Dearg Mor to Bealach a' Mhaim. It then descends a well-

constructed path more steeply to Glen Brittle. After crossing the Allt an Fhamhair, it rises slightly to meet the Glen Brittle road, near to a small car park. It is a further 6km to the beach at Loch Brittle.

SGURR NA H-UAMHA (736m)

This fascinating little peak is situated at the end of a southwards extension of the main ridge overlooking Harta Corrie. It is an extremely fine viewpoint. The easiest way off the summit by the north ridge is Moderate (Route 37).

35 South Ridge Grade 3   **

This route is in a remote setting and has some excellent rock. It was first ascended in 1896 by Naismith and Parker.

Start

Follow the path along Glen Sligachan for almost 6km. During a dry spell it is possible to cross the River Sligachan and approach from An Glas-choire (see Route 36). Otherwise follow the left (south) bank of the river to the Bloody Stone. This huge boulder makes an entertaining diversion, and can be ascended by several lines

Cross the River Sligachan further on, and ascend the steep hillside left of a prominent stream to a terrace below the south-east face.

The Route

The first part of the route ascends rocks to the left of a faint gully which slants up to a shoulder on the south ridge proper. Zigzag up a slightly intimidating band of rough rock a little to the left of the gully line. Then follow very pleasant slabby rocks parallel to the gully for some distance. The gully becomes better defined higher up.

From the shoulder it would be possible to descend the other side to easier ground, but a steep rib above and slightly to the right gives sustained and sensational scrambling on rough rock. Ascend reddish rock with downward sloping holds to a steeper section. Move up a little ramp on the left before traversing delicately back rightwards to the crest of the rib. Pass a slightly worrying section of rock with a cracked block. Then head diagonally right to an easier groove, which leads up to the crest of the ridge.

Walk up steep ground, weaving between blocks and ascending slabs. Move slightly right and scramble up delightful slabby rocks. Continue along the crest to the surprisingly broad top.

Traverse the summit and descend by the north ridge (Route 37).

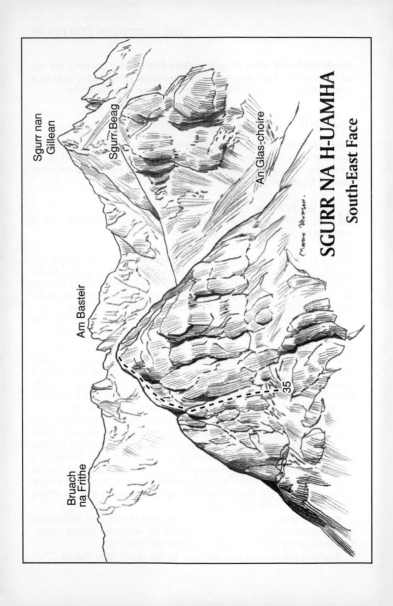

Sgurr nan Gillean

Sgurr Beag

Am BANglas-choire

An Glas-choire

Martin Moran.

SGURR NA H-UAMHA
South-East Face

Am Basteir

Bruach na Frithe

35

36 North-East Face   Grade 3 or Moderate   *
This is the face by which the peak was first climbed in 1887. Charles Pilkington described the route as a 'capital scramble'. A harder variation can be taken on the upper section.

Start
During a spell of dry weather the route can be approached by crossing the River Sligachan opposite Marsco. The floor of the glen is very boggy hereabouts. A prominent buttress at the foot of the slope (GR 487 245) has a pleasant scramble up its slabby left face. Cross over the Allt a' Ghlais-choire higher up, and continue to the foot of the north-east face. The start of the south ridge (Route 35) can be reached by traversing leftwards below the east face.

Alternatively, it is an easy matter to descend An Glas-choire from Bealach a' Ghlas-choire just south of Sgurr Beag.

The Route
The route follows an obvious right-slanting break on a face that looks more north than north-east. Ascend a conspicuous slabby ramp, then continue up a left-slanting groove (sometimes wet). Instead of continuing up a broader section of gully, slant right up slabs. Make a thinner move up a tiny corner on light green rock, and then continue up very enjoyable slabs trending very slightly left. Stay on rocks to the right of boulders and scree.

The angle eases slightly as the gully on the left appears to swing to the right higher up. Ascend short slabby ribs and more broken ground, and eventually reach a scree terrace. Traverse right to find more slabby rock, and continue to a grassy terrace.

a) **Original Finish**:   Grade 3
The first ascent party broke left across steep ground to gain the eastern flank. They then continued mainly on scree to the summit.

b) **Right-hand Finish**:   Moderate *
A more serious finish starts by slanting up right along the grassy terrace. (Purple flowers of devilsbit scabious are numerous here in late summer.) Follow narrow slabs continuing further right. Then step down into a gully in a much more exposed position. Make a few moves up the gully, then make a delicate move to get established on the slabby right wall. Ascend a crack heading away from the gully, and eventually reach a long rock band with an alcove to the left. Traverse to the right-hand end of the rock band.

The very exposed rocks above are sustained, and constitute the crux of the right-hand finish. Climb up a rib and continue up slabs just right of a dyke. Reach a ledge and step left onto the dyke where it

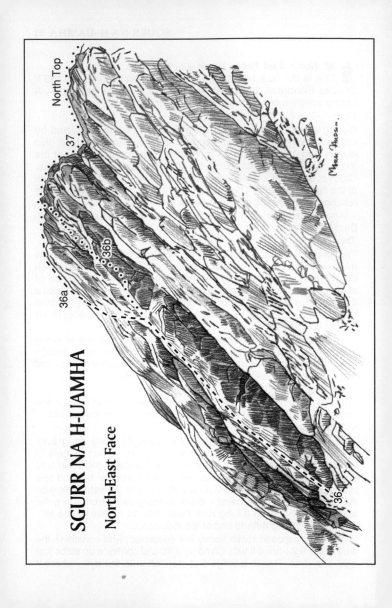

SGURR NA H-UAMHA

North-East Face

North Top

37

36b

36a

36

Mark Hudson.

leans back left slightly. Ascend the dyke for a short distance, then traverse back to slabs on the right by a juniper bush. Continue with less difficulty and join the crest a short distance north of the summit.

37 North Ridge Moderate *
This is the normal route used when bagging this peak from Sgurr Beag. There is a relatively short section of Moderate rock, but it must also be negotiated in descent when returning from the summit.
Start
From Bealach a' Ghlas-choire, which can easily be reached from the east or west side but is normally approached from Sgurr Beag.
The Route
The ridge is fairly straightforward as far as a dip just beyond the small, rocky northern top. From the dip, traverse a grassy ledge on the west (Lota Corrie) side, and scramble up rocks and grass to reach a broad rock rib. Move into a grassy alcove on the left side of the crest, and ascend rightwards to a rib. Ascend this to gain a ledge below the steep final tier. Slant rightwards along the ledge, then climb a short steep wall (crux) to gain the summit ridge. Follow this more easily to the top. Return the same way.

SGURR BEAG (764m)

This minor top lies on the ridge linking Sgurr na h Uamha and Sgurr nan Gillean. It is easily traversed from north to south.

38 North–South Traverse
Descend the continuation of the south-east ridge of Sgurr nan Gillean beyond the point where the normal route from Sligachan (Route 40) gains the crest. This is a narrow rocky arête with very steep drops on the east side. From a dip a slight detour has to be made to the east to reach the summit. The broader and steeper south ridge is descended easily to Bealach a' Ghlas-choire.

———

There is a long tongue of rocky ground forming the south-east flank of the peak. This is guarded all round its base by an overlap formed by a cone-sheet. However, it is possible to traverse a wall on the south-west side rightwards (Grade 2) to gain the tongue. This gives pleasant easy scrambling. There are dramatic views looking north from a small top just before the summit.

SGURR NAN GILLEAN (964m)

This majestic peak is among the finest in the Cuillin. It has a commanding position at the northern end of the main ridge, and is an impressive sight from Sligachan. Three fine ridges, none of which is easy, lead to its summit.

39 Eastern Spur Grade 2/3 **

This outing makes an entertaining alternative start to the normal route up the south-east ridge of the mountain (Route 40). It requires reasonably dry conditions for the approach across Glen Sligachan.

Start

Follow the path along Glen Sligachan for some 5km until directly below Fiaclan Dearg – the crag on the west face of Marsco. Head off over boggy ground at right-angles to the path, and cross the River Sligachan. Continue across the floor of the glen towards the right-hand of two buttresses situated either side of a stream.

The Route

Move to the left-hand side of what is known as Glen Sligachan Buttress, and scramble up slabs of very rough rock coated in brown lichen. Weave a way up for some distance, and eventually break out onto more open ground with a stream visible below on the left.

Slant rightwards to gain a superb sweep of slabs – one of the best sections of the route. These are quite steep at first, but then continue for some distance at a very enjoyable angle. Eventually the broad crest of the spur is gained.

Continue with plenty of interest on the rounded crest. Some slabby sections are interrupted by short, steep noses, which are best taken direct. Eventually reach more bouldery ground, where a large crag comes into view above and slightly to the right.

Ascend boulders and short sections of scree heading for the centre of some right-slanting slabby rocks well to the left of the crag. Delightful scrambling, rightwards at first and then left at the top, leads to a boulder field where the normal route up the mountain (Route 40) is joined. There are good views of Pinnacle Ridge on the skyline to the right.

The simplest option from here is to descend Route 40 back to Sligachan. The preferred option, however, is to continue up Route 40 to the summit by the south-east ridge. Another option is to traverse Sgurr Beag (Route 38) and visit Sgurr na h-Uamha (Route 37).

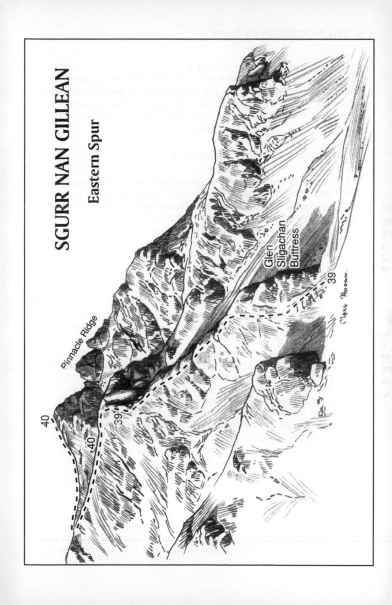

40 South-East Ridge   Grade 3 **

This is the easiest way up the mountain, but not a route to be underestimated. Route-finding can be a problem in poor visibility, and the crucial section is high up near the summit. This was the line followed by Professor James Forbes and Duncan MacIntyre when they made the first ascent of the peak in 1836.

Start

A short distance west of the Sligachan Hotel.

The Route

Pick up a path which leads to a narrow bridge over the Allt Dearg Mor. Cross this and shortly after head away from the river on a well constructed path – much improved in recent years. Eventually reach the north bank of the Allt Dearg Beag. Follow this stream for a short distance, then cross it by a narrow footbridge.

Follow a muddier path for a further kilometre to the crest of a broad shoulder. Descend slightly to cross Coire Riabhach, then climb out again more steeply on the south side. Continue on more bouldery ground, with Pinnacle Ridge prominent high up on the right. Curve up slightly rightwards on scree to reach a steeper section of rockier ground. Break through this by slanting left up a broad cleft to reach a bouldery terrace. Zigzag up stony ground for some distance (junction with Route 39) to gain the crest of the south-east ridge.

Walk and clamber over blocks on the crest at first. Then continue over distinctive volcanic breccia with large brown blocks in it. Eventually take an easy line on the left side of the crest, and ascend a shallow gully. Exit from this by bridging out rightwards at the top to regain easier ground. Do not follow a ledge leading left, but move up into a short corner and ascend rightwards by means of flakes. Then continue up slabbier rocks, zigzagging up slightly right, until a short traverse hard right can be made to reach the crest.

Make an awkward and exposed step-up, and continue on the very narrow crest. Ascend delightful red-coloured slabs, and soon reach the final section of arête where the crest starts to level off. Cross a small neck where the ridge pinches down, and shortly after reach the summit – one of the finest viewpoints in the Cuillin. The only problem now is that the easiest way down is back the same way.

41 Cooper's Gully – Bhasteir Gorge   Moderate *

The Allt Dearg Beag flows out of Coire a' Bhasteir through the Bhasteir Gorge. This spectacular ravine was first ascended in its entirety by Hastings, Hopkinson and Slingsby (Alpine Club) in 1890, but they had to swim across a 10 metre-long pool. The following route visits the main part of the gorge, but escapes by the left wall without entailing an aquatic diversion. It was first ascended by C.H. Cooper in 1913. It is best done during a spell of dry weather, when it can be used as an alternative approach to Pinnacle Ridge (Route 42).

Start

From Sligachan, follow the path to the Allt Dearg Beag as for the previous route but, instead of crossing the narrow bridge, stay on the north bank and follow it all the way to the mouth of the gorge.

The Route

Enter the gorge and make progress easily at first. Then ascend a chockstone, and traverse along a ramp on the right wall to avoid a tiny pool. Further minor difficulties, usually taken on the right, lead to a long pool where the AC party took to the water.

Now walk back along the gorge from this pool for about 30 metres and look for a gully on the east wall – i.e. on the left when heading upstream. Make a slightly awkward move to enter the gully, and ascend it fairly easily at first. When it gets a bit steeper and wetter, make a ticklish traverse across the right wall, and move further round into a more exposed position. Make a tricky move up by the edge of a block (crux) and re-enter the gully briefly before transferring to some slabby rocks on the right-hand side. These continue pleasantly for some distance before giving way to easy ground. Move up slightly left to gain a broad slabby toe leading to the start of Pinnacle Ridge.

42 Pinnacle Ridge   Moderate   **

This is the north ridge of the mountain. It is a popular outing with some sensational situations, but not on the best of rock. The normal way of tackling the crucial descent of the third pinnacle is to make a scary 22m abseil from the summit, although it can be down-climbed at Difficult. It is also possible to avoid this manoeuvre by traversing across the east face lower down. The date of the first ascent is uncertain, but it was probably in the 1880s.

Start

From Sligachan, follow Route 40 as far as the high point on the path just north of Coire Riabhach. Then head in a south-westerly direction up a broad shoulder, following traces of a path at first.

After 1km the shoulder becomes more rocky and better defined. The Bhasteir Gorge lies immediately to the west. Make directly for the steeper rocks forming the base of the first pinnacle. A faint path slants rightwards across scree at this point, and skirts all the way below

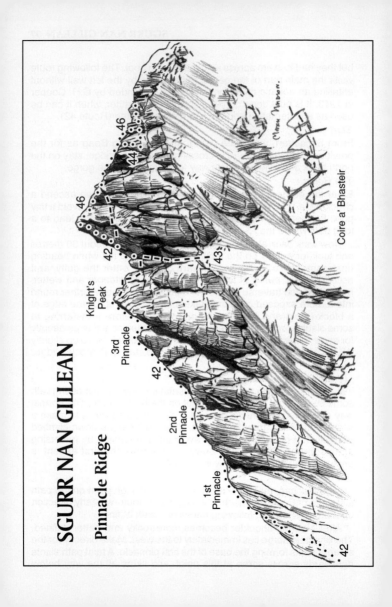

SGURR NAN GILLEAN

Pinnacle Ridge

1st Pinnacle

2nd Pinnacle

3rd Pinnacle

Knight's Peak

Coire a' Bhasteir

Sgurr Nan...

Pinnacle Ridge. It eventually leads to the start of the west ridge (Route 46) and Bealach a' Bhasteir.

The Route

Slant left on well worn ground, easily at first, then ascend a grassy groove and broken rocks. Move slightly further left and cross slabs to reach another grassy groove. Continue slightly leftwards to a ledge in a more exposed position with good views of Coire Riabhach.

Slant back right along a rake to regain the crest of the buttress. Continue slightly right again and ascend a groove. Cut back hard left along a ledge, then climb a steep nose by a narrow dyke (Grade 3). Continue more easily then, at a short horizontal section, cross over to the right-hand side of the crest. Ascend a block and a groove to regain the crest. Then follow a pleasant arête, and continue for some distance with a gully on the right. Move slightly left and eventually reach flatter ground marking the top of the first pinnacle.

Turn right and soon pass the top of a prominent gully dividing the first and second pinnacles. By heading slightly left, it is no more than walking to the dip between the second and third pinnacles. Otherwise slant hard right over slabs, and hunt out a little scrambling to gain the broad summit of the second pinnacle.

Ascend scree to where the rocks steepen at the start of the third pinnacle proper. Scramble up a small gully and pass to the right of a minor pinnacle. There are two options from here:

a) **Traverse of the Third Pinnacle** Moderate with a 22m abseil **

Trend slightly right and scramble up broken ground to reach a steep groove on the right-hand side of the crest. Climb this with one awkward move, then continue with less difficulty to the dramatic summit. A good thread belay slightly to the left allows an exciting abseil to be made into a narrow gully. This leads down to the gap before Knight's Peak. Experienced climbers may prefer to down climb from the summit at Difficult standard (by either the left or right-hand arête), but this is probably more time-consuming.

b) **Traverse of the East Face** Grade 3

A short distance above the minor pinnacle break left onto the east face. Cross slabs fairly easily at first. Then, after some orange-stained rock, stay high and ascend knobbly rock. Continue quite delicately across slabs to reach easier ground. Do not follow a grassy ledge, but descend slightly to enter a gully which is followed to the gap before Knight's Peak. Drop down 2m to a ledge on the west side.

To ascend Knight's Peak, follow an obvious ledge leading right. Stride boldly across two gaps in the ledge. Continue past a big block and round a corner to a stony ledge. Now cut back leftwards for some distance and pass an awkward nose to a point where there are good views to the east. Ascend a groove slanting back slightly right to reach the summit of Knight's Peak. This is marked by twin tops of very similar height. The south-eastern top is rather harder to ascend.

The descent from Knight's Peak gives quite sustained scrambling, and requires good route-finding. Follow a ledge on the south side slanting down to the left, and cross a tiny gap to reach a shoulder. Drop down right slightly, then slant back leftwards to a gap. A Difficult 5m chimney on the east side of this gap can be descended to reach an easy scree slope. It is surprisingly awkward in ascent.

Traverse below a sizeable pinnacle on the Coire a' Bhasteir side and reach a higher gap marking the start of the fifth and final pinnacle. Climb the slab out of the gap by using a very high foothold under an overlap and stretching up high for a good hand-hold (Moderate). Move slightly right then scramble up left to a ledge.

There are several ways on from here: i) The most direct way is to move slightly left and climb a steep rib (Moderate), then zigzag up by the easiest line on concrete-like rock. Eventually join the west ridge near a rock tower which features a 'window'. ii) The easiest option is to follow a prominent ledge a long way round to the right and join the west ridge at a lower level. Continue up the west ridge to the summit.

43 Knight's Peak via 4/5 Gully Grade 3

This gully offers perhaps the easiest way of reaching the summit of Knight's Peak. However, it is a hard scramble – at the upper limit of its grade. It is not recommended as a descent route. The preferred option is to finish up Sgurr nan Gillean, but this is Moderate.

Start

Follow the previous route to the base of the first pinnacle. Then ascend a faint path – at times on very steep scree – to reach the prominent scree fan emanating from the gully between Knight's Peak and the main summit rocks.

The Route

A large chockstone blocks the gully low down. Teeter past this by a leftwards traverse (first crux). Then scramble up rocks mainly on the left side of the gully. Take the right fork of the gully, and bridge up this with sustained interest (second crux) to slightly easier ground. Traverse left below a pinnacle to reach a gap. Slant diagonally leftwards along a break, then head back right to a shoulder. Cross a small exposed gap and slant left to the crest by the twin tops.

SGURR NAN GILLEAN

West Ridge

Knight's Peak

Missing Gendarme

46

45

44

46

Deep Chimney

Doctor's Gullies

46

WEST RIDGE

The west ridge of the mountain forms part of the main Cuillin ridge. It is guarded at its base by a section of steep rock which can only be ascended by climbing. The rest of the ridge is a pleasant scramble.

The three routes described can be approached from Bealach a' Bhasteir, either along the ridge from Am Basteir (Routes 47 and 52), or by ascending scree in Coire a' Bhasteir. Walk along the ridge, then continue along an obvious ledge on the Coire a' Bhasteir side.

44 Nicolson's Chimney Difficult *

The main chimney feature, which characterises this route, is quite short but smooth-walled. It is marginally easier to slither down than climb up. It was first descended by Alexander Nicolson in 1865. He was also in the party that made the first ascent 14 years later.

Start

Follow the ledge leftwards for 50 metres to a prominent alcove with a gully below. Then continue a short distance around the next corner.

The Route

Either scramble up directly to the foot of the chimney/groove or start slightly further left near twin gullies (Doctor's Gully Left and Right) and slant rightwards along a break more easily. Climb the rather smooth tube-like chimney with some difficulty. Move right on a shelf at the top to join the crest of the west ridge a short distance above the arête of Route 46. Follow that route to the summit.

45 Tooth Chimney Difficult *

This classic chimney offers a steep climb direct to the crest of the west ridge. The first recorded ascent was by W.M. MacKenzie in 1956 although it may well have been climbed at an earlier date.

Start

Follow the ledge leftwards for some 50 metres to the obvious recess.

The Route

At the back of the recess on the left there is a prominent chimney. This is climbed direct in one pitch using back and foot. It finishes on the crest immediately above the rickety arête of the next route.

46 West Ridge via the Tooth Arête Moderate *

This is the easiest way up the west ridge. However, the crucial section of arête on which the Tooth (or Gendarme) used to sit has very steep drops on either side and is still an intimidating obstacle.

Start

Follow the ledge leftwards to where it broadens. This point is marked by two boulders, and is just short of the recess of the previous route.

The Route

Ascend the right-hand of two parallel groove/crack lines which merge together higher up, like an inverted tuning fork. Continue up the single groove to reach the crest of the arête. Make some delicate moves in a very exposed position to pass the stub of the former Tooth. Continue on rather better holds, and pass the top of Tooth Chimney. Soon reach easier ground where Nicolson's Chimney joins the crest.

The remainder of the ridge is no more than scrambling. A fairly long but straightforward section of ridge leads to some rather more delicate scrambling on curious concrete-like rock just left of the crest. Shortly after this reach a tower marked by a window which offers an amusing through route. From a small gap at the back of the tower traverse along the right-hand side of the ridge. Regain the crest and soon after reach the small platform marking the summit.

Alexander Nicolson wrote an account of his traverse of Sgurr nan Gillean in 1865 using a quill fashioned from an eagle's feather which he found on the summit. The carpet of moss that he described at the summit has long gone, but this spot remains a superb viewpoint. The easiest descent is by the south-east ridge (Route 40).

————

At the base of the west ridge, a short spur juts out southwards into Lota Corrie. A minor top on this spur, called Sgurr Coire an Lobhta, can be reached by a Grade 1/2 scramble along a narrow ridge.

AM BASTEIR (934m)

This fine peak presents a very steep north wall to Coire a' Bhasteir. Its western end is guarded by a spectacular pinnacle known as the Bhasteir Tooth. The distinctive profile of this feature can be recognised from afar. The easiest route to the summit is by way of the east ridge, but a recent rockfall has created a 'Bad Step' part way up.

47 East Ridge Grade 2 (or Difficult) *
The direct route along the crest is now much harder than it used to be. An easier option, which skirts the difficulties on the Lota Corrie side, requires careful route-finding. There are no easy ways off from the western end of the peak.

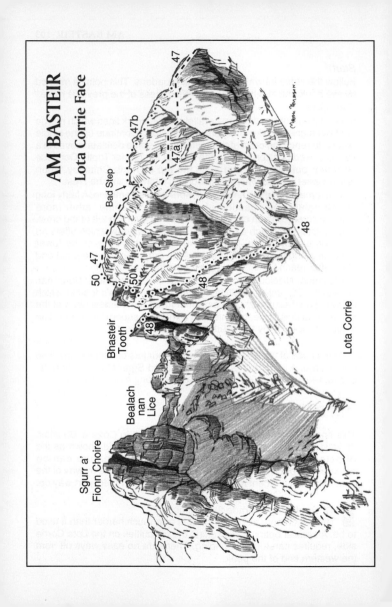

AM BASTEIR
Lota Corrie Face

47

47b

47a

Bad Step

48

50   47

50b

48

50

Bhasteir
Tooth

48

48

Bealach
nan
Lice

Sgurr a'
Fionn Choire

Lota Corrie

Start

Reach Bealach a' Bhasteir either by ascending scree in Coire a' Bhasteir or by following Route 52 below the north wall of Am Basteir.

The Route

Ascend the ridge easily until it starts to steepen slightly.

a) **Left-hand Variation** Grade 2

Look for a faint path on the left-hand side of the crest which leads to an orange-brown slab. Ascend the slab then cut horizontally leftwards for some distance. Continue round in a slightly exposed position and eventually cross a wall to join a ramp of purple-stained rock. Go up this more easily and soon reach the gap just beyond the Bad Step.

b) **Direct Route** Difficult *

Instead of leaving the ridge on the left, continue pleasantly up the crest. Some enjoyable scrambling in a fine position eventually leads to a narrow section of ridge and an abrupt drop. Although this is quite short it is at least Severe (harder for those of average reach). However, by returning a short distance from this Bad Step, it is possible to climb down the wall on the Lota Corrie side. Slant down leftwards (looking down) on small holds, and eventually step onto a tiny nose. Then climb down to the right (again looking down) to reach sloping ground at the base of wall. Walk up a short distance to reach the gap just beyond the Bad Step.

Both routes rejoin at this point. Continue more easily to the airy summit. Scramblers will now have to return the same way.

48 Lota Corrie Route Moderate *

This climb was discovered by Collie and Mackenzie when they made the first ascent of the Bhasteir Tooth in 1889. The route follows a slanting weakness across the south face of Am Basteir. It offers an easier alternative to Naismith's Route on the Tooth. The continuation onto Am Basteir is somewhat harder (see Route 50).

Start

The normal approach is made from Bealach nan Lice – an easy pass on the main ridge – which can be reached either from Fionn Choire or Coire a' Bhasteir. There is a prominent rock spike on the north-east side of this bealach. Descend into Lota Corrie by a faint path in the scree until almost level with the lowest rocks of the south face.

The Route

Head left to an obvious ramp/gully feature which has an outcrop of light-coloured intrusion near its mouth. Ascend the gully on scree and continue up a narrower groove above. Transfer to the left edge and then step down slightly and continue in the same direction with a steep drop on the left for a short section. Ascend by some small chockstones, then avoid a bigger one by rocks to the left.

It is possible to continue up the gully line but, by moving slightly left, a fine slab can be climbed in a fairly exposed position. Then move up rightwards to regain the original line. Continue until a high step up to the right allows a move left onto a boulder in a cleft.

Above are twin grooves separated by a steep boss. Start up the right-hand groove, then step hard left and follow the left-hand groove. From a grassy recess make a stride out left and ascend a slabby rib to reach easier ground.

The route to the summit of Am Basteir (Route 50) climbs a gully above and slightly right. Instead, follow an obvious traverse line leftwards and descend a cleft to reach the nick before the Bhasteir Tooth. Ascend a pleasant slab to reach the highest point of the Tooth. There is a spectacular drop on the other side.

49 Naismith's Route on the Bhasteir Tooth Very Difficult ***
This is the most intimidating route on the Cuillin main ridge. It has been the undoing of many tired climbers making a south–north traverse. It gives a sensational climb, and avoids the considerable height loss suffered by the popular alternatives (Routes 49 and 52).

The route was first climbed by Naismith and Mackay in 1898. Naismith inspected the upper section on a rope prior to his ascent.

Start

From Bealach nan Lice, either descend a short distance into Lota Corrie or scramble along the crest of a wall which overlooks Coire a' Bhasteir.

The Route

Gain a ledge, either from directly below or by a rightwards traverse. Ascend to a higher ledge and traverse along it to the right. Climb a steep wall slightly leftwards (first crux) to gain a more accommodating chimney crack. Ascend this, then traverse right and make a tricky mantelshelf onto a ledge (second crux). Finish on the slab forming the roof of the Tooth.

50 Am Basteir from the Bhasteir Tooth Very Difficult
The route linking the Bhasteir Tooth to the summit of Am Basteir is far from straightforward. The most obvious way is very strenuous.

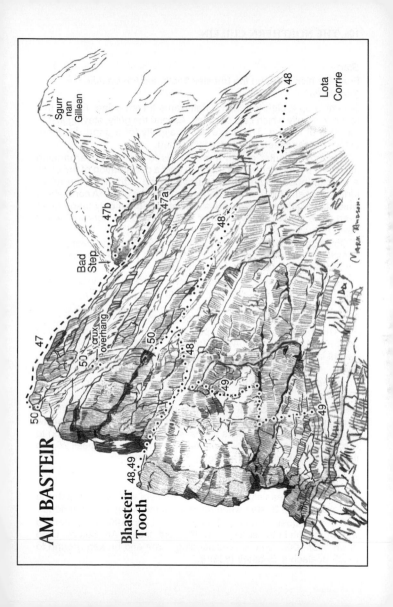

Start
From the nick between the Bhasteir Tooth and Am Basteir.
The Route
Scramble up a cleft to reach a rightwards traverse line. Follow this round to a gully which cuts back left. Ascend the gully, staying just to the right of a dyke. The angle eases slightly for a short distance, before a steeper section of rock is reached.

The most popular option from here is to climb an overhanging niche and pull up rightwards (hard) to gain a continuation of the gully. A less strenuous but more sustained option is to climb the rocks further right and make a long step left to enter the gully. A cone-sheet which leads leftwards below this crucial rock band only leads to an even more difficult groove. (Other options climb the right wall lower down.)

Continue up the gully more easily. By placing a tape over a boss of rock high on the left wall (looking down) it is possible to abseil this section when descending from the summit.

A short but enjoyable section of steep scrambling leads to the summit. The usual descent is by the east ridge (Route 47).

51 King's Cave Chimney Difficult with a 25m abseil
The route described offers perhaps the most convenient way of descending from the Bhasteir Tooth. It was the scene of an epic ascent in 1889, and was originally known as Bhasteir Nick Gully.
Start
From the nick between the Bhasteir Tooth and Am Basteir.
The Route
Head away from the Lota Corrie side and descend a broad rift with boulders. Find a small hole on the right and climb down a narrow spiral-shaped tunnel. Make a very awkward final step down (crux) to reach the floor of a cave below a massive chockstone. Abseil 25m to the foot of the gully using a lengthy thread belay.

52 Base of the North Wall 500m
This is the easiest option for scramblers wishing to reach the east ridge of Am Basteir when travelling north along the main ridge.

From the boss of rock in Bealach nan Lice (890m), descend a well-worn path in the scree below the north face of Am Basteir. Drop down over 100m before re-ascending scree and broken ground to reach Bealach a' Bhasteir (833m).

AM BASTEIR
North Face

Bhasteir Tooth

Shadbolt's Chimney

tunnel

abseil

51

King's
Cave
Chimney

To
Bealach
nan Lice

52

52

To
Bealach a'
Bhasteir

SGURR A' BHASTEIR (898m)

This peak is the high point on the ridge dividing Coire a' Bhasteir and Fionn Choire. A traverse of the summit makes a fine outing and offers unrivalled views of the Pinnacle Ridge of Sgurr nan Gillean. The approach by the north-east ridge is preferred – the north-north-west ridge being slightly looser and less pleasant in its lower section.

53 Traverse by the North-East Ridge Grade 1/2 **
This route is a good choice for newcomers to the Cuillin with limited scrambling experience. It offers some mild scrambling with superb views, and can easily be combined with Bruach na Frithe.

Start
From Sligachan, follow the path along the west bank of the Allt Dearg Beag towards the Bhasteir Gorge (as for Route 41).

The Route
Ascend a worn route over stony ground and slabby rocks, some distance above the west side of the gorge. The floor of Coire a' Bhasteir and its tiny lochan can be reached by continuing in a southerly direction. Instead, when the path levels off (some distance before a massive overhang which makes a good shelter), head right up a broad ridge on slabs and grass.

Follow the ridge – with plenty of opportunities for scrambling – to a slight shoulder. Continue up pleasant slabby rocks to reach a narrow neck, where a gully plunges down into Coire a' Bhasteir on the left. (The guide John Mackenzie had a fall from the top pitch of this gully before making the first ascent in 1902).

The going is then little more than walking for some distance. From the junction with the north-north-west ridge, head south along a very fine arête to the summit.

Continue beyond the summit, with steep drops on either side, until the ridge broadens and there are excellent views of the Bhasteir Tooth. The boss of rock marking Bealach nan Lice lies straight ahead.

There are several options at this point. The easiest option is to descend Fionn Choire on the right. A rather rougher but more direct descent can be made down Coire a' Bhasteir on the left. (At the bottom it is better to exit from the corrie by moving right onto the slabby toe of rock on the eastern side of the Bhasteir Gorge.)

However, it is easy to include an ascent of Bruach na Frithe and Sgurr a' Fionn Choire before descending as described.

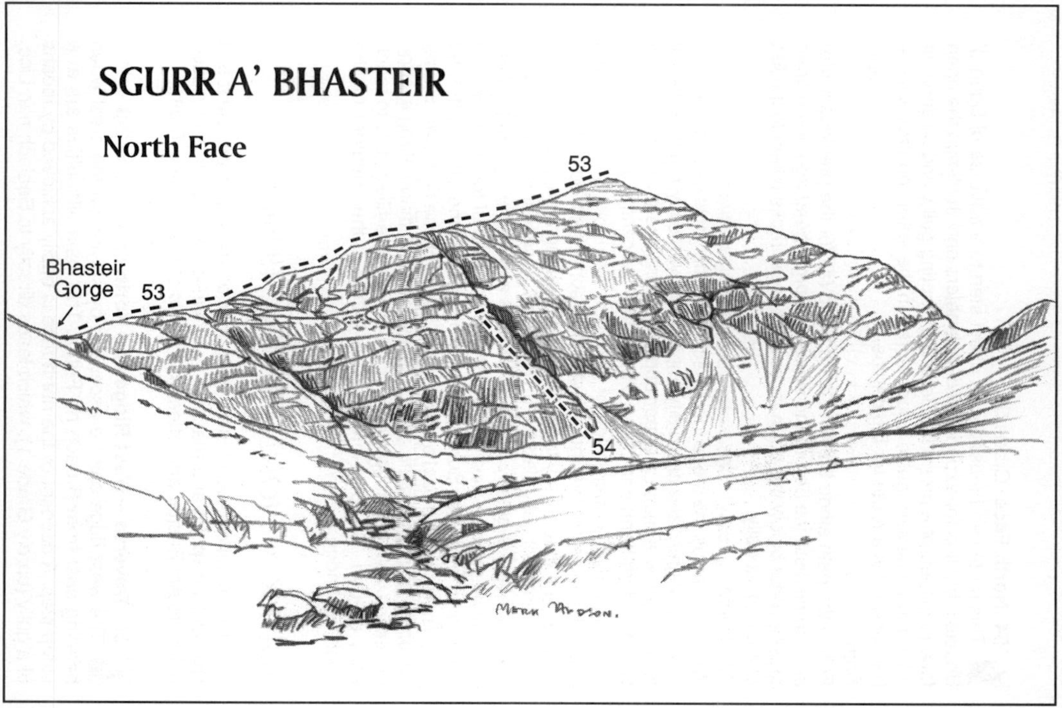

SGURR A' BHASTEIR

North Face

Bhasteir Gorge 53

53

54

Minna Marion.

54 North Face Grade 3

This route can be used as a direct start to a traverse of Sgurr a' Bhasteir, but it is for experienced scramblers only. It climbs the open face to the left of a prominent leftward slanting gully, and finishes up a hidden subsidiary gully. Loose scree in the latter requires careful handling – not a route for big parties.

Start

Follow the path along the Allt Dearg Beag (as for the previous route) and, some distance before the Bhasteir Gorge, head right to an open grassy corrie below the north face. Start at the rocks a little to the left of the central gully.

The Route

Weave a way up the steep initial section. As height is gained, the rock lies back slightly and its quality improves. Eventually reach a grassy terrace below a much steeper upper section. There are good views from the right-hand end of the terrace into the central gully.

Start some 10 metres left of the edge overlooking the gully and ascend a narrow gully/groove just right of some stacked blocks. Move slightly right to a grassy ledge, then continue up a groove to reach a more prominent gully slanting up to the left. Ascend this on its left side initially. Ignore a grassy break which cuts across the right-hand wall.

Continue up the bed of the gully on sections of loose scree with occasional bridging. Surmount a small chockstone on its left-hand side. Then climb up past a bigger chockstone on the right wall. Higher up, some devious moves allow a tricky exit to be made along a ledge on the left wall. Finish up a rib just left of the scree-filled gully to reach easy ground. The previous route is joined at the shoulder on the north-east ridge.

SGURR A' FIONN CHOIRE (935m)

This little peak can be skirted altogether on its north side, but it is a splendid viewpoint and makes a worthwhile traverse. It is of similar height to Am Basteir and offers fine views of the Bhasteir Tooth.

55 Traverse – West Ridge and North Face Grade 2/3 *

The west ridge can be ascended by staying on the crest when heading east from Bruach na Frithe. The main difficulties are at a steep step. A descent of the north face is easily achieved by means of a gully (barely Grade 1), which leads directly to Bealach nan Lice.

BRUACH NA FRITHE (958m)

The summit of Bruach na Frithe marks a change in direction of the Cuillin main ridge from north–south to east–west. It is a superb view point and boasts the only triangulation pillar in the Cuillin. It is one of the few Cuillin summits accessible to the walker. Professor Forbes made the first recorded ascent with Duncan MacIntyre in 1845.

56 East Ridge via Fionn Choire 12km *

Although this outing ascends one of the tamest corries in the Cuillin, it crosses some very rough ground. The east ridge itself is quite short and not at all exposed. The featureless nature of the terrain can cause navigation problems in poor visibility.

Start

Approach Fionn Choire by the path to Bealach a' Mhaim (Route 34). The Glen Brittle start is marginally shorter.

The Route

Head up into the open corrie for some 2km. Various paths converge as height is gained. Numerous boulders floor the corrie, and the ascent follows the general line of a stream. A small mossy spring at a height of some 820m is one of the highest sources of drinking water in the Cuillin – a fact worth knowing in scorching weather.

Steeper scree in the upper section of the corrie leads directly to Bealach nan Lice. Skirt to the right below Sgurr a' Fionn Choire on a well worn path and reach a dip on the ridge marking the start of the east ridge proper. Continue along the broader crest on bouldery ground. Move slightly left to reach the summit.

A more adventurous return to Sligachan can be made via Coire a' Bhasteir (as for Route 53). Otherwise return by the outward route.

57 North-West Ridge Grade 2 **

This very long ridge makes a fine outing. It has better views than the previous route and takes a more direct line to the summit.

Start

The shortest approach starts from Glen Brittle by the path to Bealach a' Mhaim (Route 34). Leave the path at its high point near a lochan.

The Route

Slant leftwards along a narrow stony path to gain the broad grassy crest. Continue just left of the crest overlooking a broad bowl with numerous streams. Pass an outcrop of breccia marking a volcanic

THE NORTHERN CUILLIN

Fionn Choire and Bruach na Frithe

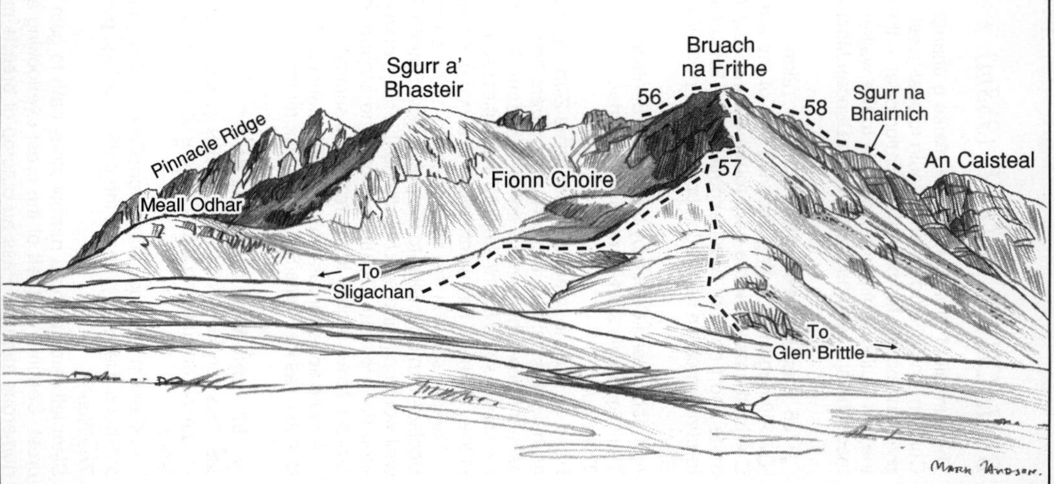

An Caisteal

Sgurr na Bhairnich

58

Bruach na Frithe

57

56

Fionn Choire

To Glen Brittle

Sgurr a' Bhasteir

To Sligachan

Pinnacle Ridge

Meall Odhar

Martin Varvoser.

vent. Then ascend a much steeper scree slope to reach a narrower section of ridge where an alternative approach from Sligachan also joins the crest.

Follow the almost level ridge to a steeper section where the scrambling begins. The rock is largely basalt and can be slippery in damp conditions. Several ledges lead off rightwards, but stay on the crest to get the best scrambling. Maintain position on the crest by moving left from time to time, but be wary of steep drops on the left-hand side. Pass the top of the only climb on the mountain (North Chimney) and reach the summit with its triangulation pillar soon after.

The easiest descent from this very fine viewpoint is by the east ridge (Route 56), but confident scramblers may prefer to reverse the next route and descend Coir' a' Tairneilear.

58 South Ridge via Sgurr na Bhairnich Grade 2 *

This long rocky ridge has only short sections of scrambling. Sgurr na Bhairnich (860m) is a minor top at the southern end of the ridge. The route starts from a deep gap on the main ridge which is reached by a long scree gully from Coir' a' Tairneilear. A more interesting approach can be made by completing a route on An Caisteal first and then descending that peak's steep north ridge (Route 59), but this involves reversing a short section of Moderate.

Start

From a small car park in Glen Brittle follow the path to Coire na Creiche along the north bank of Allt Coir' a' Tairneilear. A picturesque section of this stream – with cascades, several deep potholes and a natural rock arch – is known as The Fairy Pools. An alternative approach from Sligachan (popular in earlier times) follows a traverse line from Bealach a' Mhaim to the Allt Coir' a' Tairneilear.

There are two routes into Coir' a' Tairneilear. One climbs steep, loose ground on the left (north) bank of the stream to reach a high traverse path; the other takes a more undulating line on the right bank. The latter route is perhaps more enjoyable in descent.

From the floor of the corrie, slant slightly left and ascend a long, broad gully on rather tedious scree. In the upper section, move left and then back right. Finish up a much narrower section of gully to gain the gap below the steep north wall of An Caisteal.

The Route

Clamber out of the gap and zigzag up rocks and a stony path on the left, before slanting back right to the crest. Continue to where an orange-brown dyke crosses the crest. A short, steep wall on the north side gives a Difficult climb, but this is easily avoided by skirting round to the right. Continue more easily to the summit of Sgurr na Bhairnich.

There is a short section of scrambling on the descent from the north end of this top. Then follow a long section of rocky ridge interspersed with short sections of scrambling. The final difficulty entails crossing a small gap. Enter this from the left-hand side of the crest, go round the back of a knobble of rock, and traverse right across a slab. Continue more easily to the summit.

AN CAISTEAL (830m)

This rocky peak has a very narrow north–south summit ridge with steep flanks either side. It was aptly named by the geologist Harker.

59 North Ridge Moderate *
Only a short section at the bottom of this route is of Moderate grade. On a south–north traverse of the main ridge this gives a rather tricky descent.
Start
Reach the deep gash on the main ridge between Sgurr na Bhairnich and An Caisteal, either by ascending the long scree gully from Coir' a' Tairneilear as for the previous route or, better, by traversing Bruach na Frithe.
The Route
Climb the rather intimidating wall directly above the gap. It is steep but the holds are good. Traverse a short distance to the right, then ascend a short corner. Scramble up slabby rocks left of the crest, with an impressive wall further left. Gain a short section of horizontal ridge and turn left. Then slant up right and soon reach the airy summit.

60 South Ridge Grade 2 **
This splendid ridge becomes increasingly exposed as height is gained. Further interest is provided by three narrow gaps.
Start
Reach the floor of Coir' a' Tairneilear as for Route 58. Then slant slightly right and scramble up a slabby rock tongue between two forks of a stream – the right-hand fork lies in a small gorge.

Head up the scree shoot above and slant rightwards to gain another scree slope which leads up to one of the lowest points (760m) on the main ridge, a short distance north of Bealach Harta.

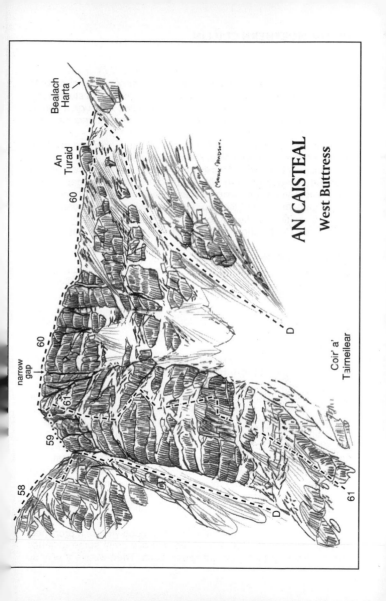

AN CAISTEAL
West Buttress

Bealach Harta

An Turaid

narrow gap

Coir' a' Tairneilear

D

D

58
59
60
61

The Route
The first feature on the ridge is a minor eminence here named An Turaid (*the turret*). At its southern end it is guarded by a steep nose. This is best ascended directly by a steep groove, although it can be skirted altogether on the left-hand side. Continue along the crest more easily.

Eventually reach the first of three gaps. This is crossed easily by ledges on the Tairneilear side. A short distance further on a second gap is negotiated in similar fashion. The ridge becomes increasingly exposed approaching the third and most spectacular gap. Either make a bold stride across it or descend a slab on the right-hand (east) side to gain the base of the gap. The summit is reached soon after.

The tricky descent by the north ridge starts from the left (west) side of the crest. Continuing directly north leads to a spectacular drop.

61 West Buttress Grade 3 *
This prominent buttress lies directly below the summit. It gives a surprisingly straightforward outing. The only difficult scrambling is on the first major rock band, which has excellent rock.

Start
Approach Coir' a' Tairneilear as for Route 58, and ascend broken ground directly to the foot of the buttress.

The Route
Head for the first slabby rock band. Start just right of centre and scramble up 5m, then traverse left along an obvious weakness. Break back right and scramble up to a steep wall. Traverse right along a narrow ledge to reach a dyke which slants very slightly left. Ascend this steeply on good holds until a stride right can be made to gain a cone-sheet which leads right to easier ground.

Continue via a minor outcrop to a much steeper rock band. This is too difficult direct, so walk right along its base and then slant back left up an easy break for some distance to reach the buttress crest.

Three closely-spaced dykes cut through the next rock outcrop. Climb the central one and move slightly left. Continue up steep but sound rock to a ledge. Then move left again and break out onto slabbier rocks. Scramble up an easy rib with slabs to the right and scree to the left.

Eventually reach a small shoulder with a good view of a prominent chimney/gully on the left side of the buttress crest some distance above. Move right and ascend easier rocks. Then weave a way up slightly steeper and more broken rocks. Climb a rib and reach a slight dip marking the top of a gully on the left side of the crest.

Follow an obvious grassy ledge to the right, then cut back left on slightly unpleasant ground. The way ahead looks rather intimidating, but rock steps just right of the steepest ground prove easier than expected. Eventually join a runnel of brown scree which leads onto the crest of the north ridge. Turn right and soon reach the summit.

EAST FACE

The east face of An Caisteal is split by two long gullies into three main buttresses. Several very long and enjoyable mountaineering routes ascend these buttresses. Both of the climbs described include long sections of scrambling. The remote setting adds a certain piquancy to the outings. The normal approach from Sligachan up Harta Corrie takes three hours.

62 South Buttress Difficult   *

This buttress was first climbed by McLaren and Shadbolt in 1911. The same pair had made the first continuous traverse of the Cuillin main ridge some three months earlier. The main difficulties are concentrated on the slabby rocks of the lower part of the buttress.

Start

Follow the path along Glen Sligachan for 5½km. Then head off to the right and pick up a faint path on the east bank of the River Sligachan. Follow this for a further kilometre to the Bloody Stone. This massive boulder is worth a few minutes diversion.

Continue along what is now the south bank of the river and eventually ascend rising ground to reach the upper section of Harta Corrie. Cross undulating terrain then head up to the mouth of South Gully, which lies immediately right of South Buttress. Some slabs to the left of the gully line can be ascended on the way.

The Route

From where the gully narrows and steepens, traverse leftwards along a cone-sheet to reach a grassy bay and belay. Ascend a prominent corner/crack to its conclusion. Trend right to another grassy bay. Ascend a narrow ramp in a superb position overlooking the gully on the right to a small rowan tree belay. Break out left for some 15 metres then up through a small overlap to more slabs.

Pleasant scrambling then ensues for a considerable distance. The buttress tapers as height is gained, with a steep drop to scree on the

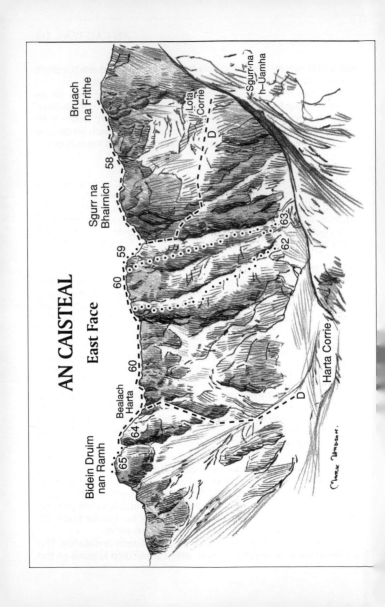

left and a gully on the right. The gully then peters out and a mossy dyke rises directly above to an arête where the buttress abuts the summit rocks. Stay just to the right of the dyke. Ascend a slab for only a few metres then break out right by the easiest line to gain the upper buttress. Easier scrambling up this leads to the crest of the south ridge. Follow that route to the summit.

The most enjoyable way of returning to Sligachan is probably to descend the North Ridge, traverse Bruach na Frithe and descend Coire a' Bhasteir. It is also possible to return to Harta Corrie by descending from Bealach Harta. (Enter a slanting scree gully a short distance south of the lowest point on the ridge.)

After Raeburn's party made the first ascent of the central buttress in 1905, they started down the gully from the gash between An Caisteal and Sgurr na Bhairnich. Just above the point where the gully steepens dramatically they crossed the left-hand wall to reach the floor of Lota Corrie.

The latter two options are marked on the diagram opposite.

63 North Buttress Difficult **

This remarkably long route (15 pitches totalling over 600m) was first climbed by Ted Wrangham in 1953. Apart from a fierce entry pitch, which is hard for its grade, the route is mainly an enjoyable mixture of scrambling and Moderate climbing on sound slabby rock.

Start

Approach from Sligachan as for the previous route

The Route

The buttress is bounded on the left by North Gully and on the right by a much deeper unnamed gully. Scramble up to the steep rocks close to North Gully. Climb up until a leftward traverse (crux) leads round and up to a good ledge overlooking North Gully. Break back right onto the crest and follow easy slabs for some distance.

When North Gully peters out, continue up a grassy ramp trending slightly right. Slant back left and find a way up steeper rocks by trending first right and then left. Continue past a green rock scar and eventually reach a grassy terrace.

Break through the steeper rocks above by slanting from left to right and continue to a short arête. Climb a groove on the left side of the tower above and then move back right at the top. Continue up a rib, then scramble up scree and a grassy gully to finish on the ridge very close to the summit. (See the previous route for options from here.)

The Central Cuillin

The central Cuillin group is here taken to extend from Bidein Druim nan Ramh to Sgurr na Banachdich. This part of the Cuillin is most readily accessible from Glen Brittle.

BIDEIN DRUIM NAN RAMH (869m)

The triple peaks of Bidein Druim nan Ramh hold a commanding position where two major side ridges join the main ridge. The traverse of all three peaks constitutes one of the more formidable sections on the main ridge. The individual peaks can be reached by scrambling routes, but a complete traverse of all three involves intricate route finding and Difficult climbing. It is possible to skirt below the peaks on the west side on scree. This is not advised in poor visibility.

64 North Peak Grade 2 *

This peak is a worthy goal in its own right, although it is normally traversed along with its two neighbours. It was first ascended by Naismith in 1880.

Start

Reach Bealach Harta from Coir' a' Tairneilear as for Route 60.

The Route

Some tricky moves on the initial slabs give way to fairly straightforward scrambling just left of the crest. A slanting ramp on the right side of the crest should be avoided. Pleasant slabs with minor rock steps soon lead to the summit (852m).

Continue towards the Central Peak by descending steep rocks on the right (west) side of the summit until an easy ledge can be followed which spirals leftwards into the gap.

65 Central Peak Grade 3 or Difficult **

This is the highest and most difficult of the three peaks. It was first climbed by Lawrence Pilkington, Hulton and Walker in 1883.

a) West flank: Grade 3

From the gap below the west peak, move up a short distance then traverse right on a narrow ledge, descending very slightly at first. When the angle above relents slightly climb up again. Cut back hard left on a ledge, and ascend a prominent chimney formed by a dyke.

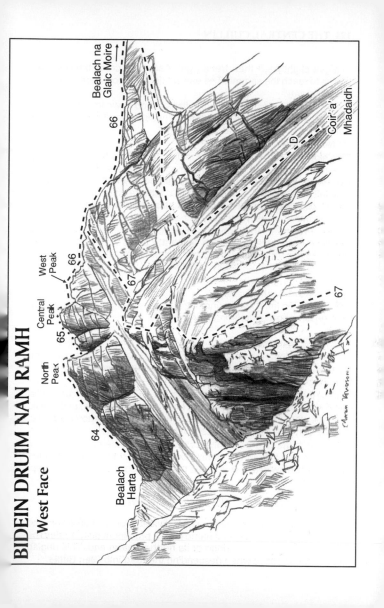

BIDEIN DRUIM NAN RAMH

West Face

Bealach na Glaic Moire →

66

Coir' a' Mhadaidh

D

67

West Peak

66

67

Central Peak

65

North Peak

64

Bealach Harta

Move slightly left then trend right. Ascend a crack between two blocks to reach the summit. The easiest descent from here is to return the same way.

To start the descent of the north flank, climb down from the summit platform and follow a ledge on the left (west) side of a narrow ridge, before crossing over to slabs on the right.

b) **North flank**: Difficult **

This side of the peak is the most testing part of the traverse. A steep face rears up from the gap below the north peak. Avoid this by a short overhanging wall further left. This is climbed by making a very long step left from a slab, using handholds at full stretch (crux) – rather stiff for Difficult. Slant further left up rock steps before cutting back hard right on easier slabs. (Many parties abseil this section in descent.)

Move round to the right of a tiny top and reach a small gap. Traverse left slightly and climb Moderate slabs via a small overlap and a crevice. At the top, cross to the right side of a crest and follow a ledge leftwards more easily to cracked blocks forming the summit.

66 West Peak Grade 2

This is the least interesting of the three peaks. Its summit (847m) is a massive boss sitting on a cone-sheet.

Start

Follow the main ridge from Bealach na Glaic Moire (see Route 70), or continue along the ridge from Sgurr an Fheadain (Route 67). The two approaches join at a slight flattening on the ridge.

The Route

Follow the ridge easily, then scramble up an orange dyke just left of the crest. Reach a flattening with a boulder and fine views of Coruisk. The boss forming the very summit of the peak gives a short scramble, but the only way off is by descending the same way.

To reach the gap below the central peak, descend a slab on the right (Coruisk) side of the summit boss. The last few moves into the gap are quite awkward. A jammed boulder bridges the top of the gap.

SGURR AN FHEADAIN (688m)

This peak lies on a side ridge which divides Coir' a' Tairneilear and Coir' a' Mhadaidh. It takes its name from a prominent gully, Waterpipe Gully, which cleaves the ridge at its north-western end. This dogleg gully is conspicuous when descending the road into Glen Brittle.

SGURR AN FHEADAIN

North–West Flank

An Caisteal

Bealach na
Glaic Moire

67

69

68

67

Waterpipe Gully

Metal Panton

67 The Spur Grade 2 **

This outing has some grand situations, although the rock on the crest could be better. Climbers may wish to combine this route with a traverse of Bidein Druim nan Ramh.

Start

Begin from a small car park in Glen Brittle and follow the path to Coire na Creiche (as for Route 58). Reach the traverse path from Bealach a' Mhaim and cross the Allt Coir' a' Tairneilear. Head up to the slabby rocks forming the left-hand toe of the ridge.

The Route

Scramble pleasantly up sound rock with numerous cone-sheets. Reach a broad terrace, then head hard right on a path across the scree. Ascend near a prominent rowan tree to gain the crest of the north-west ridge.

Follow the crest of the ridge more or less directly. Short sections of scrambling give interest from time to time. The upper section of Waterpipe Gully can be seen on the right higher up. Eventually the ridge starts to ease off slightly. There are fine views of the imposing north-east face of Sgurr a' Mhadaidh from the summit.

Move onto the right-hand side of the ridge to descend from the summit and scramble down slightly broken rocks to a dip in the ridge. There are ways off from here into the corries on either side. However, it is preferable to continue along a most enjoyable stretch of ridge.

From a small neck it is possible to traverse hard left on scree beneath Bidein Druim nan Ramh to Bealach Harta. Otherwise ascend an easier crest trending slightly right to reach the main ridge.

It is only a short distance up the ridge to the West Peak of Bidein Druim nan Ramh. If the traverse of that peak is too daunting, scramble down rocks to the right and continue more easily to Bealach na Glaic Moire. Then descend into Coir' a' Mhadaidh (see Route 70).

68 Edgeway Difficult **

This route makes a superb direct start to the previous route. It is on magnificently rough rock. It starts up the right-hand edge of Spur Gully, and was first climbed by Clive Rowland in 1980.

Start

Approach from Glen Brittle as for the previous route. A more direct line can be taken across the moor from a bend in the river. Head for the rocks well left of Waterpipe Gully. Start at the foot of a faint gully, known as Spur Gully, which has a mossy wall to its right.

The Route

Scramble up rocks slightly right of the gully/groove line to reach the left-hand end of a grassy terrace. Move left and climb a steep groove to reach a ledge below a rightward slanting crack. Slant up left along a cone-sheet to reach a recess with several rowan trees. Climb slightly steeper rocks immediately right of the narrow gully, using a foothold in the gully at one point.

The rocks then lean back slightly and a more interesting section of the gully can be seen slanting left above. Do not try and force a way up straight ahead. Instead, traverse part way along a ledge to the right and feel around for good holds on an overhanging wall. Climb this (crux) and continue delicately up slabs. Slant right to rock with white veining, and shortly after reach a ledge with a groove above.

Traverse left a short distance and climb a slab, then move back right, before slanting left up a groove. Continue more easily to join the previous route up the crest.

69 Pipeline Grade 3 *

This route finds a way up the rocks to the right of Waterpipe Gully. The upper section is fairly committing and requires good route-finding skills. It is at the upper limit of its grade.

Start

Approach from Glen Brittle by the path to Coire na Creiche. Cross the main river near a bend, and head directly for Waterpipe Gully. Move across to the rock apron on the right-hand side of the gully. Start halfway between a central weakness and the right-hand end.

The Route

Scramble up pleasant slabs for some distance. Slant left from a grassy groove to find a more interesting way up steeper rocks. Continue more easily. Scramble up slabby rocks trending slightly left.

Ascend a dyke staircase through a slightly steeper section. When this becomes grassy, continue for a short distance before traversing out left. Follow a cone-sheet further left and reach the crest of a rib with a grassy gully on its left-hand side. Scramble up this very pleasant rib for some distance. At the top, avoid a block by moving round onto the left-hand flank overlooking the gully. Soon break out onto an extensive scree slope. The upper section of the route is much harder, and those having second thoughts can escape rightwards at this point.

Head up and slightly left to a broad shoulder. Ascend a grassy weakness leading right. This narrows slightly at one point. Then make a very long traverse left in a much more serious position. Weave a way up to reach an alcove with a big slabby wall (wet?) on its left-hand side. Move right and pull up onto a blocky rib. Move right again into a recess and from a chockstone make a tricky step up to reach an easier gully above. Jink back left onto the rib. Weave to and fro to find the best way.

At another alcove climb a big step on the left and stride up and right to exit. Follow a left-slanting weakness rather than a chossy dyke/gully on the right. Leave it by stepping up and left. Continue over big blocks which lead back to the right-hand gully line. Climb a very awkward steep final runnel on its right-hand side.

Easier scrambling and walking for some distance leads to a minor top above Waterpipe Gully. Reach the summit of Sgurr an Fheadain shortly after and continue as for Route 67.

BEALACH NA GLAIC MOIRE SLABS

At the head of Coir' a' Mhadaidh there is an easy pass over to Coruisk called Bealach na Glaic Moire (760m). Directly below this pass on the Glen Brittle side there are some impressive slabs split by three gullies. The normal way to Bealach na Glaic Moire ascends loose scree to the left of these slabs, then cuts a long way right above the slabs on a slanting terrace. However, the three main sections of slab all offer more direct and interesting ways of reaching the bealach.

70 North Buttress Grade 2 *

The narrow left-hand slab is bounded on its right by North Gully. A narrow chimney (Stag Gully) splits the left-hand half of the buttress.
Start
Approach from Glen Brittle as for the previous route. To reach Coir' a' Mhadaidh, ascend a shallow scoop with a stream some distance to the right of Waterpipe Gully. Slant right and break out onto a broad shoulder. (This is a much easier route than one further right by a gorge.) Then follow a faint path which slants up left towards the scree slope left of the slabs.
The Route
The lower rocks of the buttress are fairly easy-angled, and some debris lies on ledges. When the rocks steepen, trend slightly right towards North Gully. Then cut back left to the buttress crest. Follow this, with much variation possible, to a prominent terrace.

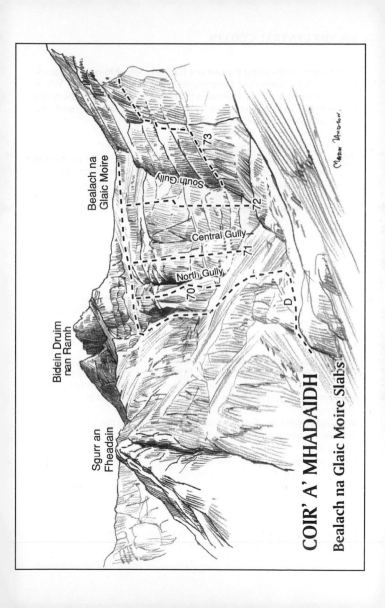

COIR' A' MHADAIDH
Bealach na Glaic Moire Slabs

Sgurr an Fheadain

Bidein Druim nan Ramh

Bealach na Glaic Moire

South Gully

Central Gully

North Gully

73

72

71

70

D

Slant hard right along the terrace for 250 metres to reach Bealach na Glaic Moire, which has superb views down to Loch Coruisk. When returning along the terrace be sure to continue all the way to the angle by the Sgurr an Fheadain ridge before scrambling down to reach the scree gully which leads into Coir' a' Mhadaidh.

71 Tuppenny Buttress Grade 2/3 **

This is the central buttress, bounded by North Gully on the left and Central Gully on the right. It gives a most enjoyable scramble.

In 1997 Willie Jeffrey found two King George V pennies part way up this route. They were half buried in grit on a minuscule ledge. One was dated 1915 – the same year that Bishop, Fraser and Hirst made an attempt on Central Gully.

Start
Approach from Glen Brittle as for the previous route. Ascend sharp scree and grass to the foot of the buttress.

The Route
Follow easy slabs to a grass terrace. Scramble up the steeper slabs above, weaving to and fro to find the easiest line. Sometimes dyke staircases offer the best way through steeper sections. The angle gradually eases as height is gained. Eventually join the terrace leading to Bealach na Glaic Moire.

72 South Buttress Grade 3 *

This is the longest and broadest of the three buttresses. The route is low in its grade and open to much variation. It is bounded on the right by South Gully, one of the best Severe gullies in the Cuillin.

Start
Approach from Glen Brittle as for Route 70. Follow the stream up the floor of the corrie towards South Gully.

The Route
Scramble up a small wedge of slabby steps just to the left of the mouth of South Gully. Then continue up slabs to a sloping grassy terrace. Just to the right at this point there is a gigantic pointed block in the bed of South Gully.

Opposite: Bidein Druim nan Ramh from Sgurr an Fheadain (Scramblers, Justine and Chris Jenner)

Next Page: Tuppenny Buttress, Coir' a' Mhadaidh (Scrambler, Willie Jeffrey)

There are various ways on from here. A slabby buttress, slightly to the right and quite close to South Gully, gives some enjoyable scrambling. Cross grass and scramble up rocks at the right-hand end of an extensive rock band. Move left onto a broad section of easier ground below the main section of buttress.

Weave a way up keeping a central position on the buttress. Large slabby blocks lie on the buttress further right. Reach a tiny grass ledge near a small muddy alcove with a distinctive green rear wall. Move up slightly right and follow a small grassy ledge rightwards.

A delightful section of padding, just to the left of a dyke, gives some of the best scrambling on the route. Move right, over a much narrower section of the dyke, and ascend to the right of a block. Follow a dyke and the rocks to its left. Then continue more easily to a terrace.

Move slightly right to find a way through the steep final tier. Trend right to reach Bealach na Glaic Moire.

SGURR A' MHADAIDH (918m)

This magnificent mountain has four tops on its summit ridge. The highest is the fourth or western top. The complex north-west face is dark and forbidding. It is crossed by several major slanting breaks formed by cone-sheets. Left of centre it harbours a huge scree-filled recess known as the Amphitheatre.

73 North-West Buttress and the Upper Rake Grade 2 *

The impressive tower-like buttress to the left of the Amphitheatre, is known as North-West Buttress. It was first ascended by Collie in 1896, but it gives a rather disappointing climb. However, various scrambling routes can be fashioned up the face hereabouts.

It should be borne in mind that continuing along the summit ridge from the top of this route may involve a short section of Difficult climbing (see Route 75).

Start

Approach from upper Glen Brittle, and reach Coir' a' Mhadaidh by the depression to the right of Waterpipe Gully as for the previous route.

Previous Page: Looking south from Sgurr a' Ghreadaidh

Opposite: Above Window Buttress, Coire na Banachdich

(Scrambler, George Archibald)

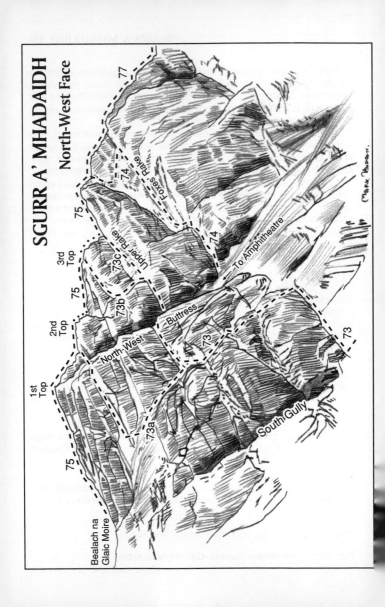

The Route

There is a gully on the left-hand side of North-West Buttress. This route starts up a buttress to the left of this gully. Follow the base of a big slabby face leftwards to the mouth of South Gully. Ascend a grassy groove just right of, and parallel to, the start of South Gully. Then scramble hard right up a slabby break to reach the crest of the buttress. Ascend the buttress on excellent rock, with scrambling to suit all tastes. Then, at a steeper section, move into the bouldery gully on the right.

a) **Left-hand Variant (The Uppermost Rake)** Grade 1/2

This is the least interesting way. Continue up the gully, and scramble up a groove right of the main gully to reach a shoulder below a more open scree slope. Ignore the first scree ledge which cuts rightwards to the crest of North-West Buttress. (It leads to a tricky Difficult nose.) Instead ascend scree for some distance, then cut hard right along the next scree shelf. This leads across the easy upper section of North-West Buttress and continues across the face to join the crest of the main ridge between the first and second tops.

b) **Upper Rake – Superior Finish** Grade 2 *

Instead of continuing up the gully, slant right on steep scree to gain a narrow rake which leads round onto the crest of North-West Buttress. This is a very fine viewpoint. Directly above is the tower-like section which gives the crux of the North-West Buttress climb. (It was first climbed direct at Very Difficult standard by W.W. King in 1901).

Go round the crest of the buttress and continue to a small shoulder. Then make a slanting descent, in a spectacular position, to reach the floor of the Amphitheatre. The start of the Upper Rake is on the opposite wall. It is possible to reach this point by ascending the Amphitheatre from directly below. (Scramble up the left-hand side of a rock band at its base – well above the start of Foxes' Rake.)

Make a steep move to get established on the Upper Rake, then continue round to the right more easily. Soon emerge onto a huge scree-covered terrace.

Curve round to the left and head for a gully breaching the rocks above. Ascend this, circumventing chockstones on the left wall. Ascend a rib on the left, and a short distance above head hard right along a narrow rake. Finish on the summit of the third top.

c) **Upper Rake – Standard Finish** Grade 1

Instead of heading for the gully breaching the upper rocks, trend rightwards up loose and tedious scree for some distance. Emerge on the ridge at the dip between the third top and the main summit.

74 Foxes' Rake Grade 3 **

This is a superb way to the summit of Sgurr a' Mhadaidh. It has better scrambling than the Upper Rake. However, the route is a natural drainage line, and is best avoided after wet weather.

Start

Cross the stream in the floor of Coir' a' Mhadaidh and ascend grass and slabs trending away from the stream. Head for the scree slope below the Amphitheatre. Ascend rocks left of the main gully then cross rightwards. Eventually reach a fairly obvious rightward sloping glacis which leads onto the start of the route.

The Route

The initial section is mainly walking. Continue on clean easy-angled slabs – scarred in places by falling rocks. Reach a platform where a wall of rock blocks the line of the rake. Move right and slant back left. Ascend a runnel, where the rocks are often wet. Climb up steeper rocks, then traverse right with sustained interest. Continue right on easier slabby rocks, along a broader section of rake, for some distance. Eventually reach a slight shoulder.

It is possible to follow a much narrower continuation of the rake, but this ends on a very rickety arête. Instead, traverse a long way left, and scramble up slabby rocks to the right of a prominent chimney. Zigzag up for some distance and finish at a small step on the north-west ridge. Scramble up a chimney/groove right of the crest. Slant rightwards on ledges to reach the summit of Sgurr a' Mhadaidh.

The easiest way off is to descend the south-west ridge to An Dorus (Route 78). Climbers will prefer to traverse the four tops (Route 75) or descend the north-west ridge (Route 77).

75 Traverse of the Four Tops Difficult **

The traverse of the complex summit ridge of Sgurr a' Mhadaidh is one of the more demanding sections on the main ridge. It is best done from west to east, thereby allowing the difficult sections to be taken in ascent. The crux is a short climb on the western end of the second top.

Start

The route is described starting from the main summit. This is most usually reached by the south-west ridge from An Dorus (Route 78).

The Route

Go north along the narrow crest towards a tower (905m) at the top of the north-west ridge. At this point the main ridge takes a dramatic

SGURR A' MHADAIDH
Viewed from the South-West

Sgurr nan Gillean

Bidein Druim nan Ramh

Bruach na Frithe

Glac Mhòr

Coire an Uaigneis

1st Top
75

2nd Top

3rd Top
75

75

Summit
78

An Dorus

78

Brown's Climb

P

turn to the east. The tower can be climbed by a steep wall from a deep notch, but in dry conditions it is slightly easier to avoid it by descending slabs on the right-hand side. Cross a small gully and continue down a fine rib with excellent views of Loch Coruisk below.

The steep nose of the third top rears up from a dip in the ridge. There are two options here – both of Moderate grade. The popular way is to descend slightly rightwards and then ascend slabby grooves on the right-hand flank back to the crest. However, confident climbers may prefer to scramble straight up from the dip and make a couple of steep moves just right of the crest. The difficulties then quickly ease and the summit of the third top is soon gained.

From the next dip weave a way up to a very steep nose. Climb this directly by a couple of Difficult moves on good rock. Then continue more easily to the summit of the second top.

A narrow dyke cuts across the ridge at the next dip. There are some awkward moves descending into and climbing out of this gap. A short distance along the ridge there is a good bivvy ledge where the uppermost rake joins the crest (see previous route). Continue pleasantly to the summit of the first top (896m).

A relatively straightforward descent from this splendid final top leads down to the broad flattening of Bealach na Glaic Moire.

76 Sgurr Thuilm via Black Slab Grade 3 *

The scree-ridden peak of Sgurr Thuilm is linked by a narrow ridge to the very fine north-west ridge of Sgurr a' Mhadaidh. The latter makes a good outing and is the next described in this guide.

The dip on the ridge between Sgurr Thuilm and Sgurr a' Mhadaidh can be accessed by steep scree from the corries either side. It is more pleasant, however, to reach this dip by traversing the summit of Sgurr Thuilm as now described.

Start

An approach is normally made by the path to Coire a' Ghreadaidh from the Youth Hostel in Glen Brittle. A more direct line can be taken from higher up Glen Brittle by ascending the steep hillside from a car park by the road bridge over the River Brittle (GR 417 246).

Head for a small crag situated on the south-west flank of Sgurr Thuilm at a height of 400m (GR 429 238).

The Route

The Black Slab route ascends the left-hand flank of the crag. It makes a pleasant easy Grade 3 scramble, although it can be avoided

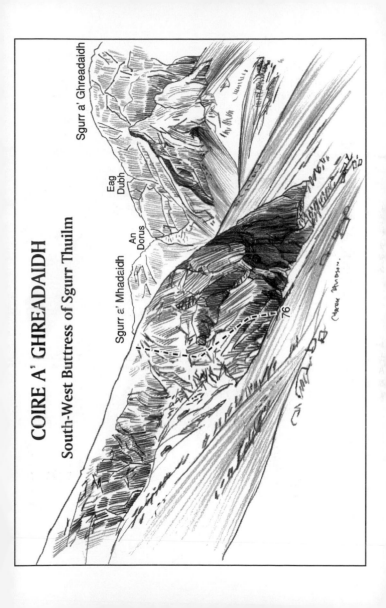

COIRE A' GHREADAIDH
South-West Buttress of Sgurr Thuilm

Sgurr a' Ghreadaidh

Eag Dubh

An Dorus

Sgurr a' Mhadaidh

76

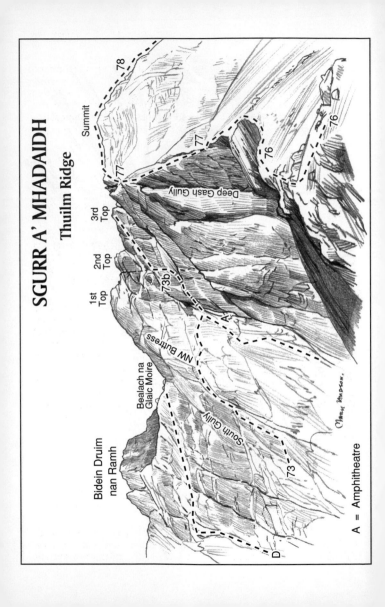

SGURR A' MHADAIDH

Thuilm Ridge

Summit

78

77

77

Deep Gash Gully

3rd Top

2nd Top

1st Top

73b

76

76

A

NW Buttress

Bealach na
Glaic Moire

Bidein Druim
nan Ramh

South Gully

73

D

A = Amphitheatre

altogether by ascending ground to the right of the crag. Start on the right-hand side of a small alcove with two dykes. Pull up rightwards and follow brown slabby rocks on good holds. Trend slightly right and make for a projecting block of orange/brown dyke rock. Pass to the right of this on grassier ground and soon reach the top of the crag.

Ascend the long slope above for several hundred metres to the fine summit of Sgurr Thuilm. Scramble down the delightful south-east ridge to the dip at the start of the north-west ridge of Sgurr a' Mhadaidh.

 77 North-West (Thuilm) Ridge Grade 2/3 **

Despite the rather devious approaches, this ridge gives an enjoyable route to the main summit of Sgurr a' Mhadaidh.

Start

The previous route gives the best approach, but a popular alternative is to gain the upper left-hand lobe of Coire a' Ghreadaidh – called Coire an Doruis – then traverse scree leftwards from below An Dorus. The start can also be reached from the Coir' a' Mhadaidh side.

The Route

Scramble up the narrow ridge with a chimney/groove further to the right. After the initial section the line is open to much variation. Staying on the exposed left-hand crest gives the best and hardest scrambling. The ground to the right of the crest is generally more amenable. If the easiest line is chosen the crux is slanting right across delicate slabs towards a groove on the right

The impressive indent of Deep Gash Gully can be viewed on the left-hand side of the crest. Eventually reach a small ledge marking the exit from Foxes' Rake. Move slightly right and scramble up by a chimney/groove, then slant rightwards on ledges to the summit.

78 South-West Ridge via An Dorus Grade 2/3 *

This is the standard way for Munro-baggers to conquer the peak.

Start

Leave the road directly opposite the Glen Brittle Youth Hostel and follow a path up the south bank of the Allt a' Choire Ghreadaidh. This stream has a gorge in its lower reaches and a delightful waterslide higher up.

To reach Coire an Doruis slant up left following a scenic section of tributary stream by its steep west bank. Then head east and cross a slabby rise before following the bed of a gully. When the stream

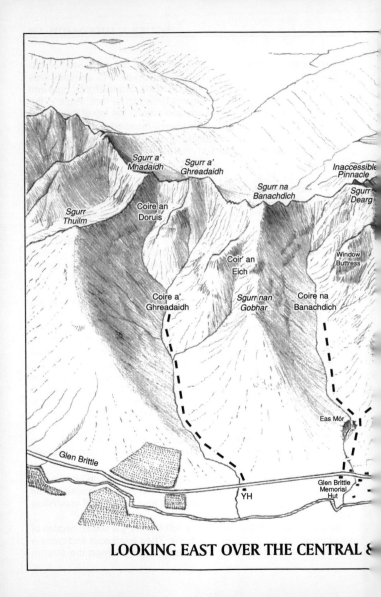

LOOKING EAST OVER THE CENTRAL &

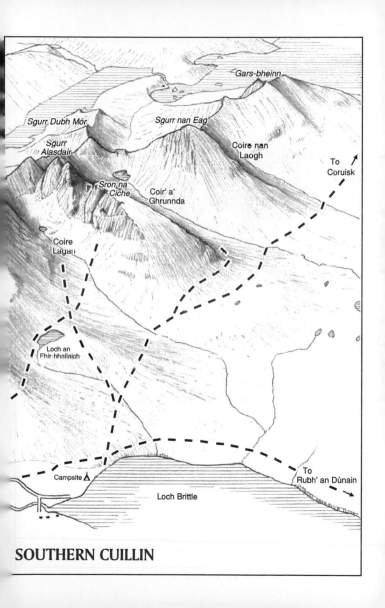

Gars-bheinn

Sgurr Dubh Mór

Sgurr nan Eag

Sgurr Alasdair

Coire nan Laogh

To Coruisk

Sron na Cìche

Coir' a' Ghrunnda

Coire Lagan

Loch an Fhir bhallaich

To Rubh' an Dùnain

Campsite ⛺

Loch Brittle

SOUTHERN CUILLIN

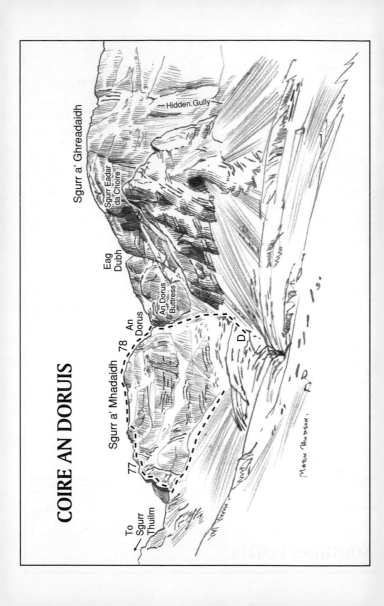

COIRE AN DORUIS

To Sgurr Thuilm

Sgurr a' Mhadaidh

77   78   An Dorus

An Dorus Buttress

Eag Dubh

Sgurr Eadar da Choire

Sgurr a' Ghreadaidh

Hidden Gully

Marin Amason.

disappears, ascend boulders and scree trending slightly left. Then scramble easily up scree and slabby rocks in a gully to reach An Dorus *(the door)*. This dip is the lowest point on the main ridge between Sgurr a' Mhadaidh and Sgurr a' Ghreadaidh and should not be confused with Eag Dubh - a deeper gash slightly further south.

Neither An Dorus nor Eag Dubh can be regarded as passes over the main ridge. Both are readily accessible from the west, but the gullies on the east (Coruisk) side involve Moderate and Difficult pitches respectively.

The Route

The main difficulty on this route is the short section of scrambling out of the north side of An Dorus. Fairly straightforward, pleasant scrambling then leads to the inclined slab forming the summit. The only easy way down from here is to return the same way. Confident scramblers may prefer to descend the north-west ridge (Route 77).

SGURR A' GHREADAIDH (973m)

This majestic mountain dominates the head of Coir'-uisg. Its superb summit ridge forms one of the most impressive and committing parts of the Cuillin main ridge. It includes a tricky section of arête linking the south top with the main summit. A subsidiary peak, called Sgurr Eadar da Choire, lies on its western flank.

79 North-North-East Ridge via An Dorus Grade 3 *

This is the easiest route to the main north summit. The crux is the scramble out of An Dorus, the remainder of the ridge being much easier. This is how W. Tribe and John Mackenzie (aged 14) first ascended the peak in 1870.

Start

Approach from the Youth Hostel in Glen Brittle as for the previous route. Ascend a well-worn line on scree to An Dorus.

The Route

The tricky south wall of An Dorus is best climbed more or less directly from the gap. Other ways can be found on either side. All these options are more difficult in descent. Cut over the crest by a dyke and ascend some slabs on the Coruisk side. Soon reach the dip of Eag Dubh, which has an impressive cleft, never more than 2–3 metres wide, on the Glen Brittle side. This is easily passed by slanting down slightly on the Coruisk side, and then slanting back right up slabs.

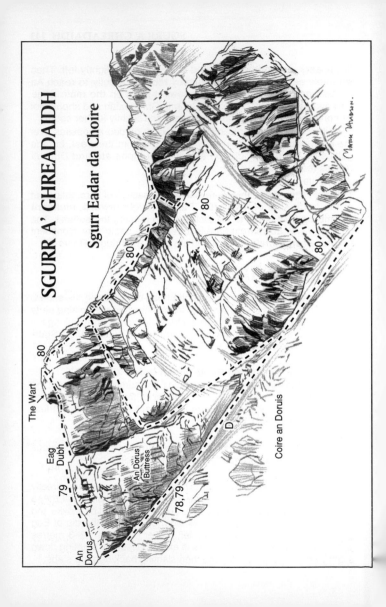

It is easy then for some distance. A large wall marks the start of a feature called 'The Wart'. This can be outflanked with surprising ease on the right, and the main north summit is reached soon after. This is the highest of the central Cuillin summits and a wonderful viewpoint for the whole ridge.

The continuation to the south (Route 81) is quite sustained and committing, and there are no easy ways off until Sgurr na Banachdich is reached. So the simplest descent is to return the same way.

80 West Flank via Sgurr Eadar da Choire Grade 3 *

The small peak of Sgurr Eadar da Choire is linked to the upper rocks of Sgurr a' Ghreadaidh by a very sharp arête. This separates Coire an Doruis from the main part of Coire a' Ghreadaidh. The direct approach to Sgurr Eadar da Choire is a Moderate rock climb on very rotten rock (King, Gibbs and Dobson 1898). The route described is more circuitous, but offers experienced scramblers an alternative way to the summit from Coire an Doruis.

Start

Approach from the Youth Hostel in Glen Brittle as for Route 78. Gain the bouldery gully some distance below An Dorus.

The Route

Go past a narrow right-trending rake. Just before a craggy wall develops on the south side of the gully, zigzag up broken rocks to reach a scree terrace parallel to the rake. Ascend this a short distance, then out up left to a higher slope. Scramble up through a rock step then trend right over boulders quite easily for some distance. Ascend a recess to a gain the ridge, then turn right and soon reach the twin tops forming the summit of Sgurr Eadar da Choire.

Return from the summit and continue along the ridge. Staying on the arête proves fairly nerve-racking. Some big blocks seem rather suspect and the situations are exciting. (The whole ridge can be avoided on the left flank if necessary.) Take two minor tops as directly as possible, but pass to the right of a gendarme. The ridge eases slightly as the summit rocks are approached. Where the main mass of the mountain is joined, a cone-sheet slants up from left to right. This point can be reached, perhaps more enjoyably, by following an easy rake rightwards from the foot of Eag Dubh.

Move right and ascend a gully formed by a dyke for 7m, then use the rocks mainly on the left side. Exit from the gully and continue more easily. Zigzag for some distance and join the summit ridge at the southern end of the Wart. Turn right and soon reach the summit.

81 South Ridge via Sgurr Thormaid Grade 3 ***

The traverse of this ridge is one of the finest outings in the Cuillin, especially when it is made part of a round of Coire a' Ghreadaidh. It is exposed and committing, and has sensational views. The scrambling is sustained but not unduly difficult.

Start

Although the route as described starts from Bealach Thormaid, the only easy way of gaining this dip on the ridge from the Glen Brittle side is by first traversing the summit of Sgurr na Banachdich (see Route 85). A much harder alternative is to ascend Route 83. An easy scree slope gives access via a forked gully on the Coruisk side.

The Route

From Bealach Thormaid negotiate some minor pinnacles, mainly on the left. Then continue along the ridge, and soon reach the summit of Sgurr Thormaid (926m). This attractive little peak (*Norman's Peak*) was named in honour of Norman Collie.

Descend pleasant slabs just right of the crest. A short distance further on an extended group of pinnacles – The Three Teeth – can be passed by easy ledges on the left or climbed directly as desired. Continue without difficulty to a broad dip in the ridge at the start of the south-west ridge of Sgurr a' Ghreadaidh. There are no easy ways of reaching this dip from the adjoining corries.

Follow the ridge which becomes narrower and more exposed as height is gained. The scrambling is absorbing and the views superb. Eventually reach the south top (970m). The continuation to the main summit gives the trickiest part of the route. Descend an exposed section of arête to a dip, then ascend the other side slightly more easily. A steep nose can be taken direct, or avoided by ledges on the left. Reach the main summit soon after. The easiest option from there is to descend the north-north-east ridge to An Dorus (Route 79).

82 Coire a' Ghreadaidh Headwall Moderate *

The main central section of Coire a' Ghreadaidh is one of the grandest corries in the Cuillin, but there are no easy ways from it onto the main ridge. With the exception of Hidden Gully Buttress (Very Difficult), which is situated in the top left-hand corner of the corrie, there are no distinguished rock climbs here either.

On the East Ridge of the Inaccessible Pinnacle, Sgurr Dearg (Climber, George Sawicki)

The route described is not very notable, but it gives an excuse to visit a magnificent corrie. It is not a rock climb as such, although it does involve some Moderate moves and some difficult route finding.

Start

Start from the Youth Hostel in Glen Brittle and follow the path on the south side of the Allt a' Choire Ghreadaidh. The main corrie has three distinct levels. The lowest level is overlooked on its south side by the north-west face of An Diallaid (714m). Here the stream from Coire an Doruis joins with the stream from the main corrie.

Access to the middle level is up delightful slabs to the right of a stream and left of a deep gorge. There are then three different ways of reaching the uppermost level. The easiest is to slant left for some distance up slabby rocks, before slanting back right. The most direct way is to ascend a steep tier of rock by a dyke just right of a stream. The third and most difficult option is to start further right and find a way up rocks to the right of a stream in a small gorge. Part way up, cut hard left over the stream along a fairly obvious break.

The route starts on an apron of slabs right of centre. Further left is the line of Diagonal Gully. This boulder-filled gully is uninteresting. However, it is guarded at the bottom by an extremely slippery scoop, which can be circumvented by Difficult rocks on either side.

The Route

The slabs are best ascended starting from the bottom left-hand side and trending up right. The easiest line is not obvious and is likely to be Grade 3 with sections of Moderate. At the top, join a grassy terrace slanting up to the right.

Now cut hard left along a fairly obvious ledge and cross a small gully. Ascend rocks trending slightly left, then zigzag up easier ground for some distance. Surmount a more difficult section by a chockstone, and slant slightly right. Eventually trend slightly left and emerge at the broad dip between Sgurr a' Ghreadaidh and Sgurr Thormaid.

83 Bealach Thormaid via Coire a' Ghreadaidh Difficult

This is not a particularly inviting way of reaching Bealach Thormaid but, like the previous route, it gives an excuse to visit this very impressive corrie. The main difficulties are concentrated in the final section of gully just below Bealach Thormaid itself.

Hart's Ledge, Sgurr Mhic Choinnich
with Sgurr Thearlaich and Sgurr Alasdair behind (Scrambler, George Sawicki)

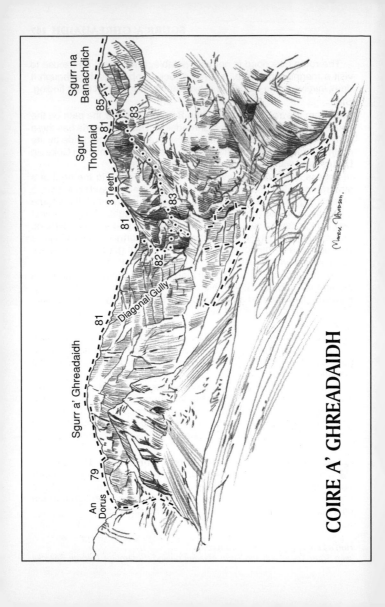

COIRE A' GHREADAIDH

Start
Reach the apron of slabs in the uppermost level of Coire a' Ghreadaidh as for the previous route.

The Route
Starting on the left, find a way up the slabs as for the previous route. Then follow the obvious terrace slanting up to the right for some distance. Ascend steep, unstable scree towards the base of a very steep rock face. Then slant right slightly more easily below the face. Turn a corner and pass below a tiny cave. Continue traversing right and eventually reach a scree gully. A rib of rock separates a narrower chimney section on the left from the main gully on the right.

Ascend this right-hand gully easily at first. Where it gets narrower, bridge up on nightmarish, shattered rock and eventually exit by the left wall. Continue more easily to the narrow dip marking Bealach Thormaid (888m). A gully drops down to Coruisk on the east, and the rocks of Sgurr na Banachdich rise immediately to the south. Turn left to reach Sgurr Thormaid (see Route 81).

84 An Diallaid – North Rib Grade 3 **
This splendid rib gives an interesting way of approaching the middle level of Coire a' Ghreadaidh. The rock is mostly very good.

Start
From the Youth Hostel in Glen Brittle as for the previous few routes. Follow the path on the south side of the Allt a' Choire Ghreadaidh to the lower level of Coire a' Ghreadaidh. Walk right to reach the foot of a well-defined rib more or less in the centre of the slabby north-west face of An Diallaid. It has a dyke gully just to its right.

The Route
Follow the rib as directly as possible staying fairly close to the gully on the right. Make a couple of moves almost in the gully at one point. Eventually traverse left for 6 metres away from the gully, and ascend big steps on the right side of a narrow runnel with clumps of grass. Bands of more angular, broken rock have to be treated carefully.

A slightly harder section involves first making a step up left onto a good foothold, with much more shattered rock further left. Then step back right onto a higher foot ledge. Continue for some distance with the angle gradually easing. There is a fair amount of debris lying on the final section.

Either traverse across for some distance to the middle level of Coire a' Ghreadaidh, or head uphill to the summit of An Diallaid.

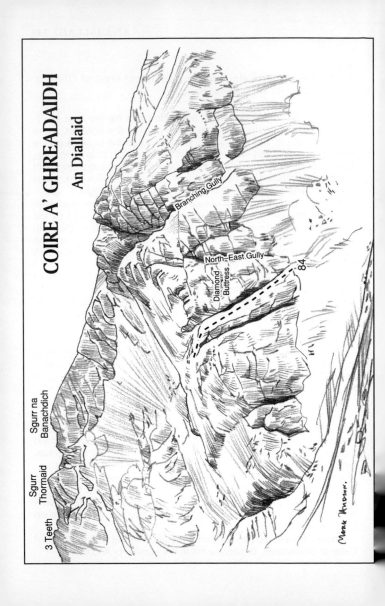

COIRE A' GHREADAIDH
An Diallaid

Branching Gully

North-East Gully

Diamond
Buttress

84

Sgurr
Thormaid

Sgurr na
Banachdich

3 Teeth

Marek Windsor.

SGURR NA BANACHDICH (965m)

The summit of Sgurr na Banachdich is a very fine viewpoint and the easiest summit on the main ridge accessible from Glen Brittle. The mountain's best feature is its south ridge. Its western ridge, which ends in a small top called Sgurr nan Gobhar, is also worthwhile.

85 North Ridge Grade 1/2

This route has no special merit and is used merely as a link between Sgurr Thormaid and Sgurr na Banachdich.

Start

Reach Bealach Thormaid by traversing Sgurr a' Ghreadaidh from An Dorus (reverse route 81). Route 83 is a less inspiring option.

The Route

Ascend scree, boulders and broken rocks on the right side of the crest. Weave to and fro to find the easiest way. Cut back left to the crest at the first opportunity to get the best scrambling. Move slightly right to join the well-worn uppermost section of the west flank route.

Continue easily to the summit. There is a sheer drop down the east face with superb views of the great basin of Coir'-uisg below. The Inaccessible Pinnacle can be seen peeking over the summit of Sgurr Dearg to the south. The easiest descent is by the next route.

86 Western Shoulder via Coir' an Eich 7km *

This is the easiest route to a major summit in the Cuillin. However, it ascends very steep scree and is far from an easy walk. The terrain above Coir' an Eich can be very confusing in bad visibility. The walk is worthwhile for the dramatic views from the summit.

Start

From the Youth Hostel in Glen Brittle. Follow the path on the south bank of the Allt a' Choire Ghreadaidh.

The Route

The scree bowl of Coir' an Eich lies on the north side of the Sgurr nan Gobhar ridge. Leave the main path to Coire a' Ghreadaidh by turning sharp right and following the west bank of the stream from Coir' an Eich. It is possible to leave the main path somewhat earlier and take a more direct line across the hillside, but this is easier to see in descent.

Eventually cross over to the left (north) bank of the Allt Coir' an Eich and ascend a worn route up steep scree. A more interesting option is to trend further left and ascend to An Diallaid (*the saddle*) on the

SGURR NA BANACHDICH

Coir' an Eich

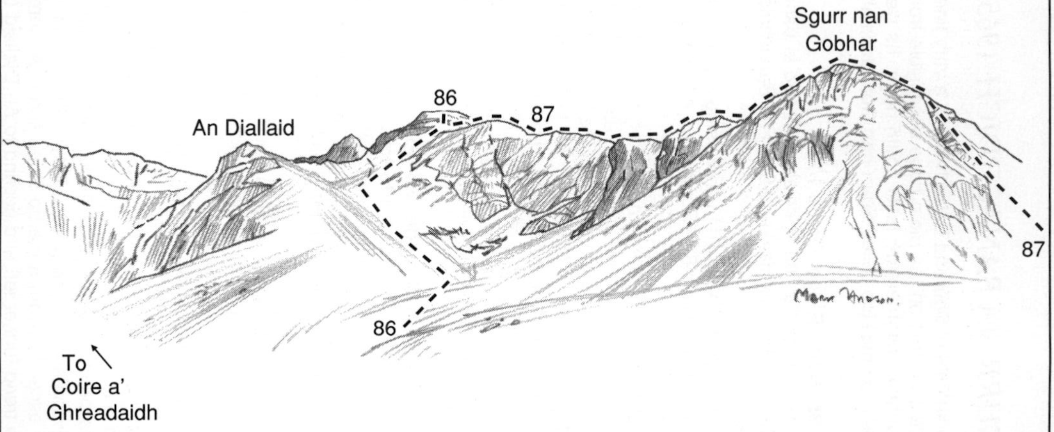

Sgurr nan Gobhar

An Diallaid

To
Coire a'
Ghreadaidh

86

87

87

86

northern side of Coir' an Eich. The ridge here has three little bumps with steep drops to the north and excellent views across Coire a' Ghreadaidh. Continue up the ridge and/or the corrie and slant right on bouldery ground to gain a slight flattening at the eastern end of the Sgurr nan Gobhar ridge. Then zigzag up the broad western shoulder on easy scree and minor rock steps for some distance. Trend slightly right towards the top to reach the summit. The spectacular views from here are the outing's chief reward.

The only option for walkers now is to return the same way. Care is needed to find the way into the top of Coir' an Eich in bad visibility. It is very easy to start down the Sgurr nan Gobhar ridge, or even head into Coire na Banachdich, by mistake.

87 Sgurr nan Gobhar Ridge Grade 2 **

A delightful ridge links the little top of Sgurr nan Gobhar (630m) with the western shoulder of Sgurr na Banachdich. It makes a most enjoyable outing and has fine views of Coire Banachdich. It is described in ascent, although it is perhaps more enjoyable in descent because of the tiresome ground at the steep western end.

Start

The start of this route is equidistant from the Youth Hostel and the Memorial Hut in Glen Brittle. The approach from the Memorial Hut is probably more popular, because it is possible to make use of a faint path on the north side of Eas Mor – a huge hollow with a spectacular waterfall.

The Route

A prominent orange-brown dyke cleaves the western flank of Sgurr nan Gobhar. The normal line of ascent is up unpleasantly steep scree and loose ground to the right (south) of this gully. However, the gully itself can be ascended in part and makes a good scramble.

Once the fine little summit has been gained the going is very much more enjoyable. The initial section is mainly walking, although the ridge is quite narrow at times. The ascent is enlivened higher up by several sections of pleasant scrambling up steps on the crest. Eventually the ridge merges with the much broader western shoulder of the previous route. This is then followed easily to the summit.

88 South Ridge Grade 2 **

This very enjoyable outing traverses three tops before reaching the main northern summit. It has steep drops on the right but generally less exposed ground to the left. It can easily be combined

SGURR NA BANACHDICH
South Ridge

Sgurr a' Ghreadaidh

Sron Bhuidhe

152

88

88

Bealach

153

Midget Ridge

88

Centre Top

88

South Top

Coire na Banachdich

with the previous route or made part of a round of Coire Banachdich. The ridge arises from Bealach Coire na Banachdich, an important pass over the main ridge between lower Glen Brittle and Coruisk. The approach to this bealach from Glen Brittle is now described.

Start

Start immediately south of the Memorial Hut in Glen Brittle by some stone sheep fanks and follow an obvious path away from the road. After a few hundred metres cross the Allt Coire na Banachdich by a footbridge and continue up the hillside to the rim of Eas Mor. Follow this uphill, but do not take the path to Coire Lagan straight ahead. Instead go left round the eastern end of Eas Mor, and follow a boggy path on the south side of the Allt Coire na Banachdich. Eventually reach the open lower part of Coire na Banachdich. Continue on more stony ground and occasional slabs.

Bealach Coire na Banachdich (851m) is the lowest point on the skyline at the head of the corrie. However, the direct route to it is blocked by a broad band of steep slabs split by a prominent gully. The route now zigzags up (left of a gorge) to pass the right-hand end of this rock band by an easy scree gully (see diagram on page 157). A more interesting line can be taken up the slabs immediately to the left of this gully. Experienced scramblers may prefer the challenge offered much further left by Banachdich Slab (Route 89).

The normal way then slants back a long way left on scree. At one point it is necessary to descend very slightly, otherwise the tendency is to scramble up loose ground towards the north ridge of Sgurr Dearg. Then ascend slightly steeper scree to the bealach, which is notable for its orange soil. A gully leads down to a broad scree slope on the Coruisk side. On the north side of the bealach there is large knobble of rock with a similar scree gully on the other side of it.

The Route

The first part of the ridge leads over an easy top (878m) above the shoulder of Sron Bhuidhe. Ledges on the Coire na Banachdich side offer the easiest options, but the best scrambling, and the best views, are on the crest itself. Pleasant scrambling then leads over the very narrow South Top (917m). A popular option is to traverse narrow ledges across the west face of the Centre Top. However, a more direct line is preferable, and probably no more time-consuming. Traverse the high point (942m), and scramble down very steeply, slightly on the west side, to the final dip. Ascend some sharp rocks then slant easily up a cone-sheet which exhibits excellent spheroidal weathering. Continue without difficulty to the main north summit.

The Southern Cuillin

The southern Cuillin group is here taken to include all the peaks from Sgurr Dearg to Gars-bheinn. These include the two highest Cuillin summits – Sgurr Alasdair and the Inaccessible Pinnacle of Sgurr Dearg. This part of the Cuillin is most readily accessible from the lower end of Glen Brittle.

SGURR DEARG (978m)

This lofty peak would not attract as much attention as it does but for an extraordinary fin of rock, known as the Inaccessible Pinnacle, that springs from the east side of its summit ridge. A complex ridge drops down further east over An Stac to the rim of Coire Lagan. The impressive and forbidding north face overlooks the scree descent from Bealach Coire na Banachdich to Coruisk.

Although the Inaccessible Pinnacle is out of bounds to all but rock climbers, the summit of Sgurr Dearg itself is an easier objective. Its north-west flank is little more than a very rough walk, and its south-western ridge is a relatively easy scramble.

The next three outings all start from Coire na Banachdich.

89 Banachdich Slab Grade 3 **

This route just qualifies as belonging to Sgurr Dearg. It can be used as a more interesting approach to Bealach Coire na Banachdich. It is sustained, at the upper limit of its grade, and is not recommended after wet weather.

Start

From the Memorial Hut, take the path up into Coire na Banachdich as for the previous route. Head for the rocks immediately to the right of Banachdich Gully. This gully gives a Very Difficult climb, best done after a dry spell (Gibbs, King and Mackenzie 1898).

The Route

Ascend a recess just right of the gully, then scramble pleasantly up a right-facing corner/groove formed by a dyke. Slant diagonally right across slabs. Make a tricky step up to the right of a rock pedestal in a tiny recess. Step right and break up onto slabs. Move right and down slightly on a grassy ledge. Then climb up and stretch for a good hold to allow a move back left onto a ledge above. Traverse left some distance, step between some big blocks and ascend to a tiny alcove

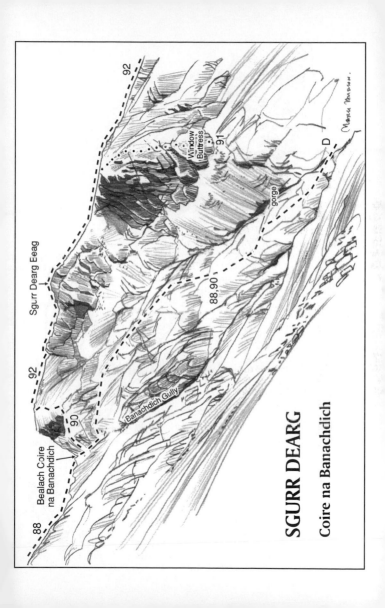

SGURR DEARG

Coire na Banachdich

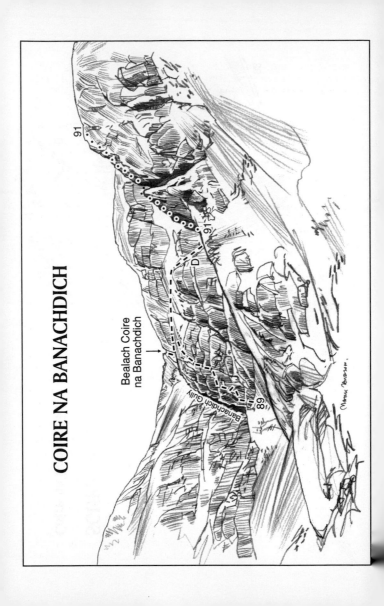

COIRE NA BANACHDICH

and juniper bush, with a slightly steeper wall above. Go to the right-hand end of a ledge and step up onto a slab. Slant slightly left by a narrow dyke and continue with further interest to a grassy terrace.

Traverse hard right along the terrace and ascend a broad dyke forming a gully. This a fairly sustained for some distance and leads to a good ledge. Move right and make one steep move left of a nose. Then either cross slabs leftwards or carry straight on up, and soon emerge onto big boulders. Continue directly to join the traverse line leading left on the normal route to Bealach Coire na Banachdich.

90 North-West Flank Grade 1

This is one of the least interesting sections of the main ridge. Apart from some mild scrambling out of Bealach Coire na Banachdich, this route is mainly a slog up steep scree. However, there are fine views looking back north. In descent it is important to go more west than north from the summit.

Start

Ascend to Bealach Coire na Banachdich as for Route 88.

The Route

Just short of the actual bealach, scramble up steep rocks on the right to gain the crest of the ridge. Soon reach a narrower section of ridge with good views across the precipitous north face. Continue to the start of a broad scree slope. Zigzag up the rather tedious scree for some distance and eventually reach the long horizontal crest forming the summit. The Inaccessible Pinnacle is close by. This is a good place to watch the antics of climbers on the West Ridge (Route 96).

The south-west ridge of Sgurr Dearg (Route 92) offers a more interesting descent. It is only slightly more difficult than the route up.

91 Window Buttress Difficult **

This prominent buttress is situated at a height of 600m on the south side of Coire na Banachdich. It has enjoyable climbing and some varied situations. It is a popular climb to do on the way up to the Inaccessible Pinnacle. It was first done by Norman Collie in 1906.

Start

Follow the path into Coire na Banachdich as for Route 88. Scramble up an obvious sweep of slabs directly to the foot of the buttress.

The Route

From the lowest rocks, climb up first slightly right, then left on good holds. Move right to a parallel groove and soon reach a ledge.

Ascend a groove past big blocks, then climb a steep corner above a ledge (crux). Continue up interesting slabs and eventually reach the nose of stacked blocks leaning against the face which gives the route its name. Direct routes up to the window are rather difficult, so move left and ascend an obvious groove to a stony ledge. Continue to the crest of the buttress. There is a gully on the other side leading to a neck, but the best option here is to stay on the crest and make some steep moves to ascend a pinnacle and so reach the highest point.

Drop down easily into the neck. Scramble up sound rocks the other side (grade 3), going first right and then back left. Continue up short blocky corners, and slabs. Then ascend a bouldery ridge for some distance. Emerge onto an extensive scree shoulder below Sgurr Dearg Beag.

92 South-West Ridge via Sgurr Dearg Beag Grade 1/2 *
This is probably the best of the easy ways to the summit of Sgurr Dearg. However, it is hard work ascending the long scree slope of Sron Dearg. This is rewarded by superb views across Coire Lagan.
Start
The outing can be started either from the Memorial Hut or from the camp site by the beach. The path to Coire Lagan from the camp site is much better (and drier). It heads uphill from the toilet block and crosses over a rough track soon after. Stay on the left-hand path where the route to Coir' a' Ghrunnda forks right across a stream.
The Route
Starting just to the east of Loch an Fhir-bhallaich, choose any convenient line up the trying scree of Sron Dearg. A popular option is to follow a brown dyke. Eventually the angle eases slightly and the scree becomes more stable. Reach a slight flattening at 800m. Then ascend steeper ground on scree, boulders and big blocks to gain the minor summit of Sgurr Dearg Beag (927m).

The remaining ridge, which curves leftwards to the summit of Sgurr Dearg, is narrower and rocky. There are short sections of interesting scrambling on the crest, or easier ledges first on the right side and later on the left. The dramatic sight of the Inaccessible Pinnacle marks the climax to the ascent.

93 South Flank – Central Buttress Grade 3
This is not the most inspiring of lines, but it offers experienced scramblers a more taxing route onto Sgurr Dearg than the previous outing. It takes full advantage of the good path into Coire Lagan.

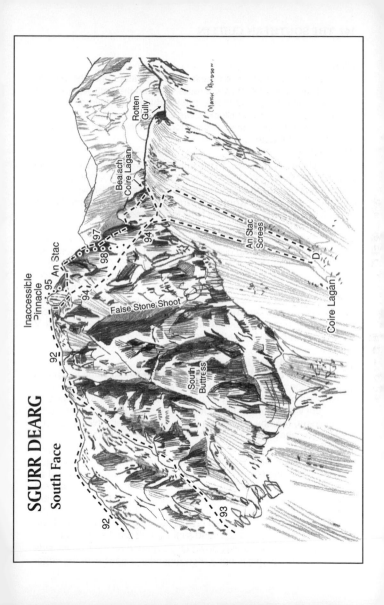

Start

From the camp site by the beach in Glen Brittle. Take the path to Coire Lagan as for the previous route. Stay on the path east of Loch an Fhir-bhallaich, and continue past a distinctive pointed boulder known as the Matterhorn Block. Eventually ascend slabs and looser ground above to reach the beautiful lochan in the ice-scooped basin of upper Coire Lagan.

The Route

Turn and face Sgurr Dearg. To the right is the prominent climbing crag called South Buttress. (This has two Difficult routes – Baly's Route, which starts up the left-bounding gully, and East Corner, which takes the right-hand edge.) Central Buttress is a rather indefinite ridge straight above with a scree gully to its left. Further left again is another rather indefinite buttress. Move slightly left and weave a way up excellent slabs to more broken ground below the left-hand buttress.

Ascend scree for some distance, then start to slant diagonally right towards a steep crag forming the lower section of Central Buttress. This is too difficult so avoid it by moving round it on the left-hand side. Tackle the next section more directly on very steep rock. The route-finding is interesting and care is required with loose blocks. Continue up the rickety ridge, which becomes less definite as height is gained. Eventually join the previous route near the crest of the south-west ridge. Turn right and follow the rocky ridge to the summit.

94 South-East Flank Grade 2 *

This is the easiest way of reaching Sgurr Dearg when traversing the main ridge northwards. It takes the line of a prominent cone-sheet which skirts below the south face of An Stac. It is not at all exposed. In descent it is important to cut left over a small shoulder marked by big boulders, thereby avoiding a 'false stone-shoot' which ends in a steep drop over broken rocks. The route is low in its grade.

Start

This route starts from Bealach Coire Lagan. This dip on the main ridge can be gained from the floor of upper Coire Lagan (reached as for the previous route), but it involves making an unpleasant ascent of the An Stac screes. A slightly better approach can be made by hard scrambling up rocky ribs further right – to the left of the lowest point on the rim of the corrie. (Rotten Gully lies on the Coruisk side.) Then traverse a broad top and descend slightly to reach the bealach.

It is possible to pick a way down steep ground on the Coruisk side of the bealach, but this is not a recommendable pass over the ridge.

The Route
From the bealach, descend broken rocks on the Coire Lagan side, then follow an obvious path on scree slanting up left. Continue in the same line by scrambling easily up slabs and stones. Eventually go through a gap by big boulders, and turn slightly right. After a short distance it is important to scramble up to a higher, parallel ramp. Continue along this until the Inaccessible Pinnacle comes into full view. Slant up a broad slabby shelf, scattered with stones, to reach the horizontal crest marking the summit of Sgurr Dearg.

THE INACCESSIBLE PINNACLE (986m)

This amazing fin of rock outstrips Sgurr Dearg by 8m and must therefore be regarded as the true summit of the mountain – much to the discomfort of many a Munro-bagger, including Sir Hugh himself. The pinnacle itself is a slice of gabbro which was originally sandwiched between two dykes. It rests on a dipping cone-sheet. It is the hardest mountain summit to attain in all the British Isles.

There are now ten climbs in total on the pinnacle, but only the two routes up the opposite ends are within the scope of this guide.

95 East Ridge Moderate ^^^

This sensational climb has good holds, but also exceptional exposure – a wonderful combination if you like that sort of thing. It was first climbed by the Pilkington brothers in 1880. Few today will approach this climb as they did from Sligachan via Coruisk. If you don't like queuing, it is best to avoid this route at Whitsun weekend.

Start
Reach the summit of Sgurr Dearg by any one of the preceding routes (90–94). Drop down slabs on the south side of the pinnacle and gain a comfortable platform below the start of the ridge.

The Route
Climb up the flank onto the crest and continue to a stance with a rather poor belay. The crux is a slightly steeper section on the first part of the next pitch. The difficulties are short-lived, but the exposure is considerable. Continue more easily to a small ledge below huge blocks forming the summit. Complete the ascent by surmounting the blocks, which are perched on a sloping slab.

The normal practice is to descend by abseiling 20m down the shorter western end from a thread belay (steel cable) at the base of a giant boulder known as the Bolster Stone.

96 West Ridge Difficult *

The route up the short end of the Inaccessible Pinnacle is steeper, and the climbing more technical, than that on the East Ridge. It has become somewhat polished, and is quite tricky for its grade. It was first climbed by Stocker and Parker in 1886.

Start

Drop down just a short distance from the summit of Sgurr Dearg.

The Route

Some rock has fallen off the base of the west ridge, and the route now starts up steep rocks on the left (north) face. Climb up to a sloping ledge, trending left, then move delicately up right. Continue more easily up ledges trending right to gain the sloping slab below the Bolster Stone. Either abseil back down or, if there is no traffic, climb down the East Ridge.

AN STAC (954m)

This is a minor top on the east ridge of Sgurr Dearg below the Inaccessible Pinnacle. It throws down an impressive buttress towards Bealach Coire Lagan, and an even more impressive face to the north. It seems to have acquired its name by mistake. (The Inaccessible Pinnacle was originally called An Stac.) John Mackenzie suggested that the top be called Sgurr na Cailleach.

The summit can be reached by a simple scramble from the foot of the East Ridge of the Inaccessible Pinnacle. It is well worth a short detour from the South-East Flank (Route 94) to take in the unusual views of the Inaccessible Pinnacle from this top.

97 East Buttress Grade 3 **

This is the preferred way up An Stac for confident scramblers. The route becomes increasingly exposed as height is gained. Gibson, Morse and Wicks descended this way in 1891. They were unaware of the easier option below the south face. It is at the upper limit of its grade.

Start

Reach Bealach Coire Lagan as for Route 94.

The Route

Slant up a left-trending ramp on the Coire Lagan side of a peaklet immediately west of the bealach. Reach a col with a broad scree-filled recess to the left (possible escape route) and steep drops to the right (north). The buttress proper now rises above.

AN STAC

South–East Face

97

98

Boulder
Nick

94

98

97

Bealach
Coire Lagan

97

94

Mark Hudson.

An Stac
Screes

Start a short distance down from the col on the Coire Lagan side. Scramble left up steps and grooves. Follow a rickety staircase slightly left instead of a groove on the right. Zigzag up a stony path to a shoulder with even steeper drops to the right. Cut back left and scramble up the narrowing arête with continuous interest to a ledge.

Follow the ledge to the right and ascend a slightly steeper groove, then cut back hard left on a glacis and spiral round to the summit. It is also possible to continue along the ledge system to the right, but there is a horrifying drop on the right-hand side. It is then necessary to backtrack slightly to reach the summit.

An easy scramble descent from the summit leads down to the dip before the Inaccessible Pinnacle.

98 Eastern Chimney Moderate *
This prominent chimney cleaves the face to the left of the previous route. It was first climbed by Goggs and Russell in 1908.
Start
From Bealach Coire Lagan. Follow the first part of the East Flank route (Route 94) until a short distance past the broad scree recess.
The Route
Scramble up a broad stone-filled groove, then a rib and slabs, to the foot of the chimney. The first part of the chimney is easy to enter. Most climbers should be able to go under one chockstone, and possibly also a second, but the chimney then becomes too narrow. The crux is climbing up exposed rocks on the right wall. Move in and out of the chimney above and eventually join the East Buttress route just before the rightward leading ledge. Finish as for that route.

SGURR MHIC CHOINNICH (948m)

The west face of this peak forms the impressive headwall of Coire Lagan. Cutting across this face some 30m below the summit is one of the most useful cone-sheet ledges in the Cuillin. The mountain's finest feature is its north ridge. The peak is named in honour of John Mackenzie, who was in the party that made the first ascent in 1887.

99 North Ridge Grade 2 **
This is a very fine ridge and, despite there being basalt on the upper section, it makes a most enjoyable scramble. This is the route taken by Charles Pilkington and his party on the first ascent.

SGURR MHIC CHOINNICH

West Face

Bealach Mhic Choinnich

102

102

100

99

101

101

100

99

99

Bealach Coire Lagan

Rotten Gully

An Stac Screes

D

(Yanik Anderson.)

Start

Gain Bealach Coire Lagan as for Route 94.

The Route

From the bealach, traverse a plateau-like top and descend easily rightwards to the lowest point on the corrie rim. The ridge proper rises above. The scrambling is interesting without being unduly difficult. Weave a way up small paths and clamber up blocks and grooves. Eventually reach the crest and follow this fairly easily at first. About two-thirds of the way along the crest look for the exit of Hart's Ledge on the Coire Lagan side. There is a slight rise on the crest immediately after this. The remainder of the ridge to the summit is narrow and delightfully exposed.

The southern end of the mountain, just beyond the summit, plunges steeply to Bealach Mhic Choinnich. The only practicable way for scramblers to reach this bealach is to return down the north ridge and follow Hart's Ledge (Route 101) across the west face. Otherwise return down the north ridge.

100 West Buttress Difficult **

This enjoyable route takes a direct line to the summit from Coire Lagan. It is mainly hard scrambling with interesting route-finding. There are a couple of climbing pitches both below and above Hart's Ledge. It was first ascended by the Abraham brothers in 1906.

Start

Reach the lochan in upper Coire Lagan as for Route 93. Start at the back of the corrie, a little to the left of the prominent scree fan forming the bottom section of the Great Stone Shoot.

The Route

At the base of the buttress there is a crag with a dark, wet left-hand wall. A start can be made either side of this crag. The left-hand option involves some tricky scrambling to reach a small neck at the back of the crag. The right-hand option is more straightforward, but entails a detour to the right across slabs and back left to the same neck.

Scramble up for some distance staying right of the crest. When the rocks start to steepen make some harder moves to break up left onto the crest. Ascend a rib until it peters out on a broader section of ridge. A grassy ledge leads rightwards off the buttress at this point.

Zigzag up a short distance, then cut hard left along a horizontal traverse line, with one awkward step onto a brown slab. Break up left, then follow a rightward slanting rake. Cut back left along a slabby groove to the centre of the buttress. Go left or right of the next rock band. The rock is somewhat mossy in places. Take a direct line up a short wall of sounder rock. Stay slightly right of the crest and weave a way up through tiny buttresses. Make some pleasant moves up a short groove with a block in it.

A choice of lines can be taken at a steepening. Going left involves an awkward move pulling up the right-hand side of a block. Eventually slant easily up right on looser ground. At a steep nose, traverse right and ascend small ledges to emerge on easier ground. Ascend some slabs to reach a steep groove with a good flake belay at the base of its right wall. Climb the corner groove on good rock, then move hard right and pull onto a ramp which slants back left. Take a belay on Hart's Ledge below another corner groove.

Climb the corner for a short distance then traverse right until it is possible to make some steep moves to gain easier rocks. Continue to a good belay. Move slightly right and take a direct line to the summit. The easiest descent is by the north ridge.

101 Hart's Ledge Grade 2 **

This remarkable ledge gives access to the north ridge of the mountain from Bealach Mhic Choinnich. It was discovered by the Irish climber Henry Hart with John Mackenzie in 1887. It is commonly known as Collie's Ledge, but Collie did not team up to do it with John Mackenzie until a year later, so the credit should really go to Hart.

Start

Reach the lochan in upper Coire Lagan as for Route 93. The approach to Bealach Mhic Choinnich starts up the Great Stone Shoot in the upper right-hand corner of the corrie. Ascend the very loose scree forming the lower half of this shoot, then, when a rock wall starts to appear directly ahead, traverse diagonally left across more stable ground. Head for a dark brown rock rib. Traverse left across this and ascend a gully the other side. Weave to and fro to find the easiest line. Higher up, find a way to break rightwards through a steeper section by interesting scrambling on good holds (Grade 2). Continue on easier ground to gain the broad bealach.

The approach to this bealach from the Coruisk side is normally made via Coir' an Lochain. Ascend a scree gully with some awkward scrambling up short rock steps in the upper section (Grade 2/3).

The Route

Hart's Ledge is a fairly obvious feature slanting up the west face from the bealach. From a terrace just on the east side of the bealach, trend

SGURR MHIC CHOINNICH

North Ridge

Rotten Gully

99

99

100
101
99

West Buttress

Jeffrey's Dyke

Sgurr Alasdair

Collie's Climb

105

Sgurr Thearlaich

103

100

Great Stone Shoot

D

Coire Lagan

slightly right on slabby ledges to a tiny recess with some scree. Ascend a steep groove by making a very high step up with the right foot. Move back left above to get established on the ledge proper. After this crux section the scrambling is fairly easy, though quite exposed at times. Stay below a steeper break which rises to the base of King's Chimney (see next route). Continue across the crest of West Buttress and round a corner in a fine position.

The way on is obvious. It is mainly exposed walking, with several short sections of scrambling where the ledge fades temporarily. One or two moves involve slight descents. Eventually ascend with surprising ease onto the crest of the north ridge.

102 King's Chimney Difficult **

This is the most enjoyable climb of its grade on the main ridge, and all the better for being easier than it looks. It allows a direct line to be taken from Bealach Mhic Choinnich to the summit of the mountain. It was first climbed by King, Douglas and Naismith in 1898.

Start

Gain Bealach Mhic Choinnich as for the previous route.

The Route

Follow the first part of Hart's Ledge, then ascend a steep, leftwards-rising break on slightly dubious rock to reach the base of the prominent corner. Ascend the corner on good holds. There is a wobbly chockstone in the corner crack. Eventually traverse out right in a fine position beneath an overhang to reach a good ledge. Continue easily up slabs to reach the delightful summit.

SGURR THEARLAICH (978m)

This is the eastern top of Sgurr Alasdair. The traverse of this summit is one of the most demanding sections of the main ridge. The mountain's south-east ridge is split by the notorious Thearlaich–Dubh gap (see Route 127), and its north ridge plunges steeply to Bealach Mhic Choinnich. It can be ascended with least difficulty from near the top of the Great Stone Shoot. The peak was first climbed in 1880 by Charles Pilkington – after whom the peak is named.

103 North Ridge Moderate **

This is quite a taxing part of the main ridge, especially when tackled, as it usually is, in descent. There are three different ways of overcoming the steep rocks above Bealach Mhic Choinnich. Each option has its advocates, but none is easy.

Start

Gain Bealach Mhic Choinnich as for Route 101.

The Route

The main option on the Coruisk side is here preferred. Although exposed, it has positive holds. Skirt the first rocks by descending slightly on the east side. Move left for some distance until the rocks can be climbed by a steep groove. Gain a traverse line leading back right. Continue up slabs and small steps trending slightly left to reach a ledge below a prominent slab. Climb this on small holds in an exposed position. Continue more easily to gain the crest of the ridge.

A popular option starting on the Coire Lagan side of the bealach ascends a gully/groove line to the left of a rock pillar, then slants right across slippery slabs to a shoulder. Continue leftwards up grooves and ledges to the crest.

Both these options finish on a fairly broad section of ridge. Continue up the ridge to a gap where a gully falls steeply into the Great Stone Shoot. Negotiate the gap and follow a ledge on the left-hand side of the crest and soon reach another gap. The remainder of the ridge is very pleasant, with much of the crest being formed by a cone-sheet dipping to the east. There are fine views to the south from the summit. Sgurr Alasdair, the highest peak on the island, is not far away to the west. The next route offers the easiest descent.

104 South Ridge via the Great Stone Shoot Grade 3 *

The south ridge of Sgurr Thearlaich forms the natural continuation of the south-east ridge from the Thearlaich–Dubh gap (Route 127). However, it can also be gained by ascending the Great Stone Shoot or by traversing Sgurr Alasdair.

Start

The easiest way to gain this ridge is by ascending the Great Stone Shoot from Coire Lagan as described for the next route.

The Route

The saddle at the top of the Great Stone Shoot has a short but rather steep wall on its eastern side. The south ridge can be gained by a number of rather strenuous little climbs directly up this wall. However, a more reasonable option is to descend on the Coir' a' Ghrunnda side by a stony path until it is possible to walk easily left onto the ridge. Do not descend too far, because the ground falls away steeply below.

Scramble up onto the crest, moving onto the right-hand side where it narrows. A sizeable section of the crest has fallen off in recent times and the rock has to be treated with care. Steady scrambling leads to the fine summit. The neighbouring peak of Sgurr Alasdair has a domineering presence on the other side of the Great Stone Shoot.

The continuation by the north ridge involves very awkward down-climbing at Moderate grade (see the previous route), so the easiest option from here is to return to the top of the Great Stone Shoot.

SGURR ALASDAIR (992m)

The highest mountain on Skye has a shapely summit, which is set apart slightly to the west of the main ridge. It lies on an important subsidiary ridge which includes Sgurr Sgumain and Sron na Ciche. It can be ascended with least difficulty via the Great Stone Shoot from Coire Lagan. On a traverse of the main ridge it is standard practice to make the short detour required to take in the wonderful views from its summit. The mountain is named after Sheriff Alexander Nicolson who first ascended the peak with A. Macrae in 1873.

105 South-East Ridge Grade 2 **
This short rocky ridge gives the easiest route to the summit. It starts from the stony saddle at the top of the Great Stone Shoot at a height of 955m.

Start
Follow the path from the camp site by the beach in Glen Brittle to upper Coire Lagan. Go round the left-hand side of the lochan, then slant right to where an obvious scree fan descends to the corrie floor. The lower part of the Great Stone Shoot consists of unstable scree and is very hard work to ascend. A slightly easier line can be found to the left of the main fan where the bouldery ground is more stable.

The upper half of the shoot is enclosed by rock walls, and the ground underfoot is badly eroded. Care is required where bedrock is exposed and some big boulders are undermined. Be aware also that, because the shoot is gently curved, it may not be possible to see other parties below. The saddle at the top of the shoot is a welcome sight.

The Route
The ridge looks intimidating but, once embarked on, it proves fairly straightforward. The rock is largely basalt, but the way is well worn

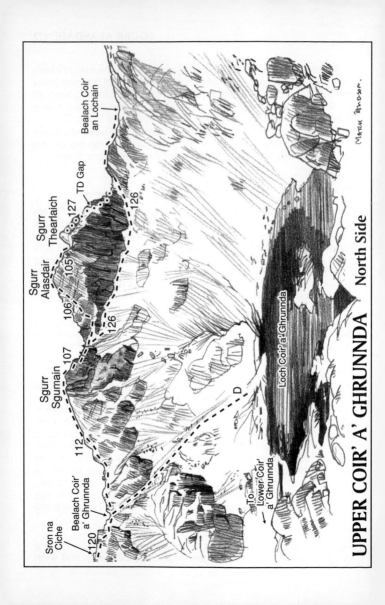

UPPER COIR' A' GHRUNNDA North Side

and there are adequate holds. Follow slabby rocks and small rock steps close to the crest. The right-hand side is rather exposed in the lower section. The views from the summit are exceptional, and many parties linger here secure in the knowledge that the Great Stone Shoot offers a rapid descent route. Note that there is no way down the Coir' a' Ghrunnda side from the saddle at the bottom of the ridge.

106 South-West Ridge Grade 3 *

This ridge offers a more interesting route to the summit than the previous one. It starts from Bealach Sgumain – a dip in the ridge between Sgurr Sgumain and Sgurr Alasdair. A nasty little wall at the start of the ridge, known as the Bad Step, can be avoided by a relatively straightforward chimney. It has become quite popular to ascend this ridge instead of negotiating the Thearlaich–Dubh gap.

Start

The ridge crest by Bealach Sgumain is marked by several troll-like pinnacles. The scree on the Coire Lagan side of the bealach is unpleasantly steep and is not recommended either in ascent or descent. The Coir' a' Ghrunnda side is also largely scree, but again this is not an attractive approach route. There are two more pleasant options; one is to traverse Sgurr Sgumain (see the next route), the other is to follow a path in the scree below the south-west face of Sgurr Thearlaich from Bealach Coir' an Lochain (see Route 126).

The Route

Ignore the obvious difficulties posed by the steep rocks near the crest. Instead follow a ledge further right which descends very slightly to reach the base of a chimney. Scramble up the chimney itself or the rocks on the left wall (crux). Above this the scrambling is fairly sustained for some distance. Slant left and right to find the easiest way. Much variation is possible and the rock is rather broken in places. Eventually move back left to the crest and follow this in a fine position to the summit. The normal descent is by the previous route.

SGURR SGUMAIN (947m)

This peak lies on the ridge between Sron na Ciche and Sgurr Alasdair. It makes an enjoyable traverse *en route* to the major summit. It has a dramatic north-west face and an extensive west buttress. The easiest way to its summit is by the south ridge from Bealach Coir' a' Ghrunnda. This bealach can be reached by the Sgumain Stone Shoot from Coire Lagan.

107 North-East Ridge Grade 2/3 *

This short, narrow ridge starts from Bealach Sgumain. It is probably done more often in descent when linking the peak with Sgurr Alasdair.

Start

The most pleasant way of reaching Bealach Sgumain is by Route 126 from Bealach Coir' an Lochain. (See also Route 106).

The Route

From the bealach, follow ledges mainly on the Coir' a' Ghrunnda side. The scrambling is quite interesting and there are one or two more awkward moves. There is a small top, with a tiny window feature, just before the much broader main summit is reached. The views northwards are especially fine. It is a simple matter to descend the south ridge (Route 112) to Bealach Coir' a' Ghrunnda.

108 North Ridge Moderate **

This route takes a fairly direct line to the summit from the lochan in upper Coire Lagan. Although it does not appear very striking from below, it is in fact a most enjoyable excursion with interesting route-finding. The rock is somewhat suspect, but not unpleasantly so. The route has much scrambling and is fairly easy for its grade. It is best done on a summer evening when the ridge catches the sun.

Start

Reach upper Coire Lagan (as for Route 93) and walk round to the opposite side of the lochan.

The Route

Ascend a fairly stable scree slope slanting left below rock outcrops. Scramble up slabs and grooves, where water trickles down, to reach a higher scree slope. Slant hard left and make for a small gap on the crest of the north ridge immediately above the steep nose forming its base. Reach this by ascending a stony gully. Part way up surmount a chockstone by rocks on the right wall and exit from the gully on very loose, fine scree.

Weave a way up the crest mainly on big blocks on the right-hand side. This gives very enjoyable scrambling. Then an easier section leads to a prominent rock band which gives the main difficulties of the ascent. The direct way is too difficult, so traverse hard left to the foot of the left-most arête. (It is possible to walk off leftwards here.)

Climb up steep rocks on good holds slanting slightly right. Make a move right at one point to a good foot ledge, and slant right past a

SGURR SGUMAIN

North-West Face

Sgurr Alasdair

Bealach
Sgumain

108

Pinnacles

109

111

108

109

Loch Coire Lagan

mossy alcove above. From a scree shelf continue slanting right to gain a broken groove which lies back slightly.

Ascend by the scree-filled groove using the rocks mainly on its right-hand side. Then follow a more definite rib on the right. When the groove starts to peter out, ascend flakes leading slightly left towards a dyke. Stay on the right side of the dyke on pleasant rocks. Eventually step left across a narrow gully and slant diagonally left to where the rocks are more amenable. When the pinnacles in Bealach Sgumain come into sight, slant right on more broken rocks. Frankland's Gully is visible further right.

Towards the top, do not go round a corner on the right but instead ascend an enjoyable rib slanting slightly left. Break out onto easy ground and soon reach the commodious summit. There are superb views south across Coir' a' Ghrunnda.

The easiest option now is to descend the south ridge to Bealach Coir' a' Ghrunnda (Route 112). However, the best combination is to traverse the summit, descend Route 107 and ascend the south-west ridge of Sgurr Alasdair (Route 106).

109 North-West Ramp Grade 3 **

This route crosses an impressive face and has some spectacular situations. The first recorded ascent was by J.S. Napier, R.G. Napier and J.H. Bell in 1896.

Start

From the lochan in upper Coire Lagan as for the previous route.

The Route

Gain the upper scree slope below the north-west face. Then, instead of slanting hard left to the North Ridge, head for the start of the obvious ramp feature that slants right below the huge face.

Follow a grassy ledge easily to the start of the slabby ramp. Ascend the slabs right of the corner, weaving to and fro to find the easiest and cleanest line. Move back closer to the corner, then reach a small alcove with wet rock to the left and a steeper wall to the right. Scramble up the alcove on small square-cut holds trending slightly left (crux). Break out onto easier slabs. Eventually trend a long way right to a flat, gritty ledge.

Move left and follow a faint ramp/weakness. Curve leftwards at first then go back right. Ascend an awkward block and continue on rough

The Cioch viewed from Amphitheatre Arête, Sron na Ciche

blocks to the crest of a ridge (West Buttress). Follow the last section of the ridge left to an impressive final tower. A small window is visible on the skyline high above. Traverse a long way right, with surprising ease, along a prominent horizontal ledge. Reach the south ridge of Sgurr Sgumain, a short distance uphill from Bealach Coir' a' Ghrunnda. Either descend by the Sgumain Stone Shoot or continue easily to the summit of Sgurr Sgumain.

110 Lochan Traverse Moderate **

There is a prominent break crossing the rocks which form the lower part of the West Buttress of Sgurr Sgumain. It marks an inward dipping contact between two different types of gabbro (dark brown above and lighter brown below). This route traverses along the break. It is best done from left to right i.e. from upper Coire Lagan to the Sgumain Stone Shoot. Although most of the route is scrambling there are some awkward moves on the first half of the traverse which just justify the climbing grade.

Start

From upper Coire Lagan, cross wonderfully ice-sculpted rocks on the right-hand (west) side of Loch Coire Lagan. Descend slightly to reach the start of the fairly obvious traverse line above an apron of steep slabs.

The Route

The start of the route is usually wet and constitutes the crux. Make some steep moves up and left to get established on the break proper. Move out of the fault by a drippy wall and traverse across delightfully rough, sound slabs. At a steeper section, make an awkward bridging move to pull up past a boulder in a slightly more exposed position.

An easier ledge is then followed to a rift with boulders. There is some vegetation in the break, and then a steeper section is reached with an overhanging left wall and damp rock. One or two tricky moves give access to a more secure rift. Then step up onto a boulder to reach more straightforward scrambling. The traverse line then starts to flatten out and an easier section is followed for some distance. There are occasional juniper bushes, and further right there are fine views of the Cioch on Sron na Ciche. After the high point of the traverse there is one further section of scrambling by a small gap, but after that it is mainly walking to reach the Sgumain Stone Shoot.

Looking down Cioch Slab Corner, Sron na Ciche (Climber, George Archibald)

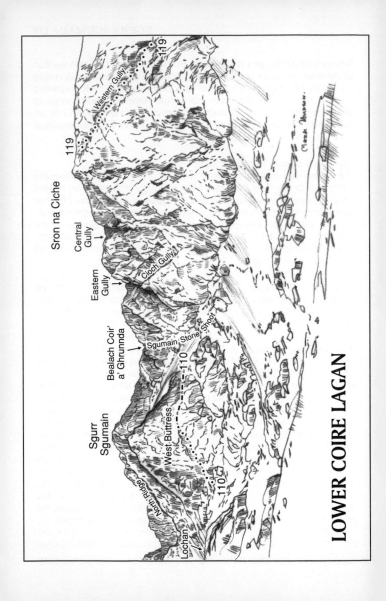

LOWER COIRE LAGAN

111 West Buttress Grade 3

There are a number of climbs on the main face of West Buttress that looks out over Coire Lagan. This route avoids the lower section of the buttress altogether on the right, and gains the crest where the angle begins to ease. However, some rickety pinnacles high up involve Difficult climbing, so an escape is suggested down the south flank. This is a rather artificial line, and the rock is worrying on the crest. Worthwhile only for the unusual views across Coire Lagan.

Start

Follow the path from the camp site to Coire Lagan. A short distance beyond Loch an Fhir-bhallaich (and before the Matterhorn block), take a less distinct right fork, and follow this across two streams towards the north face of Sron na Ciche. Do not go up to the foot of the face, but slant left and find a way up scree, big blocks and rock outcrops to gain the main Sgumain Stone Shoot. Ascend this until above the level of the Lochan Traverse (Route 110).

The Route

There are several places on the first part of the route where it is easy to escape rightwards and rejoin the stone shoot. Slant left across fairly easy ground at first. A slab with a dyke running up it has a chockstone 4m above a corner. Squeeze up under this on the left. Continue up scree, ascend a groove and move left along a thick cone-sheet. Where the terrace pinches out break right to more broken ground. Go up rocks to the right of some chockstones to more scree. Cut hard left below a grassy alcove, and ascend a shallow recess with a groove above. Break right and step up by a juniper bush onto a slab, then pass round a blocky pinnacle on its right-hand side.

Slant diagonally leftwards up slabs and grassy grooves below steeper rocks forming the tower-like crest of the buttress. Go further left and scramble up rocks to the left of a dyke. Make a tricky move left onto a slabby ledge. There are now views of the northern flank. Do not break back right to the crest until beyond the first mass of rock. Then follow the crest as closely as possible.

The shattered nature of the rock detracts from the fine position. There are excellent views of both Sgurr Mhic Choinnich and Sron na Ciche. At one point make a reverse *à cheval* move to descend a sharp arête. Shortly after this the crest becomes even more tricky, and it is left to climbers to find a way past some tottering pinnacles. Instead, pick a way down the right-hand flank, slanting right at first with some care, to gain an easier scree slope which merges with the Sgumain Stone Shoot lower down.

SGURR SGUMAIN

West Buttress

109

Final Tower

Pinnacles

111

111

Sgumain Shoot

D

Martin Jamieson

110

112 South Ridge 8km *

Some very rough ground has to be ascended to reach the start of this ridge at Bealach Coir' a' Ghrunnda (840m). The summit is a fine viewpoint, but walkers will have to return from it the same way.

Start

The most direct approach to the start of this ridge is by the Sgumain Stone Shoot from Coire Lagan (see previous route). The terrain is hard going, but fairly well-worn once the main shoot is reached. The face of Sron na Ciche is an impressive sight to the right and, high up the slope, a rocky ridge known as Ladies' Pinnacle stands out on the left. An alternative approach is to traverse Sron na Ciche (Route 120).

The Route

A prominent brown-orange peridotite dyke crosses the crest near the bealach and, shortly above this, gabbro gives way to a large intrusive sheet of grey tholeiite (here an amygdaloidal breccia). This rock forms an obvious capping to the summit of Sgurr Sgumain. Ascend the ridge without any great difficulty to the broad summit.

SRON NA CICHE (859m)

The long, wedge-like spur of Sron na Ciche separates Coire Lagan from Coir' a' Ghrunnda. On its northern and south-eastern flanks it has some of the best climbing on offer in the Cuillin. The Coire Lagan face is particularly impressive, being a full kilometre wide and 300m high. This superb precipice is the preserve of rock climbers. Not surprisingly, the routes described here have a fairly serious air about them. An extraordinary boss of rock, known as the Cioch, protrudes from the middle of the face. Most climbers will have an ambition to reach the summit platform of this unique piece of rock architecture.

The flank which overlooks Coir' a' Ghrunnda faces south-east, and seems slightly more friendly. It has two sizeable buttresses, with some very enjoyable climbs. The south-western flank, by contrast, is a broad scree and boulder slope of no great interest. The summit itself is not distinguished but it links, via Bealach Coir' a' Ghrunnda, with Sgurr Sgumain.

COIRE LAGAN FACE

The huge north-north-west face of Sron na Ciche is split by two major leftward-slanting gullies – Eastern and Central Gullies – into three main sections, Eastern Buttress on the left, Central or Cioch Buttress in the middle, and Western Buttress to the right. Most of the routes described here are on Cioch Buttress. It is possible to reach the Terrace below the Cioch itself by two different routes which involve only scrambling, but otherwise this side of the mountain is for climbers only. The face is in shadow until late in the day.

113 Collie's Route to the Cioch Moderate **

This climb was pioneered by Collie and Mackenzie when they made the first ascent of the Cioch in 1906. It takes a very devious route, but has plenty of atmosphere. The outing as described finishes by ascending the upper section of Eastern Gully to reach the summit of Sron na Ciche.

Start

Approach the face of Sron na Ciche as for Route 111. Ascend steep scree and broken ground to reach the foot of the face near the centre of Cioch Buttress. Then slant left below the face and cross a deep scoop in the scree. This was gouged out by a major rockfall in April 1999. Ascend debris with care to reach an obvious traverse line where a cone-sheet slants right. The start is harder than it used to be, but is still little more than Grade 2 scrambling.

The Route

Traverse delicately right and soon reach a more comfortable shelf. Continue right into the boulder-filled break of Eastern Gully. Make a tricky rightwards traverse across a slab – below a steep, wet wall. Move round onto the Terrace below the spectacular Cioch Slab. All the ways onto the Cioch from here involve rock climbing.

This route follows the first obvious crack slanting left up the Cioch Slab. It looks quite intimidating from below. However, the climbing is not technically difficult, although the drop into Eastern Gully on the left adds some spice. Where the rocks start to steepen, do not go straight up, but look for a ledge leading round to the left onto the wall of Eastern Gully. Ascend a section of dyke and continue traversing left across the wall until it is possible to reach the floor of the gully.

Go a short distance up the gully, then traverse right across slabs. Follow a break leading right and, after a short delicate section, descend a more secure rift known as the Shelf. Continue down the exposed right-hand crest to reach the neck behind the Cioch.

A bold step up from the neck soon leads to easier rocks and the amazing summit platform. An alternative option from the neck is to traverse slightly left along a ledge and ascend a chimney. This is possibly a touch harder but less exposed.

THE CIOCH and CIOCH SLAB

Eastern Gully

Cioch Upper Buttress

The Shelf

113

113

114

115

116

117

113

The Terrace

Eastern Buttress

113

113

Eastern Gully

Little Gully

rock scar

After enjoying the vistas from the top, some tricky moves have to be reversed to get back down to the neck. (An abseil can be arranged from a rock boss on the Coire Lagan side of the summit platform.) Follow the Shelf all the way back to Eastern Gully. It is possible to descend Eastern Gully, but this involves an abseil.

A more entertaining option is to continue up Eastern Gully. An athletic wriggle to get past a big chockstone on the left-hand side is followed by an awkward little traverse on the left wall. Higher up take the right fork. Emerge on the south-west flank of Sron na Ciche and continue without difficulty to the summit. If nothing more ambitious is planned, an easy descent can be made down the Sgumain Stone Shoot from Bealach Coir' a' Ghrunnda.

114 Arrow Route Very Difficult ***
This climb finds a way up the middle of Cioch Slab on wonderfully sound, dimpled rock – Cuillin gabbro at its best. It is not over-endowed with protection, but modern rock slippers make it a less harrowing lead than it once was. First ascent by I. Allan in 1944.
Start
Reach the Terrace below the Cioch Slab as for Route 113 (or 117).
The Route
Start directly below Cioch Slab Corner and follow a left-slanting crack to a stance by a small niche with a flake belay. Then climb boldly up, slanting slightly left, on perfect rock. Towards the top, trend right up a shallow ramp to reach the Shelf. A superb pitch.

115 Cioch Slab Corner Difficult **
This is a direct and very enjoyable way of reaching the Cioch from the Terrace. It is well protected and on delightful rock.
Start
Reach the Terrace below the Cioch Slab as for Route 113 (or 117).
The Route
Climb the introductory slab and the obvious corner above in two pitches – the second being the crux. Finish on the neck behind the Cioch. Reach the summit platform as for Collie's Route.

116 South-West Face Moderate **
This face is not as spectacular as the Cioch Slab, but it catches more of the sun. A prominent crack slanting across the face is the key to the climb.

Start

Reach the Terrace below the Cioch Slab as for Route 113 (or 117).

The Route

Continue slanting right up the Terrace beyond Cioch Slab Corner. Make a foot traverse across a short wall to reach a continuation of the Terrace. Slanting right from here leads round a corner towards Cioch Gully. Instead head up to a slight recess in the rocks above, which form the western nose of the Cioch.

Gain the recess by slanting left up a slab, then climb rightwards by a sharp-edged crack. Step down slightly and make a tricky move to get established in a very prominent crack which slants across the slabby face forming the back of the Cioch (visible in the colour plate opposite page 178). Follow this crack with interest to the ledge by the chimney which gives access to the summit of the Cioch.

117 Cioch Gully and South-West Chimney Grade 3 **

This is a very enjoyable way of reaching the Terrace below the Cioch, though only climbers will be able to progress any further up the face. Collie used this route as a way of descending from the Terrace. When combined with the previous route, it offers climbers a quick way of approaching the routes on Cioch Upper Buttress.

Start

Approach the face of Sron na Ciche as for Route 111. Ascend steep scree and broken ground to reach the foot of the face near the centre of Cioch Buttress.

The Route

To the right of a steep buttress there is a slabby gully where water trickles down. Start by scrambling up this by the rocks on the left side. Then transfer to the right and weave a way up pleasant slabs to reach easier ground. Join the main line of Cioch Gully and slant leftwards along this. A break on the right leads up to the Amphitheatre (see next route). At this point Cioch Gully becomes more defined.

Scramble pleasantly up the gully at first. Move onto the rocks to the left of the gully, then trend back right. Follow a rib and rake to the left, then ascend a crack in a steeper section of slab to gain a platform with boulders by an alcove.

At a point where a chockstone can be seen in the steeper gully above, follow a prominent break which slants left away from Cioch Gully – clearly seen in the colour plate opposite page 178. Ascend a mossy groove, surmount a chockstone and enter a chimney/rift.

SRON NA CICHE
Coire Lagan Face

Ladies' Pinnacle

Eastern Gully

Central Gully

The Cioch

The Amphitheatre

Cioch Gully

Sgumain Stone Shoot

116

117

118

118

117

113

D

Mark Andrew

Thrutch up the chimney (easier with a small sac), and break out onto a ledge on the front face of Cioch Buttress.

Traverse left a short way along the ledge and as soon as possible make an awkward step up to get established on a beautiful section of slab (crux). Continue up the slab in a fine position, and eventually reach bouldery ground below the western nose of the Cioch. The Terrace below Cioch Slab can be gained by descending slightly to the left and foot traversing a short wall. However, the natural continuation from here is to climb the nose directly above as for the previous route.

118 Amphitheatre Arête Difficult **

This route ascends a long slabby rib up an impressive section of face on Western Buttress. It is a very enjoyable route with plenty of atmosphere. The main difficulties are short-lived, and the climb is low in its grade. It was first ascended by Norman Collie in 1907.

Start

Approach the face of Sron na Ciche as for the previous route. Start at a slabby gully where water trickles down.

The Route

Scramble up to the main part of Cioch Gully as for the previous route. Leave Cioch Gully by climbing up slabs and grooves on the right. The easiest line is not obvious, and the rock is often wet. It is best not to stay in the left-hand corner. Some delicate padding on damp slabs (first crux) leads to easier ground where Central Gully cuts across the face. A broad recess in the face above is known as the Amphitheatre.

Do not continue straight up, where the rocks are often wet, but instead traverse hard right along a ledge. Ascend slabs for some 6m to easier-angled rocks, then continue traversing right to reach a ledge at the start of the broad rib or arête which is the main feature of the route. Climb easily up the arête on pleasant rock for some distance.

Eventually the arête starts to curve leftwards as a gully develops on the right. Do not follow a ledge horizontally left below steep rocks; instead move right and climb steep steps up a nose (second crux). Continue to an alcove with intimidating rocks above. Trend up left and then traverse right across a wall by a narrow ledge. Reach a break cutting back left and follow this to easier ground. The extensive summit plateau is nearby. There is a prominent pinnacle (The Finger) to the left of where the route finishes. It is sitting on a ledge which is a continuation of the same cone-sheet forming the Cioch Terrace.

Either descend boulders and scree on the south-west flank or continue to the summit of Sron na Ciche (see Route 120).

119 Western Gully Moderate *

This gully lies at the far right-hand end of Western Buttress. It offers a different kind of outing to the main face climbs, and has very fine seaward views. The route as described was first ascended by Collie and Mackenzie in 1906.

Start

Follow the path to Lower Coire Lagan as for Route 111. Once across the Allt Coire Lagan bear right and head directly towards the base of Western Gully (see diagram on Page 180). Ascend scree and slabs to the mouth of the gully.

The Route

A dyke marks the line of the gully. The initial section is rather steep so scramble up rocks to the left of the gully itself. (The direct route up the gully was climbed by Guy Barlow soon after the first ascent.) Weave a way up the left-bounding buttress for some distance. Interesting scrambling alternates with minor pitches of climbing up steeper rock steps. Eventually it becomes more attractive to traverse rightwards into the gully.

There are several short pitches in the gully with some tricky moves by chockstones. The crux pitch finishes with a delicate traverse across the right wall to regain the bed of the gully.

The gully now starts to lie back, and there are only minor pitches before the gully forks. The main gully is filled with scree, so follow the more interesting right-hand fork and then break out onto the south-west flank of Sron na Ciche. Either descend scree and boulders to join the path from Coir' a' Ghrunnda or traverse the summit as for the next route.

120 Traverse by South-West Flank 7km

The broad south-west flank is the easiest, but least inspiring, route to the summit of Sron na Ciche. It does, however, offer a convenient descent route from the neighbouring face climbs, and there are fine views of Rum and Canna from its upper reaches.

Start

Follow the path from the camp site in Glen Brittle as for Coire Lagan, but take a right fork across a stream after 800 metres. The path, which has been much improved of late, eventually crosses the Allt Coire Lagan. Shortly after this, two parallel paths cross the toe of Sron na Ciche. The lower path leads to Gars-bheinn and continues as an intermittent feature around the coast to Coruisk. The upper path is used to reach Coir' a Ghrunnda and also the start of this route.

The Route

Leave the upper path and head up between small crags to a broad slope of scree and boulders. Ascend this rather tedious ground for some distance. The angle starts to ease at about the 750m level. Continue over bouldery ground and pass indents in the left-hand rim of the plateau marking the two forks of Eastern Gully. Little more than one hundred metres of walking then leads to the summit.

Soon after the highest point a steep drop cuts across the slope, so it is necessary to move right and find a way back left down slabby steps. It is only a short distance then to Bealach Coir' a' Ghrunnda. An easy descent can then be made down the Sgumain Stone Shoot into Coire Lagan. However, it is a simple matter to visit the summit of Sgurr Sgumain first by using Route 112. A more adventurous return can be made via Coir' a' Ghrunnda (see the diagram on page 174).

COIR' A' GHRUNNDA FACE

Coir' a' Ghrunnda itself is arguably the rockiest of all the Cuillin corries. It is a magnificent example of glacial sculpturing. Three levels of superb boiler-plate slabs form the floor of the lower corrie, and much of the rock basin in the upper corrie is occupied by Loch Coir' a' Ghrunnda – at 697m, the highest body of water in the Cuillin. A visit to Coir' a' Ghrunnda alone is very rewarding. However, the easiest way to the upper corrie requires good route-finding as well as some scrambling ability.

The south-east face of Sron na Ciche, which overlooks Coir' a' Ghrunnda, has two main sections of crag separated by a broad, wet gully. The left-hand section, known as South Crag, is very impressive and has excellent climbing. Two rakes cut across this crag from right to left. The right-hand section of the face, known as North Crag, is quite complex and consists of two buttresses – Black Buttress and Slab Buttress – divided by North Crag Gully.

All the routes described on this face were first climbed by Steeple and Barlow in 1920. The routes on South Crag are described first.

121 Stony Rake Grade 1 *

This route is not a particularly worthwhile outing in its own right, but it offers a possible descent route from the climbs on South Crag, or a different way home from Coir' a' Ghrunnda.

Start

Follow the path from the camp site in Glen Brittle as described for Route 120. Shortly after crossing the Allt Coire Lagan, cut uphill to

gain a higher path which is situated above the level of a prominent boulder. Contour across the toe of Sron na Ciche for one kilometre.

There are two ways into Coir' a' Ghrunnda. The higher route is more convenient for approaching South Crag, but it is easy to miss. It breaks off from the main path just before the last section of crag on the southern flank of Sron na Ciche. Ascend an earthy gully quite steeply, with a rock wall on the left, to reach a slight flattening marked by a boggy hollow. Then ascend stony ground for some distance to gain a broad terrace below the prominent rock face of South Crag.

The Route

Slant rightwards up a weakness to gain a much narrower terrace at the foot of the main face. From the left-hand end of this terrace ascend the obvious leftward slanting rake formed by a cone-sheet. Short sections of easy scrambling lead to a more open section of face. The continuation of the rake is mainly walking on much grassier terrain. Eventually break out onto the south-western flank of Sron na Ciche. Descend diagonally across the slope in a westward direction to rejoin the approach path.

122 Central Buttress Difficult ***

This is one of the most enjoyable routes of its grade in the Cuillin. It has several pitches of delightful, open climbing on good rock. A slightly scrappy pitch above Pinnacle Rake is more than compensated for by sensational climbing on the final tower.

Start

As for the previous route.

The Route

From a slight alcove above the start of Stony Rake, climb along a narrow, leftward-slanting intrusion above and parallel to the rake. Reach a feature called the Horizontal Ledge which extends some distance across the face. The next pitch starts just left of a small projecting rib, some 3 metres to the left of the gully/groove climbed by Trap Dyke Route (Difficult). Climb a ragged crack with white veining, and weave a way up on superb rock trending slightly left. Sustained climbing by narrow dykes with very little protection leads to a stance below slightly steeper rocks.

Continue up a dyke trending slightly right at first, then cut back left to the centre of the buttress. Make an awkward step up, then take a fairly direct line up a groove with some pleasant bridging. Take a stance just below a cone-sheet which slants up leftwards below steeper rocks. Go left along the cone-sheet to the left edge of the buttress, where there are good views into a gully (Green Recess Chimneys). Climb up the left edge in a fine position. Stay on the arête apart from a couple of moves on the left-hand side. The angle gradually eases as height is gained. A stance can be taken just below Pinnacle Rake to avoid problems with rope drag.

Cross a slight neck to reach Pinnacle Rake just left of one of the two spectacular pinnacles after which it is named. Continue directly above and head for a prominent tower with gullies on either side. Start at the bottom right-hand side of the tower and step left onto its front face. Traverse left on small foot ledges to reach the centre of the face. Move up slightly then traverse hard right to near the right edge, before moving up and then returning to a central position. Climb up very steeply on jutting blocks and flakes in a fine position (crux). The climbing gradually eases above. Eventually reach a fine stance on a ledge. A further short pitch leads to the top.

To return to the foot of the face, descend the south-west flank of Sron na Ciche as far as a sharp leftward bend in its south-eastern rim. It should then be possible to identify the upper grassy section of Stony Rake (Route 121). Descend the rake to the start of the route.

123 Pinnacle Rake Grade 2 *

This rake crosses the upper part of South Crag from right to left. It is difficult to identify from below, and is best seen from the base of Stack Buttress or when descending from upper Coir' a' Ghrunnda. It is more difficult than Stony Rake and harder to follow, but like that route it offers an alternative way home from Coir' a' Ghrunnda.

Start

Approach as for Route 121. Go past the base of South Crag and slant right to just beyond where water drains from the gully dividing North and South Crags. A short section of leftward-leaning brown slab marks the best access point to the rake.

The Route

A striking pinnacle, which resembles an owl, stands out on the skyline to the left of the rake. Ascend the short slab, then traverse left across

---

Opposite: Below the Thearlaich–Dubh Gap, looking south-east (Scrambler, Tommy Archibald)

Next Page: The crux chimney on the South-West Ridge of Sgurr Alasdair (Scrambler, George Sawicki)

damp and slightly broken rocks to eventually gain the obvious break to the right of the owl-like pinnacle. The ground gradually steepens and becomes unpleasantly loose. Pick a way up rather shattered rock with care (crux) and bridge up a groove on the left. Soon gain an easier and more grassy section. Continue by a small rowan tree and, shortly after, go over boulders beside a second, finger-like pinnacle. The Central Buttress climb (Route 122) crosses the rake near here.

Turn a slight corner and traverse across a recess marking the upper part of Green Recess Chimneys. The rake now appears to peter out. By descending a grassy groove for a short distance it is possible to pick up the line of a cone-sheet which is the key to the final section of the route. Follow this with interest around several corners and eventually emerge on the south-west flank of Sron na Ciche. Descend that slope to regain the approach path.

124 Stack Buttress Direct Difficult **

This very enjoyable route offers a remarkably different style of climbing to Central Buttress. It has very interesting route-finding, and is quite hard for the grade.

Start

Approach as for Route 121, then continue beyond South Crag. Stack Buttress is set back slightly and starts at a higher level.

It is also possible to approach by the lower route into Coir' a' Ghrunnda. Slant left up veined slabs to reach a fault that runs along the base of a prominent rock band. Follow this a long way right until a short easy scramble leads to bouldery ground directly below Stack Buttress. See the diagram on page 192.

The climb starts near the centre of the buttress (well to the left of North Crag Gully) below a rightward slanting diagonal crack/break.

The Route

Climb up to the break and follow it over some awkward jutting blocks. Go horizontally right to a stance below a sloping roof. Move further right and climb over some slightly suspect flakes. Then break back up left for some distance and traverse horizontally left to a stance.

Previous Page: Looking across Coir' a' Ghrunnda from the West-South-West Flank of Sgurr nan Eag (Scrambler, George Archibald)

*Opposite: On the Dubh Slabs above Loch Coruisk
(Scramblers, George Archibald and Willie Jeffrey)*

COIR' A' GHRUNNDA
North Crag

Stack
Buttress

North Crag Gully

Slab Buttress

123

124

125

To
Upper Coir
a'Ghrunnda

Mark Hudson

Make some steep moves up a slight depression, and pull up onto a large slabby ramp overlooking North Crag Gully. Follow the ramp left for a short distance then break right, across a wall, and shortly after reach another ramp. Follow this up left to a stance.

The bulging wall above proves rather difficult. With careful footwork it is possible to use some excellent handholds above and slightly left. Soon reach a grassy rake which is followed easily up to the left. Continue up a slab to a commodious terrace.

The slabby wall above is the south face of a tapered tower known as The Stack. Start by slanting very slightly left up a gully/groove then, at the first opportunity, traverse right onto the face. The standard way is to then climb directly up a crack. However, after climbing up slightly, it is possible to traverse delicately right again and then continue fairly directly to the crest of The Stack – a superb pitch.

Weave a way up left with fine views of upper Coir' a' Ghrunnda. Finish up a rightward sweep of easy slabs. Either traverse over the summit of Sron na Ciche or descend its south-west flank (Route 120).

125 Slab Buttress Grade 3 **
This is an interesting meander up a big face, with several harder options available to climbers. The rock is generally very good.
Start
Approach as for the previous route. Slab Buttress lies immediately to the right of Stack Buttress. The route to upper Coir' a' Ghrunnda ascends a broad gully which slants below the base of the buttress.
The Route
The superb slabs forming the lower part of the buttress can be ascended by climbers. However, an easier option starts further left near the bottom of North Crag Gully, and this is now described.

Go up by the stream which issues from North Crag Gully. A short distance below the mouth of the gully, find a way onto the right-hand wall by a dyke. Move right round a corner, then traverse easily along a grassy terrace some distance to the right. Before reaching the end of the terrace, move up to a higher rock ledge. Traverse right and use a deep dimple for the left hand to ascend a steeper section by a dyke. Break back leftwards on rock which gradually gets easier as height is gained. Clamber carefully past some loose blocks, then move left from an alcove and follow a dyke trending slightly right. Eventually reach a point overlooking a damp chimney/gully on the right. Move back left and step up onto fine slabs. Follow these to easier ground.

Reach a big slanting terrace where an easy escape is available off to the right. Continue up fairly easy rocks in the same general direction, and eventually reach another big slanting terrace. This time the rocks directly ahead are too steep, so go right and ascend coarse scree. Then cut back hard left up the higher of two sloping rock shelves. From the top of the shelf there are views across into North Crag Gully.

The next tier gives very sustained scrambling. Go back down the shelf a short distance. Ascend a broken groove to the right of a more prominent groove near a corner. Then move left to gain the left-hand groove. Follow this on slightly slimy rock for a short distance, then traverse right and follow an arête to the right of a slab. Move right along a crack-line and ascend to a ledge. Traverse left and ascend a crack behind a huge block to reach a sloping grassy terrace.

Ascend a prominent slab by moving left and scrambling pleasantly up a rightward-trending break. Reach another terrace and follow this up left. There is a prominent tower directly above. The scrambling option avoids this by continuing round to the left. However, the slabs and corner below and right of the tower offer climbers some additional fun (Moderate/Difficult). Either option leads to the bouldery plateau of Sron na Ciche. The top of Eastern Gully lies directly across the slope. It is a simple matter to visit the summit of Sron na Ciche before descending. See Route 120.

SGURR THEARLAICH (978m)

This peak was described earlier, along with the peaks surrounding Coire Lagan (see pages 171–173). However, its south-east ridge is described here because it overlooks Coir' a' Ghrunnda. This ridge is cleaved by one of the most formidable obstacles on the Cuillin main ridge – the Thearlaich–Dubh Gap.

126 Traverse below the South-West Face 450m
This route has become quite a popular way of avoiding the Thearlaich–Dubh Gap. However, the natural continuation to the summit of Sgurr Alasdair is a Grade 3 scramble.

Start

The route starts from Bealach Coir' an Lochain. It is most likely to be approached along the main ridge. See Route 127 for a description of how to approach Bealach Coir' an Lochain from Coir' a' Ghrunnda.

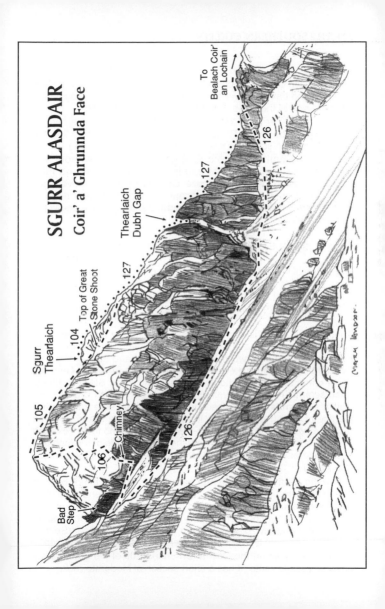

The Route
From Bealach Coir' an Lochain follow the south-east ridge for a short distance, and traverse over a very minor rise. Then find a way off the left-hand side of the ridge. See the diagram on page 199.

Pick up a faint path which crosses the scree fan below the Thearlaich–Dubh Gap. (The gully which leads directly up to the gap is mainly a loose scramble with a short section of Moderate.)

Follow the path close to a rock wall on the right without any difficulty. Towards the upper end it curves gently left and then ascends scree to the right of a cave. Continuing directly above leads to Bealach Sgumain. The normal route up the south-west ridge of Sgurr Alasdair follows a ledge to the right, a short distance below the bealach itself (see Route 106).

127 South-East Ridge via the Thearlaich–Dubh Gap
Very Difficult (with an abseil) **

This is one of the hardest obstacles on the Cuillin main ridge traverse. Only Naismith's Route on the Bhasteir Tooth is of a similar standard. The problem of the gap was first solved by Collie, King and Mackenzie when they scaled both its walls on the same day in 1891.

Start
Although this route is normally reached along the main ridge, the approach from Coir' a' Ghrunnda is described for completeness. Follow either of the two routes up the left-hand side of Coir' a' Ghrunnda (see Route 124) to the base of Slab Buttress. Gain the upper corrie by first slanting up a broad gully below Stack Buttress. Then scramble up rocks well left of the stream which drains Loch Coir' a' Ghrunnda. (When descending this way be sure not to follow the line of the stream.) Then clamber over boulders and traverse across rough ground to where the stream leaves the loch. To reach Bealach Coir' an Lochain, go round the left-hand side of the loch and ascend extremely rough ground forming the headwall of the corrie.

The Route
Follow the crest of the ridge and pass to the left of a minor boss of rock. Then climb up a section of much steeper rock, trending slightly left at first, to arrive at the lip of the gap. The normal practice is then to abseil some 10m down the south-east wall directly into the gap. In ascent this wall gives a very steep climb of Very Difficult/Severe standard. The best line is just to the left of centre when looking up.

The loose gully on the Coir' a' Ghrunnda side of the gap offers a possible escape route. It has a short section of Moderate rock.

The climb up the north-west side of the gap is longer (25m) but slightly easier than the one on the other side. In perfect conditions it may seem easy for its grade. However, it is rather polished and becomes extremely treacherous in the wet. The lower section is a steep chimney/crack with an awkward jamming move halfway up which is easier in boots. The upper section follows a slightly less steep groove. Scramble pleasantly up the remainder of the ridge until it is possible to slant left and ascend on scree to the saddle at the top of the Great Stone Shoot. It is normal then to make a detour to the summit of Sgurr Alasdair (Route 105).

SGURR DUBH AN DA BHEINN *(938m)*

This shapely peak is composed of peridotite – a rock which is even rougher than gabbro. The three ridges radiating from the summit separate three spectacular corries. On a traverse of the main ridge it is now common practice to make a detour from this summit to visit Sgurr Dubh Mor – a Munro.

128 North-West Ridge Grade 1
This is the easiest of the mountain's three ridges.
Start
Approach Bealach Coir' an Lochain as for the previous route. This bealach can also be reached from the Coir' an Lochain side.
The Route
Fairly straightforward walking and some easy scrambling soon lead to the summit of this peak. It is an excellent viewpoint.

129 East Ridge to Sgurr Dubh Mor Grade 2 or 3 *
Since this route is frequently used to visit Sgurr Dubh Mor from the main ridge, it is described starting from Sgurr Dubh an Da Bheinn.
The Route
From the summit, scramble down the fairly narrow east ridge without great difficulty to a low point at 886m. Pass some sizeable pinnacles on the right side, or take them more directly to add extra interest.

The south-west spur of Sgurr Dubh Mor rises ahead. Weave a way up ledges starting on the right (Grade 2), or climb more directly up steep walls in a spectacular position (at least Grade 3). The summit lies a short distance along the chisel-like crest. Return the same way. See also the Dubh Slabs (Route 147).

130 South Ridge Grade 2 **
This ridge gives an enjoyable scramble. It is characterised by massive blocks of rough rock.

Start

It is possible to reach the dip on the north side of Caisteal a' Garbh-choire (see below) by scrambling up very rough ground from either of the neighbouring corries. Scrabble under a huge leaning block to reach the start from the Coir' a' Ghrunnda side.

The Route

Clamber up huge blocks close to the crest but generally just on the Coir' a' Ghrunnda side. Much variation is possible. At one point move left along a good ledge and then back right to a nose. Continue for some distance with the angle gradually easing. Curve rightwards to reach the summit.

CAISTEAL A' GARBH-CHOIRE (828m)

To the west of Loch Coir' a' Ghrunnda there is a pass over to Coruisk called Bealach an Garbh-choire (797m). An impressive rock bastion, called Caisteal a' Garbh-choire, is situated in the bealach. The feature is well named *(castle of the rough corrie)*. It is built from extremely rough peridotite. Its distinctive profile can be recognised even from the landing stage in Loch na Cuilce by the Coruisk Hut.

The summit is accessible only to climbers. The whole mass can be bypassed most easily by a path on the east side. When crossing to Coruisk, the best option is to gain the ridge at the southern end of Caisteal a' Garbh-choire, skirt round by this path on the east side and then descend into An Garbh-choire from the northern end.

131 North-East Ridge Difficult *
This route was climbed by Naismith and Arthur in 1912, when they traversed the peak from north to south. Confident climbers can descend this way, though it should not be confused with the overhanging northern end, which is sometimes abseiled.

Start

From the dip at the northern end of Caisteal a' Garbh-choire, move down very slightly left onto the An Garbh-choire side.

The Route

Climb steeply up the rather indefinite ridge for some 8m, then continue with slightly less difficulty. Slant right to gain the summit

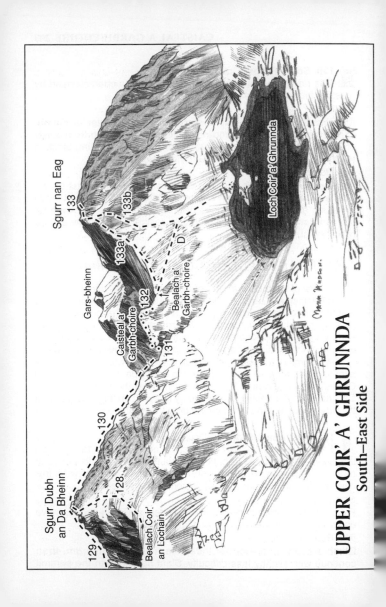

UPPER COIR' A' GHRUNNDA
South–East Side

Sgurr nan Eag

133

133b

133a

Gars-bheinn

Loch Coir' a' Ghrunnda

132

Caisteal a' Garbh-choire

Bealach a' Garbh-choire

D

131

130

Sgurr Dubh an Da Bheinn

128

129

Bealach Coir' an Lochain

crest. The highest point is towards the southern end. Descend by the south ridge or west face as described for the next route.

132 South Ridge and West Face Moderate **

This combination gives a most enjoyable way of traversing this fine little peak. The grade would be harder but for the superbly adhesive quality of the rock.

Start

From Bealach a' Garbh-choire at the southern end of Caisteal a' Garbh-choire. There are big blocks set in the rock hereabouts.

The Route

Scramble up the crest to where it steepens. Climb amazing rock in a superb position. The easiest line lies slightly left of the crest. From the summit continue down the crest then climb down the middle of the west face. Scramble around the north-western side and ascend loose ground to the tunnel by the leaning block.

SGURR NAN EAG (924m)

This bulky mountain is the most southerly Munro in the Cuillin. There are superb views from its 400 metre-long and almost level summit ridge. It has a steep face to the north overlooking An Garbh-choire, and a broad and uninteresting south-western flank. It is normally traversed by its east and north ridges.

133 North Ridge Grade 1 or 2 **

This is the usual way of bagging the peak from Glen Brittle. The easiest way has only mild scrambling and is well worn.

Start

Approach Coir' a' Ghrunnda as described for Routes 120/121. Either ascend the left-hand side of the lower corrie by the fault along the base of the rock band or by the higher terrace which slants below the base of South Crag. Continue past Slab Buttress and scramble up rocks some distance left of the stream which spills from Loch Coir' a' Ghrunnda. Once in the upper corrie, walk round the south side of the loch and slant up rough ground to one of the two possible starts.

An alternative approach can be taken up the superb slabby floor of the lower corrie. Scramble up a cleft formed by a wide dyke which cuts through the right-hand end of the rock bands close to the west flank of Sgurr nan Eag. Continue directly to gain the upper corrie.

The Route

a) The best scrambling line starts from Bealach a' Garbh-choire and follows the crest as closely as possible (Grade 2). Scramble up extremely rough ground to reach the bealach. The rock at the start is peridotite with conspicuous fragments (xenoliths) set in it, but this soon gives way to gabbro. The middle section has slightly more awkward route-finding over big blocks. Higher up, where the crest coincides with a cone-sheet, the going is easier. A minor top is crossed just before the long summit ridge is reached. There are several rocky eminences on the crest, the second of which has a steep drop at the far end. The third one is marginally the highest.

b) An easier option starts by slanting up rightwards on broken ground some distance below Bealach a' Garbh-choire (Grade 1). Follow scree paths with only minor sections of scrambling to the right of the crest. Join the route up the ridge where the angle starts to ease some distance before the summit. It is possible to cut left to join the crest at several places on the ascent.

The simplest option now is to return the same way. The broad south-western flank is an unattractive alternative. However, the continuation to Gars-bheinn at the far end of the ridge presents no difficulties (see Routes 135 and 137–139), and it is possible to avoid Sgurr nan Eag on the return by using one of Harker's short cuts. This starts from the dip in the ridge (774m) between Sgurr a' Choire Bhig and Sgurr nan Eag. Drop down only a short distance on the north side into An Garbh-choire. Then traverse across the north-east flank of Sgurr nan Eag. The main difficulty involves crossing a slab at the start which may be wet. Then continue below the gash of The Chasm – a classic Very Difficult climb. After that, pick a way carefully over very rough boulders for some distance. The line more or less contours the slope, with only a slight rise towards the end to reach Bealach a' Garbh-choire (797m).

134 West-South-West Flank Grade 2/3 *

This scramble takes a fairly direct way up Sgurr nan Eag from the lower floor of Coir' a' Ghrunnda. In dry conditions a long, hidden gully towards the top offers an interesting finish.

Start

Use the normal approach to Coir' a' Ghrunnda (see Routes 120/121) but, instead of ascending the gully by the rock wall, follow the more obvious lower route round into the mouth of the corrie. Then head right and cross the stream in the corrie floor.

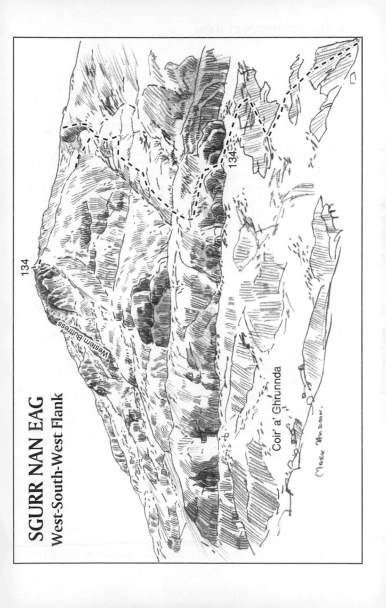

SGURR NAN EAG
West-South-West Flank

134

Western Buttress

134

134

Coir' a' Ghrunnda

The Route

A leftward-slanting grassy gully cuts through the steep rock band at the base of the face. It is difficult to see from below. Approach it by scrambling pleasantly up some introductory slabs. The biggest slab below the rock band is ascended by following a cone-sheet slanting right. High up this, make an awkward move to break back left onto an easier section of slab. Then slant leftwards onto easier ground.

The grassy gully lies immediately to the right of two massive stacked blocks and a squat pinnacle. Ascend the gully without difficulty and then slant hard left on a very narrow grassy ledge for some distance. Scramble up short rock steps to reach easier-angled ground, where a broad terrace slants leftwards across the face.

Walk up to a rock band which lies a short distance to the right of a gully. Pull up to gain a cone-sheet slanting right, and follow this to reach a grassy ledge below another rock band. There is a scoop to the right of a steeper section of wall. Gain the scoop and slant delicately left to reach a crack with a good finger slot. Continue to a more continuous sweep of slabs. Ascend this by a prominent rightward-slanting cone-sheet for some distance. Slant back left along a cracked weakness, then follow another cone-sheet slanting right. Break up through slabs more directly, then move left again. Weave to and fro more easily for some distance.

Slant right along another cone-sheet to reach a scree slope. Go hard right and ascend stepped rocks pleasantly back left. Follow a grassy rake slanting right and, when it levels off slightly, break diagonally left. Ascend the rocks to the right of a grassy runnel, and then weave to and fro on easier ground.

Scramble up steps of rock with vertical banding, a short distance right of where water trickles down. The water originates from a gully which slants a long way left further up the face. In dry conditions it is possible to move left and scramble steeply up a drainage line to gain the main gully. Otherwise continue directly to eventually reach the edge of the south-west flank. Follow this to the summit.

The gully can also be entered from above, near the point where the south-west flank is first reached. Drop down a short distance and cross a rounded, bouldery rib. Then slant left down a prominent grassy rake to reach the bed of the gully. Scramble up the gully for some distance over boulders, slabs and small chockstones. Several steep, wet rock walls cross the gully in its upper section, and these bring a more serious air to the ascent. Move right then back left slightly. Ascend a 2m rock wall, using a wet foothold to reach the platform above. Soon after, cut hard left to exit the gully. Gain the left-bounding arête and go further left round the corner. Break back right onto the crest almost immediately by ascending some fine rock steps. Reach easier ground soon after.

Slant right to join the other finish. Continue up the south-west flank and negotiate a way through some gigantic boulders. Finish by the first (north-western) of the three eminences on the summit ridge. Continue as for the previous route.

135 East Ridge Grade 1

This is a straightforward section of the main ridge which is normally ascended as part of a traverse from Gars-bheinn. It is therefore described starting from the dip between Sgurr a' Choire Bhig and Sgurr na Eag. See also the next route.

The Route

There are short sections of very easy scrambling early on, but the upper section is just a steep walk on scree. Interest can be added by looking for some holes on the Coire nan Laogh side of the crest about two-thirds of the way up the ridge. They mark the exit from a Very Difficult climb called The Chasm. The climb starts on the An Garbh-choire side (see Route 133). After a tricky entry pitch, it turns into a very unusual subterranean excursion. It was largely filled with snow and ice when it was first climbed by Steeple and Barlow in 1915. They returned in 1919 with Doughty to make the first summer ascent.

136 Coire nan Laogh Slabs Grade 2/3 *

This route finds a way up one of the least-frequented corries in the Cuillin. It wanders up slabs to the left of the steep rock band in the centre of the corrie, and it finishes on the lower part of the East Ridge of Sgurr nan Eag. The route is not recommended in descent.

Start

Follow the path from the camp site in Glen Brittle as for Route 120. Stay on the lower path across the base of Sron na Ciche and eventually cross the Allt Coir' a' Ghrunnda some distance below Coir' a' Ghrunnda itself. Continue on the path for a further kilometre then slant left up the hillside and follow the stream up into Coire nan Laogh. Stags may be seen and heard here during the rutting season.

Two prominent gullies cleave the main rock band in the centre of the corrie. The left-hand one, called West Gully, has one Moderate pitch but is otherwise an uninteresting scramble over boulders. The right-hand one, called Central Gully, is a more attractive Very Difficult

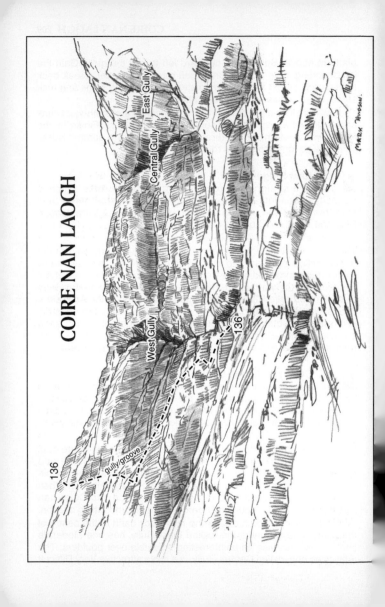
COIRE NAN LAOGH

climb. A less obvious gully further right, called East Gully, gives a pleasant Difficult. All three gullies were climbed in 1912 by Herford and Laycock. Herford found fame on the Central Buttress of Scafell two years later. Laycock – a gritstone expert of his day – was very enthusiastic about Central Gully in a Fell & Rock Climbing Club Journal; " ... *a remarkable place, of the most romantic, and a very worthy climb. I would almost say it is unique within my experience.*"

The Route

The lower floor of the corrie is largely heather-covered, but some small rock bands of almost flint-like basalt give short sections of scrambling. West Gully has a conspicuous chockstone part way up. Slant left from a grassy terrace to reach the mouth of this gully.

Scramble diagonally left up surprisingly awkward slabs. Traverse right into a groove, and ascend this for two or three moves, before breaking back left onto the slabs. Follow these to a big terrace. Head up to a rock band and pull up steeply at the left-hand end of a long flake. Traverse right along a foot ledge and climb up by a tiny dyke. Continue more easily, then slant a long way left along a scree terrace.

A key feature on the next section of the route is a leftward leaning gully/groove. The scramble goes up rocks a little further left. Slant left up a grassy cleft heading towards the groove, but then traverse left along an intrusion to reach a ledge with a small juniper bush. Now weave a way up slabs trending slightly right (crux) in the general direction of a boulder on the skyline above. Join a faint buttress, which lies to the left of the groove, and follow this pleasantly for some distance. Ascend a short wall from a recess with junipers.

When the groove on the right starts to peter out, slant right across slabs and soon reach easier ground. Continue up easy slabs, staying slightly left rather than following bouldery ground further right. Reach a rock band with a long roof and slant right with surprising ease to gain a good ledge. Traverse right past a steep wall then ascend a corner to reach easier slabs and soon break left to a grassy ledge. Scramble over an overlap by trending slightly right. Take a direct line up slabs then follow an enjoyable leftward trending slabby ramp. Break back right and soon join the lower section of the East Ridge.

Previous Page : Peridotite Buttress, Sron Bhuidhe, Coireachan Ruadha
(Scrambler, George Archibald)

Opposite : Collie's Route on Sgurr a' Ghreadaidh, above Coir'-uisg
(Climber, George Archibald)

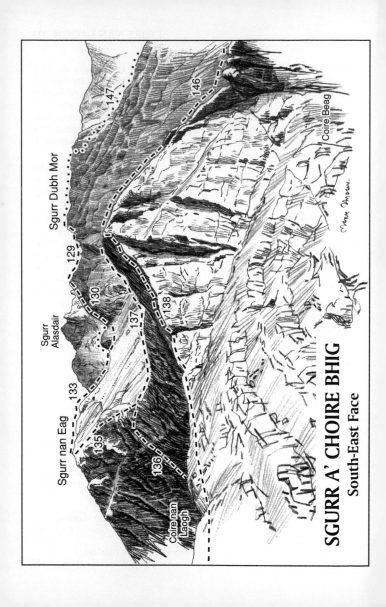

SGURR A' CHOIRE BHIG
South-East Face

Coire Beag

Sgurr Dubh Mor

Sgurr Alasdair

Sgurr nan Eag

Coire nan Laogh

147

146

129

130

137

138

133

135

136

SGURR A' CHOIRE BHIG (875m)

This peak is frequently hurried over early in the morning by parties starting a traverse of the main ridge. However, its shapely summit warrants a more leisurely treatment. It offers excellent views and can be traversed without difficulty by its south and north-west ridges. The mountain's finest feature is its north-east ridge, which is described later in the Coruisk chapter (see Route 146).

137 North-West Ridge ½km
The usual way to approach the start of this ridge would be to first traverse Sgurr nan Eag (see Routes 133–135). The previous route offers a possible alternative.

The Route
From the dip between Sgurr nan Eag and Sgurr a' Choire Bhig ascend the ridge to a broad flat section of whale-back slabs and boulders. This is a better place to bivvy before tackling the main ridge than the more cramped locations around the summit of Gars-bheinn.

Continue pleasantly up the ridge. Although the upper section narrows dramatically, it is no more than walking. From the summit there are fine views of Gars-bheinn, as well as Sgurr Dubh Beag and Sgurr Dubh Mor on the other side of An Garbh-choire.

138 South Ridge Grade 1 *
This short, rocky ridge is the natural continuation from the north-west ridge of Gars-bheinn – see the next route described.

The Route
Follow the narrow ridge crest with only short sections of very mild scrambling up short steps early on. Reach the summit abruptly. Continue by descending the previous route.

GARS-BHEINN (895m)

The most southerly mountain on the Cuillin main ridge is a fine peak with magnificent views. On a clear day most of the main ridge can be seen, as well as many mainland mountains such as Ben Nevis. Unfortunately, the normal approach from Glen Brittle involves the ascent of 500m of purgatorial scree on the mountain's south-west flank. Some rather more pleasant approaches are described in the Coruisk chapter.

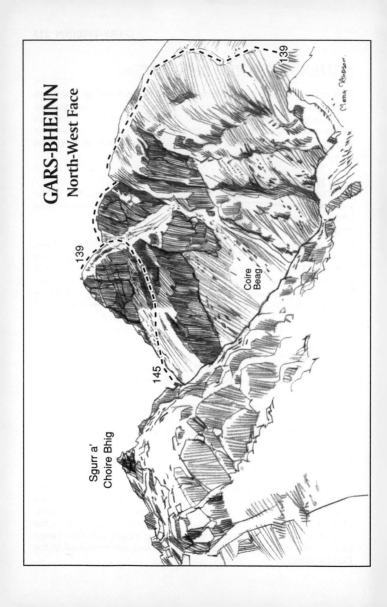

GARS-BHEINN
North-West Face

139

139

145

Coire Beag

Sgurr a'
Choire Bhig

Marin Anderson.

139 North-West Ridge Grade 1 *

The ridge itself is pleasant enough, but the approach from the Glen Brittle side is hard going. Two minor tops before the main summit can cause confusion in bad visibility.

Start

Follow the path from the camp site in Glen Brittle as for Route 120. Take the lower path across the base of Sron na Ciche, and continue for a further 2km – crossing the streams from Coir' a' Ghrunnda and Coire nan Laogh on the way. Ascend the steep south-west flank on loose scree and rubble. Fine views of Soay and Rum offer some distraction from the tedium. The ridge crest is normally gained (with great relief) midway between the dip below Sgurr a' Choire Bhig and the summit of Gars-bheinn.

The Route

Walk along the pleasant grassy crest over the first minor top. Pass the top of a narrow scree-filled gully which lies on the north or Coire Beag side of the ridge. Traverse a second top and scramble down to a dip before the main summit. (Another branch of the scree gully leads down into Coire Beag from here.) Easy scrambling on steeper ground leads up to the fine summit. Superb views can be obtained of Loch Scavaig by walking a short distance down the south-east ridge.

Before describing the routes which are approached from the Coruisk side of the Cuillin, it is convenient to mention here some low-level outings from Glen Brittle. The 'Fairy Pools' in Coire na Creiche, and the spectacular waterfall of Eas Mor below Coire na Banachdich, have already been referred to (see Routes 58 and 88 respectively). They both make enjoyable short walks. The easy hills above the forest on the west side of Glen Brittle are also worthwhile and offer unusual views of the Cuillin. One delightful outing, however, deserves a separate description.

140 Rubh' an Dunain 13km **

The headland of Rubh' an Dunain lies between Loch Brittle and Soay Sound, and to the south of the Glen Brittle camp site. It harbours several fascinating sites of historical and archaeological significance. The walk is fairly long, and allowance should also be made for dallying at the various localities of interest. The most useful map for this outing is the OS *Outdoor Leisure Map 8*.

Start

Park near the beach and walk along a track through the camp site. Cross a stile behind the toilet block.

The Route

There are two options on the first part of this walk. Either turn right and follow a gently undulating footpath near to the shore, or go uphill a short distance (pass to the left of some water storage tanks) and join a vehicular track which takes a higher route parallel to the path. Taking the path on the way out, and the track on the way back, makes a good combination.

After 1½km the route crosses the Allt Coire Lagan. This stream may be a problem to cross when in spate, in which case a small wooden footbridge situated halfway between the path and the track may offer the best solution. Continue for some distance until the track peters out by a stream. Carry on in the same direction and take the left fork which slants gradually uphill. Pass by a small lochan and go to the left of a small top called Creag Mhor (120m). From the southern end of this rocky knoll there are good views of the way ahead. A wide dyke, which cuts all the way across the headland, has formed a linear depression known as Slochd Dubh (*black ditch*).

Drop down and slant leftwards across this feature, heading in the direction of Rum. Go through a wall and continue in the same general direction across fairly featureless ground. Eventually descend slightly to a hollow where the remains of a building and an enclosure can be seen. This is Rhundunan, a former home of the MacAskills.

Now start to slant right, in the direction of Canna, and find a way through the high bracken towards Loch na h-Airde. Go left along the shore of this loch, which is only a very short distance above sea level. Follow the east side of its outlet channel. This was deepened at some time in the past to allow boats to be brought up to the safe anchorage inside. Ascend to a promontory where the remains of an Iron Age dun can be inspected.

Go round the western tip of Rubh an Dunain and, on the return, visit the north side of Loch na h-Airde. A chambered cairn is situated very close to the loch on the east side of a wall. It is hard to see until close up to it. When it was excavated in the 1930s the remains of six adults and fragments of Beaker pottery were found.

Return by a more northerly path with fine views of the Cuillin in the distance. After crossing the end of Slochd Dubh, skirt left below Creag Mhor to eventually rejoin the path used on the approach.

Coruisk

The great hollow known as Coruisk lies in the heart of the Cuillin. It is enclosed by the southern and central sections of the Cuillin main ridge, and the long side ridge of Druim nan Ramh. Lying in the floor of this huge corrie is Loch Coruisk – a 2½ kilometre-long freshwater loch, the ice-scooped floor of which lies over 30m below sea level. Coruisk is the anglicised version of Coir'-uisg, which means *water corrie*. The term 'Coir'-uisg' tends to be associated with that part of the corrie upstream of Loch Coruisk. Whereas the term 'Coruisk' is used rather more loosely to refer to the whole basin which contains Loch Coruisk, and also the area around its outflow into Loch na Cuilce at the head of Loch Scavaig.

The water draining out of Loch Coruisk flows along the River Scavaig for only 400 metres before it spills down slabs into the sea. There is an important crossing point over the River Scavaig at its outflow from Loch Coruisk, but the stepping stones there can quickly become submerged in spate conditions. The Coruisk Memorial Hut is situated below a long crag near the mouth of the River Scavaig. It is a private hut and is kept locked when not in use. There is plenty of scope for camping on slightly boggy ground nearby. However, on occasions when wind is funnelled into this area, conditions can become very difficult for camping.

Coruisk was first described in rapturous terms early in the nineteenth century by MacCulloch the geologist. It has attracted sightseers ever since. Among the early visitors were several artists and poets – such as Scott, Daniell and Turner – who tried, with mixed success, to portray the awesome grandeur of the scenery.

There is certainly a special atmosphere about this part of the Cuillin, although it may be hard to appreciate when thick cloud obscures all the tops, and heavy rain transforms all the streams into white, foaming torrents. In good weather, however, this is one of the finest mountain locations in the country, and its delights can only be enjoyed properly at first hand.

In the summer months there is a busy boat service between Elgol and the little landing stage in Loch na Cuilce. These popular trips allow visitors ashore for only an hour, unless special arrangements are made in advance. Boats can also be chartered from Arisaig and Mallaig. Sailing into Loch na Cuilce in fine weather is one of the best possible ways of experiencing this part of the Cuillin.

It is also feasible to reach Coruisk by crossing the main ridge from several places in Glen Brittle – the three main options being via:

Bealach na Glaic Moire, 760m ....(p128 / diags pp129 & 234)
Bealach Coire na Banachdich, 851m ....(p155 / diag p157)
Bealach a' Garbh-choire, 797m ....(p203 / diags pp204 & 224).

In addition, there are three low-level approaches on foot from Glen Brittle in the west, Sligachan in the north and Camasunary in the east. These last three approaches are now described, as well as the link between Sligachan and Camasunary.

141 Glen Brittle to Coruisk via the coast 11km *

The first half of this route is reasonably well-worn, since it is also used to approach Gars-bheinn at the southern end of the main ridge. The second half is also worn, but not so obvious, and requires good route-finding through some tricky terrain. It is something of a misnomer to describe this as a coastal route since for most of the way it lies some distance from the shore and more than 200m above sea level. Not a route to be underestimated.

Start
From the camp site in Glen Brittle.

The Route
Head up the hillside and after 800 metres take a right fork across a stream. Follow the path towards the base of Sron na Ciche. Stay on the lower path, which eventually crosses the Allt Coir' a' Ghrunnda well below the mouth of the corrie. Continue below the broad flank of Sgurr nan Eag, and cross the Allt Coire nan Laogh. Shortly after this, do not take the higher route that slants left up to the base of Gars-bheinn, instead keep traversing at the 225m level for a full kilometre, then slant gently uphill on grassy ground for some 300 metres.

There are two main ways of rounding the more broken ground on the south-east shoulder of Gars-bheinn. The upper way cuts the corner slightly by gaining and losing height. It slants up across a depression, and continues ascending the hillside to a shelf with a tiny lochan at a height of 315m. This lochan is the source of the Allt an Fhraoich (named only on OS 1:25 000 map). Continue for some 200 metres beyond the lochan, then make a gradual descent leftwards away from the stream. The lower route contours around the shoulder and eventually slants up beside the same stream before crossing it and heading in a northerly direction to join the other route.

Continue north at roughly the 280m level for a further 700 metres until almost directly above Eilean Reamhar in Loch Scavaig below. At this point it is possible to maintain height and continue northwards to gain a slightly higher, grassy terrace which eventually leads to An Garbh-choire (see Route 147). However, the way down to the coast now slants down steeply to the right on grass and heather. Halfway down it crosses over the Allt Coir' a' Chruidh and then passes below a steep crag. Soon after this it rises slightly to cross a neck behind a small knoll (GR 481 192), before continuing down to the shore.

Cross a stream which descends from a grassy depression and shortly after cross the more impressive Allt a' Chaoich (Mad Burn). This stream can become impassable when in spate. Continue along the coast on awkward rock slabs (Grade 1?), or use the shore when the tide is out, and soon reach the more open ground near the Coruisk Hut. Cross short sections of rock slab and head up a path to eventually reach the stepping stones over the River Scavaig, by the mouth of Loch Coruisk.

142 Sligachan to Coruisk via Druim Hain 11½km **

This is the most straightforward of the walking routes into Coruisk, though it is still a long outing. It rises to a height of 317m on Druim Hain. (Some prefer to visit a superb viewpoint on Sgurr na Stri instead of losing height to reach the shore of Loch Coruisk – see Route 156.) The easiest way back is to return the same way.
Start
From the old road bridge by the Sligachan Hotel.
The Route
Follow the path along Glen Sligachan for 3km, then cross the Allt na Measarroch and continue south past some big boulders with rowan trees. The path rises slightly as it continues below the impressive west face of Marsco. When the path starts to descend slightly, some 6km from Sligachan, take a right fork and head south across the floor of the glen. Then ascend steadily by a well-worn path for some distance and eventually reach the crest of Druim Hain, from where there are dramatic views of the Cuillin. Volcanic breccia gives way to gabbro just as the crest is reached.

A popular option at this point is to slant across the west flank of Sgurr Hain to an excellent viewpoint below Sgurr na Stri. It gives magnificent views of Coruisk and most of the Cuillin. A short detour can also be made about halfway along this leg to visit Captain Maryon's Monument (GR 498 205). This well-constructed cairn lies

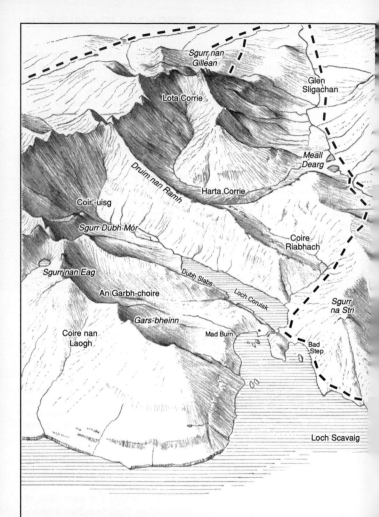

LOOKING NORTH OVER CORUISK & BLA BHEINN

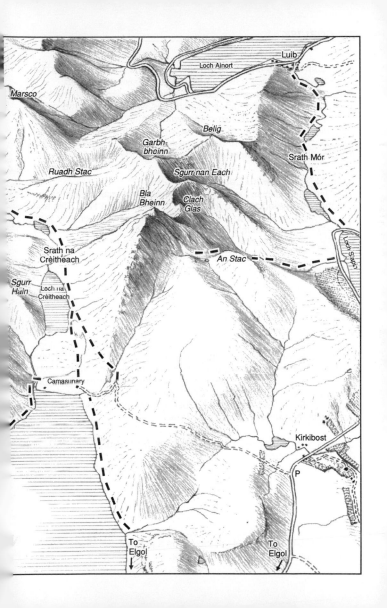

some 50m below the path, at the spot where the captain lay dead for almost two years before his remains were discovered in 1948.

Otherwise drop down into Coire Riabhach, staying above the loch in its floor. The path becomes less obvious where the ground drops more steeply, and there are some awkward little sections of slab. Stay slightly left and eventually follow one of a number of paths all the way down to the shore of Loch Coruisk. Continue around a tiny bay to reach the stepping stones at the outlet from the loch.

143 Sligachan to Camasunary 12½km *

This route follows the long defile between the main Cuillin range and the hills immediately to the east (i.e. the Western Red Hills and Cuillin Outliers). Although it rises to a maximum height of only 90m at the halfway point, it is a fairly demanding outing. This is especially true if it is made part of a circuit with routes 142 and 144.

Start

From the old road bridge by the Sligachan Hotel.

The Route

Follow the path along Glen Sligachan for 6km as for the previous route, then take the left fork which continues below the south-west flank of Ruadh Stac to Loch an Athain. There are fine views of Clach Glas and Bla Bheinn from here.

Walk along the flat floor of Srath na Creitheach and continue along the east side of Loch na Creitheach. Part way along this loch a path slants off on the left to cross a small bealach to the east of An t-Sron. It eventually joins the track over Am Mam to the Broadford–Elgol road (see Route 5). However, the route to Camasunary stays beside the loch, and then continues south for just over a kilometre to reach the very welcome grassy haven by the beach.

144 Camasunary to Coruisk via the Bad Step Grade 1/2 **

The route from Camasunary around the coast to Coruisk is mainly a walk. It is only 4km in total distance, although it can seem longer when part of a bigger outing. The scrambling on the Bad Step is very short-lived, and not difficult if the correct line is taken.

Start

The shortest approach to Camasunary starts from near Kilmarie on the Broadford–Elgol road (Route 5), but see also Routes 4 and 143. The bothy on the west side of the bay is a popular overnight base. It has several rooms and a concrete floor.

The Route

From the bothy, go west a short distance to the bank of the Abhainn Camas Fhionnairigh. It is usually necessary to walk upstream for about 250 metres to find a suitable crossing place above the tidal limit. Then walk back along the west bank and continue round the coast to Rubha Ban. After a further kilometre, cut over a neck on the north side of a small knoll above Rubha Buidhe, and continue on a well-worn path below the west flank of Sgurr na Stri. Eventually the ground becomes more rocky approaching the Bad Step. A prominent islet can be seen a short distance out in Loch Scavaig at this point.

The best advice on the Bad Step is not to go too high. Follow a ledge to a slab which slopes down into the sea. Ascend a slanting crack, forming a natural gangway up the slab, until about halfway up. Then break left and soon reach a narrow shelf which leads horizontally left to much easier ground. Continue around the edge of Loch nan Leachd without further difficulty and pass through a low gap between large rock masses. Arrive suddenly at the mouth of Loch Coruisk. This is perhaps the most dramatic of the three approaches.

The routes originating on the Coruisk side of the main ridge are now described in a clockwise direction. The major subsidiary corries, which give access to bealachs on the main ridge, are also mentioned.

GARS-BHEINN *(895m)*

The most southerly peak on the main ridge can be attained in a number of ways from Coruisk. Fairly careful route-finding is needed to reach the south-east ridge via Coir' a' Chruidh. It is also possible to ascend Coire Beag and gain the north-west ridge by either one of two scree gullies. A third and more direct option is now described.

145 North-East Ridge Grade 1 *

The ridge is fairly straightforward apart from a steep section early on which is easily avoided on the right. A narrow shelf is used to outflank the fearsome summit headwall. The route was ascended by Sidney Williams and John Mackenzie in 1896.

Start

Go along the coast from the Coruisk Hut and cross the Mad Burn. Ascend the next grassy depression with a stream and eventually

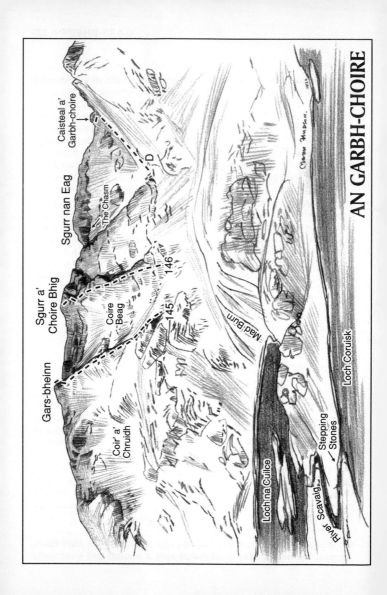

AN GARBH-CHOIRE

Caisteal a' Garbh-choire

Sgurr nan Eag

The Chasm

D

Sgurr a' Choire Bhig

146

Coire Beag

Gars-bheinn

145

Coir' a' Chruidh

Mad Burn

Clach Hudson

Loch Coruisk

Loch na Cuilce

Stepping Stones

River Scavaig

reach the broad and rather featureless lower level of An Garbh-choire. Head up to the left passing small outcrops and boulders of the distinctive peridotite rock which characterises this corrie.

The Route

Ascend a long stretch of hillside to a narrow nose forming the left-hand side of Coire Beag at the 600m level. This can be taken directly or outflanked more easily on the right. Continue up the fairly narrow crest to a level section. Ascend the much broader crest without difficulty for some distance. A small pinnacle, with a capping of luxurious moss on its summit, is passed easily to the right. Continue on broken basaltic rocks and scree.

At the very steep rocks below the summit, traverse right and descend ever so slightly. Look for a narrow shelf below a rock band on the right flank (see diagram on page 214). Follow this round to a gully with boulders leading left to a dip on the crest just west of the summit. Easy scrambling then leads to the top.

It is possible to descend by scree gullies back into Coire Beag from either of the two dips on the ridge a short distance west of the summit.

SGURR A' CHOIRE BHIG (875m)

The finest feature of this peak is its north-east ridge. It offers similar scrambling to the Dubh Slabs, but is much shorter. The peak has a cap of brittle basalt, but most of the northern side is excellent gabbro.

146 North-East Ridge Grade 3 **

This ridge provides a good alternative for those unsure about 'doing the Dubhs' (see the next route). It is slightly easier than the Dubh Slabs and does not involve an abseil. It was probably first ascended by Sidney Williams in 1896.

Start

Gain the lower level of An Garbh-choire as described for the previous route. Slant up slightly right towards the sweep of slabs forming the right-hand border of Coire Beag.

The Route

The superbly rough slabs give very enjoyable scrambling and can be ascended by any number of lines. There is a prominent curving overlap on the right-hand side of the crest at about half height.

Higher up, some stumpy pinnacles are taken on the right. Then a steep rock band, with an outward-dipping cone-sheet at its base, blocks the direct line up the ridge. Traverse a short distance to the right and ascend a short gully until it is possible to climb out on the left. Continue on more broken rocks to the shapely summit.

The quickest descent off the summit is via Coire Beag as described for the previous route. Another option is to scramble down into An Garbh-choire from the dip between Sgurr a' Choire Bhig and Sgurr nan Eag, staying left at first.

An Garbh-choire can be approached from halfway along the southern side of Loch Coruisk, as well as by the stream immediately south of the Mad Burn. The terrain in the upper part of An Garbh-choire is one of the most extraordinary in the Cuillin. The floor is covered with a jumble of giant peridotite boulders. Great care is needed when clambering over and between these very rough blocks. It would be easy to break a leg here. The normal route taken to Bealach a' Garbh-choire stays slightly closer to Sgurr Dubh Mor in the upper part of the corrie. See also Caisteal a' Garbh-choire (Page 203).

SGURR DUBH MOR (944m)

The mighty mountain of Sgurr Dubh Mor lies to the east of the main Cuillin ridge. It has a long summit ridge running east–west and an extensive north-north-east flank. The mountain is linked by a fine ridge to its small eastern top called Sgurr Dubh Beag (733m). A magnificent sweep of slabs falls from this summit to Loch Coruisk.

147 The Dubh Slabs and Sgurr Dubh Beag Moderate ***
The unique combination of easy climbing on immaculate slabs, a superb setting, a scary abseil and a Munro tick, makes this arguably the finest outing of its grade in the country. An ascent by two past presidents of the SMC inspired a much quoted piece of verse:

Said Maylard to Solly one day in Glen Brittle,
'All serious climbing, I vote, is a bore;
Just for once, I Dubh Beag you'll agree to do little,
And, as less we can't do, let's go straight to Dubh Mor.'

So now when they seek but a day's relaxation,
With no thought in the world but of viewing the views,
And regarding the mountains in mute adoration,
They call it not 'climbing', but 'doing the Dubhs'.

Those of more modest climbing ability may not find some parts of the outing quite as relaxing as this poem suggests. The abseil from the summit of Sgurr Dubh Beag is certainly far from straightforward, and the continuation onto Sgurr Dubh Mor also has its moments. This is not a good route to choose for a first abseil. Fortunately there is an alternative way which avoids the abseil, although it begins more than 100 metres lower down the route. This latter option was used until Douglas, Lamont and Rennie made the first direct descent by abseil from the summit in 1896.

Start

Follow a path on the south side of Loch Coruisk over ice-smoothed slabs and some boggier ground until directly below the slabs. An approach can also be made by descending An Garbh-choire, either from Bealach a' Garbh-choire or from the so-called coast path from Glen Brittle (Route 141). From the lower level of the corrie, descend a broad depression with a stream, on the south side of the slabs, to reach an area peppered by tiny lochans close to Loch Coruisk.

The Route

The slabs extend for well over one kilometre at an average angle of almost 30°, from just above the shore of Loch Coruisk to the summit of Sgurr Dubh Beag. The hardest unavoidable section is getting established on the main sweep of slabs at the bottom. Ascend a grassy gully immediately to the right of a toe of steep slabs, and emerge on a broad platform with good views down Loch Coruisk.

Turn right to face a wall of steeper rock, then move to the left-hand end of the ledge and follow widely spaced steps up leftwards from a leaning block. After some awkward moves trend slightly right and soon reach the crest of the ridge where the difficulties quickly ease.

A prominent rock band rises above a grassy terrace. Either move left and weave a way up steep rocks in a rather exposed position, or ascend slabs more easily at the right-hand end of the rock band. After this, the slabs can be climbed almost anywhere for some considerable distance. It is only rarely that hands are needed for lengthy sections. Occasional grassy depressions running across the crest give ample opportunities to take in the magnificent views. In one or two places slanting grassy gullies on the left flank offer escape routes into An Garbh-choire.

A stretch of excellent slabs higher up has a slanting grassy gully on its right-hand side. From the lush grassy depression above this, ascend slightly steeper slabs to the left of a more lichenous section. Then follow more broken rocks with boulders for some distance. A splendid crack up a short clean slab gives the last scrambling before the delightful summit of Sgurr Dubh Beag is reached.

Descend carefully for some 6m to a small ledge, and arrange an abseil off tapes round a slightly dubious block. A doubled 45m rope is required to reach the deck. The take-off is rather awkward and two sections are completely free. A short distance further down the ridge it is necessary to face in to descend a tricky rock step.

The option which avoids the abseil starts some 120 metres before the summit. It descends an easy gully on the left (south) for a short distance, and then picks a way easily round broken rocks to reach a broad ramp line. This leads up diagonally, parallel to the ridge. It comes out just by the final descent after the abseil off Sgurr Dubh Beag, at the dip on the ridge leading to Sgurr Dubh Mor. There is an escape route from the north side of this dip down Coir' a' Chaoruinn.

The ridge which continues onto Sgurr Dubh Mor is very different in character. A short distance along it there is another rather awkward descent. Interesting scrambling on the crest then alternates with easier ledges on the left. Higher up, a scar on the right side of the crest marks a recent rockfall.

Eventually the more intimidating rocks guarding the summit ridge are reached. The natural tendency is to follow sloping stony ledges up leftwards, taking higher options wherever possible. If this is done, it leads to an exposed move past a boulder perched on a slab. Immediately after this, there is an alcove with a very steep and tricky (Very Difficult) groove above it. The easiest way avoids this groove by ascending a much less obvious line starting from a muddy and gritty slope further right and slightly lower down (i.e. before the boulder). Step rightwards at first, then go up a short distance before cutting back left to reach a slabby rake slanting left. Emerge on the crest of the ridge at a slight dip not far from the steep eastern end. Clamber along the crest with steep drops to the left and a gentler slope to the right. Cut back left to descend a steep drop before reaching the final section of mossy rocks forming the summit.

Turn left at the western end and descend the south-west nose with care (Route 129). A recent rockfall has left a green scar. Weave a way down to a small dip before a pinnacle. It is possible to descend grassy rakes slanting down leftwards into An Garbh-choire from this first dip. Otherwise continue to the lowest point on the ridge. (Do not descend the gully on the left at this point. It is horribly loose.) Then scramble up the east ridge of Sgurr Dubh an Da Bheinn. To return to An Garbh-choire from here, descend the south ridge (Route 130).

COIREACHAN RUADHA
Sgurr Coir' an Lochain

Sgurr Alasdair

Sgurr Dubh Mor

Sgurr Dubh Beag

Loch Scavaig

Coir' a' Chaoruinn

Poiten Gully

147

150

147

148

147

148 North-North-East Flank Grade 3 *

The broad northern flank of Sgurr Dubh Mor forms the eastern border of Coir' an Lochain. It does not bear comparison with the previous route, but it does offer a fairly direct way to the summit from the upper end of Loch Coruisk.

Start

Follow the path along the south side of Loch Coruisk and slant left across the lower half of Coir' a' Chaoruinn, crossing streams as necessary. Head for a fairly obvious slanting grassy terrace which cuts across the shoulder of Sgurr Dubh Mor at about the 500m level. This is the approach route to Coir' an Lochain.

The Route

When in full view of the northern flank, set off up grass and slabby rocks to the main section of slabs. Ascend these without undue difficulty by any number of lines. A steeper nose high up gives the crux. Thereafter the angle soon eases and a broad slope can be ascended almost anywhere to reach the summit crest. Finish as for the previous route. It is possible to descend into Coir' an Lochain from the dip between Sgurr Dubh Mor and Sgurr Dubh an Da Bheinn. This is the way Sheriff Nicolson began his epic descent in 1874

SGURR THEARLAICH (978m)

The delightful lochan in Coir' an Lochain is rarely visited. Sgurr Thearlaich is the highest peak overlooking the corrie. Its north and south-east ridges have been mentioned previously (Routes 103 and 127). It would be very unusual to approach them from the Coruisk side. One way of avoiding the difficult traverse of this peak is to descend from Bealach Coir' an Lochain, skirt below the east face and scramble up the gully leading to Bealach Mhic Choinnich. A more interesting way of reaching this bealach is now described.

149 North-East Rib Grade 3 **

There is a prominent slabby rib on the left side of the gully leading to Bealach Mhic Choinnich. It was first ascended by Harold Raeburn and party in 1913.

Start

Follow the approach to the start of the previous route. Continue further right along the grassy terrace and follow the stream uphill to the lochan in Coir' an Lochain. Ascend the right-hand slope behind the lochan and so gain a dip on the south ridge of Sgurr Coir' an Lochain. Turn left and follow the broad crest easily, over a minor top (787m), to the foot of the rib.

The Route

Starting left of centre, steep scrambling leads onto the broad slabby rib. The rib can also be gained, less satisfactorily, from the gully on the right. The slabs give pleasant upper-grade scrambling by a variety of lines. They eventually peter out below the steeper rocks marking the start of the north ridge (see Route 103). Bealach Mhic Choinnich lies a short distance to the right.

SGURR COIR' AN LOCHAIN (729m)

There are several minor bumps on the low ridge forming the west side of Coir' an Lochain. At the northern end of this ridge there is a small gap and then a tiny top with steep rock on three sides. This top is thought to have been the last mountain summit to be conquered in the British Isles, when Collie, Howell, Mackenzie and Naismith first climbed its north face in 1896. They made a day of it by also climbing the Inaccessible Pinnacle and continuing along the ridge to Sgurr a' Mhadaidh, before descending by the Thuilm ridge.

150 South Ridge Difficult *

The grade only applies if the top itself is reached. The ridge is only a walk as far as the last top (759m) before the gap.

Start

Follow the same approach as for the previous route, but turn right on reaching the crest of the ridge behind the lochan.

The Route

The crest is followed without difficulty until the drop into the gap. Climb down carefully into the gap (712m), then scramble more easily onto the small summit – a superb viewpoint. Return the same way, or pick a way carefully down the gully on the east side of the gap.

SGURR MHIC CHOINNICH (948m)

There are two main ways of reaching the summit of Sgurr Mhic Choinnich from the Coruisk side. One option is to gain Bealach Mhic Choinnich, either by an obvious gully with some short Grade 2/3 rock steps, or by Route 149. Then follow King's Chimney (Route 102) or

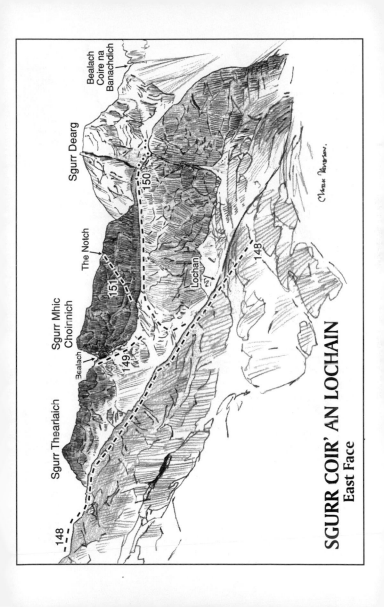

SGURR COIR' AN LOCHAIN
East Face

Bealach Coire na Banachdich

Sgurr Dearg

The Notch

Sgurr Mhic Choinnich

Sgurr Thearlaich

Bealach

Lochan

148

149

150

151

148

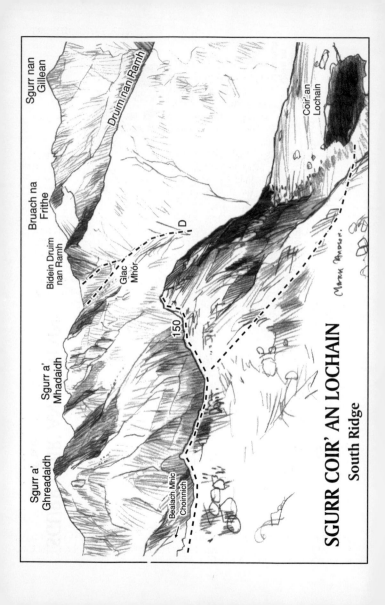

SGURR COIR' AN LOCHAIN
South Ridge

Hart's Ledge (Route 101) on the west face. The other main option is to gain the north ridge by the next route.

151 East Face Rake Grade 1/2 *

This is a surprisingly easy way onto the summit ridge of Sgurr Mhic Choinnich. It joins the north ridge at a prominent notch.

Start

Gain the south ridge of Sgurr Coir' an Lochain as for Route 149. Slant rightwards across a bouldery slope to the left-hand end of the east face of Sgurr Mhic Choinnich. Start below Forgotten Groove – a Very Difficult climb with a slabby face and a vertical right-hand wall.

The Route

A scree gully slants rightwards through small rock buttresses. The worst of the scree can be avoided by traversing right along a terrace for a short distance, and then ascending slabs trending slightly left. Follow an easy, rightward-slanting grass rake for some distance with only one slightly awkward rocky section.

Eventually a prominent pinnacle can be seen on the skyline with a scree gully to its left. Again the worst of the scree at the bottom can be avoided by traversing right a short distance. Scramble up the right-hand side of a rib, and then cut back left into the gully. Ascend scree and boulders to a notch on the north ridge (see Route 99).

SGURR NA BANACHDICH (965m)

The east face of Sgurr na Banachdich, which overlooks Coireachan Ruadha, is impressively steep. Unfortunately the rock here is generally not as good as elsewhere. However, the next two routes, especially if done in combination, give an enjoyable way up this face.

SRON BHUIDHE

The small top (878m) just north of Bealach Coire na Banachdich has a ridge, called Sron Bhuidhe, projecting into Coireachan Ruadha. This ridge is distinguished at half height by a buttress of peridotite – the most northerly outcrop of the band that crosses the Cuillin.

152 Peridotite Buttress Grade 3 **

The superb rock which characterises this route justifies making the rather lengthy approach. The scrambling is reminiscent of Honeycomb Arête on Rum.

SGURR A' GHREADAIDH South-East Ridge

Glac Mhòr

Coir' an Uaigneis

154

152

Peridotite Buttress

Terrace Gully

The Terrace

Sron Bhuidhe

154

Start
The best approach is from Glen Brittle via Bealach Coire na Banachdich (see Route 88). From the bealach, drop down steep scree into Coireachan Ruadha for 250m, and slant left by some massive boulders to reach a broad terrace at the 600m level.

The Route
A prominent orange/brown buttress is situated a short distance above the terrace. It has a V-shaped central face and a leftward-leaning slabby section to the left. The scramble ascends the central face.

Clamber over boulders to reach the central depression. Start quite close to a rightward-slanting groove. Scramble up fairly directly, but make some steep moves left early on to get past some small overlaps. Then take a direct line up the steep face using reassuringly deep slots for the hands and feet. The rock is superb and the situation is exhilarating. The buttress peters out all too soon

Continue up the ridge more easily until near the steep upper rocks. Then follow an obvious narrow ledge across the right flank to easier ground. It would be possible to scramble up from here to the dip between the 878m top and the south top of Sgurr na Banachdich (917m). However, the best option now is to traverse a long way right along a terrace to the start of the next route.

153 Midget Ridge Difficult *
This fine little ridge was first climbed by Patey and Brooker in 1953. They did three other routes hereabouts on the same day. There are occasional loose holds and the climb could do with more traffic.

Start
The ridge is best done after the previous route, but it can also be reached by dropping down from the dip on the ridge north of the 878m top. Traverse along the terrace to the foot of a rightward-leaning arête with a gully on its left-hand side.

The Route
Make some steep moves to get established on the front of the arête. Continue slightly more easily. A second pitch up the arête leads to a stance below an alcove. Bridge up carefully by suspect blocks and make some strenuous moves to exit from the alcove. Take a stance after half a rope length to avoid rope drag. Continue up a slightly broader section of ridge with some fine climbing. An easier arête then leads to the main ridge a few metres north of the south top.

A good continuation is to traverse Sgurr na Banachdich (Route 88).

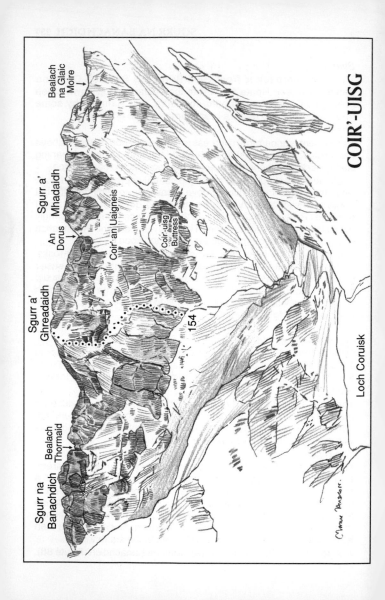

COIR'-UISG

Bealach na Glaic Moire

Sgurr a' Mhadaidh

An Dorus

Coir' an Uaigneis

Sgurr a' Ghreadaidh

Coir'-uisg Buttress

154

Bealach Thormaid

Sgurr na Banachdich

Loch Coruisk

SGURR A' GHREADAIDH (973m)

The south-east face of this mountain dominates the head of Coir'-uisg. One famous route up this face may appeal to climbers seeking a full day's mountaineering in secluded surroundings.

154 South-East Ridge Very Difficult **

This is reputed to be the longest rock climb in the country, although in fact it is a somewhat disjointed outing. The lower third gives good climbing on ice-smoothed slabs, whilst the middle section is just a walk. The upper section is more nerve-racking. It weaves an intricate line up a narrow ridge on some rather suspect rock. The route was pioneered by Collie and Howell in 1896.

Start

It is a long way to the start of this route. Perhaps the quickest approach is to cross Bealach na Glaic Moire from upper Glen Brittle. Another option is to use Bealach Coire na Banachdich from lower Glen Brittle. One attraction of an approach by Loch Coruisk is that a quick return can be made to Coir'-uisg from Bealach Thormaid.

The climb starts at a height of about 400m, where a stream from a prominent gully meets two other tiny streams in a slabby depression. A short distance up the slope to the left there is a recess with a rowan tree. When this part of the face is viewed from Loch Coruisk, the prominent gully is seen to curve rightwards higher up and join with another gully to form an inverted U.

The Route

The lower part of the route is open to variation. The original start ascended rocks to the left of the prominent gully, but a more direct alternative start is now described. Climb a pitch up a slabby rib immediately to the right of the main gully. Continue on slightly easier rock, then cross a cleft with water in it and belay below steeper rocks.

The next pitch gives the crux. Traverse right and then back left across a wall. Follow slanting slabby rocks with scant protection for some distance to a stance with a poor belay. Step right and follow a slanting groove. Then break right and soon reach easier ground. Slant diagonally right across slabs and continue to a ledge with an overlap above. Traverse right over blocks and continue up a groove on the left side of a gully. Break left onto superb slabs and follow these, eventually passing to the left of a big boulder, and so reach easy ground. Walk a long way leftwards and pass to the left of the lowest rocks forming the bottom of the south-east ridge.

From the south side of the ridge – with good views of the extensive terrace further left – cut back right very slightly to gain the crest. Follow the crest then continue by climbing a series of short walls linked by leftward-slanting cone-sheets. Great care is needed with the rock at times, and the easiest way is not always obvious. Eventually make a slightly longer traverse left, and ascend a recess directly to reach somewhat easier ground. Continue up the crest for some distance on more mossy rock and join the main ridge a short distance before the south top (see Route 81).

BIDEIN DRUIM NAN RAMH *(869m)*

Druim nan Ramh is the longest side ridge projecting from the main Cuillin chain. It originates from the complex triple peaks of Bidein Druim nan Ramh, and overlooks the north-east side of Loch Coruisk.

155 Druim nan Ramh Grade 1 or 3 **

This 5km long ridge is the easiest continuous stretch of ridge in the Cuillin. It is mainly a walk, apart from short problems near the start and finish. It offers superb views of the whole Cuillin range.

Start

Go around the eastern end of Loch Coruisk and cross the Allt a' Choire Riabhaich. Head up the hillside to the start of the ridge.

The Route

Either scramble directly up a steep nose at the base of the ridge (Grade 3) or ascend an easy gully on the right flank. Then walk up onto the crest, and continue without any difficulty for some distance. The ridge broadens out as the high point of 500m is reached at one third distance. There are a number of tiny lochans scattered about the summit plateau, and fine views in all directions. The ridge gently undulates then narrows as it drops to a low point of 450m.

The final third of the ridge rises more steeply, and a deep cleft gives the main unavoidable difficulties of the day. Scramble down 8m into the gap on rather crumbly rock, and slant out the other side along a ledge. Then skirt below the Druim Pinnacle on its left flank.

The Central Peak of Bidein Druim nan Ramh lies straight ahead. This can be ascended by a Grade 3 scramble (Route 65). Otherwise follow ledges leading left to the gully below the West Peak and slant out left up slabs. Drop down the main ridge to Bealach na Glaic Moire. Slant down easy scree and then descend by a stream to Coir'-uisg.

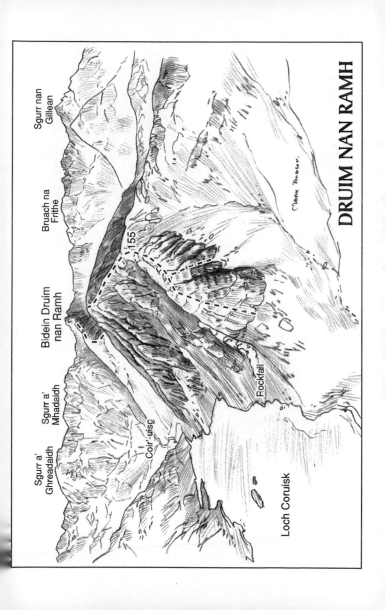

DRUIM NAN RAMH

Sgurr nan Gillean

Bruach na Frithe

155

Bidein Druim nan Ramh

Sgurr a' Mhadaidh

Sgurr a' Ghreadaidh

Coir'-uisg

Rockfall

Loch Coruisk

BIDEIN DRUIM NAN RAMH

South-West Flank

West Peak

Central Peak

Druim Pinnacle

cleft

155

MALCOLM MADDEN.

SGURR NA STRI (494m)

This lowly but rugged peak is well seen from Elgol. It has twin tops of similar height, separated by a long trench-like depression. The western top offers breathtaking views of Loch Coruisk.

156 North Ridge 12km (from Sligachan) *

The most straightforward way of ascending this peak is to divert from Druim Hain *en route* from Sligachan to Coruisk.

Start

When approaching from Sligachan (Route 142), follow the path which carries straight on from the crest of Druim Hain. If starting from Loch Coruisk, follow the path from the stepping stones towards Druim Hain and cut back along a broad ramp on the north-west flank.

The Route

Traverse across the west flank of Sgurr Hain and gain the crest of the north ridge a short distance after a minor rounded summit. Some paths trending round to the right just lead to viewing points for Loch Coruisk. Instead, hold the highest ground and eventually reach the fine western top. Fragments of a crashed jet aircraft can be found hereabouts. It is worth visiting the eastern top, which lies 100 metres away on the other side of the trench-like depression. The easiest descent is to return the same way. See the next route for a description of a descent route to Camasunary.

157 South-South-East Buttress Grade 2/3 **

There is a prominent gully on the southern flank of the peak, which is a continuation of the depression that splits the summit. This route ascends the buttress on the right-hand side of the gully. It gives a very fine scramble on excellent rock, and is open to much variation.

Start

The easiest way to identify the buttress is from the coast path between Camasunary and Coruisk (Route 144) just north-west of Rubha Ban, where a stream from the gully reaches the coast. The route starts at a height of 150m by a prominent slab, which rises from a broad, grassy saddle (GR 504 186) just west of a lochan.

Previous Page : MacLeod's Maidens, Idrigill Point, Duirinish

Opposite : Sron Vourlinn and Fingal's Pinnacles, Trotternish

The Route

Ascend the delightful slab, moving right to a crack high up. Then continue more easily for some distance to the start of the buttress proper. Scramble up slabs to the right of a grassy groove and gain a ledge. Follow steps up a steep rock rib on the left side of a recess.

Ascend a broad leftward-trending dyke as far as a cone-sheet, then follow very pleasant slabs on the right for some distance. Move back left into the dyke for a short stretch, then scramble up slabs of very rough rock to a recess with big boulders. Follow the slabby crest trending left. Step up from a boulder on the right and make some interesting moves left to ascend the left-hand end of an overhanging wall. From a platform of stripy rock, go to the left-hand end of the wall, then slant right up a broken ramp.

Trend left up slabby rocks to reach a steeper section of buttress, which provides the crux. Starting on the left-hand side, make an awkward move up, then step delicately left onto a slab. Move slightly left again and break up through to easier ground. Slant back right to stay on the crest. Ascend sound rocks two metres right of a small overhang. From a terrace, some more fun can be had by finding a way up a small headwall via a recess. Then traverse four metres right along a cone-sheet and ascend some tricky slabs on the right side of a left-slanting gully. Either step out left from the top of an alcove, or ascend the rib on the left more easily. Climb to the top of a flake/block and pull onto a wall. Step left, move up, then back right before continuing straight up to another terrace. Follow easier rocks and a broad, undulating ridge to the eastern summit, from where there are excellent views of Bla Bheinn and Camasunary.

Slant left to find a way down into the central depression and soon gain the western top. After enjoying the wonderful views, it is possible to descend to Loch Coruisk by slanting off left from the north ridge in the vicinity of Captain Maryon's Monument. Descend a grassy depression with a stream to join the path from Druim Hain.

To descend to Camasunary, enter the depression between the summits and follow the gully in a southerly direction until it steepens and becomes choked with large boulders. (The gully marks the line of a light-coloured vein rather than the more usual dolerite dyke.) Then exit the gully on the left-hand side and cross over the crest of the buttress – previously ascended – by a terrace. Descend a slanting grassy rake fairly steeply down the south-eastern flank of the hill. Eventually head east over less steep grassy ground to where the Abhainn Camas Fhionnairigh can be forded.

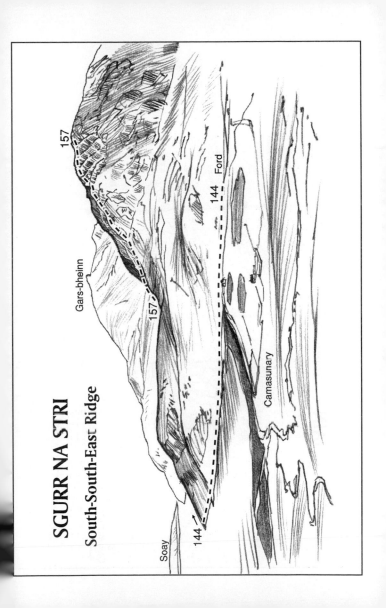

SGURR NA STRI
South-South-East Ridge

Soay

144

Gars-bheinn

157

157

144

Ford

Camasunary

SGURR HAIN   South-East Ridge

158

158

159

Loch na Crèitheach

An-t-Sròn

Sgurr nan Gillean

Marsco

To Camasunary

SGURR HAIN (420m)

The summit of this rocky hill is often bypassed to the west. However, it is well worth diverting from the path over Druim Hain to pay it a visit. The extraordinary panoramic view from the summit includes the whole Cuillin range as well as Bla Bheinn and Marsco. The next two routes offer interesting approaches from the Camasunary side.

158 South-East Ridge Grade 1 *
For those based at Camasunary this makes an excellent little outing. The scrambling does not amount to much, but the views from the summit ridge are exceptional.

Start

Follow the east bank of the Abhainn Camas Fhionnairigh upstream. Pass some pleasant slabs in the stream bed, and eventually cross a fork of the stream by some stepping stones. Follow the left-hand fork for a short distance, then cross that as well by stepping stones. Go past an impressive crag with two buttresses, and continue beyond its more slabby right-hand wing.

The Route

Slant rightwards up a grassy ramp, staying to the left of a broad slabby nose. Move left to join a grassy ramp slanting left below a rock band. Make a very long rising traverse left along the ramp. Eventually ascend a short rib to reach the crest of the ridge above the main right-hand buttress. This point can also be reached more steeply from the corrie to the west.

Turn right and ascend the crest on delightful slabby rocks. There are some very minor rock bands but the main interest is the ever-improving view. The first top has a tiny lochan just below it, but the highest point lies 250 metres away across a slight dip. The views from the main summit are stupendous. A straightforward descent by the north ridge leads to the path over Druim Hain (Route 142). By traversing back across the west flank of Sgurr Hain it is possible to cross the ridge and descend a nameless corrie to the starting point.

159 South-East Slabs Moderate *
The slabby right-hand wing of the crag mentioned in the previous route offers a rather tricky direct start. The climbing involves some quite intricate route-finding above half height, where the exposure also becomes more noticeable.

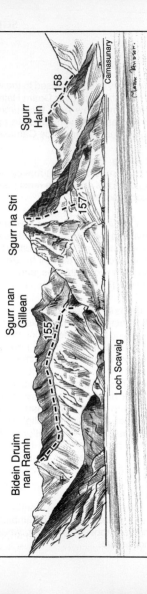

THE CUILLIN FROM ELGOL

Bidein Druim nan Ramh

Sgurr nan Gillean

Sgurr na Stri

Sgurr Hain

155

157

158

Loch Scavaig

Camasunary

The Main Ridge Traverse

The traverse of the Cuillin main ridge is undoubtedly the finest outing of its type in the British Isles. No other ridge is as narrow, as rocky and of such sustained difficulty. To complete the full traverse demands a high level of physical fitness, agility and mountaineering skill, as well as good fortune with the weather. An ability to scramble comfortably in exposed situations is essential. The direct route along the crest involves climbing of Very Difficult standard, and even taking all the easier options will still involve making some moves graded Difficult. The sustained level of difficulty can take its toll mentally as well as physically in the later stages of the outing.

The ridge is usually done from south to north, but a good case can be made for doing it in the opposite direction. Both of these options involve problems with transport at the finish. It is slightly easier to complete the circuit on foot by starting from a base at Coruisk. Bivvying out on the ridge is a wonderful experience in settled weather, but this does mean carrying extra gear.

May and June are generally the best months for the ridge weather-wise, although this is far from being true every year. In warm weather dehydration can also become quite a problem. Two litres of water is a popular amount to carry, but this may not be enough in heatwave conditions.

Fuller details of the individual sections of the ridge can be found earlier in this guide, but a brief summary is also now given of the main difficulties encountered when making a south to north traverse. The normal approach from Glen Brittle follows the first part of the coast route to Coruisk, and then ascends the bing-like south-eastern flank of Gars-bheinn. This start is an early test of character.

Gars-bheinn to Sgurr nan Eag – mainly pleasant ridge walking with only short sections of Grade 1 scrambling.

Sgurr nan Eag to Bealach a' Garbh-choire – Grade 2 scrambling if the crest is followed, otherwise mainly rough walking and easy scrambling on the Coir' a' Ghrunnda side.

Caisteal a' Garbh-choire – this fine rock bastion is easily bypassed on its eastern side. Purists will need to be competent climbers to ascend the south ridge and descend by the north-east end (Difficult).

Sgurr Dubh an Da Bheinn from Caisteal a' Garbh-choire – a pleasant Grade 2 scramble. Not exposed, but on very rough rock.

Sgurr Dubh an Da Bheinn to Sgurr Dubh Mor (and return) – this is becoming an obligatory detour. Be prepared for up to Grade 3 scrambling on the steep south-western nose of Sgurr Dubh Mor.

Sgurr Dubh an Da Bheinn to Sgurr Alasdair – although Sgurr Alasdair is not on the main ridge, it is rarely missed out, since it is the highest peak on the island. The easiest option skirts below the south-west face of Sgurr Thearlaich and ascends the south-west ridge of Sgurr Alasdair by a Grade 3 chimney. The classic option is to abseil into the Thearlaich–Dubh gap and climb out by one of the hardest pitches on the ridge (Very Difficult). Then scramble up Sgurr Alasdair from the top of the Great Stone Shoot.

Sgurr Thearlaich – not a peak to be underestimated. The upper section of the south ridge, starting from the saddle at the top of the Great Stone Shoot, is a Grade 3 scramble, and the two main ways of descending to Bealach Mhic Choinnich at the end of the north ridge are at least Moderate. The slabs on the Coruisk side are very exposed, but involve perhaps the least troublesome route-finding.

Sgurr Mhic Choinnich from Bealach Mhic Choinnich – either follow Hart's Ledge across the Coire Lagan face at easy Grade 2 and backtrack along the north ridge to the summit, or part way along Hart's Ledge scramble up to a higher ledge and climb the spectacular King's Chimney (Difficult) more directly to the summit.

Sgurr Mhic Choinnich to An Stac – the descent of the north ridge of Sgurr Mhic Choinnich is an enjoyable Grade 2 scramble. The best continuation is to take the direct route up the east ridge of An Stac (upper Grade 3), but an easier slabby ramp can be followed around the base of the south face at Grade 1/2.

The Inaccessible Pinnacle – can easily be avoided on the left, but this is not a very satisfying option, unless there are long queues. The east ridge is surely the most sensational, but also one of the easiest, of Moderate rock climbs. Not to be missed. Most climbers will then abseil down the shorter, but more difficult, western end.

Profile along the Southern Cuillin

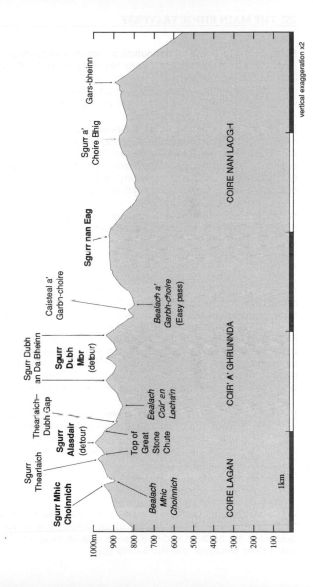

Sgurr Mhic Choinnich

Sgurr Thearlaich

Sgurr Alasdair (detour)

Thear'aich–Dubh Gap

Sgurr Dubh an Da Bheinn

Sgurr Dubh Mor (detour)

Caisteal a' Garbh-choire

Sgurr nan Eag

Sgurr a' Choire Bhig

Gars-bheinn

Bealach Mhic Choinnich

Top of Great Stone Chute

Eealach Coir' an Lochain

Bealach a' Garbh-choire (Easy pass)

COIRE LAGAN

COIR' A' GHRUNNDA

COIRE NAN LAOGH

1000m
900
800
700
600
500
400
300
200
100

1km

vertical exaggeration x2

Sgurr Dearg to Sgurr na Banachdich – an easy descent on scree from the summit of Sgurr Dearg leads to Bealach Coire na Banachdich – an important crossing point over the main ridge to Coruisk. The south ridge of Sgurr na Banachdich gives a superb Grade 2 scramble over two tops before the major summit is reached.

Sgurr na Banachdich to Sgurr a' Ghreadaidh – this is one of the most committing sections of the ridge. Scramble down loose ground to Bealach Thormaid, and continue over Sgurr Thormaid. Three teeth are normally bypassed on the west side. Then follow the south ridge of Sgurr a' Ghreadaidh with increasing interest. An absorbing section of Grade 3 scrambling links the south top and the main summit.

Sgurr a' Ghreadaidh to An Dorus – rather easier scrambling leads down from the main summit of Sgurr a' Ghreadaidh past the Wart to an easy gap called Eag Dubh. A little further down the ridge, a short but tricky Grade 2 scramble leads into the gap of An Dorus, from where an escape can be made into Coire a' Ghreadaidh.

From An Dorus over the four tops of Sgurr a' Mhadaidh – another committing and difficult section, best done in this direction. The ridge takes a sharp turn to the east shortly after the main summit of Sgurr a' Mhadaidh. The third top can be climbed direct, but the usual route finds a way up further right. The crux on this section is the direct ascent of the second top by a short, steep nose (Difficult). After crossing a narrow gap, the traverse of the first (and final!) top proves more straightforward. Bealach na Glaic Moire is a broad, easy pass between Glen Brittle and Coruisk. It is the lowest point on the ridge.

Bidein Druim nan Ramh – this complex peak has three tops. The Western top is not a problem, but the traverse of the Central top calls for considerable expertise in route-finding and down climbing. The crux is the descent into the gap before the North top, which is at least Difficult if done without resort to an abseil. The traverse of the North top proves relatively straightforward and finishes at Bealach Harta – a fairly easy, but rarely used pass over the main ridge.

An Caisteal – the narrow ridge leading to this summit is famous for its three gaps, the last of which can be crossed by a bold leap. The descent at the northern end of the peak is quite tricky and finishes with a steep Moderate wall into a deep gap.

Profile along the Central Cuillin

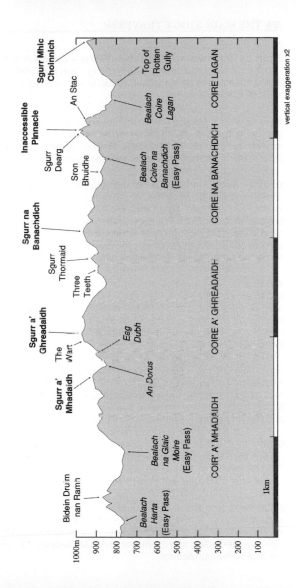

Bidein Druim nan Ramh

Bealach Harta (Easy Pass)

Sgurr a' Mhadaidh

An Dorus

Bealach na Glaic Moire (Easy Pass)

COIR' A' MHADAIDH

Sgurr a' Ghreadaidh

The Wart

Eag Dubh

COIRE A' GHREADAIDH

Three Teeth

Sgurr Thormaid

Sgurr na Banachdich

COIRE NA BANACHDICH

Sron Bhuidhe

Sgurr Dearg

Bealach Coire na Banachdich (Easy Pass)

Inaccessible Pinnacle

An Stac

Bealach Coire Lagan

COIRE LAGAN

Sgurr Mhic Choinnich

Top of Rotten Gully

1000m
900
800
700
600
500
400
300
200
100

1km

vertical exaggeration x2

Sgurr na Bhairnich and Bruach na Frithe – the technical difficulties relent for the next kilometre, and nothing more than pleasant Grade 2 scrambling need be encountered as far as the small peak of Sgurr a' Fionn Choire.

Sgurr a' Fionn Choire – although it can be bypassed easily on the north side, this fine peak is well worth traversing. The west ridge has an awkward step on it (Grade 2/3). An easy scramble down the north flank leads to Bealach nan Lice – another easy pass over the ridge.

Bhasteir Tooth – the ascent of this peak is for climbers only. Many a tired climber is fazed by the sensational face climbing on Naismith's Route (Very Difficult). Lota Corrie Route (Moderate) is a much longer but easier alternative. The continuation onto Am Basteir also has a sting in the tail in the form of an undercut chimney (Very Difficult). The masses will prefer to avoid this top by following a path in the scree below the north face of Am Basteir to Bealach a' Bhasteir.

Am Basteir – the simplest way up to this summit is by the east ridge from Bealach a' Bhasteir, but a recent rockfall has turned a fairly easy step down on the crest into a formidable Bad Step. This is now tackled by climbing down a Difficult wall on the Lota Corrie side. However, with careful route-finding it can be avoided altogether at a lower level (Grade 2).

Sgurr nan Gillean – there are a number of options at the start of the west ridge. The most popular is to climb Tooth Groove followed by an exposed and rather tricky Moderate arête past the stump of the former tooth. The remainder of the ridge is little more than Grade 2, and the very shapely summit makes a superb finale.

The first part of the descent by the south-east ridge is exposed Grade 3 scrambling, but it eases fairly quickly lower down. Most parties then descend northwards and pick up a path back across Coire Riabhach to Sligachan. The chance of a drink before closing time is an added spur, but purists will visit two extra peaks first.

Sgurr Beag and Sgurr na h-Uamha – a narrow but straightforward ridge is followed to the first top, from where an easy descent leads to Bealach a' Ghlas-choire. After crossing a small northern top, some careful route-finding and a move or two of Moderate grade soon bring the final summit underfoot.

Profile along the Northern Cuillin

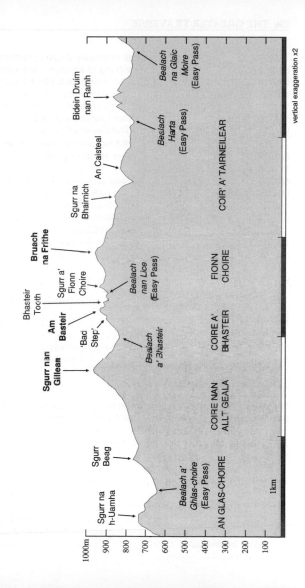

vertical exaggeration x2

The time taken for the traverse will obviously depend, among other things, on exactly which tops are visited and which route is taken. The time of 12 hours 18 minutes from first peak to last taken by Shadbolt and McLaren on the first complete traverse of the ridge in 1911 is still a good time to aim for. There have been some remarkable times achieved by subsequent parties. Ben Humble summarised some of these up to 1951 in his fine book, *The Cuillin of Skye*.

Eric Beard set an amazing time of 4 hours 9 minutes in 1967. When Andy Hyslop bettered this time by five minutes in 1984 he took pains to specify his route in some detail. Del Davies and Paul Stott smashed the four hour barrier by some ten minutes just two years later, and finished their traverse by descending Pinnacle Ridge. Martin Moran and Andy Hyslop have both since lowered the record even further to just over 3 hours 32 minutes.

These astonishing times were achieved by soloing all the climbing sections and running wherever possible. A more leisurely pace will suit most people.

THE GREATER TRAVERSE

Those looking for a more extended challenge can go on to complete a traverse of the Cuillin Outliers. This was first done by Charleson and Forde in 1939, when they added Clach Glas and Bla Bheinn in a total ridge time of 20 hours. It is more usual nowadays to include Garbh-bheinn as well. A fair amount of willpower is needed to set off again from the floor of Glen Sligachan to tackle the eastern peaks.

THE CUILLIN ROUND

The ultimate Cuillin circuit, which combines a traverse of the Red Hills overlooking Glen Sligachan with the Cuillin Outliers and all the Cuillin main ridge, was first done by Rob Woodall in June 1999. He took 23½ hours to complete the round, which started and finished in Glen Sligachan.

A remark made by Colin Kirkus to Alf Bridge on the summit of Sgurr Alasdair puts the case for a more relaxed approach to enjoying the mountains:

> *"You know, Alf, going to the right place, at the right time, with the right people is all that really matters. What one does is purely incidental."*

Minginish

There are other attractions in Minginish beyond the Cuillin – notably in the more desolate northern part of the region where there are some spectacular sea cliffs. About 7km west of Carbost lies beautiful Talisker Bay and its two sea stacks. This is an idyllic place to visit on a fine summer's evening. Access is through the grounds of Talisker House. It is 1½km from the parking place to the sandy beach.

Boswell and Johnson were guests at Talisker during their tour of the Hebrides in 1773. Boswell noted that *"Talisker is a better place than one commonly finds in Sky[e]."* Towering above Talisker House is the steep western end of a basaltic hill called Preshal More (317m).

160 Preshal More – Boswell's Buttress Grade 2 **

Boswell ascended Preshal More with Donald Maclean, the young Laird of Coll. He remarked on the fine views from the summit.

Start

Leave the road in Gleann Oraid just where it starts to drop down more steeply to Talisker. Slant right and traverse around the western end of the hill. Start just to the left of the lowest rocks, near the bottom end of a prominent leftward-slanting earthy ramp.

The Route

Scramble up a small buttress with leftward-leaning columnar rocks. Move left slightly and ascend steps of brown, lichenous rock. Stay below a small overhang and slant right to gain a sloping ledge with junipers. Then move up diagonally leftwards, passing just to the right of a detached 2m high pillar. Care is needed with the rock for 4m. The going gradually eases above. Follow a long, leftward-slanting slope on broken rock, scree and heather to reach a heathery shoulder.

Head up the superb rock directly above. Start by trending right slightly and then back left. Instead of slanting easily left higher up, a more interesting option is to make a delicate traverse diagonally rightwards on excellent rock. Then trend back left slightly. Numerous lines are possible as the angle gradually eases.

Reach a large heathery ledge with views of the big craggy face further right. Higher up, break through a small crag by a V-groove and continue easily to the summit from where there are superb views.

Head east from the summit and descend a broad grassy gully on the north side or, better, descend a gully southwards and cross Sleadale to ascend Preshal Beg (Grade 1) and visit a ruined broch.

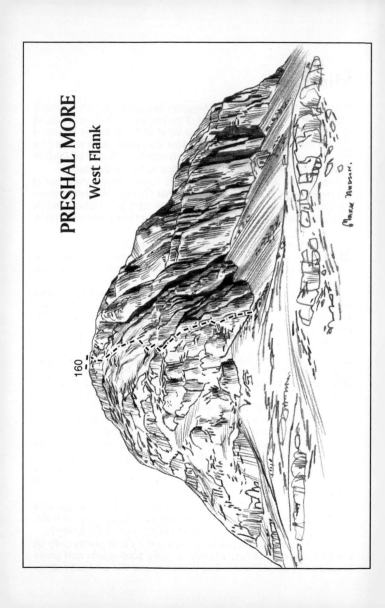

PRESHAL MORE
West Flank

160

Duirinish

The most westerly peninsula of the island, known as Duirinish, is accessed by a single-track road just south of Dunvegan. It is built of flat-lying basalt lavas. These have been eroded to produce two very distinctive flat-topped hills, Healabhal Mhor and Healabhal Bheag – better known as MacLeod's Tables. The area is also renowned for its spectacular coastal scenery.

161 MacLeod's Tables – the round of Glen Osdale 11km **
An ascent of either Healabhal Mhor or Healabhal Bheag alone is an enjoyable outing, but the anti-clockwise circuit which includes them both is particularly rewarding.

Start
Park near a small bridge over the Osdale River (GR 248 459).

The Route
Follow a fence on the west bank of the river at first, then cross heather moorland, which is boggy in places. Ascend gently rising ground on the north side of Glen Osdale for some distance. Follow sheep tracks which zigzag up the first section of steeper slope. Continue up a series of long, gentle stretches succeeded by short steeper slopes. Go to the left of a rock band with a rockfall at its left-hand end. Eventually ascend steepish grass to gain the summit plateau of Healabhal Mhor. It is a further 300 metres up a very gentle slope to the pile of rocks marking the summit (469m). The ground is slightly boggy in places and the views are rather disappointing, although Waterstein Head stands out to the north-west.

Leave the summit plateau and descend the grassy south-western flank to An Sgurran. Small rock bands are easily dealt with on the way. Negotiate a route through some peat hags, then either ascend a small rounded top or contour across its eastern face to reach the bealach below the steep north-west flank of Healabhal Bheag.

Ascend the long grassy slope to reach the summit plateau. There is a trig point inside a stone wall in the centre of the plateau, but the highest point (489m) lies at the southern end. It is marked by a cairn, which is almost completely overgrown by grass. There are excellent views of the glen below and all the islands in Loch Bracadale.

Return to the trig point and head north-east to leave the summit. The ridge gradually pinches down. Continuing over a slight rise leads to a fearsome drop, so backtrack slightly and drop down steep broken

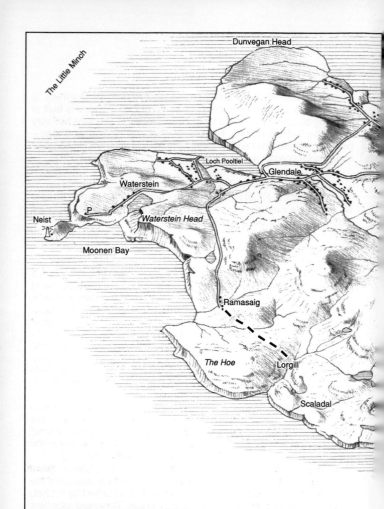

LOOKING NORTH OVER DUIRINISH

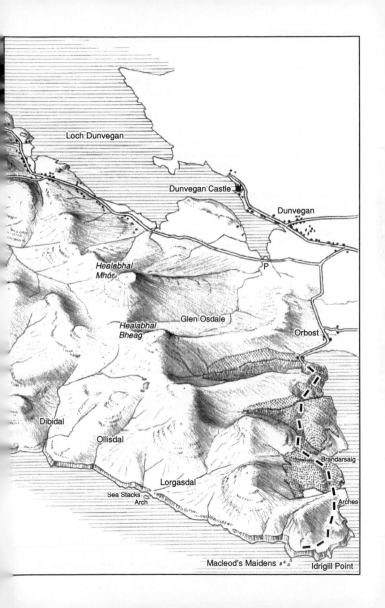

ground on the north-west flank. Zigzag down, then curve round to the right and gain easier grassy ground. A long descent over the moor, on the east side of a large stream, eventually leads back to the start.

———

There is some delightful walking around the coast of Duirinish. Two locations which offer short but very spectacular outings are Neist Point and Waterstein Head on the most westerly tip of the island. However, the most outstanding walk in the area follows the coast around the southern half of the peninsula.

162 Duirinish coast walk – Orbost to Ramasaig 21km ***
This very long cliff-top walk is quite a serious undertaking. The distance from the finish back to the start by road is 20km, so transport has to be well organised. It is worth the effort, however, for this walk follows one of the most dramatic sections of coastline in the country.
Start
Turn off the main road at Heribost and drive through Roag. It is best to get dropped off at Orbost House because parking space is limited.
The Route
Walk along a rough track to some buildings by Loch Bharcasaig. Continue into the forest and, when the track peters out after a kilometre or so, follow a faint path through younger plantations. Pass over a small col and take the uphill side of a deer fence for a short distance. Descend slightly to cross Brandarsaig Burn near some crofting ruins, and continue for a further kilometre to the ruins of the larger community of Idrigill. It is worth diverting from here to see the natural arches and sea caves directly below, although good views are also obtained when looking back on the rise to Ard Beag.

Some will be content to return to Orbost after viewing the three sea stacks known as MacLeod's Maidens to the west of Idrigill Point. The continuation to the north-west takes on a different character. The ground underfoot is generally firm and grassy, but the route lies close to the edge of high sea cliffs, and there are only occasional sheep tracks to show the way. Numerous short diversions have to be made inland to cross streams and rivers flowing from the various dals.

A fine arch and several sea stacks can be seen where the Lorgasdal River plunges over the cliffs in a spectacular waterfall. The Ollisdal bothy makes a welcome stopping place. The last difficulty is crossing the ravine of the Scaladal Burn. Then crest a rise before dropping down to Lorgill Bay. Pass the ruins of the cleared community of Lorgill and pick up a track for the last 3km to Ramasaig.

Trotternish

The great northern finger of Skye has the longest continuous ridge on the island – the Trotternish Ridge. It forms the crest of a 30km long, east-facing escarpment, on the east flank of which are numerous massive landslides – the largest in Britain. The landslipped masses have been eroded to form some extraordinary scenery.

Trotternish lies to the north of Portree – the principal town on the island. A short distance further south, and just outwith Trotternish proper, there is a hill which offers a delightful excursion.

163 Ben Tianavaig 7km **
The ascent of this modest hill is surprisingly enjoyable. There is easy walking on the firm, grassy ground which forms the crest, and there are fine views of Raasay, Portree and The Storr.
Start
A few kilometres south of Portree, take a minor road leading to the Braes. Turn off to Camastianavaig and park by Tianavaig Bay.
The Route
Walk round the north side of the bay near the high-tide mark and ascend the steepish slope using sheep tracks where possible. Cross more heathery ground and eventually reach the closely-cropped grassy ground leading up the crest of the south ridge. Look for signs of a path joining the crest from the eastern flank – this marks the return route. Continue up the delightful crest to the summit (413m).

Descend northwards from the trig point and, at a height of about 350m, cut down to the right to reach an eastern shoulder. Head back southwards through landslipped terrain and make for a finger-like pinnacle. Continue south and eventually descend fairly steeply in a south-easterly direction. Look for a faint path which contours the slope and eventually regains the crest of the ridge used in ascent. Retrace your steps back to the starting point.

***

The traverse of the whole Trotternish Ridge is a major undertaking, perhaps best done north to south. The section south of the Uig to Staffin road is quite committing. The going is generally quite pleasant underfoot, so, despite being more than twice the length of the Cuillin main ridge, the Trotternish Ridge can be completed in a similar time. It can be done in lightweight style as an extended hill run, or at a more leisurely pace by backpacking along it over two days.

The next three outings are much less demanding in comparison. They wander among some of the gigantic landslides on the eastern flank of the Trotternish Ridge.

164 Old Man of Storr and The Storr 7km ***

A visit to the Old Man of Storr is one of the most popular walks on Skye. The amazing terrain in the vicinity of this giant obelisk is fascinating to explore. In good weather it is well worth extending the outing to ascend The Storr (719m), the highest summit in Trotternish.

Start

The walk starts 10km north of Portree. There are two main approach routes. Perhaps the best combination is to start at GR 511 532 and ascend open ground on the north side of a large conifer plantation, leaving the well-constructed path through the forest for the descent.

The Route

Follow the slightly boggy path directly up the hillside. Once above the forest join the other approach route and continue up steeper ground. It is tempting to head straight for the base of the 50m high pinnacle referred to as the Old Man, but it is perhaps best to first trend up leftwards to visit an area known as 'The Sanctuary'. This gives excellent views of the Old Man and the other pinnacles.

Raeburn and Russell ascended *"a small pinnacle near the Old Man"* in 1898, but it wasn't until 1955 that the Old Man itself was first climbed by Don Whillans. It is still very rarely ascended, because of the difficulty of the climbing and the appalling nature of the rock.

Follow a track on the uphill side of the Old Man beneath towering cliffs of basalt. A little further north is another distinctive pinnacle with window-like holes in it known as 'The Cathedral'. To ascend The Storr, continue northwards beyond the Cathedral until the cliffs diminish in size and there are views of Loch Scamadal below. Turn back left and ascend the upper scoop of Coire Scamadal near the rim overlooking the Storr cliffs. Skirt round the tops of gullies, and trend right near the top to find a way up to the summit.

After enjoying the remarkable views of the whole Trotternish ridge from the summit, the simplest option is to return the same way. Another option is to make a detour to the north for almost 2km to view the amazing boulder-field below Carn Liath. (This is the debris from an unusually large rock avalanche.) Yet another option is to descend the steep south-western flank of The Storr to Bealach Beag. Drop down from the escarpment by the left bank of a stream. Slant across the hillside and descend to the road by the edge of the forest.

165 Quiraing 7km ***

This section of the Trotternish escarpment lies just north of the road between Staffin and Uig. It harbours some of the most remarkable scenic features on the island, and more than justifies making the long journey north.

Start

The most popular approach starts from a sharp bend near the high point on the Staffin–Uig road, but a more pleasant approach starts lower down the road from a tiny parking space (GR 444 682).

The Route

Head in a north-westerly direction below the increasingly impressive cliffs. The first sizeable knoll on the right is called Cnoc a' Mheirlich, *hill of the robber*. Eventually slant up to join the higher path that contours across the steep slope. The next large mass on the right-hand side of the path is called 'The Prison'. It is worth ascending this impressive hillock to get good views of the way up to the Quiraing proper. An ascent of the highest tower involves a tricky scramble.

A tall, slender pinnacle in the cliffs high above, called 'The Needle', points the way into the hidden sanctuary of the Quiraing (*pillared enclosure*). Ascend the steep slope directly below the Needle and then pass around it on the left-hand side. Weave a way up through the cliffs behind. Eventually slant left and break out onto the flat, grassy surface of a colossal landslipped block known as 'The Table'.

There is no way of reaching the plateau above from here. So drop down from the middle of the eastern rim of The Table and descend a gully leading north. Continue down to join a path skirting below the escarpment. (Turning right leads back round to the Prison.) Follow this north for just over a kilometre. It eventually rises gently to gain the crest of the ridge on the left. Then follow the rim of the escarpment as it rises in a southerly direction. There are fine views overlooking the Quiraing. The summit of Meall na Suiramach (543m) lies about 350 metres back from the edge. Descend the long south-western flank, then drop down steeply southwards back to the road.

166 Leac nan Fionn and Sron Vourlinn 5km **

This outing visits some very impressive landslipped ground, but does not attract many walkers, so shows little signs of wear.

Start

Instead of taking the road over to Uig, continue north on the Duntulm road for just over 3km. Look for a faint track – on the west side of the road – which leads to hidden Loch Langaig.

The Route
Follow the track round the north side of the loch and continue by a faint path which ascends in a south-westerly direction to Loch Hasco. Above this second loch are the cliffs of Leac nan Fionn. These are too steep to take direct, so ascend steep ground to outflank them on the left. Find a way up from the back onto the sloping table-top of Leac nan Fionn *(Fingal's tombstone)*. Go to its northern end to view the shear cliffs of Sron Vourlinn, below which is a hollow peppered with pinnacles.

Descend off the back of the summit plateau and head for a dip on the ridge further west. Ascend the slope, which overlooks Coire Mhic Eachainn, in a north-easterly direction to the summit (378m). There is a horrifying drop on the eastern side. Return the same way, but find a way down on the north side of Leac nan Fionn to the hollow with the pinnacles seen earlier. Head east to rejoin the route of approach.

———

Trotternish has some spectacular sea cliffs, particularly along its eastern coast. There is a popular viewing place for Kilt Rock, for example, just to the south of Staffin. The final outing lies further north near Duntulm.

167 **Rubha Hunish** 7km **
This walk visits a beautiful headland forming the most northerly tip of the island. On a fine day, the views of the Shiants and the Western Isles are superb.

Start
Take the road to Duntulm. There are two possible starts. Either head north-west from a telephone box on a bend in the road (GR 422 742) or follow a track past some former coastguard buildings on the west side of a lochan (GR 415 741).

The Route
The second approach gives easier walking. Go through a gate and over a style, and eventually slant down to the shore in Tulm Bay. After about a kilometre, cross a fence and ascend a steep slope. Continue over heathery ground to the summit of Meall Deas (101m). There are steep cliffs below with fine views across Loch Hunish. Turn right and follow the cliff top along to a trench-like hollow. There is a way down slanting rightwards through the cliffs from here to the headland below. Several sea stacks are hidden on the north-east side of the headland. When returning to the cliff top turn left to visit an old coastguard lookout on Meall Tuath (117m), before returning to the start.

Further Reading

Climbing and Walking

Abraham, A.P. 1908. *Rock Climbing in Skye*. London.

Humble, B.H. 1952. *The Cuillin of Skye*. Facsimile Edition, 1986.
The Ernest Press.

Humble, B.H. 1947. *Tramping in Skye*. William MacLellan, Glasgow.

Mackenzie, J.R. and Williams, N. 1996. *Skye and the Hebrides :
Rock & Ice Climbs, Volume 1, The Isle of Skye*.
Scottish Mountaineering Trust.

Marsh, T., 1996. *The Isle of Skye : A Walker's Guide*. Cicerone Press.

Steeple, E.W., Barlow, G. et al. 1923. *Island of Skye*. 2nd Edition
1948, 3rd Edition 1954. Scottish Mountaineering Club.

Storer, R. 1989. *Skye : Walking, Scrambling and Exploring*.
David & Charles.

Photographic Studies

Poucher, W.A. 1949. *The Magic of Skye*. Chapman and Hall.

Stainforth, G. 1994. *The Cuillin : Great Mountain Ridge of Skye*.
Constable.

Caving

Ryder, P.F. 1995. *Caves of Skye : The Limestone Caves of Scotland,
Part 5*. Grampian Speleological Group.

Biographies

Cunningham, F.F. 1990. *James David Forbes : Pioneer Scottish
Glaciologist*. Scottish Academic Press.

Mill, C. 1987. *Norman Collie : A Life in Two Worlds*. Aberdeen University
Press.

Macpherson, G.W. *John Macpherson : The Skye Martyr*.
West Highland Publishing Company.

Douglas, H. 1994. *Flora MacDonald : The Most Loyal Rebel*. Mandarin.

Fauna and Flora

Birks, H.J.B. 1973. *Past and present vegetation of the Isle of Skye
– a palaeoecological study*. Cambridge University Press.

Boyd, J.M. and Boyd, I.L. 1990. *The Hebrides : A Natural History*.
Collins.

Murray, C.W. & Birks H.J.B. 1980. *The Botanist in Skye*.
Botanical Society of the British Isles.

Geology

Anderson, F.W. and Dunham, K.C. 1966. *The geology of northern Skye. Memoir of the Geological Survey of Great Britain.* Her Majesty's Stationery Office, Edinburgh.

Ballantyne, C.K., Benn, D.I., Lowe, J.J. and Walker, M.J.C. 1991. *The Quaternary of the Isle of Skye : Field Guide.* Quaternary Research Association, Cambridge.

Bell, B.R. and Harris, J.W. 1986. *An excursion guide to the geology of the Isle of Skye.* Geological Society of Glasgow.

Craig, G.Y. (Ed.) 1991. *Geology of Scotland.* 3rd Edition. The Geological Society, London.

Richey, J.E. (Revised by MacGregor, A.G. and Anderson, F.W.) 1987. *British Regional Geology : The Tertiary Volcanic Districts of Scotland.* Her Majesty's Stationery Office, Edinburgh.

Stephenson, D. & Merritt, J. *Skye : A Landscape Fashioned by Geology.* Scottish Natural Heritage/British Geological Survey.

Whittow, J.B. 1977. *Geology and Scenery in Scotland.* Penguin Books.

History and General Interest

Cooper, D. 1995. *Skye.* Birlinn Ltd.

Devine, T.M. 1988. *The Great Highland Famine.* John Donald, Edinburgh.

Donaldson-Blyth, I. 1995. *In Search of Prehistoric Skye.* ThistlePress.

Johnson, S. and Boswell, J. (Introduction by McGowan, I.) 1996. *Journey to the Hebrides.* Canongate.

MacCulloch, J.A. 1905. *The Misty Isle of Skye.* (several subsequent editions) Eneas Mackay, Stirling.

MacLean, M. and Carrell, C. (Eds). 1986. *As an Fhearann / From the Land.* Mainstream Publishing/An Lanntair/Third Eye Centre.

Nicolson, A. 1994. *History of Skye.* 2nd Edition. MacLean Press.

Ritchie, G. and Harman, M. 1985. *Exploring Scotland's Heritage – Argyll and the Western Isles.* Her Majesty's Stationery Office.

Hill Names

Drummond, P. 1991. *Scottish Hill and Mountain Names.* Scottish Mountaineering Trust.

Dwelly, E. 1977. *The Illustrated Gaelic-English Dictionary.* 9th Edition. Gairm Publications.

MacDonald, J. *The Place Names of Skye : A Visitors Guide.*

Humour (For when it rains!)

Besley, R. 1999. *Skye for Beginners.* Neil Wilson Publishing, Glasgow.

List of Routes

Note : Entries are grouped by area or peak, and refer only to the
pages on which route descriptions are given

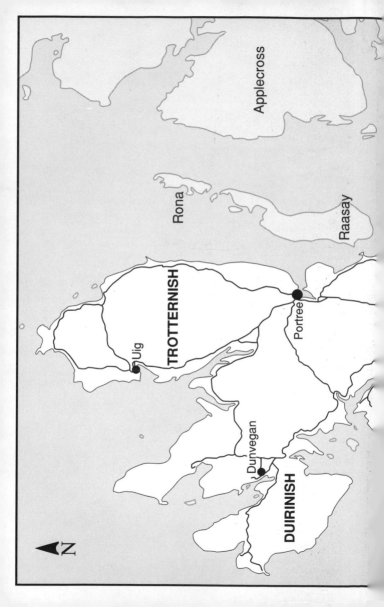

· A ·
· GOOD · BOOK ·
· IS · THE ·
· PRECIOUS ·
· LIFE-BLOOD ·
· OF · A ·
· MASTER ·
SPIRIT
Milton

PRINTED IN   GREAT BRITAIN

The KINGS TREASURIES
OF LITERATURE

GENERAL EDITOR
Sir A·T· QUILLER COUCH

LONDON : J·M·DENT & SONS LTD.

AN
INLAND VOYAGE
and

TRAVELS
WITH A DONKEY
in the
Cevennes

by

R·L·Stevenson

R. L. S.

ROBERT LOUIS STEVENSON was born in Edinburgh in 1850, and there he was educated. His father was secretary to the Commissioners of Northern Lighthouses; his grandfather had built the Bell Rock lighthouse; and he, too, would have entered some active, practical profession but for ill-health. Instead, he turned first to law, and then to literature, leading a wandering life in search of health and experiences. The books of adventure he wrote are, as it were, a compensation, making up by their vigour, and bloodshed, and thrill, for the more active life that he was not strong enough to face. *Treasure Island* is the greatest of all pirate stories; and even if to the modern ear Stevenson's style is sometimes a little precious and studied, it is probable, from the way he is standing the test of time, that "R. L. S." is among the immortals.

He was at very great pains to develop his wonderful style. First he steeped himself in the work of great prose writers such as Sir Thomas Browne, and John Bunyan, and Charles Lamb, and the translators of the Bible, and from them he learnt the use of the right word, the telling phrase, the wonderful effects of delicate prose rhythm. He took what he needed from them, and then evolved a style of his own which came upon the reading public as a revelation.

In 1876 he made, with his friend Sir Walter Simpson, the "inland voyage" from Antwerp to Pontoise des-

cribed in the following pages, and this was his first
published book.   The same year in which he published
it—1878—he travelled through southern France with a
donkey and a sleeping-sack; and again he kept a little
discursive journal full of reflections, and character
sketches, and delicious whimsical homilies; and this too
was published.   Other writers, such as Henry Fielding,
W. M. Thackeray, and Mark Twain, have written little
discursive travel books of this kind; but it is to be
doubted whether any succeeded as R. L. S. has done in
touching every scene, every conversation, every little
adventure, with such delicate enchantment, so boy-like
a feeling for romance in little things.   And Stevenson
never outgrew his boyhood.   All the great adventure
stories which came later from his pen are eager with a
boy's romantic expectation, and zest for dangerous life.
He never outlived his essential youthfulness, and he
died young.

                                        G. N. P.

AN INLAND VOYAGE

Thus sang they in the English boat.

MARVELL.

TO

SIR WALTER GRINDLAY SIMPSON, Bart.

My Dear "Cigarette,"

It was enough that you should have shared so liberally in the rains and portages of our voyage; that you should have had so hard a paddle to recover the derelict *Arethusa* on the flooded Oise; and that you should thenceforth have piloted a mere wreck of mankind to Origny Sainte-Benoîte and a supper so eagerly desired. It was perhaps more than enough, as you once somewhat piteously complained, that I should have set down all the strong language to you, and kept the appropriate reflections for myself. I could not in decency expose you to share the disgrace of another and more public shipwreck. But now that this voyage of ours is going into a cheap edition, that peril, we shall hope, is at an end, and I may put your name on the burgee.

But I cannot pause till I have lamented the fate of our two ships. That, sir, was not a fortunate day when we projected the possession of a canal barge; it was not a fortunate day when we shared our day-dream with the most hopeful of day-dreamers. For a while, indeed, the world looked smilingly. The barge was procured and christened, and, as the *Eleven Thousand Virgins of Cologne*, lay for some months, the admired of all admirers, in a pleasant river and under the walls of an ancient town. M. Mattras, the accomplished carpenter of Moret, had made her a centre of emulous labour; and you will not have forgotten the amount of sweet champagne consumed in the inn at the bridge end, to give zeal to the workmen and speed to the work. On the financial aspect I would not willingly dwell. The *Eleven Thousand Virgins of Cologne* rotted in the stream where she was beautified. She felt not the impulse of the breeze; she was never harnessed to the patient track-horse. And when at length she was sold, by the indignant carpenter of Moret, there were sold along with her the *Arethusa* and the *Cigarette*, she of cedar, she, as we knew so keenly on a portage, of solid-hearted English oak. Now these historic vessels fly the tricolour and are known by new and alien names.

R. L. S.

PREFACE TO FIRST EDITION

To equip so small a book with a preface is, I am half afraid, to sin against proportion. But a preface is more than an author can resist, for it is the reward of his labours. When the foundation-stone is laid, the architect appears with his plans, and struts for an hour before the public eye. So with the writer in his preface: he may have never a word to say, but he must show himself for a moment in the portico, hat in hand, and with an urbane demeanour.

It is best, in such circumstances, to represent a delicate shade of manner between humility and superiority: as if the book had been written by some one else, and you had merely run over it and inserted what was good. But for my part I have not yet learned the trick to that perfection; I am not yet able to dissemble the warmth of my sentiments towards a reader; and if I meet him on the threshold, it is to invite him in with country cordiality.

To say truth, I had no sooner finished reading this little book in proof, than I was seized upon by a distressing apprehension. It occurred to me that I might not only be the first to read these pages, but the last as well; that I might have pioneered this very smiling tract of country all in vain, and find not a soul to follow in my steps. The more I thought, the more I disliked the notion; until the distaste grew into a sort of panic terror, and I rushed into this Preface, which is no more than an advertisement for readers.

What am I to say for my book? *Caleb* and *Joshua* brought back from *Palestine* a formidable bunch of grapes; alas! my book produces naught so nourishing; and for the matter of that, we live in an age when people prefer a definition to any quantity of fruit.

I wonder, would a negative be found enticing? for, from the negative point of view, I flatter myself this volume has a certain stamp. Although it runs to considerably upwards of two hundred pages, it contains not a single reference to the imbecility of *God's* universe, nor so much as a single hint that I could have made a better one myself.—I really do not know where my head can have been. I seem to have forgotten all that makes it glorious to be man.—'Tis an omission that renders the book philosophically unimportant; but I am in hopes the eccentricity may please in frivolous circles.

To the friend who accompanied me I owe many thanks already, indeed I wish I owed him nothing else; but at this moment I feel towards him an almost exaggerated tenderness. He, at least, will become my reader:—if it were only to follow his own travels alongside of mine.

R. L. S.

CONTENTS

AN INLAND VOYAGE

ANTWERP TO BOOM

WE made a great stir in *Antwerp Docks*. A stevedore and a lot of dock porters took up the two canoes, and ran with them for the slip. A crowd of children followed cheering. The *Cigarette* went off in a splash and a bubble of small breaking water. Next moment the *Arethusa* was after her. A steamer was coming down, men on the paddle-box shouted hoarse warnings, the stevedore and his porters were bawling from the quay. But in a stroke or two the canoes were away out in the middle of the *Scheldt*, and all steamers, and stevedores, and other 'long-shore vanities were left behind.

The sun shone brightly; the tide was making—four jolly miles an hour, the wind blew steadily, with occasional squalls. For my part, I had never been in a canoe under sail in my life; and my first experiment out in the middle of this big river was not made without some trepidation. What would happen when the wind first caught my little canvas? I suppose it was almost as trying a venture into the regions of the unknown as to publish a first book, or to marry. But my doubts were not of long duration; and in five minutes you will not be surprised to learn that I had tied my sheet.

I own I was a little struck by this circumstance myself; of course, in company with the rest of my fellow-men, I had always tied the sheet in a sailing-boat; but in so little and crank a concern as a canoe, and with these charging squalls, I was not prepared to find myself follow the same principle; and it inspired me with some contemptuous views of our regard for life. It is certainly easier to smoke with the sheet fastened; but I had never before weighed a comfortable pipe of tobacco against an obvious risk, and gravely elected for the comfortable pipe. It is a commonplace, that we cannot answer for ourselves before we have been tried. But it is not so common a reflection, and surely more consoling, that we usually find ourselves a great deal braver and better than we thought. I believe this is every one's experience: but an apprehension that they may belie themselves in the future prevents mankind from trumpeting this cheerful sentiment abroad. I wish sincerely, for it would have saved me much trouble, there had been some one to put me in a good heart about life when I was younger; to tell me how dangers are most portentous on a distant sight; and how the good in a man's spirit will not suffer itself to be overlaid, and rarely or never deserts him in the hour of need. But we are all for tootling on the sentimental flute in literature; and not a man among us will go to the head of the march to sound the heady drums.

It was agreeable upon the river. A barge or two went past laden with hay. Reeds and willows bordered on the stream; and cattle and grey venerable horses came and hung their mild heads over the embankment. Here and there was a pleasant village among trees, with a noisy shipping yard; here and there a villa in a lawn. The wind served us well up the *Scheldt* and thereafter up the *Rupel*; and we were running pretty free when we began to sight the brickyards of *Boom*, lying for a long way on the right bank of the river. The left bank was still green and pastoral, with alleys of trees along the embankment, and here and there a flight of steps to serve a ferry, where perhaps there sat a woman with her elbows on her knees, or an old gentleman with a staff and silver spectacles. But *Boom* and its brickyards grew smokier and shabbier with every minute; until a great church with a clock, and a wooden bridge over the river, indicated the central quarters of the town.

Boom is not a nice place, and is only remarkable for one thing: that the majority of the inhabitants have a private opinion that they can speak English, which is not justified by fact. This gave a kind of haziness to our intercourse. As for the *Hôtel de la Navigation*, I think it is the worst feature of the place. It boasts of a sanded parlour, with a bar at one end, looking on the street; and another sanded parlour, darker and colder, with an empty birdcage and a tricolour subscription box by way of sole adornment, where we made shift to dine in the company of three uncommunicative engineer apprentices and a silent bagman. The food, as usual in *Belgium*, was of a nondescript occasional character; indeed I have never been able to detect anything in the nature of a meal among this pleasing people; they seem to peck and trifle with viands all day long in an amateur spirit: tentatively French, truly German, and somehow falling between the two.

The empty birdcage, swept and garnished, and with no trace of the old piping favourite, save where two wires had been pushed apart to hold its lump of sugar, carried with it a sort of graveyard cheer. The engineer apprentices would have nothing to say to us, nor indeed to the bagman; but talked low and sparingly to one another, or raked us in the gaslight with a gleam of spectacles. For though handsome lads, they were all (in the Scotch phrase) barnacled.

There was an English maid in the hotel, who had been long enough out of *England* to pick up all sorts of funny foreign idioms, and all sorts of curious foreign ways, which need not here be specified. She spoke to us very fluently in her jargon, asked us information as to the manners of the present day in *England*, and obligingly corrected us when we attempted to answer. But as we were dealing with a woman, perhaps our information was not so much thrown away as it appeared. The sex likes to pick up knowledge and yet preserve its superiority. It is good policy, and almost necessary in the circumstances. If a man finds a woman admire him, were it only for his acquaintance with geography, he will begin at once to build upon the admiration. It is only by unintermittent snubbing that the pretty ones can keep us in our place. Men, as Miss *Howe* or Miss *Harlowe* would have said, "are such *encroachers*." For my part, I am body and soul with the women; and after a well-married couple, there is nothing so beautiful in the world as the myth of the divine huntress. It is no use for a man to take to the woods; we know him; *Anthony* tried the same thing long ago, and had a pitiful time of it by all accounts. But there is this about some women, which overtops the best gymnosophist among men, that they suffice to themselves, and can walk in a high and cold zone without the countenance of any trousered being. I declare, although the reverse of a professed ascetic, I am more obliged to women for this ideal than I should be to the majority of them, or indeed to any but one, for a spontaneous kiss. There is nothing so encouraging as the spectacle of self-sufficiency. And when I think of the slim and lovely

maidens, running the woods all night to the note of
Diana's horn; moving among the old oaks, as fancy-
free as they; things of the forest and the starlight, not
touched by the commotion of man's hot and turbid life
—although there are plenty other ideals that I should
prefer—I find my heart beat at the thought of this one.
'Tis to fail in life, but to fail with what a grace! That
is not lost which is not regretted. And where—here
slips out the male—where would be much of the glory
of inspiring love if there were no contempt to overcome?

ON THE WILLEBROEK CANAL

Next morning, when we set forth on the *Willebroek
Canal*, the rain began heavy and chill. The water of the
canal stood at about the drinking temperature of tea;
and under this cold aspersion, the surface was covered
with steam. The exhilaration of departure, and the
easy motion of the boats under each stroke of the
paddles, supported us through this misfortune while it
lasted; and when the cloud passed and the sun came
out again, our spirits went up above the range of stay-
at-home humours. A good breeze rustled and shivered
in the rows of trees that bordered the canal. The
leaves flickered in and out of the light in tumultuous
masses. It seemed sailing weather to eye and ear;
but down between the banks, the wind reached us only
in faint and desultory puffs. There was hardly enough
to steer by. Progress was intermittent and unsatis-
factory. A jocular person, of marine antecedents,
hailed us from the tow-path with a *"C'est vite, mais
c'est long."*

The canal was busy enough. Every now and then

we met or overtook a long string of boats, with great green tillers; high sterns with a window on either side of the rudder, and perhaps a jug or a flower-pot in one of the windows; a dinghy following behind; a woman busied about the day's dinner, and a handful of children. These barges were all tied one behind the other with tow-ropes, to the number of twenty-five or thirty; and the line was headed and kept in motion by a steamer of strange construction. It had neither paddle-wheel nor screw; but by some gear not rightly comprehensible to the unmechanical mind, it fetched up over its bow a small bright chain which lay along the bottom of the canal, and paying it out again over the stern, dragged itself forward, link by link, with its whole retinue of loaded scows. Until one had found out the key to the enigma, there was something solemn and uncomfortable in the progress of one of these trains, as it moved gently along the water with nothing to mark its advance but an eddy alongside dying away into the wake.

Of all the creatures of commercial enterprise, a canal barge is by far the most delightful to consider. It may spread its sails, and then you see it sailing high above the tree-tops and the windmill, sailing on the aqueduct, sailing through the green corn-lands: the most picturesque of things amphibious. Or the horse plods along at a foot-pace as if there were no such thing as business in the world; and the man dreaming at the tiller sees the same spire on the horizon all day long. It is a mystery how things ever get to their destination at this rate; and to see the barges waiting their turn at a lock affords a fine lesson of how easily the world may be taken. There should be many contented spirits on board, for such a life is both to travel and to stay at home.

The chimney smokes for dinner as you go along; the banks of the canal slowly unroll their scenery to contemplative eyes; the barge floats by great forests and through great cities with their public buildings and their lamps at night; and for the bargee, in his floating home, "travelling abed," it is merely as if he were listening to another man's story or turning the leaves of a picture-book in which he had no concern. He may take his afternoon walk in some foreign country on the banks of the canal, and then come home to dinner at his own fire-side.

There is not enough exercise in such a life for any high measure of health; but a high measure of health is only necessary for unhealthy people. The slug of a fellow, who is never ill nor well, has a quiet time of it in life, and dies all the easier.

I am sure I would rather be a bargee than occupy any position under Heaven that required attendance at an office. There are few callings, I should say, where a man gives up less of his liberty in return for regular meals. The bargee is on shipboard— he is master in his own ship—he can land whenever he will—he can never be kept beating off a lee-shore a whole frosty night when the sheets are as hard as iron; and so far as I can make out, time stands as nearly still with him as is compatible with the return of bed-time or the dinner-hour. It is not easy to see why a bargee should ever die.

Half-way between *Willebroek* and *Villevorde*, in a beautiful reach of canal like a squire's avenue, we went ashore to lunch. There were two eggs, a junk of bread, and a bottle of wine on board the *Arethusa*; and two eggs and an Etna cooking apparatus on board the *Cigarette*. The master of the latter boat smashed one of the eggs in the course of disembarkation; but observing pleasantly that it might still be cooked *à la papier*, he dropped it into the Etna, in its covering of Flemish newspaper. We landed in a blink of fine weather; but we had not been two minutes ashore before the wind freshened into half a gale, and the rain began to patter on our shoulders. We sat as close about the Etna as we could. The spirits burned with great ostentation; the grass caught flame every minute or two, and had to be trodden out; and before long there were several burnt fingers of the party. But the solid quantity of cookery accomplished was out of proportion with so much display; and when we desisted, after two applications of the fire, the sound egg was little more than loo-warm; and as for *à la papier*, it was a cold and sordid *fricassée* of printer's ink and broken egg-shell. We made shift to roast the other two, by putting them close to the burning spirits; and that with better success. And then we uncorked the bottle of wine, and sat down in a ditch with our canoe aprons over our knees. It rained smartly. Discomfort, when it is honestly uncomfortable and makes no nauseous pretensions to the contrary, is a vastly humorous business; and people well steeped and stupefied in the open air are in a good vein for laughter. From this point of view, even egg *à la papier* offered by way of food may pass muster as a sort of accessory to the fun. But this manner of jest, although it may be taken in good part, does not invite repetition; and from that time forward, the Etna voyaged like a gentleman in the locker of the *Cigarette*.

It is almost unnecessary to mention that when lunch was over and we got aboard again and made sail, the wind promptly died away. The rest of the journey to *Villevorde* we still spread our canvas to the unfavouring air; and with now and then a puff, and now and then a spell of paddling, drifted along from lock to lock, between the orderly trees.

It was a fine, green, fat landscape; or rather a mere green water-lane, going on from village to village. Things had a settled look, as in places long lived in. Crop-headed children spat upon us from the bridges as we went below, with a true conservative feeling. But even more conservative were the fishermen, intent upon their floats, who let us go by without one glance. They perched upon starlings and buttresses and along the slope of the embankment gently occupied. They were indifferent like pieces of dead nature. They did not move any more than if they had been fishing in an old Dutch print. The leaves fluttered, the water lapped, but they continued in one stay like so many churches established by law. You might have trepanned every one of their innocent heads, and found no more than so much coiled fishing line below their skulls. I do not care for your stalwart fellows in india-rubber stockings breasting up mountain torrents with a salmon rod; but I do dearly love the class of man who plies his unfruitful art, for ever and a day, by still and depopulated waters.

At the last lock just beyond *Villevorde* there was a lock mistress who spoke French comprehensibly, and told us we were still a couple of leagues from *Brussels*. At the same place, the rain began again. It fell in straight, parallel lines; and the surface of the canal was thrown up into an infinity of little crystal fountains. There were no beds to be had in the neighbourhood. Nothing for it but to lay the sails aside and address ourselves to steady paddling in the rain.

Beautiful country houses, with clocks and long lines of

shuttered windows, and fine old trees standing in groves and avenues, gave a rich and sombre aspect in the rain and the deepening dusk to the shores of the canal. I seem to have seen something of the same effect in engravings: opulent landscapes, deserted and overhung with the passage of storm. And throughout we had the escort of a hooded cart, which trotted shabbily along the tow-path, and kept at an almost uniform distance in our wake.

THE ROYAL SPORT NAUTIQUE

THE rain took off near *Laeken*. But the sun was already down; the air was chill; and we had scarcely a dry stitch between the pair of us. Nay, now we found ourselves near the end of the *Allée Verte*, and on the very threshold of *Brussels* we were confronted by a serious difficulty. The shores were closely lined by canal boats waiting their turn at the lock. Nowhere was there any convenient landing-place; nowhere so much as a stable-yard to leave the canoes in for the night. We scrambled ashore and entered an *estaminet* where some sorry fellows were drinking with the landlord. The landlord was pretty round with us; he knew of no coach-house or stable-yard, nothing of the sort; and seeing we had come with no mind to drink, he did not conceal his impatience to be rid of us. One of the sorry fellows came to the rescue. Somewhere in the corner of the basin there was a slip, he informed us, and something else besides, not very clearly defined by him, but hopefully construed by his hearers.

Sure enough there was the slip in the corner of the basin; and at the top of it two nice-looking lads in boating clothes. The *Arethusa* addressed himself to these. One of them said there would be no difficulty about a night's lodging for our boats; and the other, taking a cigarette from his lips, inquired if they were made by *Searle and Son*. The name was quite an introduction. Half a dozen other young men came out of a boat-house bearing the superscription ROYAL SPORT NAUTIQUE, and joined in the talk. They were all very polite, voluble and enthusiastic; and their discourse was interlarded with English boating terms, and the names of English boat-builders and English clubs. I do not know, to my shame, any spot in my native land where I should have been so warmly received by the same number of people. We were English boating-men, and the Belgian boating-men fell upon our necks. I wonder if French Huguenots were as cordially greeted by English Protestants when they came across the Channel out of great tribulation. But after all, what religion knits people so closely as a common sport?

The canoes were carried into the boat-house; they were washed down for us by the Club servants, the sails were hung out to dry, and everything made as snug and tidy as a picture. And in the meanwhile we were led upstairs by our new-found brethren, for so more than one of them stated the relationship, and made free of their lavatory. This one lent us soap, that one a towel, a third and fourth helped us to undo our bags. And all the time such questions, such assurances of respect and sympathy! I declare I never knew what glory was before.

"Yes, yes, the *Royal Sport Nautique* is the oldest club in *Belgium*."

"We number two hundred."

"We"—this is not a substantive speech, but an

abstract of many speeches, the impression left upon my mind after a great deal of talk; and very youthful, pleasant, natural and patriotic it seems to me to be— "We have gained all races, except those where we were cheated by the *French.*"

"You must leave all your wet things to be dried."

"O! *entre frères!* In any boat-house in *England* we should find the same." (I cordially hope they might.)

"*En Angleterre, vous employez des sliding-seats, n'est-ce pas?*"

"We are all employed in commerce during the day; but in the evening, *voyez vous, nous sommes sérieux.*"

These were the words. They were all employed over the frivolous mercantile concerns of *Belgium* during the day; but in the evening they found some hours for the serious concerns of life. I may have a wrong idea of wisdom, but I think that was a very wise remark. People connected with literature and philosophy are busy all their days in getting rid of second-hand notions and false standards. It is their profession, in the sweat of their brows, by dogged thinking, to recover their old fresh view of life, and distinguish what they really and originally like from what they have only learned to tolerate perforce. And these *Royal Nautical Sportsmen* had the distinction still quite legible in their hearts. They had still those clean perceptions of what is nice and nasty, what is interesting and what is dull, which envious old gentlemen refer to as illusions. The nightmare illusion of middle age, the bear's hug of custom gradually squeezing the life out of a man's soul, had not yet begun for these happy-star'd young *Belgians.* They still knew that the interest they took in their business was a trifling affair compared to their spontaneous, long-suffering affection for nautical sports.

To know what you prefer, instead of humbly saying Amen to what the world tells you you ought to prefer, is to have kept your soul alive. Such a man may be generous! he may be honest in something more than the commercial sense; he may love his friends with an elective, personal sympathy, and not accept them as an adjunct of the station to which he has been called. He may be a man, in short, acting on his own instincts, keeping his own shape that *God* made him in; and not a mere crank in the social engine-house, welded on principles that he does not understand, and for purposes that he does not care for.

For will anyone dare to tell me that business is more entertaining than fooling among boats? He must have never seen a boat, or never seen an office, who says so. And for certain the one is a great deal better for the health. There should be nothing so much a man's business as his amusements. Nothing but money-grubbing can be put forward to the contrary; no one but

> Mammon, the least erected spirit that fell
> From Heaven,

durst risk a word in answer. It is but a lying cant that would represent the merchant and the banker as people disinterestedly toiling for mankind, and then most useful when they are most absorbed in their transactions; for the man is more important than his services. And when my *Royal Nautical Sportsman* shall have so far fallen from his hopeful youth that he cannot pluck up an enthusiasm over anything but his ledger, I venture to doubt whether he will be near so nice a fellow, and whether he would welcome, with so good a grace, a couple of drenched *Englishmen* paddling into *Brussels* in the dusk.

When we had changed our wet clothes and drunk a glass of pale ale to the Club's prosperity, one of their number escorted us to an hotel. He would not join us at our dinner, but he had no objection to a glass of wine. Enthusiasm is very wearing; and I begin to understand why prophets were unpopular in *Judæa*, where they were best known. For three stricken hours did this excellent young man sit beside us to dilate on boats and boat-races; and before he left he was kind enough to order our bed-room candles.

We endeavoured now and again to change the subject; but the diversion did not last a moment, the *Royal Nautical Sportsman* bridled, shied, answered the question, and then breasted once more into the swelling tide of his subject. I call it his subject; but I think it was he who was subjected. The *Arethusa*, who holds all racing as a creature of the devil, found himself in a pitiful dilemma. He durst not own his ignorance for the honour of Old *England*, and spoke away about English clubs and English oarsmen whose fame had never before come to his ears. Several times, and, once above all, on the question of sliding-seats, he was within an ace of exposure. As for the *Cigarette*, who has rowed races in the heat of his blood, but now disowns these slips of his wanton youth, his case was still more desperate; for the *Royal Nautical* proposed that he should take an oar in one of their eights on the morrow, to compare the English with the Belgian stroke. I could see my friend per-spiring in his chair whenever that particular topic came up. And there was yet another proposal which had the same effect on both of us. It appeared that the champion canoeist of *Europe* (as well as most other champions) was a *Royal Nautical Sportsman*. And if we would only wait until the *Sunday*, this infernal paddler would be so

condescending as to accompany us on our next stage.
Neither of us had the least desire to drive the coursers
of the sun against *Apollo*.

When the young man was gone, we countermanded
our candles, and ordered some brandy and water. The
great billows had gone over our head. The *Royal
Nautical Sportsmen* were as nice young fellows as a
man would wish to see, but they were a trifle too young
and a thought too nautical for us. We began to see that
we were old and cynical; we liked ease and the agreeable
rambling of the human mind about this and the other
subject; we did not want to disgrace our native land
by messing an eight, or toiling pitifully in the wake of
the champion canoeist. In short, we had recourse to
flight. It seemed ungrateful, but we tried to make that
good on a card loaded with sincere compliments. And
indeed it was no time for scruples; we seemed to feel
the hot breath of the champion on our necks.

AT MAUBEUCE

PARTLY from the terror we had of our good friends the
Royal Nauticals, partly from the fact that there were
no fewer than fifty-five locks between *Brussels* and
Charleroi, we concluded that we should travel by train
across the frontier, boats and all. Fifty-five locks in
a day's journey was pretty well tantamount to trudging
the whole distance on foot, with the canoes upon our
shoulders, an object of astonishment to the trees on the
canal side, and of honest derision to all right-thinking
children.

To pass the frontier, even in a train, is a difficult
matter for the *Arethusa*. He is somehow or other a

marked man for the official eye. Wherever he journeys,
there are the officers gathered together. Treaties are
solemnly signed, foreign ministers, ambassadors, and
consuls sit throned in state from *China* to *Peru*, and the
Union Jack flutters on all the winds of heaven. Under
these safeguards, portly clergymen, schoolmistresses,
gentlemen in grey tweed suits, and all the ruck and
rabble of British touristry pour unhindered, *Murray*
in hand, over the railways of the Continent, and yet
the slim person of the *Arethusa* is taken in the meshes,
while these great fish go on their way rejoicing. If
he travels without a passport, he is cast, without any
figure about the matter, into noisome dungeons: if his
papers are in order, he is suffered to go his way indeed,
but not until he has been humiliated by a general
incredulity. He is a born British subject, yet he has
never succeeded in persuading a single official of his
nationality. He flatters himself he is indifferent honest;
yet he is rarely taken for anything better than a spy,
and there is no absurd and disreputable means of live-
lihood but has been attributed to him in some heat
of official or popular distrust. . . .

For the life of me I cannot understand it. I too
have been knolled to church, and sat at good men's
feasts; but I bear no mark of it. I am as strange as a
Jack Indian to their official spectacles. I might home
from any part of the globe, it seems, except from where
I do. My ancestors have laboured in vain, and the
glorious Constitution cannot protect me in my walks
abroad. It is a great thing, believe me, to present a
good normal type of the nation you belong to.

) Nobody else was asked for his papers on the way to
Maubeuge; but I was; and although I clung to my
rights, I had to choose at last between accepting the

humiliation and being left behind by the train. I was sorry to give way; but I wanted to get to *Maubeuge*.

Maubeuge is a fortified town, with a very good inn, the *Grand Cerf*. It seemed to be inhabited principally by soldiers and bagmen; at least, these were all that we saw, except the hotel servants. We had to stay there some time, for the canoes were in no hurry to follow us, and at last stuck hopelessly in the custom-house until we went back to liberate them. There was nothing to do, nothing to see. We had good meals, which was a great matter; but that was all.

The *Cigarette* was nearly taken up upon a charge of drawing the fortifications: a feat of which he was hopelessly incapable. And besides, as I suppose each belligerent nation has a plan of the other's fortified places already, these precautions are of the nature of shutting the stable door after the steed is away. But I have no doubt they help to keep up a good spirit at home. It is a great thing if you can persuade people that they are somehow or other partakers in a mystery. It makes them feel bigger. Even the Freemasons, who have been shown up to satiety, preserve a kind of pride; and not a grocer among them, however honest, harmless and empty-headed he may feel himself to be at bottom, but comes home from one of their cœnacula with a portentous significance for himself.

It is an odd thing, how happily two people, if there are two, can live in a place where they have no acquaintance. I think the spectacle of a whole life in which you have no part paralyses personal desire. You are content to become a mere spectator. The baker stands in his door; the colonel with his three medals goes by to the *café* at night; the troops drum and trumpet and man the ramparts, as bold as so many lions. It would

task language to say how placidly you behold all this.
In a place where you have taken some root, you are
provoked out of your indifference; you have a hand in
the game; your friends are fighting with the army.
But in a strange town, not small enough to grow too
soon familiar, nor so large as to have laid itself out for
travellers, you stand so far apart from the business, that
you positively forget it would be possible to go nearer;
you have so little human interest around you, that you
do not remember yourself to be a man. Perhaps, in a
very short time, you would be one no longer! Gymnoso-
phists go into a wood, with all Nature seething around
them, with romance on every side; it would be much
more to the purpose if they took up their abode in a dull
country town, where they should see just so much of
humanity as to keep them from desiring more, and only
the stale externals of man's life. These externals are as
dead to us as so many formalities, and speak a dead
language in our eyes and ears. They have no more
meaning than an oath or a salutation. We are so
much accustomed to see married couples going to church
of a *Sunday* that we have clean forgotten what they
represent; and novelists are driven to rehabilitate
adultery, no less, when they wish to show us what a
beautiful thing it is for a man and a woman to live for
each other.

One person in *Maubeuge*, however, showed me something more than his outside. That was the driver of
the hotel omnibus: a mean-enough looking little man, as
well as I can remember, but with a spark of something
human in his soul. He had heard of our little journey,
and came to me at once in envious sympathy. How he
longed to travel! he told me. How he longed to be
somewhere else, and see the round world before he went

into the gravel! "Here I am," said he. "I drive to the
station. Well. And then I drive back again to the
hotel. And so on every day and all the week round.
My *God*, is that life?" I could not say I thought it was
—for him. He pressed me to tell him where I had
been, and where I hoped to go; and as he listened, I
declare the fellow sighed. Might not this have been a
brave African traveller, or gone to the *Indies* after *Drake*?
But it is an evil age for the gipsily inclined among men.
He who can sit squarest on a three-legged stool, he it is
who has the wealth and glory.

I wonder if my friend is still driving the omnibus for
the *Grand Cerf*? Not very likely, I believe; for I think
he was on the eve of mutiny when we passed through,
and perhaps our passage determined him for good.
Better a thousand times that he should be a tramp, and
mend pots and pans by the wayside, and sleep under
trees, and see the dawn and the sunset every day above
a new horizon. I think I hear you say that it is a
respectable position to drive an omnibus? Very well.
What right has he who likes it not to keep those who
would like it dearly out of this respectable position?
Suppose a dish were not to my taste, and you told me
that it was a favourite among the rest of the company,
what should I conclude from that? Not to finish the
dish against my stomach, I suppose.

Respectability is a very good thing in its way, but it
does not rise superior to all considerations. I would
not for a moment venture to hint that it was a matter
of taste; but I think I will go as far as this: that if a
position is admittedly unkind, uncomfortable, unnecessary, and superfluously useless, although it were as
respectable as the Church of *England*, the sooner a man
is out of it, the better for himself and all concerned.

B

ON THE SAMBRE CANALISED:

TO QUARTES

ABOUT three in the afternoon the whole establishment of the *Grand Cerf* accompanied us to the water's edge. The man of the omnibus was there with haggard eyes. Poor cagebird! Do I not remember the time when I myself haunted the station, to watch train after train carry its complement of freemen into the night, and read the names of distant places on the time-bills with indescribable longings?

We were not clear of the fortifications before the rain began. The wind was contrary, and blew in furious gusts; nor were the aspects of Nature any more clement than the doings of the sky. For we passed through a stretch of blighted country, sparsely covered with brush, but handsomely enough diversified with factory chimneys. We landed in a soiled meadow among some pollards, and there smoked a pipe in a flaw of fair weather. But the wind blew so hard, we could get little else to smoke. There were no natural objects in the neighbourhood, but some sordid workshops. A group of children headed by a tall girl stood and watched us from a little distance all the time we stayed. I heartily wonder what they thought of us.

At *Hautmont*, the lock was almost impassable! the landing-place being steep and high, and the launch at a long distance. Near a dozen grimy workmen lent us a hand. They refused any reward; and, what is much better, refused it handsomely, without conveying any sense of insult. "It is a way we have in our country-side," said they. And a very becoming way it is. In

Scotland, where also you will get services for nothing, the good people reject your money as if you had been trying to corrupt a voter. When people take the trouble to do dignified acts, it is worth while to take a little more, and allow the dignity to be common to all concerned. But in our brave Saxon countries, where we plod threescore years and ten in the mud, and the wind keeps singing in our ears from birth to burial, we do our good and bad with a high hand and almost offensively; and make even our alms a witness-bearing and an act of war against the wrong.

After *Hautmont*, the sun came forth again and the wind went down; and a little paddling took us beyond the iron-works and through a delectable land. The river wound among low hills, so that sometimes the sun was at our backs, and sometimes it stood right ahead, and the river before us was one sheet of intolerable glory. On either hand, meadows and orchards bordered, with a margin of sedge and water flowers, upon the river. The hedges were of great height, woven about the trunks of hedgerow elms; and the fields, as they were often very small, looked like a series of bowers along the stream. There was never any prospect; sometimes a hill-top with its trees would look over the nearest hedgerow, just to make a middle distance for the sky; but that was all. The heaven was bare of clouds. The atmosphere, after the rain, was of enchanting purity. The river doubled among the hillocks, a shining strip of mirror glass; and the dip of the paddles set the flowers shaking along the brink.

In the meadows wandered black and white cattle fantastically marked. One beast, with a white head and the rest of the body glossy black, came to the edge to drink, and stood gravely twitching his ears at me as

I went by, like some sort of preposterous clergyman in a play. A moment after I heard a loud plunge, and, turning my head, saw the clergyman struggling to shore. The bank had given way under his feet.

Besides the cattle, we saw no living things except a few birds and a great many fishermen. These sat along the edges of the meadows, sometimes with one rod, sometimes with as many as half a score. They seemed stupefied with contentment; and when we induced them to exchange a few words with us about the weather, their voices sounded quiet and far-away. There was a strange diversity of opinion among them as to the kind of fish for which they set their lures; although they were all agreed in this, that the river was abundantly supplied. Where it was plain that no two of them had ever caught the same kind of fish, we could not help suspecting that perhaps not any one of them had ever caught a fish at all. I hope, since the afternoon was so lovely, that they were one and all rewarded; and that a silver booty went home in every basket for the pot. Some of my friends would cry shame on me for this; but I prefer a man, were he only an angler, to the bravest pair of gills in all *God's* waters. I do not affect fishes unless when cooked in sauce; whereas an angler is an important piece of river scenery, and hence deserves some recognition among canoeists. He can always tell you where you are after a mild fashion; and his quiet presence serves to accentuate the solitude and stillness, and remind you of the glittering citizens below your boat.

The *Sambre* turned so industriously to and fro among his little hills, that it was past six before we drew near the lock at *Quartes*. There were some children on the tow-path, with whom the *Cigarette* fell into a chaffing

talk as they ran along beside us. It was in vain that I
warned him. In vain I told him, in English, that boys
were the most dangerous creatures; and if once you
began with them, it was safe to end in a shower of
stones. For my own part, whenever anything was
addressed to me, I smiled gently and shook my head
as though I were an inoffensive person inadequately
acquainted with French. For indeed I have had such
experience at home, that I would sooner meet many
wild animals than a troop of healthy urchins.

But I was doing injustice to these peaceable young
Hainaulters. When the *Cigarette* went off to make
inquiries, I got out upon the bank to smoke a pipe
and superintend the boats, and became at once the
centre of much amiable curiosity. The children had
been joined by this time by a young woman and a mild
lad who had lost an arm; and this gave me more security.
When I let slip my first word or so in French, a little
girl nodded her head with a comical grown-up air. "Ah,
you see," she said, "he understands well enough now;
he was just making believe." And the little group
laughed together very good-naturedly.

They were much impressed when they heard we came
from *England*; and the little girl proffered the information that *England* was an island "and a far way from
here—*bien loin d'ici.*"

"Ay, you may say that, a far way from here," said the
lad with one arm.

I was as nearly homesick as ever I was in my life;
they seemed to make it such an incalculable distance
to the place where I first saw the day.

They admired the canoes very much. And I observed
one piece of delicacy in these children which is worthy
of record. They had been deafening us for the last

hundred yards with petitions for a sail; ay, and they
deafened us to the same tune the next morning when
we came to start; but then, when the canoes were lying
empty, there was no word of any such petition.
Delicacy? or perhaps a bit of fear for the water in so
crank a vessel? I hate cynicism a great deal worse
than I do the devil; unless perhaps the two were the
same thing? And yet 'tis a good tonic; the cold tub
and bath-towel of the sentiments; and positively necessary to life in cases of advanced sensibility.

From the boats they turned to my costume. They
could not make enough of my red sash; and my knife
filled them with awe.

"They make them like that in *England*," said the boy
with one arm. I was glad he did not know how badly
we make them in *England* nowadays. "They are for
people who go away to sea," he added, "and to defend
one's life against great fish."

I felt I was becoming a more and more romantic
figure to the little group at every word. And so I
suppose I was. Even my pipe, although it was an
ordinary French clay, pretty well "trousered," as they
call it, would have been a rarity in their eyes, as a thing
coming from so far away. And if my feathers were
not very fine in themselves, they were all from overseas.
One thing in my outfit, however, tickled them out of
all politeness; and that was the bemired condition of
my canvas shoes. I suppose they were sure the mud
at any rate was a home product. The little girl (who
was the genius of the party) displayed her own sabots
in competition; and I wish you could have seen how
gracefully and merrily she did it.

The young woman's milk-can, a great amphora of
hammered brass, stood some way off upon the sward.

I was glad of an opportunity to divert public attention from myself, and return some of the compliments I had received. So I admired it cordially both for form and colour, telling them, and very truly, that it was as beautiful as gold. They were not surprised. The things were plainly the boast of the countryside. And the children expatiated on the costliness of these amphoræ, which sell sometimes as high as thirty francs apiece; told me how they were carried on donkeys, one on either side of the saddle, a brave caparison in themselves; and how they were to be seen all over the district, and at the larger farms in great number and of great size.

PONT-SUR-SAMBRE

WE ARE PEDLARS

THE *Cigarette* returned with good news. There were beds to be had some ten minutes' walk from where we were, at a place called *Pont*. We stowed the canoes in a granary, and asked among the children for a guide. The circle at once widened round us, and our offers of reward were received in dispiriting silence. We were plainly a pair of *Bluebeards* to the children; they might speak to us in public places, and where they had the advantage of numbers; but it was another thing to venture off alone with two uncouth and legendary characters, who had dropped from the clouds upon their hamlet this quiet afternoon, sashed and beknived, and with a flavour of great voyages. The owner of the granary came to our assistance, singled out one little fellow and threatened him with corporalities; or I suspect we should have had to find the way for ourselves.

As it was, he was more frightened at the granary man
than the strangers, having perhaps had some experience of the former. But I fancy his little heart must
have been going at a fine rate; for he kept trotting at a
respectful distance in front, and looking back at us
with scared eyes. Not otherwise may the children of
the young world have guided *Jove* or one of his *Olympian*
compeers on an adventure.

A miry lane led up from *Quartes* with its church and
bickering windmill. The hinds were trudging home-
wards from the fields. A brisk little old woman passed
us by. She was seated across a donkey between a pair
of glittering milk-cans; and, as she went, she kicked
jauntily with her heels upon the donkey's side, and
scattered shrill remarks among the wayfarers. It was
notable that none of the tired men took the trouble to
reply. Our conductor soon led us out of the lane
and across country. The sun had gone down, but the
west in front of us was one lake of level gold. The
path wandered a while in the open, and then passed
under a trellis like a bower indefinitely prolonged. On
either hand were shadowy orchards; cottages lay low
among the leaves and sent their smoke to heaven;
every here and there, in an opening, appeared the great
gold face of the west.

I never saw the *Cigarette* in such an idyllic frame of
mind. He waxed positively lyrical in praise of country
scenes. I was little less exhilarated myself; the mild
air of the evening, the shadows, the rich lights and the
silence, made a symphonious accompaniment about our
walk; and we both determined to avoid towns for the
future and sleep in hamlets.

At last the path went between two houses, and turned
the party out into a wide muddy high-road, bordered,

as far as the eye could reach on either hand, by an
unsightly village. The houses stood well back, leaving
a ribbon of waste land on either side of the road, where
there were stacks of firewood, carts, barrows, rubbish
heaps, and a little doubtful grass. Away on the left, a
gaunt tower stood in the middle of the street. What
it had been in past ages I know not: probably a hold
in time of war; but nowadays it bore an illegible dial-
plate in its upper parts, and near the bottom an iron
letter-box.

The inn to which we had been recommended at
Quartes was full, or else the landlady did not like our
looks. I ought to say, that with our long, damp india-
rubber bags we presented rather a doubtful type of
civilisation: like rag and bone men, the *Cigarette* imagined.
"These gentlemen are pedlars?"—*Ces messieurs sont des
marchands?*—asked the landlady. And then, without
waiting for an answer, which I suppose she thought
superfluous in so plain a case, recommended us to a
butcher who lived hard by the tower and took in
travellers to lodge.

Thither went we. But the butcher was flitting, and
all his beds were taken down. Or else he didn't like our
look. As a parting shot, we had " These gentlemen are
pedlars?"

It began to grow dark in earnest. We could no
longer distinguish the faces of the people who passed
us by with an inarticulate "Good evening." And the
householders of *Pont* seemed very economical with their
oil; for we saw not a single window lighted in all that
long village. I believe it is the longest village in the
world; but I daresay in our predicament every pace
counted three times over. We were much cast down
when we came to the last *auberge*; and looking in at the

dark door, asked timidly if we could sleep there for the
night. A female voice assented in no very friendly
tones. We clapped the bags down and found our way
to chairs.

The place was in total darkness, save a red glow in the
chinks and ventilators of the stove. But now the landlady lit a lamp to see her new guests; I suppose the
darkness was what saved us another expulsion; for I
cannot say she looked gratified at our appearance.
We were in a large bare apartment, adorned with two
allegorical prints of *Music* and *Painting*, and a copy
of the Law against Public Drunkenness. On one side
there was a bit of a bar, with some half a dozen bottles.
Two labourers sat waiting supper in attitudes of extreme
weariness; a plain-looking lass bustled about with a
sleepy child of two; and the landlady began to derange
the pots upon the stove and set some beefsteak to grill.

"These gentlemen are pedlars?" she asked sharply.
And that was all the conversation forthcoming. We
began to think we might be pedlars after all. I never
knew a population with so narrow a range of conjecture
as the innkeepers of *Pont-sur-Sambre*. But manners
and bearing have not a wider currency than banknotes.
You have only to get far enough out of your beat, and
all your accomplished airs will go for nothing. These
Hainaulters could see no difference between us and the
average pedlar. Indeed we had some grounds for
reflection while the steak was getting ready, to see how
perfectly they accepted us at their own valuation, and
how our best politeness and best eff rts at entertainment
seemed to fit quite suitably with the character of pack-
men. At least it seemed a good account of the profession in *France*, that even before such judges we could
not beat them at our own weapons.

At last we were called to table. The two hinds (and
one of them looked sadly worn and white in the face, as
though sick with overwork and underfeeding) supped
off a single plate of some sort of bread-berry, some
potatoes in their jackets, a small cup of coffee sweetened
with sugar candy, and one tumbler of swipes. The
landlady, her son, and the lass aforesaid took the same.
Our meal was quite a banquet by comparison. We had
some beefsteak, not so tender as it might have been,
some of the potatoes, some cheese, an extra glass of the
swipes, and white sugar in our coffee.

You see what it is to be a gentleman—I beg your
pardon, what it is to be a pedlar. It had not before
occurred to me that a pedlar was a great man in a
labourer's ale-house; but now that I had to enact that
part for an evening, I found that so it was. He has
in his hedge quarters somewhat the same pre-eminency
as the man who takes a private parlour in a hotel.
The more you look into it, the more infinite are the
class distinctions among men; and possibly, by a happy
dispensation, there is no one at all at the bottom of the
scale; no one but can find some superiority over somebody else, to keep up his pride withal.

We were pleased enough with our fare. Particularly
the *Cigarette*; for I tried to make believe that I was
amused with the adventure, tough beefsteak and all.
According to the *Lucretian* maxim, our steak should
have been flavoured by the look of the other people's
bread-berry. But we did not find it so in practice.
You may have a head knowledge that other people live
more poorly than yourself, but it is not agreeable—
I was going to say it is against the etiquette of the
universe—to sit at the same table and pick your own
superior diet from among their crusts. I had not seen

such a thing done since the greedy boy at school with
his birthday cake. It was odious enough to witness,
I could remember; and I had never thought to play the
part myself. But there again you see what it is to be a
pedlar.

There is no doubt that the poorer classes in our
country are much more charitably disposed than their
superiors in wealth. And I fancy it must arise a great
deal from the comparative indistinction of the easy and
the not so easy in these ranks. A workman or a pedlar
cannot shutter himself off from his less comfortable
neighbours. If he treats himself to a luxury, he must
do it in the face of a dozen who cannot. And what
should more directly lead to charitable thoughts? . . .
Thus the poor man, camping out in life, sees it as it is,
and knows that every mouthful he puts in his belly
has been wrenched out of the fingers of the hungry.

But at a certain stage of prosperity, as in a balloon
ascent, the fortunate person passes through a zone of
clouds, and sublunary matters are thenceforward hidden
from his view. He sees nothing but the heavenly bodies,
all in admirable order and positively as good as new.
He finds himself surrounded in the most touching manner
by the attentions of *Providence*, and compares himself
involuntarily with the lilies and the skylarks. He does
not precisely sing, of course; but then he looks so un-
assuming in his open *Landau*! If all the world dined at
one table, this philosophy would meet with some rude
knocks.

PONT-SUR-SAMBRE

THE TRAVELLING MERCHANT

LIKE the lackeys in *Molière's* farce, when the true noble-
man broke in on their high life below stairs, we were
destined to be confronted with a real pedlar. To make
the lesson still more poignant for fallen gentlemen like
us, he was a pedlar of infinitely more consideration than
the sort of scurvy fellows we were taken for: like a lion
among mice, or a ship of war bearing down upon two
cock-boats. Indeed, he did not deserve the name of
pedlar at all: he was a travelling merchant.

I suppose it was about half-past eight when this
worthy, Monsieur *Hector Gilliard* of *Maubeuge*, turned
up at the ale-house door in a tilt-cart drawn by a donkey,
and cried cheerily on the inhabitants. He was a lean,
nervous flibbertigibbet of a man, with something the
look of an actor, and something the look of a horse
jockey. He had evidently prospered without any of
the favours of education; for he adhered with stern
simplicity to the masculine gender, and in the course of
the evening passed off some fancy futures in a very
florid style of architecture. With him came his wife, a
comely young woman with her hair tied in a yellow
kerchief, and their son, a little fellow of four, in a blouse
and military *képi*. It was notable that the child was
many degrees better dressed than either of the parents.
We were informed he was already at a boarding school;
but the holidays having just commenced, he was off to
spend them with his parents on a cruise. An enchanting
holiday occupation, was it not? to travel all day with
father and mother in the tilt-cart full of countless

treasures: the green country rattling by on either side and the children in all the villages contemplating him with envy and wonder? It is better fun, during the holidays, to be the son of a travelling merchant, than son and heir to the greatest cotton spinner in creation. And as for being a reigning prince—indeed I never saw one if it was not Master *Gilliard*!

While M. *Hector* and the son of the house were putting up the donkey, and getting all the valuables under lock and key, the landlady warmed up the remains of our beefsteak, and fried the cold potatoes in slices, and Madame *Gilliard* set herself to waken the boy, who had come far that day, and was peevish and dazzled by the light. He was no sooner awake than he began to prepare himself for supper by eating galette, unripe pears and cold potatoes—with, so far as I could judge, positive benefit to his appetite.

The landlady, fired with motherly emulation, awoke her own little girl; and the two children were confronted. Master *Gilliard* looked at her for a moment, very much as a dog looks at his own reflection in a mirror before he turns away. He was at that time absorbed in the galette. His mother seemed crestfallen that he should display so little inclination towards the other sex; and expressed her disappointment with some candour and a very proper reference to the influence of years.

Sure enough a time will come when he will pay more attention to the girls, and think a great deal less of his mother: let us hope she will like it as well as she seemed to fancy. But it is odd enough; the very women who profess most contempt for mankind as a sex, seem to find even its ugliest particulars rather lively and high-minded in their own sons.

The little girl looked longer and with more interest, probably because she was in her own house, while he was a traveller and accustomed to strange sights. And besides, there was no galette in the case with her.

All the time of supper, there was nothing spoken of but my young lord. The two parents were both absurdly fond of their child. Monsieur kept insisting on his sagacity: how he knew all the children at school by name; and when this utterly failed on trial, how he was cautious and exact to a strange degree, and if asked anything, he would sit and think—and think, and if he did not know it, "my faith, he wouldn't tell you at all—*ma foi, il ne vous le dira pas.*" Which is certainly a very high degree of caution. At intervals, M. *Hector* would appeal to his wife, with his mouth full of beefsteak, as to the little fellow's age at such or such a time when he had said or done something memorable; and I noticed that Madame usually pooh-poohed these inquiries. She herself was not boastful in her vein; but she never had her fill of caressing the child; and she seemed to take a gentle pleasure in recalling all that was fortunate in his little existence. No schoolboy could have talked more of the holidays which were just beginning and less of the black schooltime which must inevitably follow after. She showed, with a pride perhaps partly mercantile in origin, his pockets preposterously swollen with tops and whistles and string. When she called at a house in the way of business, it appeared he kept her company; and whenever a sale was made, received a sou out of the profit. Indeed they spoiled him vastly, these two good people. But they had an eye to his manners for all that, and reproved him for some little faults in breeding which occurred from time to time during supper.

On the whole, I was not much hurt at being taken for
a pedlar. I might think that I ate with greater delicacy,
or that my mistakes in French belonged to a different
order; but it was plain that these distinctions would
be thrown away upon the landlady and the two labourers.
In all essential things, we and the *Gilliards* cut very
much the same figure in the ale-house kitchen. M.
Hector was more at home, indeed, and took a higher
tone with the world; but that was explicable on the
ground of his driving a donkey-cart, while we poor
bodies tramped afoot. I daresay the rest of the company thought us dying with envy, though in no ill sense,
to be as far up in the profession as the new arrival.

And of one thing I am sure: that everyone thawed
and became more humanised and conversible as soon
as these innocent people appeared upon the scene.
I would not very readily trust the travelling merchant
with any extravagant sum of money; but I am sure his
heart was in the right place. In this mixed world, if
you can find one or two sensible places in a man, above
all, if you should find a whole family living together on
such pleasant terms, you may surely be satisfied, and
take the rest for granted; or, what is a great deal better,
boldly make up your mind that you can do perfectly
well without the rest; and that ten thousand bad traits
cannot make a single good one any the less good.

It was getting late. M. *Hector* lit a stable lantern and
went off to his cart for some arrangements; and my
young gentleman proceeded to divest himself of the
better part of his raiment, and play gymnastics on his
mother's lap, and thence on to the floor, with accompaniment of laughter.

"Are you going to sleep alone?" asked the servant lass.

"There's little fear of that," says Master *Gilliard*.

"You sleep alone at school," objected his mother.
"Come, come, you must be a man."

But he protested that school was a different matter
from the holidays; that there were dormitories at school;
and silenced the discussion with kisses: his mother
smiling, no one better pleased than she.

There certainly was, as he phrased it, very little fear
that he should sleep alone; for there was but one bed
for the trio. We, on our part, had firmly protested
against one man's accommodation for two; and we had a
double-bedded pen in the loft of the house, furnished,
beside the beds, with exactly three hat-pegs and one
table. There was not so much as a glass of water. But
the window would open, by good fortune.

Some time before I fell asleep the loft was full of the
sound of mighty snoring: the *Gilliards*, and the labourers,
and the people of the inn, all at it, I suppose, with one
consent. The young moon outside shone very clearly
over *Pont-sur-Sambre*, and down upon the ale-house
where all we pedlars were abed.

ON THE SAMBRE CANALISED:

TO LANDRECIES

In the morning, when we came downstairs, the landlady
pointed out to us two pails of water behind the street-
door. *"Voilà de l'eau pour vous débarbouiller,"* says she.
And so there we made shift to wash ourselves, while
Madame *Gilliard* brushed the family boots on the outer
doorstep, and M. *Hector*, whistling cheerily, arranged
some small goods for the day's campaign in a portable
chest of drawers, which formed a part of his baggage.

Meanwhile the child was letting off *Waterloo* crackers all over the floor.

I wonder, by-the-by, what they call *Waterloo* crackers in *France*; perhaps *Austerlitz* crackers. There is a great deal in the point of view. Do you remember the *Frenchman* who, travelling by way of *Southampton*, was put down in *Waterloo* Station, and had to drive across *Waterloo* Bridge? He had a mind to go home again, it seems.

Pont itself is on the river, but whereas it is ten minutes' walk from *Quartes* by dry land, it is six weary kilometres by water. We left our bags at the inn, and walked to our canoes through the wet orchards unencumbered. Some of the children were there to see us off, but we were no longer the mysterious beings of the night before. A departure is much less romantic than an unexplained arrival in the golden evening. Although we might be greatly taken at a ghost's first appearance, we should behold him vanish with comparative equanimity.

The good folk of the inn at *Pont*, when we called there for the bags, were overcome with marvelling. At sight of these two dainty little boats, with a fluttering Union Jack on each, and all the varnish shining from the sponge, they began to perceive that they had entertained angels unawares. The landlady stood upon the bridge, probably lamenting she had charged so little; the son ran to and fro, and called out the neighbours to enjoy the sight; and we paddled away from quite a crowd of rapt observers. These gentlemen pedlars, indeed! Now you see their quality too late.

The whole day was showery, with occasional drenching plumps. We were soaked to the skin, then partially dried in the sun, then soaked once more. But there were some calm intervals, and one notably, when we

were skirting the forest of *Mormal*, a sinister name to
the ear, but a place most gratifying to sight and smell.
It looked solemn along the river-side, drooping its
boughs into the water, and piling them up aloft into a
wall of leaves. What is a forest but a city of Nature's
own, full of hardy and innocuous living things, where
there is nothing dead and nothing made with the hands,
but the citizens themselves are the houses and public
monuments? There is nothing so much alive, and yet
so quiet, as a woodland; and a pair of people, swinging
past in canoes, feel very small and bustling by comparison.

And surely of all smells in the world, the smell of many
trees is the sweetest and most fortifying. The sea has
a rude, pistolling sort of odour, that takes you in
the nostrils like snuff, and carries with it a fine sentiment
of open water and tall ships; but the smell of a forest,
which comes nearest to this in tonic quality, surpasses
it by many degrees in the quality of softness. Again,
the smell of the sea has little variety, but the smell of
a forest is infinitely changeful; it varies with the hour of
the day, not in strength merely, but in character; and
the different sorts of trees, as you go from one zone of
the wood to another, seem to live among different kinds
of atmosphere. Usually the resin of the fir predomin-
ates. But some woods are more coquettish in their
habits; and the breath of the forest of *Mormal*, as it
came aboard upon us that showery afternoon, was
perfumed with nothing less delicate than sweetbriar.

I wish our way had always lain among woods. Trees
are the most civil society. An old oak that has been
growing where he stands since before the Reformation,
taller than many spires, more stately than the greater
part of mountains, and yet a living thing, liable to sick-

nesses and death, like you and me: is not that in itself
a speaking lesson in history? But acres on acres full
of such patriarchs contiguously rooted, their green tops
billowing in the wind, their stalwart younglings pushing
up about their knees: a whole forest, healthy and beautiful, giving colour to the light, giving perfume to the air:
what is this but the most imposing piece in Nature's
repertory? *Heine* wished to lie like *Merlin* under the
oaks of *Broceliande.* I should not be satisfied with one
tree; but if the wood grew together like a banyan grove,
I would be buried under the tap-root of the whole; my
parts should circulate from oak to oak; and my consciousness should be diffused abroad in all the forest, and give a
common heart to that assembly of green spires, so that
it also might rejoice in its own loveliness and dignity.
I think I feel a thousand squirrels leaping from bough
to bough in my vast mausoleum; and the birds and the
winds merrily coursing over its uneven leafy surface.

Alas! the forest of *Mormal* is only a little bit of a wood,
and it was but for a little way that we skirted by its
boundaries. And the rest of the time the rain kept
coming in squirts and the wind in squalls, until one's
heart grew weary of such fitful, scolding weather. It
was odd how the showers began when we had to carry
the boats over a lock, and must expose our legs. They
always did. This is a sort of thing that readily begets a
personal feeling against Nature. There seems no reason
why the shower should not come five minutes before or
five minutes after, unless you suppose an intention
to affront you. The *Cigarette* had a mackintosh which
put him more or less above these contrarieties. But
I had to bear the brunt uncovered. I began to remember
that Nature was a woman. My companion, in a rosier
temper, listened with great satisfaction to my jeremiads,

and ironically concurred. He instanced, as a cognate matter, the action of the tides, "Which," said he, "was altogether designed for the confusion of canoeists, except in so far as it was calculated to minister to a barren vanity on the part of the moon."

At the last lock, some little way out of *Landrecies*, I refused to go any further; and sat in a drift of rain by the side of the bank, to have a reviving pipe. A vivacious old man, whom I take to have been the devil, drew near and questioned me about our journey. In the fulness of my heart, I laid bare our plans before him. He said, it was the silliest enterprise that ever he heard of. Why, did I not know, he asked me, that it was nothing but locks, locks, locks, the whole way? not to mention that, at this season of the year, we should find the *Oise* quite dry? "Get into a train, my little young man," said he, "and go you away home to your parents." I was so astounded at the man's malice, that I could only stare at him in silence. A tree would never have spoken to me like this. At last, I got out with some words. We had come from *Antwerp* already, I told him, which was a good long way; and we should do the rest in spite of him. Yes, I said, if there were no other reason, I would do it now, just because he had dared to say we could not. The pleasant old gentleman looked at me sneeringly, made an allusion to my canoe, and marched off, wagging his head.

I was still inwardly fuming, when up came a pair of young fellows, who imagined I was the *Cigarette's* servant, on a comparison, I suppose, of my bare jersey with the other's mackintosh, and asked me many questions about my place and my master's character. I said he was a good enough fellow, but had this absurd voyage on the head. "O no, no," said one, "you must not say that; it is not absurd; it is very courageous of him." I believe these were a couple of angels sent to give me heart again. It was truly fortifying to reproduce all the old man's insinuations, as if they were original to me in my character of a malcontent footman, and have them brushed away like so many flies by these admirable young men.

When I recounted this affair to the *Cigarette*, "They must have a curious idea of how English servants behave," says he, dryly, "for you treated me like a brute-beast at the lock."

I was a good deal mortified; but my temper had suffered, it is a fact.

AT LANDRECIES

AT *Landrecies* the rain still fell and the wind still blew; but we found a double-bedded room with plenty of furniture, real water-jugs with real water in them, and dinner: a real dinner, not innocent of real wine. After having been a pedlar for one night, and a butt for the elements during the whole of the next day, these comfortable circumstances fell on my heart like sunshine. There was an English fruiterer at dinner, travelling with a Belgian fruiterer; in the evening at the *café*, we watched out compatriot drop a good deal of money at corks; and I don't know why, but this pleased us.

It turned out that we were to see more of *Landrecies* than we expected; for the weather next day was simply bedlamite. It is not the place one would have chosen for a day's rest; for it consists almost entirely of fortifications. Within the ramparts, a few blocks of houses, a long row of barracks, and a church, figure, with what

countenance they may, as the town. There seems to
be no trade; and a shopkeeper from whom I bought a
sixpenny flint and steel was so much affected, that he
filled my pockets with spare flints into the bargain. The
only public buildings that had any interest for us were
the hotel and the *café*. But we visited the church.
There lies Marshal *Clarke*. But as neither of us had ever
heard of that military hero, we bore the associations
of the spot with fortitude.

In all garrison towns, guard-calls, and *réveilles* and
such like, make a fine romantic interlude in civic business.
Bugles, and drums, and fifes, are of themselves most
excellent things in nature; and when they carry the
mind to marching armies, and the picturesque vicissi-
tudes of war, they stir up something proud in the heart.
But in a shadow of a town like *Landrecies*, with little
else moving, these points of war made a proportionate
commotion. Indeed, they were the only things to
remember. It was just the place to hear the round
going by night in the darkness, with the solid tramp of
men marching, and the startling reverberations of the
drum. It reminded you that even this place was a
point in the great warfaring system of *Europe*, and might
on some future day be ringed about with cannon smoke
and thunder, and make itself a name among strong towns.

The drum, at any rate, from its martial voice and
notable physiological effect, nay even from its cumbrous
and comical shape, stands alone among the instruments
of noise. And if it be true, as I have heard it said, that
drums are covered with asses' skin, what a picturesque
irony is there in that! As if this long-suffering animal's
hide had not been sufficiently belaboured during life,
now by Lyonnese costermongers, now by presumptuous
Hebrew prophets, it must be stripped from his poor

hinder quarters after death, stretched on a drum, and beaten night after night round the streets of every garrison town in *Europe*. And up the heights of *Alma* and *Spicheren*, and wherever death has his red flag a-flying, and sounds his own potent tuck upon the cannons, there also must the drummer-boy, hurrying with white face over fallen comrades, batter and bemaul this slip of skin from the loins of peaceable donkeys.

Generally a man is never more uselessly employed than when he is at this trick of bastinadoing asses' hide. We know what effect it has in life, and how your dull ass will not mend his pace with beating. But in this state of mummy and melancholy survival of itself, when the hollow skin reverberates to the drummer's wrist, and each dub-a-dub goes direct to a man's heart, and puts madness there, and that disposition of the pulses which we, in our big way of talking, nickname Heroism:—is there not something in the nature of a revenge upon the donkey's persecutors? Of old, he might say, you drubbed me up hill and down dale, and I must endure; but now that I am dead, those dull thwacks that were scarcely audible in country lanes have become stirring music in front of the brigade; and for every blow that you lay on my old great-coat, you will see a comrade stumble and fall.

Not long after the drums had passed the *café*, the *Cigarette* and the *Arethusa* began to grow sleepy, and set out for the hotel which was only a door or two away. But although we had been somewhat indifferent to *Landrecies*, *Landrecies* had not been indifferent to us. All day, we learned, people had been running out between the squalls to visit our two boats. Hundreds of persons, so said report, although it fitted ill with our idea of the town—hundreds of persons had inspected them

where they lay in a coal-shed. We were becoming lions
in *Landrecies*, who had been only pedlars the night
before in *Pont*.

And now, when we left the *café*, we were pursued and
overtaken at the hotel door by no less a person than the
Juge de Paix: a functionary, as far as I can make out,
of the character of a Scotch *Sheriff Substitute*. He gave
us his card and invited us to sup with him on the spot,
very neatly, very gracefully, as *Frenchmen* can do these
things. It was for the credit of *Landrecies*, said he;
and although we knew very well how little credit we
could do the place, we must have been churlish fellows
to refuse an invitation so politely introduced.

The house of the Judge was close by; it was a well-
appointed bachelor's establishment with a curious
collection of old brass warming-pans upon the walls.
Some of these were most elaborately carved. It seemed
a picturesque idea for a collector. You could not help
thinking how many nightcaps had wagged over these
warming-pans in past generations; what jests may have
been made, and kisses taken, while they were in service;
and how often they had been uselessly paraded in the
bed of death. If they could only speak, at what absurd,
indecorous and tragical scenes had they not been present!

The wine was excellent. When we made the Judge
our compliments upon a bottle, "I do not give it you
as my worst," said he. I wonder when *Englishmen* will
learn these hospitable graces. They are worth learning;
they set off life, and make ordinary moments ornamental.

There were two other *Landrecienses* present. One
was the collector of something or other, I forget what;
the other, we were told, was the principal notary of the
place. So it happened that we all five more or less
followed the law. At this rate, the talk was pretty

certain to become technical. The *Cigarette* expounded
the Poor Laws very magisterially. And a little later I
found myself laying down the Scotch Law of Illegitimacy,
of which I am glad to say I know nothing. The collector
and the notary, who were both married men, accused
the Judge, who was a bachelor, of having started the
subject. He deprecated the charge, with a conscious,
pleased air, just like all the men I have ever seen, be
they French or English. How strange that we should
all, in our unguarded moments, rather like to be thought
a bit of a rogue with the women!

As the evening went on, the wine grew more to my
taste; the spirits proved better than the wine; the company was genial. This was the highest water-mark of
popular favour on the whole cruise. After all, being
in a Judge's house, was there not something semi-official
in the tribute? And so, remembering what a great
country *France* is, we did full justice to our entertainment. *Landrecies* had been a long while asleep before
we returned to the hotel; and the sentries on the ramparts
were already looking for daybreak.

SAMBRE AND OISE CANAL:

CANAL BOATS

NEXT day we made a late start in the rain. The Judge
politely escorted us to the end of the lock under an
umbrella. We had now brought ourselves to a pitch
of humility in the matter of weather, not often attained
except in the Scotch *Highlands*. A rag of blue sky or
a glimpse of sunshine set our hearts singing; and when
the rain was not heavy, we counted the day almost fair.

Long lines of barges lay one after another along the canal; many of them looking mighty spruce and ship-shape in their jerkin of *Archangel* tar picked out with white and green. Some carried gay iron railings, and quite a parterre of flower-pots. Children played on the decks, as heedless of the rain as if they had been brought up on *Loch Carron* side; men fished over the gunwale, some of them under umbrellas; women did their washing; and every barge boasted its mongrel cur by way of watch-dog. Each one barked furiously at the canoes, running alongside until he had got to the end of his own ship, and so passing on the word to the dog aboard the next. We must have seen something like a hundred of these embarkations in the course of that day's paddle, ranged one after another like the houses in a street; and from not one of them were we disappointed of this accompaniment. It was like visiting a menagerie, the *Cigarette* remarked.

These little cities by the canal side had a very odd effect upon the mind. They seemed, with their flower-pots and smoking chimneys, their washings and dinners, a rooted piece of Nature in the scene; and yet if only the canal below were to open, one junk after another would hoist sail or harness horses and swim away into all parts of *France*; and the impromptu hamlet would separate, house by house, to the four winds. The children who played together to-day by the *Sambre* and *Oise* Canal, each at his own father's threshold, when and where might they next meet?

For some time past the subject of barges had occupied a great deal of our talk, and we had projected an old age on the canals of *Europe*. It was to be the most leisurely of progresses, now on a swift river at the tail of a steamboat, now waiting horses for days together on some inconsiderable junction. We should be seen pottering on deck in all the dignity of years, our white beards falling into our laps. We were ever to be busied among paint-pots; so that there should be no white fresher, and no green more emerald than ours, in all the navy of the canals. There should be books in the cabin, and tobacco jars, and some old *Burgundy* as red as a *November* sunset and as odorous as a violet in *April*. There should be a flageolet whence the *Cigarette*, with cunning touch, should draw melting music under the stars; or perhaps, laying that aside, upraise his voice—somewhat thinner than of yore, and with here and there a quaver, or call it a natural grace note—in rich and solemn psalmody.

All this simmering in my mind, set me wishing to go aboard one of these ideal houses of lounging. I had plenty to choose from, as I coasted one after another, and the dogs bayed at me for a vagrant. At last I saw a nice old man and his wife looking at me with some interest, so I gave them good day and pulled up alongside. I began with a remark upon their dog, which had somewhat the look of a pointer; thence I slid into a compliment on Madame's flowers, and thence into a word in praise of their way of life.

If you ventured on such an experiment in *England* you would get a slap in the face at once. The life would be shown to be a vile one, not without a side shot at your better fortune. Now, what I like so much in *France* is the clear unflinching recognition by everybody of his own luck. They all know on which side their bread is buttered, and take a pleasure in showing it to others, which is surely the better part of religion. And they scorn to make a poor mouth over their poverty, which I take to be the better part of manliness. I have heard a woman in quite a better position at home, with

a good bit of money in hand, refer to her own child with
a horrid whine as "a poor man's child." I would not
say such a thing to the Duke of *Westminster*. And the
French are full of this spirit of independence. Perhaps it is
the result of republican institutions, as they call them.
Much more likely it is because there are so few people
really poor that the whiners are not enough to keep
each other in countenance.

The people on the barge were delighted to hear that
I admired their state. They understood perfectly well,
they told me, how Monsieur envied them. Without
doubt Monsieur was rich; and in that case he might
make a canal-boat as pretty as a villa—*joli comme un
château*. And with that they invited me on board their
own water villa. They apologised for their cabin;
they had not been rich enough to make it as it ought
to be.

"The fire should have been here, at this side," explained
the husband. "Then one might have a writing-table in
the middle—books—and" (comprehensively) "all. It
would be quite coquettish—*ça serait tout-à-fait coquet*."
And he looked about him as though the improvements
were already made. It was plainly not the first time
that he had thus beautified his cabin in imagination;
and when next he makes a hit, I should expect to see the
writing-table in the middle.

Madame had three birds in a cage. They were no
great thing, she explained. Fine birds were so dear.
They had sought to get a *Hollandais* last winter in
Rouen (*Rouen?* thought I; and is this whole mansion,
with its dogs and birds and smoking chimneys, so far
a traveller as that? and as homely an object among the
cliffs and orchards of the *Seine* as on the green plains of
Sambre?)—they had sought to get a *Hollandais* last

winter in *Rouen*; but these cost fifteen francs apiece—
picture it—fifteen francs!

"*Pour un tout petit oiseau*—For quite a little bird,"
added the husband.

As I continued to admire, the apologetics died away,
and the good people began to brag of their barge, and
their happy condition in life, as if they had been Em-
peror and Empress of the *Indies*. It was, in the Scotch
phrase, a good hearing, and put me in good humour
with the world. If people knew what an inspiriting
thing it is to hear a man boasting, so long as he boasts
of what he really has, I believe they would do it more
freely and with a better grace.

They began to ask about our voyage. You should
have seen how they sympathised. They seemed half
ready to give up their barge and follow us. But these
canaletti are only gipsies semi-domesticated. The semi-
domestication came out in rather a pretty form. Suddenly Madame's brow darkened. "*Cependant*," she began,
and then stopped; and then began again by asking
me if I were single?

"Yes," said I.

"And your friend who went by just now?"

He also was unmarried.

O then—all was well. She could not have wives left
alone at home; but since there were no wives in the
question, we were doing the best we could.

"To see about one in the world," said the husband,
"*il n'y a que ça*—there is nothing else worth while. A
man, look you, who sticks in his own village like a bear,"
he went on,—"very well, he sees nothing. And then
death is the end of all. And he has seen nothing."

Madame reminded her husband of an *Englishman*
who had come up this canal in a steamer.

"Perhaps Mr. *Moens* in the *Ytene*," I suggested.

"That's it," assented the husband. "He had his wife and family with him, and servants. He came ashore at all the locks and asked the name of the villages, whether from boatmen or lock-keepers; and then he wrote, wrote them down. O he wrote enormously! I suppose it was a wager."

A wager was a common enough explanation for our own exploits, but it seemed an original reason for taking notes.

THE OISE IN FLOOD

BEFORE nine next morning the two canoes were installed on a light country cart at *Étreux*: and we were soon following them along the side of a pleasant valley full of hop-gardens and poplars. Agreeable villages lay here and there on the slope of the hill; notably *Tupigny*, with the hop-poles hanging their garlands in the very street, and the houses clustered with grapes. There was a faint enthusiasm on our passage; weavers put their heads to the windows; children cried out in ecstasy at sight of the two "boaties"—*barquettes*: and bloused pedestrians, who were acquainted with our charioteer, jested with him on the nature of his freight.

We had a shower or two, but light and flying. The air was clean and sweet among all these green fields and green things growing. There was not a touch of autumn in the weather. And when, at *Vadencourt*, we launched from a little lawn opposite a mill, the sun broke forth and set all the leaves shining in the valley of the *Oise*.

The river was swollen with the long rains. From *Vadencourt* all the way to *Origny* it ran with ever-quick-

ening speed, taking fresh heart at each mile, and racing
as though it already smelt the sea. The water was
yellow and turbulent, swung with an angry eddy among
half-submerged willows, and made an angry clatter
along stony shores. The course kept turning and turning
in a narrow and well-timbered valley. Now, the river
would approach the side, and run gliding along the
chalky base of the hill, and show us a few open colza
fields among the trees. Now, it would skirt the garden-
walls of houses, where we might catch a glimpse through
a doorway, and see a priest pacing in the chequered
sunlight. Again, the foliage closed so thickly in front,
that there seemed to be no issue; only a thicket of
willows, overtopped by elms and poplars, under which
the river ran flush and fleet, and where a kingfisher flew
past like a piece of the blue sky. On these different
manifestations the sun poured its clear and catholic
looks. The shadows lay as solid on the swift surface of
the stream as on the stable meadows. The light sparkled
golden in the dancing poplar leaves, and brought the
hills into communion with our eyes. And all the while
the river never stopped running or took breath; and the
reeds along the whole valley stood shivering from top
to toe.

There should be some myth (but if there is, I know it
not) founded on the shivering of the reeds. There are
not many things in Nature more striking to man's eye.
It is such an eloquent pantomime of terror; and to see
such a number of terrified creatures taking sanctuary
in every nook along the shore, is enough to infect a silly
human with alarm. Perhaps they are only a-cold, and
no wonder, standing waist deep in the stream. Or perhaps
they have never got accustomed to the speed and fury
of the river's flux, or the miracle of its continuous body.

Pan once played upon their forefathers; and so, by the hands of his river, he still plays upon these later generations down all the valley of the *Oise*; and plays the same air, both sweet and shrill, to tell us of the beauty and the terror of the world.

The canoe was like a leaf in the current. It took it up and shook it, and carried it masterfully away, like a Centaur carrying off a nymph. To keep some command on our direction required hard and diligent plying of the paddle. The river was in such a hurry for the sea! Every drop of water ran in a panic, like as many people in a frightened crowd. But what crowd was ever so numerous, or so single-minded? All the objects of sight went by at a dance measure; the eyesight raced with the racing river; the exigencies of every moment kept the pegs screwed so tight, that our being quivered like a well-tuned instrument; and the blood shook off its lethargy, and trotted through all the highways and byeways of the veins and arteries, and in and out of the heart, as if circulation were but a holiday journey, and not the daily moil of threescore years and ten. The reeds might nod their heads in warning, and with tremulous gestures tell how the river was as cruel as it was strong and cold, and how death lurked in the eddy underneath the willows. But the reeds had to stand where they were; and those who stand still are always timid advisers. As for us, we could have shouted aloud. If this lively and beautiful river were, indeed, a thing of death's contrivance, the old ashen rogue had famously outwitted himself with us. I was living three to the minute. I was scoring points against him every stroke of my paddle, every turn of the stream. I have rarely had better profit of my life.

For I think we may look upon our little private war

c

with death somewhat in this light. If a man knows he
will sooner or later be robbed upon a journey, he will
have a bottle of the best in every inn, and look upon all
his extravagances as so much gained upon the thieves.
And above all, where instead of simply spending, he
makes a profitable investment for some of his money,
when it will be out of risk of loss. So every bit of brisk
living, and above all when it is healthful, is just so much
gained upon the wholesale filcher, death. We shall have
the less in our pockets, the more in our stomach, when
he cries stand and deliver. A swift stream is a favourite
artifice of his, and one that brings him in a comfortable
thing per annum; but when he and I come to settle our
accounts, I shall whistle in his face for these hours upon
the upper *Oise*.

Towards afternoon we got fairly drunken with the
sunshine and the exhilaration of the pace. We could no
longer contain ourselves and our content. The canoes
were too small for us; we must be out and stretch ourselves on shore. And so in a green meadow we bestowed
our limbs on the grass, and smoked deifying tobacco
and proclaimed the world excellent. It was the last
good hour of the day, and I dwell upon it with extreme
complacency.

On one side of the valley, high upon the chalky summit
of the hill, a ploughman with his team appeared and
disappeared at regular intervals. At each revelation
he stood still for a few seconds against the sky: for all
the world (as the *Cigarette* declared) like a toy *Burns*
who had just ploughed up the *Mountain Daisy*. He
was the only living thing within view, unless we are to
count the river.

On the other side of the valley a group of red roofs
and a belfrey showed among the foliage. Thence some

inspired bell-ringer made the afternoon musical on a chime of bells. There was something very sweet and taking in the air he played; and we thought we had never heard bells speak so intelligibly, or sing so melodiously, as these. It must have been to some such measure that the spinners and the young maids sang, "Come away, Death," in the Shakespearean *Illyria*. There is so often a threatening note, something blatant and metallic, in the voice of bells, that I believe we have fully more pain than pleasure from hearing them; but these, as they sounded abroad, now high, now low, now with a plaintive cadence that caught the ear like the burthen of a popular song, were always moderate and tunable, and seemed to fall in with the spirit of still, rustic places, like the noise of a waterfall or the babble of a rookery in spring. I could have asked the bell-ringer for his blessing, good, sedate old man, who swung the rope so gently to the time of his meditations. I could have blessed the priest or the heritors, or whoever may be concerned with such affairs in *France*, who had left these sweet old bells to gladden the afternoon, and not held meetings, and made collections, and had their names repeatedly printed in the local paper, to rig up a peal of brand-new, brazen, *Birmingham*-hearted substitutes, who should bombard their sides to the provocation of a brand-new bell-ringer, and fill the echoes of the valley with terror and riot.

At last the bells ceased, and with their note the sun withdrew. The piece was at an end; shadow and silence possessed the valley of the *Oise*. We took to the paddle with glad hearts, like people who have sat out a noble performance and return to work. The river was more dangerous here; it ran swifter, the eddies were more sudden and violent. All the way down we had had our fill of difficulties. Sometimes it was a weir which could be shot, sometimes one so shallow and full of stakes that we must withdraw the boats from the water and carry them round. But the chief sort of obstacle was a consequence of the late high winds. Every two or three hundred yards a tree had fallen across the river and usually involved more than another in its fall. Often there was free water at the end, and we could steer round the leafy promontory and hear the water sucking and bubbling among the twigs. Often, again, when the tree reached from bank to bank, there was room, by lying close, to shoot through underneath, canoe and all. Sometimes it was necessary to get out upon the trunk itself and pull the boats across; and sometimes, where the stream was too impetuous for this, there was nothing for it but to land and "carry over." This made a fine series of accidents in the day's career, and kept us aware of ourselves.

Shortly after our re-embarkation, while I was leading by a long way, and still full of a noble, exulting spirit in honour of the sun, the swift pace, and the church bells, the river made one of its leonine pounces round a corner, and I was aware of another fallen tree within a stone-cast. I had my backboard down in a trice, and aimed for a place where the trunk seemed high enough above the water, and the branches not too thick to let me slip below. When a man has just vowed eternal brotherhood with the universe, he is not in a temper to take great determinations coolly, and this, which might have been a very important determination for me, had not been taken under a happy star. The tree caught me about the chest, and while I was yet struggling to make less of myself and get through, the river took the matter out of my hands and bereaved me of my boat. The

Arethusa swung round broadside on, leaned over, ejected so much of me as still remained on board, and thus disencumbered, whipped under the tree, righted, and went merrily away down-stream.

I do not know how long it was before I scrambled on to the tree to which I was left clinging, but it was longer than I cared about. My thoughts were of a grave and almost sombre character, but I still clung to my paddle. The stream ran away with my heels as fast as I could pull up my shoulders, and I seemed, by the weight, to have all the water of the *Oise* in my trouser pockets. You can never know, till you try it, what a dead pull a river makes against a man. Death himself had me by the heels, for this was his last ambuscade, and he must now join personally in the fray. And still I held to my paddle. At last I dragged myself on to my stomach on the trunk, and lay there a breathless sop, with a mingled sense of humour and injustice. A poor figure I must have presented to *Burns* upon the hill-top with his team. But there was the paddle in my hand. On my tomb, if ever I have one, I mean to get these words inscribed: "He clung to his paddle."

The *Cigarette* had gone past a while before; for, as I might have observed, if I had been a little less pleased with the universe at the moment, there was a clear way round the tree-top at the farther side. He had offered his services to haul me out, but as I was then already on my elbows, I had declined, and sent him down-stream after the truant *Arethusa*. The stream was too rapid for a man to mount with one canoe, let alone two, upon his hands. So I crawled along the trunk to shore, and proceeded down the meadows by the river-side. I was so cold that my heart was sore. I had now an idea of my own, why the reeds so bitterly shivered. I could have given any of them a lesson. The *Cigarette* remarked facetiously, that he thought I was "taking exercise" as I drew near, until he made out for certain that I was only twittering with cold. I had a rub down with a towel, and donned a dry suit from the india-rubber bag. But I was not my own man again for the rest of the voyage. I had a queasy sense that I wore my last dry clothes upon my body. The struggle had tired me; and perhaps, whether I knew it or not, I was a little dashed in spirit. The devouring element in the universe had leaped out against me, in this green valley quickened by a running stream. The bells were all very pretty in their way, but I had heard some of the hollow notes of *Pan's* music. Would the wicked river drag me down by the heels, indeed? and look so beautiful all the time? Nature's good-humour was only skin-deep after all.

There was still a long way to go by the winding course of the stream, and darkness had fallen, and a late bell was ringing in *Origny Sainte-Benoîte*, when we arrived.

ORIGNY SAINTE-BENOÎTE

A BY-DAY

The next day was *Sunday*, and the church bells had little rest; indeed I do not think I remember anywhere else so great a choice of services as were here offered to the devout. And while the bells made merry in the sunshine, all the world with his dog was out shooting among the beets and colza.

In the morning a hawker and his wife went down the street at a foot-pace, singing to a very slow, lamentable music, "*O France, mes amours.*" It brought everybody

to the door; and when our landlady called in the man to
buy the words, he had not a copy of them left. She
was not the first nor the second who had been taken with
the song. There is something very pathetic in the love
of the French people, since the war, for dismal patriotic
music-making. I have watched a forester from *Alsace*
while someone was singing "*Les malheurs de la France*"
at a baptismal party in the neighbourhood of *Fontainebleau*. He arose from the table and took his son aside,
close by where I was standing. "Listen, listen," he said,
bearing on the boy's shoulder, "and remember this, my
son." A little after he went out into the garden suddenly, and I could hear him sobbing in the darkness.

The humiliation of their arms and the loss of *Alsace*
and *Lorraine* made a sore pull on the endurance of this
sensitive people; and their hearts are still hot, not so
much against *Germany* as against the Empire. In what
other country will you find a patriotic ditty bring all the
world into the street? But affliction heightens love; and
we shall never know we are *Englishmen* until we have
lost *India*. Independent *America* is still the cross of
my existence; I cannot think of *Farmer George* without
abhorrence; and I never feel more warmly to my own
land than when I see the stars and stripes, and remember
what our empire might have been.

The hawker's little book, which I purchased, was a
curious mixture. Side by side with the flippant, rowdy
nonsense of the *Paris* music-halls, there were many
pastoral pieces, not without a touch of poetry, I thought,
and instinct with the brave independence of the poorer
class in *France*. There you might read how the wood-
cutter gloried in his axe, and the gardener scorned to be
ashamed of his spade. It was not very well written,
this poetry of labour, but the pluck of the sentiment

redeemed what was weak or wordy in the expression. The martial and the patriotic pieces, on the other hand, were tearful, womanish productions one and all. The poet had passed under the *Caudine Forks*; he sang for an army visiting the tomb of its old renown, with arms reversed; and sang not of victory, but of death. There was a number in the hawker's collection called *Conscrits Française* which may rank amongst the most dissuasive war-lyrics on record. It would not be possible to fight at all in such a spirit. The bravest conscript would turn pale if such a ditty were struck up beside him on the morning of battle; and whole regiments would pile their arms to its tune.

If *Fletcher* of *Saltoun* is in the right about the influence of national songs, you would say *France* was come to a poor pass. But the thing will work its own cure, and a sound-hearted and courageous people weary at length of snivelling over their disasters. Already *Paul Déroulède* has written some manly military verses. There is not much of the trumpet note in them, perhaps, to stir a man's heart in his bosom; they lack the lyrical elation, and move slowly; but they are written in a grave, honourable, stoical spirit, which should carry soldiers far in a good cause. One feels as if one would like to trust *Déroulède* with something. It will be happy if he can so far inoculate his fellow-countrymen that they may be trusted with their own future. And in the meantime, here is an antidote to "French Conscripts" and much other doleful versification.

We had left the boats over-night in the custody of one whom we shall call *Carnival*. I did not properly catch his name, and perhaps that was not unfortunate for him, as I am not in a position to hand him down with honour to posterity. To this person's premises we strolled in the course of the day, and found quite a little deputation inspecting the canoes. There was a stout gentleman with a knowledge of the river, which he seemed eager to impart. There was a very elegant young gentleman in a black coat, with a smattering of English, who led the talk at once to the *Oxford* and *Cambridge* boat race. And then there were three handsome girls from fifteen to twenty; and an old gentleman in a blouse, with no teeth to speak of, and a strong country accent. Quite the pick of *Origny*, I should suppose.

The *Cigarette* had some mysteries to perform with his rigging in the coach-house; so I was left to do the parade single-handed. I found myself very much of a hero whether I would or not. The girls were full of little shudderings over the dangers of our journey. And I thought it would be ungallant not to take my cue from the ladies. My mishap of yesterday, told in an off-hand way, produced a deep sensation. It was *Othello* over again, with no less than three *Desdemonas* and a sprinkling of sympathetic senators in the background. Never were the canoes more flattered, or flattered more adroitly.

"It is like a violin," cried one of the girls in an ecstasy.

"I thank you for the word, mademoiselle," said I. "All the more since there are people who call out to me, that it is like a coffin."

"O! but it is really like a violin. It is finished like a violin," she went on.

"And polished like a violin," added a senator.

"One has only to stretch the cords," concluded another, "and then tum-tumty-tum"—he imitated the result with spirit.

Was not this a graceful little ovation? Where this people finds the secret of its pretty speeches, I cannot imagine; unless the secret should be no other than a sincere desire to please? But then no disgrace is attached in *France* to saying a thing neatly; whereas in *England*, to talk like a book is to give in one's resignation to society.

The old gentleman in the blouse stole into the coach-house, and somewhat irrelevantly informed the *Cigarette* that he was the father of the three girls and four more; quite an exploit for a *Frenchman*.

"You are very fortunate," answered the *Cigarette* politely.

And the old gentleman, having apparently gained his point, stole away again.

We all got very friendly together. The girls proposed to start with us on the morrow, if you please! And jesting apart, everyone was anxious to know the hour of our departure. Now, when you are going to crawl into your canoe from a bad launch, a crowd, however friendly, is undesirable; and so we told them not before twelve, and mentally determined to be off by ten at latest.

Towards evening, we went abroad again to post some letters. It was cool and pleasant; the long village was quite empty, except for one or two urchins who followed us as they might have followed a menagerie; the hills and the tree-tops looked in from all sides through the clear air; and the bells were chiming for yet another service.

Suddenly, we sighted the three girls standing, with a fourth sister, in front of a shop on the wide selvage of the roadway. We had been very merry with them a little while ago, to be sure. But what was the etiquette of *Origny*? Had it been a country road, of course we should have spoken to them; but here, under the eyes of all the gossips, ought we to do even as much as bow? I consulted the *Cigarette*.

"Look," said he.

I looked. There were the four girls on the same spot; but now four backs were turned to us, very upright and conscious. Corporal Modesty had given the word of command, and the well-disciplined picket had gone right-about-face like a single person. They maintained this formation all the while we were in sight; but we heard them tittering among themselves, and the girl whom we had not met laughed with open mouth, and even looked over her shoulder at the enemy. I wonder was it altogether modesty after all? or in part a sort of country provocation?

As we were returning to the inn, we beheld something floating in the ample field of golden evening sky, above the chalk cliffs and the trees that grow along their summit. It was too high up, too large and too steady for a kite; and as it was dark, it could not be a star. For although a star were as black as ink and as rugged as a walnut, so amply does the sun bathe heaven with radiance that it would sparkle like a point of light for us. The village was dotted with people with their heads in air; and the children were in a bustle all along the street and far up the straight road that climbs the hill, where we could still see them running in loose knots. It was a balloon, we learned, which had left *Saint Quentin* at half-past five that evening. Mighty composedly the majority of the grown people took it. But we were English, and were soon running up the hill with the best. Being travellers ourselves in a small way, we would fain have seen these other travellers alight.

The spectacle was over by the time we gained the top of the hill. All the gold had withered out of the sky, and the balloon had disappeared. Whither? I ask myself; caught up into the seventh heaven? or come safely to land somewhere in that blue uneven distance, into which the roadway dipped and melted before our eyes? Probably the aeronauts were already warming themselves at a farm chimney, for they say it is cold in these unhomely regions of the air. The night fell swiftly. Roadside trees and disappointed sightseers, returning through the meadows, stood out in black against a margin of low red sunset. It was cheerfuller to face the other way, and so down the hill we went, with a full moon, the colour of a melon, swinging high above the wooded valley, and the white cliffs behind us faintly reddened by the fire of the chalk kilns.

The lamps were lighted, and the salads were being made in *Origny Sainte-Benoîte* by the river.

ORIGNY SAINTE-BENOÎTE

THE COMPANY AT TABLE

ALTHOUGH we came late for dinner, the company at table treated us to sparkling wine. "That is how we are in *France*," said one. "Those who sit down with us are our friends." And the rest applauded.

They were three altogether, and an odd trio to pass the *Sunday* with.

Two of them were guests like ourselves, both men of the north. One ruddy, and of a full habit of body, with copious black hair and beard, the intrepid hunter of *France*, who thought nothing so small, not even a lark or a minnow, but he might vindicate his prowess by its capture. For such a great, healthy man, his hair flourishing like *Samson's*, his arteries running buckets of red blood, to boast of these infinitesimal exploits produced a feeling of disproportion in the world, as when a steam-hammer is set to cracking nuts. The other was a quiet, subdued person, blond and lymphatic and sad, with something the look of a Dane: *"Tristes têtes de Danois!"* as *Gaston Lafenestre* used to say.

I must not let that name go by without a word for the best of all good fellows now gone down into the dust. We shall never again see *Gaston* in his forest costume—he was *Gaston* with all the world, in affection, not in disrespect—nor hear him wake the echoes of *Fontaine-bleau* with the woodland horn. Never again shall his kind smile put peace among all races of artistic men, and make the *Englishman* at home in *France*. Never more shall the sheep, who were not more innocent at heart than he, sit all unconsciously for his industrious pencil. He died too early, at the very moment when he was beginning to put forth fresh sprouts, and blossom into something worthy of himself; and yet none who knew him will think he lived in vain. I never knew a man so little, for whom yet I had so much affection; and I find it a good test of others, how much they had learned to understand and value him. His was indeed a good influence in life while he was still among us; he had a fresh laugh, it did you good to see him; and however sad he may have been at heart, he always bore a bold and cheerful countenance, and took fortune's worst as it were the showers of spring. But now his mother sits alone by the side of *Fontainebleau* woods, where he gathered mushrooms in his hardy and penurious youth.

Many of his pictures found their way across the Channel: besides those which were stolen, when a dastardly *Yankee* left him alone in *London* with two English pence, and perhaps twice as many words of English. If anyone who reads these lines should have a scene of sheep, in the manner of *Jacques*, with this fine creature's signature, let him tell himself that one of the kindest and bravest of men has lent a hand to decorate his lodging. There may be better pictures in the *National Gallery*; but not a painter among the generations had a better heart. Precious in the sight of the *Lord* of humanity, the *Psalms* tell us, is the death of His saints. It had need to be precious; for it is very costly, when by the stroke a mother is left desolate, and the peacemaker, and *peace-looker*, of a whole society is laid in the ground with *Cæsar* and the *Twelve Apostles*.

There is something lacking among the oaks of *Fontainebleau*; and when the dessert comes in at *Barbizon*, people look to the door for a figure that is gone.

The third of our companions at *Origny* was no less a person than the landlady's husband: not properly the landlord, since he worked himself in a factory during the day, and came to his own house at evening as a guest: a man worn to skin and bone by perpetual excitement, with baldish head, sharp features, and swift, shining eyes. On *Saturday*, describing some paltry adventure at a duck-hunt, he broke a plate into a score of fragments. Whenever he made a remark, he would look all round the table, with his chin raised, and a spark of green light in either eye, seeking approval. His wife appeared now and again in the doorway of the room, where she was superintending dinner, with a *"Henri*, you forget yourself," or a *"Henri*, you can surely talk without making such a noise." Indeed, that was what the honest fellow could not do. On the most trifling matter, his eyes kindled, his fist visited the table, and his voice rolled abroad in changeful thunder. I never saw such a petard of a man; I think the devil was in him. He had two favourite expressions: "it is logical," or illogical as the case might be: and this other, thrown out with a certain bravado, as a man might unfurl a banner, at the beginning of many a long and sonorous story: "I am a proletarian, you see." Indeed, we saw it very well. *God* forbid that ever I should find him handling a gun in *Paris* streets. That will not be a good moment for the general public.

I thought his two phrases very much represented the good and evil of his class, and to some extent of his country. It is a strong thing to say what one is, and not be ashamed of it; even although it be in doubtful taste to repeat the statement too often in one evening. I should not admire it in a duke, of course; but as times go, the trait is honourable in a workman. On the other hand, it is not at all a strong thing to put one's reliance upon logic; and our own logic particularly, for it is generally wrong. We never know where we are to end, if once we begin following words or doctors. There is an upright stock in a man's own heart, that is trustier than any syllogism; and the eyes, and the sympathies and appetites, know a thing or two that have never yet been stated in controversy. Reasons are as plentiful as blackberries; and like fisticuffs, they serve impartially with all sides. Doctrines do not stand or fall by their proofs, and are only logical in so far as they are cleverly put. An able controversialist no more than an able general demonstrates the justice of his cause. But *France* is all gone wandering after one or two big words; it will take some time before they can be satisfied that they are no more than words, however big; and when once that is done, they will perhaps find logic less diverting.

The conversation opened with details of the day's shooting. When all the sportsmen of a village shoot over the village territory *pro indiviso*, it is plain that many questions of etiquette and priority must arise.

"Here now," cried the landlord, brandishing a plate, "here is a field of beetroot. Well. Here am I then. I advance, do I not? *Eh bien! sacristi*," and the statement, waxing louder, rolls off into a reverberation of oaths, the speaker glaring about for sympathy, and everybody nodding his head to him in the name of peace.

The ruddy *Northman* told some tales of his own prowess in keeping order: notably one of a Marquis. "Marquis," I said, "if you take another step I fire upon you. You have committed a dirtiness, Marquis." Whereupon, it appeared, the Marquis touched his cap and withdrew.

The landlord applauded noisily. "It was well done," he said. "He did all that he could. He admitted he was wrong." And then oath upon oath. He was no marquis-lover either, but he had a sense of justice in him, this proletarian host of ours.

From the matter of hunting, the talk veered into a general comparison of *Paris* and the country. The proletarian beat the table like a drum in praise of *Paris*. "What is *Paris*? *Paris* is the cream of *France*. There are no Parisians: it is you and I and everybody who are Parisians. A man has eighty chances per cent. to get on in the world in *Paris*." And he drew a vivid sketch of the workman in a den no bigger than a dog-hutch, making articles that were to go all over the world. "*Eh bien, quoi, c'est magnifique, ça!*" cried he.

The sad *Northman* interfered in praise of a peasant's life; he thought *Paris* bad for men and women; "Centralisation," said he——

But the landlord was at his throat in a moment. It

was all logical, he showed him; and all magnificent.
"What a spectacle! What a glance for an eye!" And
the dishes reeled upon the table under a cannonade of
blows.

Seeking to make peace, I threw in a word in praise of
the liberty of opinion in *France*. I could hardly have
shot more amiss. There was an instant silence, and a
great wagging of significant heads. They did not fancy
the subject, it was plain; but they gave me to understand that the sad *Northman* was a martyr on account
of his views. "Ask him a bit," said they. "Just ask
him."

"Yes, sir," said he in his quiet way, answering me,
although I had not spoken. "I am afraid there is less
liberty of opinion in *France* than you may imagine."
And with that he dropped his eyes, and seemed to consider the subject at an end.

Our curiosity was mightily excited at this. How, or
why, or when, was this lymphatic bagman martyred?
We concluded at once it was on some religious question,
and brushed up our memories of the *Inquisition*, which
were principally drawn from *Poe's* horrid story, and the
sermon in *Tristram Shandy*, I believe.

On the morrow we had an opportunity of going
further into the question; for when we rose very early
to avoid a sympathising deputation at our departure,
we found the hero up before us. He was breaking his
fast on white wine and raw onions, in order to keep up
the character of martyr, I conclude. We had a long
conversation, and made out what we wanted in spite of
his reserve. But here was a truly curious circumstance.
It seems possible for two *Scotchmen* and a *Frenchman*
to discuss during a long half-hour, and each nationality
have a different idea in view throughout. It was not

till the very end that we discovered his heresy had been political, or that he suspected our mistake. The terms and spirit in which he spoke of his political beliefs were, in our eyes, suited to religious beliefs. And *vice versa*.

Nothing could be more characteristic of the two countries. Politics are the religion of *France*; as *Nanty Ewart* would have said, "A d—d bad religion"; while we, at home, keep most of our bitterness for little differences about a hymn-book, or a Hebrew word which, perhaps, neither of the parties can translate. And perhaps the misconception is typical of many others that may never be cleared up: not only between people of different race, but between those of different sex.

As for our friend's martyrdom, he was a Communist, or perhaps only a Communard, which is a very different thing; and had lost one or more situations in consequence. I think he had also been rejected in marriage; but perhaps he had a sentimental way of considering business which deceived me. He was a mild, gentle creature, anyway; and I hope he has got a better situation, and married a more suitable wife since then.

DOWN THE OISE: TO MOY

CARNIVAL notoriously cheated us at first. Finding us easy in our ways, he regretted having let us off so cheaply; and taking me aside, told me a cock-and-bull story with the moral of another five francs for the narrator. The thing was palpably absurd; but I paid up, and at once dropped all friendliness of manner, and kept him in his place as an inferior with freezing British dignity. He saw in a moment that he had gone too far, and killed a willing horse; his face fell; I am sure he

would have refunded if he could only have thought of a
decent pretext. He wished me to drink with him, but
I would none of his drinks. He grew pathetically tender
in his professions; but I walked beside him in silence or
answered him in stately courtesies; and when we got to
the landing-place, passed the word in English slang to
the *Cigarette*.

In spite of the false scent we had thrown out the day
before, there must have been fifty people about the
bridge. We were as pleasant as we could be with all
but *Carnival*. We said good-bye, shaking hands with
the old gentleman who knew the river and the young
gentleman who had a smattering of English; but never
a word for *Carnival*. Poor *Carnival*, here was a humiliation. He who had been so much identified with the
canoes, who had given orders in our name, who had
shown off the boats and even the boatmen like a private
exhibition of his own, to be now so publicly shamed by
the lions of his caravan! I never saw anybody look
more crestfallen than he. He hung in the background,
coming timidly forward ever and again as he thought he
saw some symptom of a relenting humour, and falling
hurriedly back when he encountered a cold stare. Let
us hope it will be a lesson to him.

I would not have mentioned *Carnival's* peccadillo had
not the thing been so uncommon in *France*. This, for
instance, was the only case of dishonesty or even sharp
practice in our whole voyage. We talk very much about
our honesty in *England*. It is a good rule to be on your
guard wherever you hear great professions about a very
little piece of virtue. If the English could only hear
how they are spoken of abroad, they might confine
themselves for a while to remedying the fact; and perhaps even when that was done, give us fewer of their airs.

The young ladies, the graces of *Origny*, were not present at our start, but when we got round to the second bridge, behold it was black with sightseers! We were loudly cheered, and for a good way below young lads and lasses ran along the bank still cheering. What with current and paddling, we were flashing along like swallows. It was no joke to keep up with us upon the woody shore. But the girls picked up their skirts, as if they were sure they had good ankles, and followed until their breath was out. The last to weary were the three graces and a couple of companions; and just as they too had had enough, the foremost of the three leaped upon a tree stump and kissed her hand to the canoeists. Not *Diana* herself, although this was more of a *Venus* after all, could have done a graceful thing more gracefully. "Come back again!" she cried; and all the others echoed her; and the hills about *Origny* repeated the words, "Come back." But the river had us round an angle in a twinkling, and we were alone with the green trees and running water.

Come back? There is no coming back, young ladies, on the impetuous stream of life.

> The merchant bows unto the seaman's star,
> The ploughman from the sun his season takes.

And we must all set our pocket watches by the clock of fate. There is a headlong, forthright tide, that bears away man with his fancies like a straw, and runs fast in time and space. It is full of curves like this, your winding river of the *Oise*; and lingers and returns in pleasant pastorals; and yet, rightly thought upon, never returns at all. For though it should revisit the same acre of meadow in the same hour, it will have made an ample sweep between whiles; many little streams will

have fallen in; many exhalations risen towards the sun;
and even although it were the same acre, it will no more
be the same river of *Oise*. And thus, O graces of *Origny*,
although the wandering fortune of my life should carry
me back again to where you await death's whistle by
the river, that will not be the old I who walks the street;
and those wives and mothers, say, will those be you?

There was never any mistake about the *Oise*, as a
matter of fact. In these upper reaches, it was still in
a prodigious hurry for the sea. It ran so fast and
merrily, through all the windings of its channel, that I
strained my thumb fighting with the rapids, and had to
paddle all the rest of the way with one hand turned up.
Sometimes, it had to serve mills; and being still a little
river, ran very dry and shallow in the meanwhile. We
had to put our legs out of the boat, and shove ourselves
off the sand of the bottom with our feet. And still it
went on its way singing among the poplars, and making
a green valley in the world. After a good woman, and
a good book, and tobacco, there is nothing so agreeable
on earth as a river. I forgave it its attempt on my life;
which was after all one part owing to the unruly winds
of heaven that had blown down the tree, one part to my
own mismanagement, and only a third part to the river
itself, and that not out of malice, but from its great
pre-occupation over its business of getting to the sea.
A difficult business, too; for the detours it had to make
are not to be counted. The geographers seem to have
given up the attempt; for I found no map represent the
infinite contortion of its course. A fact will say more
than any of them. After we had been some hours, three
if I mistake not, flitting by the trees at this smooth,
breakneck gallop, when we came upon a hamlet and
asked where we were, we had got no farther than four

kilometres (say two miles and a half) from *Origny*. If
it were not for the honour of the thing (in the Scotch
saying), we might almost as well have been standing still.

We lunched on a meadow inside a parallelogram of
poplars. The leaves danced and prattled in the wind all
round about us. The river hurried on meanwhile, and
seemed to chide at our delay. Little we cared. The
river knew where it was going; not so we: the less our
hurry, where we found good quarters and a pleasant
theatre for a pipe. At that hour, stockbrokers were
shouting in *Paris* Bourse for two or three per cent.; but
we minded them as little as the sliding stream, and
sacrificed a hecatomb of minutes to the gods of tobacco
and digestion. Hurry is the resource of the faithless.
Where a man can trust his own heart, and those of his
friends, to-morrow is as good as to-day. And if he die
in the meanwhile, why then, there he dies, and the
question is solved.

We had to take to the canal in the course of the afternoon; because, where it crossed the river, there was not
a bridge, but a siphon. If it had not been for an excited
fellow on the bank, we should have paddled right into
the siphon, and thenceforward not paddled any more.
We met a man, a gentleman, on the tow-path, who was
much interested in our cruise. And I was witness to a
strange seizure of lying suffered by the *Cigarette*; who,
because his knife came from *Norway*, narrated all sorts
of adventures in that country, where he has never been.
He was quite feverish at the end, and pleaded demoniacal
possession.

Moy (pronounce Moÿ) was a pleasant little village,
gathered round a *château* in a moat. The air was perfumed with hemp from neighbouring fields. At the
Golden Sheep we found excellent entertainment. Ger-

man shells from the siege of *La Fère, Nürnberg* figures, gold fish in a bowl, and all manner of knick-knacks, embellished the public room. The landlady was a stout, plain, short-sighted, motherly body, with something not far short of a genius for cookery. She had a guess of her excellence herself. After every dish was sent in, she would come and look on at the dinner for a while, with puckered, blinking eyes. *"C'est bon, n'est-ce pas?"* she would say; and when she had received a proper answer, she disappeared into the kitchen. That common French dish, partridge and cabbages, became a new thing in my eyes at the *Golden Sheep*; and many subsequent dinners have bitterly disappointed me in consequence. Sweet was our rest in the *Golden Sheep* at *Moy*.

LA FÈRE OF CURSED MEMORY

WE lingered in *Moy* a good part of the day, for we were fond of being philosophical, and scorned long journeys and early starts on principle. The place, moreover, invited to repose. People in elaborate shooting costumes sallied from the *château* with guns and game-bags; and this was a pleasure in itself to remain behind while these elegant pleasure-seekers took the first of the morning. In this way, all the world may be an aristocrat, and play the duke among marquises, and the reigning monarch among dukes, if he will only outvie them in tranquillity. An imperturbable demeanour comes from perfect patience. Quiet minds cannot be perplexed or frightened, but go on in fortune or misfortune at their own private pace, like a clock during a thunderstorm.

We made a very short day of it to *La Fère*; but the dusk was falling, and a small rain had begun before we

stowed the boats. *La Fère* is a fortified town in a plain,
and has two belts of rampart. Between the first and
the second extends a region of waste land and cultivated
patches. Here and there along the wayside were posters
forbidding trespass in the name of military engineering.
At last, a second gateway admitted us to the town itself.
Lighted windows looked gladsome, whiffs of comfortable
cookery came abroad upon the air. The town was full
of the military reserve, out for the French *Autumn*
manœuvres, and the reservists walked speedily and wore
their formidable greatcoats. It was a fine night to be
within doors over dinner, and hear the rain upon the
windows.

The *Cigarette* and I could not sufficiently congratulate
each other on the prospect, for we had been told there
was a capital inn at *La Fère*. Such a dinner as we were
going to eat! such beds as we were to sleep in!—and all
the while the rain raining on houseless folk over all the
poplared country-side! It made our mouths water.
The inn bore the name of some woodland animal, stag,
or hart, or hind, I forget which. But I shall never forget
how spacious and how eminently habitable it looked as
we drew near. The carriage entry was lighted up, not
by intention, but from the mere superfluity of fire and
candle in the house. A rattle of many dishes came to
our ears; we sighted a great field of tablecloth; the
kitchen glowed like a forge and smelt like a garden of
things to eat.

Into this, the inmost shrine, and physiological heart,
of a hostelry, with all its furnaces in action, and all its
dressers charged with viands, you are now to suppose us
making our triumphal entry, a pair of damp rag-and-
bone men, each with a limp india-rubber bag upon his
arm. I do not believe I have a sound view of that

kitchen; I saw it through a sort of glory: but it seemed to me crowded with the snowy caps of cookmen, who all turned round from their saucepans and looked at us with surprise.   There was no doubt about the landlady, however: there she was, heading her army, a flushed, angry woman, full of affairs.   Her I asked politely—too politely, thinks the *Cigarette*—if we could have beds: she surveying us coldly from head to foot.

"You will find beds in the suburb," she remarked. "We are too busy for the like of you."

If we could make an entrance, change our clothes, and order a bottle of wine, I felt sure we could put things right; so said I: "If we cannot sleep, we may at least dine"—and was for depositing my bag.

What a terrible convulsion of nature was that which followed in the landlady's face!   She made a run at us, and stamped her foot.

"Out with you—out of the door!" she screeched. "*Sortez! sortez! sortez par la porte!*"

I do not know how it happened, but next moment we were out in the rain and darkness, and I was cursing before the carriage entry like a disappointed mendicant. Where were the boating men of *Belgium*? where the Judge and his good wines? and where the graces of *Origny*?   Black, black was the night after the firelit kitchen; but what was that to the blackness in our heart?   This was not the first time that I have been refused a lodging.   Often and often have I planned what I should do if such a misadventure happened to me again.   And nothing is easier to plan.   But to put in execution, with the heart boiling at the indignity?   Try it; try it only once; and tell me what you did.

It is all very fine to talk about tramps and morality. Six hours of police surveillance (such as I have had) or one brutal rejection from an inn door, change your views upon the subject like a course of lectures. As long as you keep in the upper regions, with all the world bowing to you as you go, social arrangements have a very handsome air; but once get under the wheels, and you wish society were at the devil. I will give most respectable men a fortnight of such a life, and then I will offer them twopence for what remains of their morality.

For my part, when I was turned out of the *Stag*, or the *Hind*, or whatever it was, I would have set the temple of *Diana* on fire, if it had been handy. There was no crime complete enough to express my disapproval of human institutions. As for the *Cigarette*, I never knew a man so altered. "We have been taken for pedlars again," said he. "Good *God*, what it must be to be a pedlar in reality!" He particularised a complaint for every joint in the landlady's body. *Timon* was a philanthropist alongside of him. And then, when he was at the top of his maledictory bent, he would suddenly break away and begin whimperingly to commiserate the poor. "I hope to *God*," he said—and I trust the prayer was answered, —"that I shall never be uncivil to a pedlar." Was this the imperturbable *Cigarette*? This, this was he. O change beyond report, thought, or belief!

Meantime the heaven wept upon our heads; and the windows grew brighter as the night increased in darkness. We trudged in and out of *La Fère* streets; we saw shops, and private houses where people were copiously dining; we saw stables where carters' nags had plenty of fodder and clean straw; we saw no end of reservists, who were very sorry for themselves this wet night, I doubt not, and yearned for their country homes; but had they not each man his place in *La Fère* barracks? And we, what had we?

There seemed to be no other inn in the whole town. People gave us directions, which we followed as best we could, generally with the effect of bringing us out again upon the scene of our disgrace. We were very sad people indeed by the time we had gone all over *La Fère*; and the *Cigarette* had already made up his mind to lie under a poplar and sup off a loaf of bread. But right at the other end, the house next the towngate was full of light and bustle. *"Bazin, aubergiste, loge à pied,"* was the sign. *"A la Croix de Malte."* There were we received.

The room was full of noisy reservists drinking and smoking; and we were very glad indeed when the drums and bugles began to go about the streets, and one and all had to snatch shakoes and be off for the barracks.

Bazin was a tall man, running to fat: soft-spoken, with a delicate, gentle face. We asked him to share our wine; but he excused himself, having pledged reservists all day long. This was a very different type of the workman-innkeeper from the bawling disputatious fellow at *Origny*. He also loved *Paris*, where he had worked as a decorative painter in his youth. There were such opportunities for self-instruction there, he said. And if anyone has read *Zola's* description of the workman's marriage party visiting the *Louvre*, they would do well to have heard *Bazin* by way of antidote. He had delighted in the museums in his youth. "One sees there little miracles of work," he said; "that is what makes a good workman; it kindles a spark." We asked him how he managed in *La Fère*. "I am married," he said, "and I have my pretty children. But frankly, it is no life at all. From morning to night, I pledge a pack of good enough fellows who know nothing."

It faired as the night went on, and the moon came out

of the clouds. We sat in front of the door, talking softly
with *Bazin*. At the guard-house opposite, the guard
was being for ever turned out, as trains of field artillery
kept clanking in out of the night, or patrols of horsemen
trotted by in their cloaks. Madame *Bazin* came out
after a while; she was tired with her day's work, I suppose; and she nestled up to her husband and laid her
head upon his breast. He had his arm about her and
kept gently patting her on the shoulder. I think *Bazin*
was right and he was really married. Of how few people
can the same be said!

Little did the *Bazins* know how much they served us.
We were charged for candles, for food and drink, and
for the beds we slept in. But there was nothing in the
bill for the husband's pleasant talk; nor for the pretty
spectacle of their married life. And there was yet
another item uncharged. For these people's politeness
really set us up again in our own esteem. We had a
thirst for consideration; the sense of insult was still hot
in our spirits; and civil usage seemed to restore us to our
position in the world.

How little we pay our way in life! Although we have
our purses continually in our hand, the better part of
service goes still unrewarded. But I like to fancy that
a grateful spirit gives as good as it gets. Perhaps the
Bazins knew how much I liked them? perhaps they,
also, were healed of some slights by the thanks that I
gave them in my manner?

DOWN THE OISE: THROUGH THE GOLDEN VALLEY

BELOW *La Fère* the river runs through a piece of open pastoral country; green, opulent, loved by breeders; called the *Golden Valley*. In wide sweeps, and with a swift and equable gallop, the ceaseless stream of water visits and makes green the fields. Kine, and horses, and little humorous donkeys, browse together in the meadows, and come down in troops to the riverside to drink. They make a strange feature in the landscape; above all when startled, and you see them galloping to and fro, with their incongruous forms and faces. It gives a feeling as of great, unfenced pampas, and the herds of wandering nations. There were hills in the distance upon either hand; and on one side, the river sometimes bordered on the wooded spurs of *Coucy* and *St. Gobain*.

The artillery were practising at *La Fère*; and soon the cannon of heaven joined in that loud play. Two continents of cloud met and exchanged salvos overhead; while all round the horizon we could see sunshine and clear air upon the hills. What with the guns and the thunder, the herds were all frighted in the *Golden Valley*. We could see them tossing their heads, and running to and fro in timorous indecision; and when they had made up their minds, and the donkey followed the horse, and the cow was after the donkey, we could hear their hooves thundering abroad over the meadows. It had a martial sound, like cavalry charges. And altogether, as far as the ears are concerned, we had a very rousing battle-piece performed for our amusement.

At last, the guns and the thunder dropped off; the sun shone on the wet meadows; the air was scented with the breath of rejoicing trees and grass; and the river kept unweariedly carrying us on at its best pace.

There was a manufacturing district about *Chauny*; and after that the banks grew so high that they hid the adjacent country, and we could see nothing but clay sides, and one willow after another. Only, here and there, we passed by a village or a ferry, and some wondering child upon the bank would stare after us until we turned the corner. I daresay we continued to paddle in that child's dreams for many a night after.

Sun and shower alternated like day and night, making the hours longer by their variety. When the showers were heavy I could feel each drop striking through my jersey to my warm skin; and the accumulation of small shocks put me nearly beside myself. I decided I should buy a mackintosh at *Noyon*. It is nothing to get wet; but the misery of these individual pricks of cold all over my body at the same instant of time made me flail the water with my paddle like a madman. The *Cigarette* was greatly amused by these ebullitions. It gave him something else to look at, besides clay banks and willows.

All the time, the river stole away like a thief in straight places, or swung round corners with an eddy; the willows nodded and were undermined all day long; the clay banks tumbled in; the *Oise*, which had been so many centuries making the *Golden Valley*, seemed to have changed its fancy, and be bent upon undoing its performance. What a number of things a river does, by simply following Gravity in the innocence of its heart!

NOYON CATHEDRAL

Noyon stands about a mile from the river, in a little plain surrounded by wooded hills, and entirely covers an eminence with its tile roofs, surmounted by a long, straight-backed cathedral with two stiff towers. As we got into the town, the tile roofs seemed to tumble uphill one upon another, in the oddest disorder; but for all their scrambling, they did not attain above the knees of the cathedral, which stood, upright and solemn, over all. As the streets drew near to this presiding genius, through the market-place under the *Hôtel de Ville*, they grew emptier and more composed. Blank walls and shuttered windows were turned to the great edifice, and grass grew on the white causeway. "Put off thy shoes from off thy feet, for the place whereon thou standest is holy ground." The *Hôtel du Nord*, nevertheless, lights its secular tapers within a stone-cast of the church; and we had the superb east end before our eyes all morning from the window of our bedroom. I have seldom looked on the east end of a church with more complete sympathy. As it flanges out in three wide terraces, and settles down broadly on the earth, it looks like the poop of some great old battleship. Hollow-backed buttresses carry vases, which figure for the stern lanterns. There is a roll in the ground, and the towers just appear above the pitch of the roof, as though the good ship were bowling lazily over an *Atlantic* swell. At any moment it might be a hundred feet away from you, climbing the next billow. At any moment a window might open, and some old admiral thrust forth a cocked hat, and proceed to take an observation. The old admirals sail the sea no longer; the old ships of battle are all broken up, and live only in pictures; but this that was a church before ever they were thought upon, is still a church, and makes as brave an appearance by the *Oise*. The cathedral and the river are probably the two oldest things for miles around; and certainly they have both a grand old age.

The *Sacristan* took us to the top of one of the towers,

and showed us the five bells hanging in their loft.   From
above, the town was a tessellated pavement of roofs and
gardens; the old line of rampart was plainly traceable;
and the *Sacristan* pointed out to us, far across the plain,
in a bit of gleaming sky between two clouds, the towers
of *Château Coucy*.

I find I never weary of great churches.   It is my
favourite kind of mountain scenery.   Mankind was never
so happily inspired as when it made a cathedral: a thing
as single and specious as a statue to the first glance, and
yet, on examination, as lively and interesting as a forest
in detail.   The height of spires cannot be taken by
trigonometry; they measure absurdly short, but how tall
they are to the admiring eye!   And where we have so
many elegant proportions, growing one out of the other,
and all together into one, it seems as if proportion tran-
scended itself and became something different and more
imposing.   I could never fathom how a man dares to
lift up his voice to preach in a cathedral.   What is he
to say that will not be an anti-climax?   For though I
have heard a considerable variety of sermons, I never
yet heard one that was so expressive as a cathedral.   'Tis
the best preacher itself, and preaches day and night; not
only telling you of man's art and aspirations in the past,
but convicting your own soul of ardent sympathies; or
rather, like all good preachers, it sets you preaching to
yourself;—and every man is his own doctor of divinity
in the last resort.

As I sat outside of the hotel in the course of the afternoon, the sweet groaning thunder of the organ floated
out of the church like a summons.   I was not averse,
liking the theatre so well, to sit out an act or two of the
play, but I could never rightly make out the nature of
the service I beheld.   Four or five priests and as many

choristers were singing *Miserere* before the high altar
when I went in. There was no congregation but a few
old women on chairs and old men kneeling on the pavement. After a while a long train of young girls, walking
two and two, each with a lighted taper in her hand, and
all dressed in black with a white veil, came from behind
the altar and began to descend the nave; the four first
carrying a Virgin and Child upon a table. The priests
and choristers arose from their knees and followed after,
singing "Ave Mary" as they went. In this order, they
made the circuit of the cathedral, passing twice before
me where I leaned against a pillar. The priest who
seemed of most consequence was a strange, down-look-
ing old man. He kept mumbling prayers with his lips;
but as he looked upon me darkling, it did not seem as if
prayer were uppermost in his heart. Two others, who
bore the burthen of the chaunt, were stout, brutal,
military-looking men of forty, with bold, overfed eyes;
they sang with some lustiness, and trolled forth "Ave
Mary" like a garrison catch. The little girls were timid
and grave. As they footed slowly up the aisle, each one
took a moment's glance at the *Englishman*; and the big
nun who played marshal fairly stared him out of countenance. As for the choristers, from first to last they
misbehaved as only boys can misbehave; and cruelly
marred the performance with their antics.

I understood a great deal of the spirit of what went on.
Indeed it would be difficult not to understand the
Miserere, which I take to be the composition of an
atheist. If it ever be a good thing to take such despondency to heart, the *Miserere* is the right music and a
cathedral a fit scene. So far I am at one with the
Catholics:—an odd name for them, after all! But why,
in *God's* name, these holiday choristers? why these priests

D

who steal wandering looks about the congregation while they feign to be at prayer? why this fat nun, who rudely arranges her procession and shakes delinquent virgins by the elbow? why this spitting, and snuffing, and forgetting of keys, and the thousand and one little misadventures that disturb a frame of mind, laboriously edified with chaunts and organings? In any play-house reverend fathers may see what can be done with a little art, and how, to move high sentiments, it is necessary to drill the supernumeraries and have every stool in its proper place.

One other circumstance distressed me. I could bear a *Miserere* myself, having had a good deal of open-air exercise of late; but I wished the old people somewhere else. It was neither the right sort of music not the right sort of divinity for men and women who have come through most accidents by this time, and probably have an opinion of their own upon the tragic element in life. A person up in years can generally do his own *Miserere* for himself; although I notice that such an one often prefers *Jubilate Deo* for his ordinary singing. On the whole, the most religious exercise for the aged is probably to recall their own experience; so many friends dead, so many hopes disappointed, so many slips and stumbles, and withal so many bright days and smiling providences; there is surely the matter of a very eloquent sermon in all this.

On the whole, I was greatly solemnised. In the little pictorial map of our whole *Inland Voyage*, which my fancy still preserves, and sometimes unrolls for the amusement of odd moments, *Noyon* cathedral figures on a most preposterous scale, and must be nearly as large as a department. I can still see the faces of the priests as if they were at my elbow, and hear *Ave Maria, ora pro*

nobis sounding through the church. All *Noyon* is blotted
out for me by these superior memories; and I do not care
to say more about the place. It was but a stack of
brown roofs at the best, where I believe people live very
reputably in a quiet way; but the shadow of the church
falls upon it when the sun is low, and the five bells are
heard in all quarters, telling that the organ has begun.
If ever I join the church of *Rome*, I shall stipulate to be
Bishop of *Noyon* on the *Oise*.

DOWN THE OISE: TO COMPIÈGNE

THE most patient people grow weary at last with being
continually wetted with rain; except of course in the
Scotch *Highlands*, where there are not enough fine intervals to point the difference. That was like to be our
case the day we left *Noyon*. I remember nothing of the
voyage; it was nothing but clay banks and willows, and
rain; incessant, pitiless, beating rain: until we stopped
to lunch at a little inn at *Pimprez*, where the canal ran
very near the river. We were so sadly drenched that
the landlady lit a few sticks in the chimney for our comfort; there we sat in a steam of vapour, lamenting our
concerns. The husband donned a game-bag and strode
out to shoot; the wife sat in a far corner watching us. I
think we were worth looking at. We grumbled over the
misfortune of *La Fère*; we forecast other *La Fères* in the
future;—although things went better with the *Cigarette*
for spokesman; he had more aplomb altogether than I;
and a dull, positive way of approaching a landlady that
carried off the india-rubber bags. Talking of *La Fère*
put us talking of the reservists.

"Reservery," said he, "seems a pretty mean way to spend one's autumn holiday."

"About as mean," returned I dejectedly, "as canoeing."

"These gentlemen travel for their pleasure?" asked the landlady, with unconscious irony.

It was too much. The scales fell from our eyes. Another wet day, it was determined, and we put the boats into the train.

The weather took the hint. That was our last wetting. The afternoon faired up: grand clouds still voyaged in the sky, but now singly, and with a depth of blue around their path; and a sunset, in the daintiest rose and gold, inaugurated a thick night of stars and a month of unbroken weather. At the same time, the river began to give us a better outlook into the country. The banks were not so high, the willows disappeared from along the margin, and pleasant hills stood all along its course and marked their profile on the sky.

In a little while the canal, coming to its last lock, began to discharge its water-houses on the *Oise*; so that we had no lack of company to fear. Here were all our old friends; the *Deo Gratias* of *Condé* and the *Four Sons of Aymon* journeyed cheerily down-stream along with us; we exchanged waterside pleasantries with the steersman perched among the lumber, or the driver hoarse with bawling to his horses; and the children came and looked over the side as we paddled by. We had never known all this while how much we missed them; but it gave us a fillip to see the smoke from their chimneys.

A little below this junction, we made another meeting of yet more account. For there we were joined by the *Aisne*, already a far-travelled river and fresh out of *Champagne*. Here ended the adolescence of the *Oise*;

this was his marriage day; thenceforward he had a
stately, brimming march, conscious of his own dignity
and sundry dams. He became a tranquil feature in the
scene. The trees and towns saw themselves in him, as
in a mirror. He carried the canoes lightly on his broad
breast; there was no need to work hard against an eddy;
but idleness became the order of the day, and mere
straightforward dipping of the paddle, now on this side,
now on that, without intelligence or effort. Truly we
were coming into halcyon weather upon all accounts,
and were floated towards the sea like gentlemen.

We made *Compiègne* as the sun was going down: a fine
profile of a town above the river. Over the bridge, a
regiment was parading to the drum. People loitered on
the quay, some fishing, some looking idly at the stream.
And as the two boats shot in along the water, we could
see them pointing them out and speaking one to another.
We landed at a floating lavatory, where the washerwomen were still beating the clothes.

AT COMPIÈGNE

WE put up at a big, bustling hotel in *Compiègne*, where
nobody observed our presence.

Reservery and general militarismus (as the Germans
call it) were rampant. A camp of conical white tents
without the town looked like a leaf out of a picture
Bible; sword-belts decorated the walls of the *cafés*; and
the streets kept sounding all day long with military
music. It was not possible to be an *Englishman* and
avoid a feeling of elation; for the men who followed the
drums were small, and walked shabbily. Each man
inclined at his own angle, and jolted to his own con-

venience, as he went. There was nothing of the superb gait with which a regiment of tall Highlanders moves behind its music, solemn and inevitable, like a natural phenomenon. Who, that has seen it, can forget the drum-major pacing in front, the drummers' tiger-skins, the pipers' swinging plaids, the strange elastic rhythm of the whole regiment footing it in time—and the bang of the drum, when the brasses cease, and the shrill pipes take up the martial story in their place?

A girl, at school in *France*, began to describe one of our regiments on parade, to her French schoolmates; and as she went on, she told me, the recollection grew so vivid, she became so proud to be the countrywoman of such soldiers, and so sorry to be in another country, that her voice failed her and she burst into tears. I have never forgotten that girl; and I think she very nearly deserves a statue. To call her a young lady, with all its niminy associations, would be to offer her an insult. She may rest assured of one thing; although she never should marry a heroic general, never see any great or immediate result of her life, she will not have lived in vain for her native land.

But though French soldiers show to ill-advantage on parade, on the march they are gay, alert, and willing like a troop of fox-hunters. I remember once seeing a company pass through the forest of *Fontainebleau*, on the *Chailly* road, between the *Bas Bréau* and the *Reine Blanche*. One fellow walked a little before the rest and sang a loud, audacious marching song. The rest bestirred their feet, and even swung their muskets in time. A young officer on horseback had hard ado to keep his countenance at the words. You never saw anything so cheerful and spontaneous as their gait; schoolboys do not look more eagerly at hare and hounds;

and you would have thought it impossible to tire such
willing marchers.

My great delight in Compiègne was the town-hall. I
doted upon the town-hall. It is a monument of Gothic
insecurity, all turreted, and gargoyled, and slashed, and
bedizened with half a score of architectural fancies.
Some of the niches are gilt and painted; and in a great
square panel in the centre, in black relief on a gilt
ground, Louis XII rides upon a pacing horse, with hand
on hip, and head thrown back. There is royal arrogance
in every line of him; the stirruped foot projects insolently
from the frame; the eye is hard and proud; the very
horse seems to be treading with gratification over prostrate serfs, and to have the breath of the trumpet in his
nostrils. So rides for ever, on the front of the town-hall,
the good king Louis XII, the father of his people.

Over the king's head, in the tall centre turret, appears
the dial of a clock; and high above that, three little
mechanical figures, each one with a hammer in his hand,
whose business it is to chime out the hours and halves
and quarters for the burgesses of Compiègne. The centre
figure has a gilt breastplate; the two others wear gilt
trunk-hose; and they all three have elegant, flapping
hats like cavaliers. As the quarter approaches, they
turn their heads and look knowingly one to the other;
and then kling go the three hammers on three little bells
below. The hour follows, deep and sonorous, from the
interior of the tower; and the gilded gentlemen rest from
their labours with contentment.

I had a great deal of healthy pleasure from their
manœuvres, and took good care to miss as few perform-
ances as possible; and I found that even the Cigarette,
while he pretended to despise my enthusiasm, was more
or less a devotee himself. There is something highly

absurd in the exposition of such toys to the outrages of
winter on a housetop. They would be more in keeping
in a glass case before a *Nürnberg* clock. Above all, at
night, when the children are abed, and even grown
people are snoring under quilts, does it not seem imper-
tinent to leave these gingerbread figures winking and
tinkling to the stars and the rolling moon? The gar-
goyles may fitly enough twist their ape-like heads; fitly
enough may the potentate bestride his charger, like a
centurion in an old German print of the *Via Dolorosa*;
but the toys should be put away in a box among some
cotton, until the sun rises, and the children are abroad
again to be amused.

In *Compiègne* post-office a great packet of letters
awaited us; and the authorities were, for this occasion
only, so polite as to hand them over upon application.

In some ways, our journey may be said to end with
this letter-bag at *Compiègne*. The spell was broken.
We had partly come home from that moment.

No one should have any correspondence on a journey;
it is bad enough to have to write, but the receipt of
letters is the death of all holiday feeling.

"Out of my country and myself I go." I wish to take
a dive among new conditions for awhile, as into another
element. I have nothing to do with my friends or my
affections for the time; when I came away, I left my
heart at home in a desk, or sent it forward with my
portmanteau to await me at my destination. After my
journey is over, I shall not fail to read your admirable
letters with the attention they deserve. But I have paid
all this money, look you, and paddled all these strokes,
for no other purpose than to be abroad; and yet you
keep me at home with your perpetual communications.
You tug the string, and I feel that I am a tethered bird.

You pursue me all over *Europe* with the little vexations that I came away to avoid. There is no discharge in the war of life, I am well aware; but shall there not be so much as a week's furlough?

We were up by six the day we were to leave. They had taken so little note of us that I hardly thought they would have condescended on a bill. But they did, with some smart particulars too; and we paid in a civilised manner to an uninterested clerk, and went out of that hotel, with the india-rubber bags, unremarked. No one cared to know about us. It is not possible to rise before a village; but *Compiègne* was so grown a town that it took its ease in the morning; and we were up and away while it was still in dressing-gown and slippers. The streets were left to people washing door-steps; nobody was in full dress but the cavaliers upon the town-hall; they were all washed with dew, spruce in their gilding, and full of intelligence and a sense of professional responsibility. *Kling* went they on the bells for the half-past six, as we went by. I took it kind of them to make me this parting compliment; they never were in better form, not even at noon upon a *Sunday*.

There was no one to see us off but the early washer-women—early and late—who were already beating the linen in their floating lavatory on the river. They were very merry and matutinal in their ways; plunged their arms boldly in, and seemed not to feel the shock. It would be dispiriting to me, this early beginning and first cold dabble of a most dispiriting day's work. But I believe they would have been as unwilling to change days with us, as we could be to change with them. They crowded to the door to watch us paddle away into the thin sunny mists upon the river and shouted heartily after us till we were through the bridge.

CHANGED TIMES

THERE is a sense in which those mists never rose from
off our journey; and from that time forth they lie very
densely in my note-book. As long as the *Oise* was a
small, rural river, it took us near by people's doors, and
we could hold a conversation with natives in the riparian
fields. But now that it had grown so wide, the life
along shore passed us by at a distance. It was the
same difference as between a great public highway and
a country bypath that wanders in and out of cottage
gardens. We now lay in towns, where nobody troubled
us with questions; we had floated into civilised life,
where people pass without salutation. In sparsely
inhabited places, we make all we can of each encounter;
but when it comes to a city, we keep to ourselves, and
never speak unless we have trodden on a man's toes.
In these waters we were no longer strange birds, and
nobody supposed we had travelled farther than from the
last town. I remember, when we came into *L'Isle
Adam*, for instance, how we met dozens of pleasure-boats
outing it for the afternoon, and there was nothing to
distinguish the true voyager from the amateur, except,
perhaps, the filthy condition of my sail. The company
in one boat actually thought they recognised me for a
neighbour. Was there ever anything more wounding?
All the romance had come down to that. Now, on the
upper *Oise*, where nothing sailed as a general thing but
fish, a pair of canoeists could not be thus vulgarly
explained away; we were strange and picturesque
intruders; and out of people's wonder sprang a sort of
light and passing intimacy all along our route. There
is nothing but tit for tat in this world, though sometimes

it be a little difficult to trace: for the scores are older than we ourselves, and there has never yet been a settling-day since things were. You get entertainment pretty much in proportion as you give. As long as we were a sort of odd wanderers, to be stared at and followed like a quack doctor or a caravan, we had no want of amusement in return; but as soon as we sank into commonplace ourselves, all whom we met were similarly disenchanted. And here is one reason of a dozen why the world is dull to dull persons.

In our earlier adventures there was generally something to do, and that quickened us. Even the showers of rain had a revivifying effect, and shook up the brain from torpor. But now, when the river no longer ran in a proper sense, only glided seaward with an even, outright, but imperceptible speed, and when the sky smiled upon us day after day without variety, we began to slip into that golden doze of the mind which follows upon much exercise in the open air. I have stupefied myself in this way more than once; indeed, I dearly love the feeling; but I never had it to the same degree as when paddling down the *Oise*. It was the apotheosis of stupidity.

We ceased reading entirely. Sometimes when I found a new paper, I took a particular pleasure in reading a single number of the current novel; but I never could bear more than three instalments; and even the second was a disappointment. As soon as the tale became in any way perspicuous, it lost all merit in my eyes; only a single scene, or, as is the way with these *feuilletons*, half a scene, without antecedent or consequence, like a piece of a dream, had the knack of fixing my interest. The less I saw of the novel, the better I liked it: a pregnant reflection. But for the most part, as I said, we neither of us read anything in the world, and employed the very little while we were awake between bed and dinner in poring upon maps. I have always been fond of maps, and can voyage in an atlas with the greatest enjoyment. The names of places are singularly inviting; the contour of coasts and rivers is enthralling to the eye, and to hit, in a map, upon some place you have heard of before, makes history a new possession. But we thumbed our charts, on these evenings, with the blankest unconcern. We cared not a fraction for this place or that. We stared at the sheet as children listen to their rattle; and read the names of towns or villages to forget them again at once. We had no romance in the matter; there was nobody so fancy-free. If you had taken the maps away while we were studying them most intently, it is a fair bet whether we might not have continued to study the table with the same delight.

About one thing we were mightily taken up, and that was eating. I think I made a god of my belly. I remember dwelling in imagination upon this or that dish till my mouth watered, and long before we got in for the night my appetite was a clamant, instant annoyance. Sometimes we paddled alongside for awhile and whetted each other with gastronomical fancies as we went. Cake and sherry, a homely refection, but not within reach upon the *Oise*, trotted through my head for many a mile; and once, as we were approaching *Verberie*, the *Cigarette* brought my heart into my mouth by the suggestion of oyster patties and *Sauterne*.

I suppose none of us recognise the great part that is played in life by eating and drinking. The appetite is so imperious, that we can stomach the least interesting viands, and pass off a dinner hour thankfully enough on bread and water; just as there are men who must read something, if it were only *Bradshaw's Guide*. But there is a romance about the matter after all. Probably the table has more devotees than love; and I am sure that food is much more generally entertaining than scenery. Do you give in, as *Walt Whitman* would say, that you are any the less immortal for that? The true materialism is to be ashamed of what we are. To detect the flavour of an olive is no less a piece of human perfection than to find beauty in the colours of the sunset.

Canoeing was easy work. To dip the paddle at the proper inclination, now right, now left; to keep the head down-stream; to empty the little pool that gathered in the lap of the apron; to screw up the eyes against the glittering sparkles of sun upon the water; or now and again to pass below the whistling tow-rope of the *Deo Gratias* of *Condé*, or the *Four Sons of Aymon*—there was not much art in that; certain silly muscles managed it between sleep and waking; and meanwhile the brain had a whole holiday, and went to sleep. We took in, at a glance, the larger features of the scene, and beheld, with half an eye, bloused fishers and dabbling washerwomen on the bank. Now and again we might be half wakened by some church spire, by a leaping fish, or by a trail of river grass that clung about the paddle and had to be plucked off and thrown away. But these luminous intervals were only partially luminous. A little more of us was called into action, but never the whole. The central bureau of nerves, what in some moods we call *Ourselves*, enjoyed its holiday without disturbance like a Government Office. The great wheels of intelligence turned idly in the head, like fly-wheels, grinding no grist. I have gone on for half an hour at a time, counting my strokes and forgetting the hundreds. flatter myself the beasts that perish could not underbid that, as a low form of consciousness. And what a pleasure it was! What a hearty, tolerant temper did it bring about! There is nothing captious about a man who has attained to this, the one possible apotheosis in life, the Apotheosis of Stupidity; and he begins to feel dignified and longœvous like a tree.

There was one odd piece of practical metaphysics which accompanied what I may call the depth, if I must not call it the intensity, of my abstraction. What philosophers call *me* and *not me, ego* and *non ego*, pre-occupied me whether I would or no. There was less *me* and more *not me* than I was accustomed to expect. I looked on upon somebody else, who managed the paddling; I was aware of somebody else's feet against the stretcher; my own body seemed to have no more intimate relation to me than the canoe, or the river, or the river banks. Nor this alone: something inside my mind, a part of my brain, a province of my proper being, had thrown off allegiance and set up for itself, or per-haps for the somebody else who did the paddling. I had dwindled into quite a little thing in a corner of myself. I was isolated in my own skull. Thoughts presented themselves unbidden; they were not my thoughts, they were plainly someone else's; and I considered them like a part of the landscape. I take it, in short, that I was about as near *Nirvana* as would be convenient in practical life; and if this be so, I make the Buddhists my sincere compliments; 'tis an agreeable state, not very consistent with mental brilliancy, not exactly profitable in a money point of view, but very calm, golden and incurious, and one that sets a man superior to alarms. It may be best figured by supposing yourself to get dead drunk, and yet keep sober to enjoy it. I have a notion that open-air labourers must spend a large portion of their days in this ecstatic stupor, which explains their high composure and endurance. A pity to go to the expense of laudanum, when here is a better paradise for nothing!

This frame of mind was the great exploit of our voyage, take it all in all. It was the farthest piece of travel accomplished. Indeed, it lies so far from the beaten paths of language, that I despair of getting the reader into sympathy with the smiling, complacent idiocy of my condition; when ideas came and went like motes in a sunbeam; when trees and church spires along the bank surged up from time to time into my notice, like solid objects through a rolling cloudland; when the rhythmical swish of boat and paddle in the water became a cradle-song to lull my thoughts asleep; when a piece of mud on the deck was sometimes an intolerable eyesore, and sometimes quite a companion for me, and the object of pleased consideration;—and all the time, with the river running and the shores changing upon either hand, I kept counting my strokes and forgetting the hundreds, the happiest animal in *France*.

DOWN THE OISE: CHURCH INTERIORS

WE made our first stage below *Compiègne* to *Pont Sainte Maxence*. I was abroad a little after six the next morning. The air was biting and smelt of frost. In an open place, a score of women wrangled together over the day's market; and the noise of their negotiation sounded thin and querulous like that of sparrows on a winter's morning. The rare passengers blew into their hands, and shuffled in their wooden shoes to set the blood agog. The streets were full of icy shadow, although the chimneys were smoking overhead in golden sunshine. If you wake early enough at this season of the year, you may get up in *December* to break your fast in *June*.

I found my way to the church; for there is always something to see about a church, whether living worshippers or dead men's tombs; you find there the deadliest earnest, and the hollowest deceit; and even where it is not a piece of history, it will be certain to leak out some contemporary gossip. It was scarcely so cold in the church as it was without, but it looked colder. The white nave was positively arctic to the eye; and the tawdriness of a continental altar looked more forlorn than usual in the solitude and the bleak air. Two priests sat in the chancel, reading and waiting penitents; and out in the nave, one very old woman was engaged in her devotions. It was a wonder how she was able to pass her beads when healthy young people were breathing in their palms and slapping their chest; but though this concerned me, I was yet more dispirited by the nature of her exercises. She went from chair to chair, from altar to altar, circumnavigating the church. To each shrine she dedicated an equal number of beads and an equal length of time. Like a prudent capitalist with a somewhat cynical view of the commercial prospect, she desired to place her supplications in a great variety of heavenly securities. She would risk nothing on the credit of any single intercessor. Out of the whole company of saints and angels, not one but was to suppose himself her champion elect against the Great Assizes! I could only think of it as a dull, transparent jugglery, based upon unconscious unbelief.

She was as dead an old woman as ever I saw; no more than bone and parchment, curiously put together. Her eyes, with which she interrogated mine, were vacant of sense. It depends on what you call seeing, whether you might not call her blind. Perhaps she had known love; perhaps borne children, suckled them and given them pet names. But now that was all gone by, and had left her neither happier nor wiser; and the best she could do with her mornings was to come up here into the cold church and juggle for a slice of heaven. It was not without a gulp that I escaped into the streets and the keen morning air. Morning? why, how tired of it she would be before night! and if she did not sleep, how then? It is fortunate that not many of us are brought up publicly to justify our lives at the bar of threescore years and ten; fortunate that such a number are knocked opportunely on the head in what they call the flower of their years, and go away to suffer for their follies in private somewhere else. Otherwise, between sick children and discontented old folk, we might be put out of all conceit of life.

I had need of all my cerebral hygiene during that day's paddle: the old devotee stuck in my throat sorely. But I was soon in the seventh heaven of stupidity; and knew nothing but that somebody was paddling a canoe, while I was counting his strokes and forgetting the hundreds. I used sometimes to be afraid I should remember the hundreds; which would have made a toil of a pleasure; but the terror was chimerical, they went out of my mind by enchantment, and I knew no more than the man in the moon about my only occupation.

At *Creil*, where we stopped to lunch, we left the canoes in another floating lavatory, which as it was high

noon was packed with washerwomen, red-handed and
loud-voiced; and they and their broad jokes are about
all I remember of the place. I could look up my
history books, if you were very anxious, and tell you a
date or two; for it figured rather largely in the English
wars. But I prefer to mention a girls' boarding-school,
which had an interest for us because it was a girls'
boarding-school, and because we imagined we had
rather an interest for it. At least—there were the
girls about the garden; and here were we on the river;
and there was more than one handkerchief waved as
we went by. It caused quite a stir in my heart; and
yet how we should have wearied and despised each
other, these girls and I, if we had been introduced at a
croquet party! But this is a fashion I love: to kiss
the hand or wave a handkerchief to people I shall never
see again, to play with possibility, and knock in a peg
for fancy to hang upon. It gives the traveller a jog,
reminds him that he is not a traveller everywhere, and
that his journey is no more than a siesta by the way on
the real march of life.

The church at *Creil* was a nondescript place in the
inside, splashed with gaudy lights from the windows,
and picked out with medallions of the *Dolorous Way*.
But there was one oddity, in the way of an *ex voto*,
which pleased me hugely; a faithful model of a canal
boat swung from the vault, with a written aspiration
that *God* should conduct the *Saint Nicolas* of *Creil*
to a good haven. The thing was neatly executed, and
would have made the delight of a party of boys on the
waterside. But what tickled me was the gravity of the
peril to be conjured. You might hang up the model
of a sea-going ship, and welcome: one that is to plough
a furrow round the world, and visit the tropic or the

frosty poles, runs dangers that are well worth a candle
and a mass. But the *Saint Nicolas* of *Creil*, which was
to be tugged for some ten years by patient draught-
horses, in a weedy canal, with the poplars chattering
overhead, and the skipper whistling at the tiller; which
was to do all its errands in green, inland places, and
never got out of sight of a village belfry in all its cruising;
why, you would have thought if anything could be done
without the intervention of Providence, it would be
that! But perhaps the skipper was a humorist: or
perhaps a prophet, reminding people of the seriousness
of life by this preposterous token.

At *Creil*, as at *Noyon*, Saint *Joseph* seemed a favourite
saint on the score of punctuality. Day and hour can
be specified; and grateful people do not fail to specify
them on a votive tablet, when prayers have been punctually and neatly answered. Whenever time is a consideration, Saint *Joseph* is the proper intermediary. I
took a sort of pleasure in observing the vogue he had in
France, for the good man plays a very small part in
my religion at home. Yet I could not help fearing that,
where the Saint is so much commended for exactitude,
he will be expected to be very grateful for his tablet.

This is foolishness to us Protestants; and not of great
importance anyway. Whether people's gratitude for
the good gifts that come to them be wisely conceived
or dutifully expressed, is a secondary matter, after all,
so long as they feel gratitude. The true ignorance is
when a man does not know that he has received a good
gift, or begins to imagine that he has got it for himself.
The self-made man is the funniest windbag after all!
There is a marked difference between decreeing light in
chaos, and lighting the gas in a metropolitan back-
parlour with a box of patent matches; and do what we

will, there is always something made to our hand, if it were only our fingers.

But there was something worse than foolishness placarded in *Creil* Church. *The Association of the Living Rosary* (of which I had never previously heard) is responsible for that. This association was founded, according to the printed advertisement, by a brief of Pope *Gregory* Sixteenth, on the 17th of *January*, 1832: according to a coloured bas-relief, it seems to have been founded, sometime or other, by the *Virgin* giving one rosary to Saint *Dominic* and the Infant *Saviour* giving another to Saint *Catherine* of *Sienna*. Pope *Gregory* is not so imposing, but he is nearer hand. I could not distinctly make out whether the association was entirely devotional, or had an eye to good works; at least it is highly organised: the names of fourteen matrons and misses were filled in for each week of the month as associates, with one other, generally a married woman, at the top for *Zélatrice*: the choragus of the band. Indulgences, plenary and partial, follow on the performance of the duties of the association. "The partial indulgences are attached to the recitation of the rosary." On "the recitation of the required *dizaine*," a partial indulgence promptly follows. When people serve the kingdom of Heaven with a pass-book in their hands, I should always be afraid lest they should carry the same commercial spirit into their dealings with their fellowmen, which would make a sad and sordid business of this life.

There is one more article, however, of happier import. "All these indulgences," it appeared, "are applicable to souls in purgatory." For *God's* sake, ye ladies of *Creil*, apply them all to the souls in purgatory without delay! *Burns* would take no hire for his last songs, preferring to serve his country out of unmixed love. Suppose you

were to imitate the exciseman, mesdames, and even if
the souls in purgatory were not greatly bettered, some
souls in *Creil* upon the *Oise* would find themselves none
the worse either here or hereafter.

I cannot help wondering, as I transcribe these notes,
whether a Protestant born and bred is in a fit state to
understand these signs, and do them what justice they
deserve; and I cannot help answering that he is not.
They cannot look so merely ugly and mean to the
faithful as they do to me. I see that as clearly as a
proposition in *Euclid*. For these believers are neither
weak nor wicked. They can put up their tablet com-
mending Saint *Joseph* for his despatch, as if he were
still a village carpenter; they can "recite the required
dizaine," and metaphorically pocket the indulgence, as
if they had done a job for heaven; and then they can
go out and look down unabashed upon this wonderful
river flowing by, and up without confusion at the pin-
point stars, which are themselves great worlds full of
flowing rivers greater than the *Oise*. I see it as plainly,
I say, as a proposition in *Euclid*, that my Protestant
mind has missed the point, and that there goes with
these deformities some higher and more religious spirit
than I dream.

I wonder if other people would make the same allow-
ances for me? Like the ladies of *Creil*, having recited
my rosary of toleration, I look for my indulgence on the
spot.

PRÉCY AND THE MARIONETTES

WE made *Précy* about sundown. The plain is rich with
tufts of poplar. In a wide, luminous curve, the *Oise*
lay under the hillside. A faint mist began to rise and

confound the different distances together. There was
not a sound audible but that of the sheep-bells in some
meadows by the river, and the creaking of a cart down
the long road that descends the hill. The villas in their
gardens, the shops along the street, all seemed to have
been deserted the day before; and I felt inclined to walk
discreetly as one feels in a silent forest. All of a sudden,
we came round a corner, and there, in a little green
round the church, was a bevy of girls in Parisian costumes playing croquet. Their laughter and the hollow
sound of ball and mallet made a cheery stir in the
neighbourhood; and the look of these slim figures, all
corseted and ribboned, produced an answerable disturbance in our hearts. We were within sniff of *Paris*,
it seemed. And here were females of our own species
playing croquet, just as if *Précy* had been a place in
real life, instead of a stage in the fairy land of travel.
For, to be frank, the peasant woman is scarcely to be
counted as a woman at all, and after having passed by
such a succession of people in petticoats digging and
hoeing and making dinner, this company of coquettes
under arms made quite a surprising feature in the landscape, and convinced us at once of being fallible males.

The inn at *Précy* is the worst inn in *France*. Not
even in *Scotland* have I found worse fare. It was kept
by a brother and sister, neither of whom was out of their
teens. The sister, so to speak, prepared a meal for us;
and the brother, who had been tippling, came in and
brought with him a tipsy butcher, to entertain us as
we ate. We found pieces of loo-warm pork among the
salad, and pieces of unknown yielding substance in the
ragoût. The butcher entertained us with pictures of
Parisian life, with which he professed himself well
acquainted; the brother sitting the while on the edge

of the billiard table, toppling precariously, and sucking the stump of a cigar. In the midst of these diversions, bang went a drum past the house, and a hoarse voice began issuing a proclamation. It was a man with marionettes announcing a performance for that evening.

He had set up his caravan and lighted his candles on another part of the girls' croquet green, under one of those open sheds which are so common in *France* to shelter markets; and he and his wife, by the time we strolled up there, were trying to keep order with the audience.

It was the most absurd contention. The show-people had set out a certain number of benches; and all who sat upon them were to pay a couple of *sous* for the accommodation. They were always quite full—a bumper house—as long as nothing was going forward; but let the show-woman appear with an eye to a collection, and at the first rattle of her tambourine, the audience slipped off the seats, and stood round on the outside with their hands in their pockets. It certainly would have tried an angel's temper. The showman roared from the proscenium; he had been all over *France*, and nowhere, nowhere, "not even on the borders of *Germany*," had he met with such misconduct. Such thieves and rogues and rascals, as he called them! And every now and again, the wife issued on another round, and added her shrill quota to the tirade. I remarked here, as elsewhere, how far more copious is the female mind in the material of insult. The audience laughed in high good humour over the man's declamations; but they bridled and cried aloud under the woman's pungent sallies. She picked out the sore points. She had the honour of the village at her mercy. Voices answered her angrily out of the crowd, and received

a smarting retort for their trouble. A couple of old
ladies beside me, who had duly paid for their seats,
waxed very red and indignant, and discoursed to each
other audibly about the impudence of these mountebanks; but as soon as the show-woman caught a whisper
of this, she was down upon them with a swoop: if mesdames could persuade their neighbours to act with
common honesty, the mountebanks, she assured them,
would be polite enough: mesdames had probably had
their bowl of soup, and perhaps a glass of wine that
evening; the mountebanks also had a taste for soup and
did not choose to have their little earnings stolen from
them before their eyes. Once, things came as far as a
brief personal encounter between the showman and
some lads, in which the former went down as readily
as one of his own marionettes to a peal of jeering laughter.

I was a good deal astonished at this scene because I
am pretty well acquainted with the ways of French
strollers, more or less artistic; and have always found
them singularly pleasing. Any stroller must be dear to
the right-thinking heart; if it were only as a living
protest against offices and the mercantile spirit, and
as something to remind us that life is not by necessity
the kind of thing we generally make it. Even a German band, if you see it leaving town in the early morning
for a campaign in country places, among trees and
meadows, has a romantic flavour for the imagination.
There is nobody, under thirty, so dead but his heart
will stir a little at sight of a gypsies' camp. "We are
not cotton-spinners all"; or, at least, not all through.
There is some life in humanity yet: and youth will
now and again find a brave word to say in dispraise of
riches, and throw up a situation to go strolling with a
knapsack.

An Englishman has always special facilities for intercourse with French gymnasts; for *England* is the natural home of gymnasts. This or that fellow, in his tights and spangles, is sure to know a word or two of English, to have drunk English *aff-'n-aff*, and perhaps performed in an English music-hall. He is a countryman of mine by profession. He leaps, like the Belgian boating men, to the notion that I must be an athlete myself.

But the gymnast is not my favourite; he has little or no tincture of the artist in his composition; his soul is small and pedestrian, for the most part, since his profession makes no call upon it, and does not accustom him to high ideas. But if a man is only so much of an actor that he can stumble through a farce, he is made free of a new order of thoughts. He has something else to think about beside the money-box. He has a pride of his own, and, what is of far more importance, he has an aim before him that he can never quite attain. He has gone upon a pilgrimage that will last him his life long, because there is no end to it short of perfection. He will better upon himself a little day by day; or even if he has given up the attempt, he will always remember that once upon a time he had conceived this high ideal, that once upon a time he had fallen in love with a star. "'Tis better to have loved and lost." Although the moon should have nothing to say to *Endymion*, although he should settle down with *Audrey* and feed pigs, do you not think he would move with a better grace, and cherish higher thoughts to the end? The louts he meets at church never had a fancy above *Audrey's* snood, but there is a reminiscence in *Endymion's* heart that, like a spice, keeps it fresh and haughty.

To be even one of the outskirters of art leaves a fine stamp on a man's countenance. I remember once dining with a party in the inn at *Château Landon*. Most of them were unmistakable bagmen; others well-to-do peasantry; but there was one young fellow in a blouse whose face stood out from among the rest surprisingly. It looked more finished; more of the spirit looked out through it; it had a living, expressive air, and you could see that his eyes took things in. My companion and I wondered greatly who and what he could be. It was fair time in *Château Landon*, and when we went along to the booths, we had our question answered; for there was our friend busily fiddling for the peasants to caper to. He was a wandering violinist.

A troop of strollers once came to the inn where I was staying, in the department of *Seine et Marne*. There was a father and mother; two daughters, brazen, blowsy huzzies who sang and acted, without an idea of how to set about either; and a dark young man, like a tutor, a recalcitrant house-painter, who sang and acted not amiss. The mother was the genius of the party, so far as genius can be spoken of with regard to such a pack of incompetent humbugs; and her husband could not find words to express his admiration for her comic countryman. "You should see my old woman," said he, and nodded his beery countenance. One night they performed in the stable-yard, with flaring lamps: a wretched exhibition, coldly looked upon by a village audience. Next night, as soon as the lamps were lighted, there came a plump of rain, and they had to sweep away their baggage as fast as possible, and make off to the barn where they harboured, cold, wet, and supperless. In the morning, a dear friend of mine, who has as warm a heart for strollers as I have myself, made a little collection and sent it by my hands to comfort them for their disappointment. I gave it to the father; he thanked me cordially, and we drank a cup together in the kitchen, talking of roads, and audiences, and hard times.

When I was going, up got my old stroller, and off with his hat. "I am afraid," said he, "that Monsieur will think me altogether a beggar; but I have another demand to make upon him." I began to hate him on the spot. "We play again to-night," he went on. "Of course, I shall refuse to accept any more money from Monsieur and his friends, who have been already so liberal. But our programme of to-night is something truly creditable; and I cling to the idea that Monsieur will honour us with his presence." And then, with a shrug and a smile: "Monsieur understands—the vanity of an artist!" Save the mark! The vanity of an artist! That is the kind of thing that reconciles me to life: a ragged, tippling, incompetent old rogue, with the manners of a gentleman and the vanity of an artist, to keep up his self-respect!

But the man after my own heart is M. de *Vauversin*. It is nearly two years since I saw him first, and indeed I hope I may see him often again. Here is his first programme, as I found it on the breakfast table, and have kept it ever since as a relic of bright days:

"Mesdames et Messieurs,

"Mademoiselle Ferrario et M. de Vauversin auront l'honneur de chanter ce soir les morceaux suivants:

"Mademoiselle Ferrario chantera—Mignon—Diseaux Légers—France—Des Français dorment là—Le château bleu—Où voulez-vous aller?

"M. de Vauversin—Madame Fontaine et M. Robinet —Les plongeurs à cheval—Le Mari mécontent—Tais-toi, gamin—Mon voisin l'original—Heureux comme ça— Comme on est trompé."

They made a stage at one end of the *salle-à-manger*. And what a sight it was to see M. de *Vauversin*, with a cigarette in his mouth, twanging a guitar, and following Mademoiselle *Ferrario's* eyes with the obedient, kindly look of a dog! The entertainment wound up with a tombola, or auction of lottery tickets: an admirable amusement, with all the excitement of gambling, and no hope of gain to make you ashamed of your eagerness; for there, all is loss; you make haste to be out of pocket; it is a competition who shall lose most money for the benefit of M. de *Vauversin* and Mademoiselle *Ferrario*.

M. de *Vauversin* is a small man, with a great head of black hair, a vivacious and engaging air, and a smile that would be delightful if he had better teeth. He was once an actor in the *Châtelet*; but he contracted a nervous affection from the heat and glare of the footlights, which unfitted him for the stage. At this crisis Mademoiselle *Ferrario*, otherwise Mademoiselle *Rita* of the *Alcazar*, agreed to share his wandering fortunes. "I could never forget the generosity of that lady," said he. He wears trousers so tight that it has long been a problem to all who knew him how he manages to get in and out of them. He sketches a little in water-colours; he writes verses; he is the most patient of fishermen, and spent long days at the bottom of the inn-garden fruitlessly dabbling a line in the clear river.

You should hear him recounting his experiences over a bottle of wine; such a pleasant vein of talk as he has, with a ready smile at his own mishaps and every now and then a sudden gravity, like a man who should hear the surf roar while he was telling the perils of the deep. For it was no longer ago than last night, perhaps, that the receipts only amounted to a franc and a half, to cover three francs of railway fare and two of board and lodging.

The *Maire*, a man worth a million of money, sat in the front seat, repeatedly applauding Mdlle *Ferrario*, and yet gave no more than three *sous* the whole evening. Local authorities look with such an evil eye upon the strolling artist. Alas! I know it well, who have been myself taken for one, and pitilessly incarcerated on the strength of the misapprehension. Once, M. de *Vauversin* visited a commissary of police for permission to sing. The commissary, who was smoking at his ease, politely doffed his hat upon the singer's entrance. "Mr. Commissary," he began, "I am an artist." And on went the commissary's hat again. No courtesy for the companions of *Apollo*! "They are as degraded as that," said M. de *Vauversin*, with a sweep of his cigarette.

But what pleased me most was one outbreak of his, when we had been talking all the evening of the rubs, indignities, and pinchings of his wandering life. Someone said it would be better to have a million of money down, and Mddle *Ferrario* admitted that she would prefer that mightily. *"Eh bien, moi non,"*—not I," cried De *Vauversin*, striking the table with his hand. "If anyone is a failure in the world, is it not I? I had an art, in which I have done things well—as well as some—better perhaps than others; and now it is closed against me. I must go about the country gathering coppers and singing nonsense. Do you think I regret my life? Do you think I would rather be a fat burgess, like a calf? Not I! I have had moments when I have been applauded on the boards: I think nothing of that; but I have known in my own mind sometimes, when I had not a clap from the whole house, that I had found a true intonation, or an exact and speaking gesture; and then, messieurs, I have known what pleasure was, what it was to do a thing well, what it was to be an artist."

And to know what art is, is to have an interest for ever, such as no burgess can find in his petty concerns. *Tenez, messieurs, je vais vous le dire*—it is like a religion."

Such, making some allowance for the tricks of memory and the inaccuracies of translation, was the profession of faith of M. de *Vauversin*. I have given him his own name, lest any other wanderer should come across him, with his guitar and cigarette, and Mademoiselle *Ferrario*; for should not all the world delight to honour this unfortunate and loyal follower of the Muses? May *Apollo* send him rimes hitherto undreamed of; may the river be no longer scanty of her silver fishes to his lure; may the cold not pinch him on long winter rides, nor the village jack-in-office affront him with unseemly manners; and may he never miss Mademoiselle *Ferrario* from his side, to follow with his dutiful eyes and accompany on the guitar!

The marionettes made a very dismal entertainment. They performed a piece, called *Pyramus and Thisbe*, in five mortal acts, and all written in Alexandrines fully as long as the performers. One marionette was the king; another the wicked counsellor; a third, credited with exceptional beauty, represented *Thisbe*; and then there were guards, and obdurate fathers, and walking gentlemen. Nothing particular took place during the two or three acts that I sat out; but you will be pleased to learn that the unities were properly respected, and the whole piece, with one exception, moved in harmony with classical rules. That exception was the comic countryman, a lean marionette in wooden shoes, who spoke in prose and in a broad *patois* much appreciated by the audience. He took unconstitutional liberties with the person of his sovereign; kicked his fellow-marionettes in the mouth with his wooden shoes, and whenever none of the versifying suitors were about, made love to *Thisbe* on his own account in comic prose.

This fellow's evolutions, and the little prologue, in which the showman made a humorous eulogium of his troop, praising their indifference to applause and hisses, and their single devotion to their art, were the only circumstances in the whole affair that you could fancy would so much as raise a smile. But the villagers of *Précy* seemed delighted. Indeed, so long as a thing is an exhibition, and you pay to see it, it is nearly certain to amuse. If we were charged so much a head for sunsets, or if *God* sent round a drum before the hawthorns came in flower, what a work should we not make about their beauty! But these things, like good companions, stupid people early cease to observe: and the Abstract Bagman tittups past in his spring gig, and is positively not aware of the flowers along the lane or the scenery of the weather overhead.

BACK TO THE WORLD

OF the next two days' sail little remains in my mind, and nothing whatever in my note-book. The river streamed on steadily through pleasant riverside lanscapes. Washerwomen in blue dresses, fishers in blue blouses, diversified the green banks; and the relation of the two colours was like that of the flower and the leaf in the *forget-me-not*. A symphony in *forget-me-not*; I think *Théophile Gautier* might thus have characterised that two days' panorama. The sky was blue and cloudless; and the sliding surface of the river held up, in smooth places, a mirror to the heaven and the shores. The washerwomen hailed us laughingly; and the noise of trees and water made an accompaniment to our dozing thoughts, as we fleeted down the stream.

The great volume, the indefatigable purpose of the river, held the mind in chain. It seemed now so sure of its end, so strong and easy in its gait, like a grown man full of determination. The surf was roaring for it on the sands of *Havre*.

For my own part, slipping along this moving thoroughfare in my fiddle-case of a canoe I also was beginning to grow aweary for my ocean. To the civilised man there must come, sooner or later, a desire for civilisation. I was weary of dipping the paddle; I was weary of living on the skirts of life; I wished to be in the thick of it once more; I wished to get to work; I wished to meet people who understood my own speech, and could meet with me on equal terms, as a man, and no longer as a curiosity.

And so a letter at *Pontoise* decided us, and we drew up our keels for the last time out of that river of *Oise* that had faithfully piloted them, through rain and sunshine, for so long. For so many miles had this fleet and footless beast of burthen charioted our fortunes, that we turned our back upon it with a sense of separation. We had made a long detour out of the world, but now we were back in the familiar places, where life itself makes all the running, and we are carried to meet adventure without a stroke of the paddle. Now we were to return, like the voyager in the play, and see what rearrangements fortune had perfected the while in our surroundings; what surprises stood ready made for us at home; and whither and how far the world had voyaged in our absence. You may paddle all day long; but it is when you come back at nightfall, and look in at the familiar room, that you find Love or Death awaiting you beside the stove; and the most beautiful adventures are not those we go to seek.

LITERARY ALLUSIONS IN AN INLAND VOYAGE

AUDREY: A country girl in *As You Like It* (Shakespeare).

CHINA TO PERU:

> "Let observation with extensive view
> Survey mankind from China to Peru."
> —From Samuel Johnson's *Vanity of Human Wishes.*

"COME AWAY DEATH": From a song in Shakespeare's *Twelfth Night.*

GAUTIER, THÉOPHILE: Wrote among other poems *A Symphony in White.*

HEINE: Great German lyric poet; lived 1797–1856.

MISS HOWE and MISS HARLOWE: The two friends in Samuel Richardson's novel *Clarissa Harlowe.*

JUBILATE DEO: Psalm c.

LUCRETIAN MAXIM: Lucretius was a great Latin poet who lived in the first century B.C. He wrote *De Rerum Natura.*

MAMMON: The God of Riches. See the New Testament, Milton's *Paradise Lost,* and Spenser's *Faerie Queene.*

THE MERCHANT BOWS UNTO THE SEAMAN'S STAR . . .: From a song by William Davenant.

MERLIN: The mysterious enchanter in the Arthurian Legend.

MISERERE: Miserere mei, Domine. Psalm li.

MOLIÈRE: The great French writer of Comedy. The "farce" here referred to is *Les Précieuses Ridicules.*

POE'S HORRID STORY: *The Pit and the Pendulum* in *Tales of Mystery and Imagination.*

PUT OFF THY SHOES . . .: See Exodus iii. 5.

PYRAMUS AND THISBE: The play on this story is done in burlesque in Shakespeare's *A Midsummer Night's Dream.*

'TIS BETTER TO HAVE LOVED AND LOST than never to have loved at all: From Tennyson's *In Memoriam,* XXVII.

TRISTRAM SHANDY: The title of a book by Laurence Sterne.

WALT WHITMAN: American poet of the nineteenth century, who broke away from European traditions and wrote free verse. R. L. S. wrote an essay about him in *Familiar Studies of Men and Books*.

ZOLA: A French novelist of the nineteenth century. Famous also as the champion of Dreyfus.

QUESTIONS ON AN INLAND VOYAGE

ANTWERP TO BOOM

1. Explain "In five minutes I had tied my sheet."
2. Explain "For though handsome lads they were all (in Scots phrase) barnacled." Who were they?

ON THE WILLEBROEK CANAL

3. What are the arguments in favour of the profession of bargee?
4 Comment on "They did not move any more than if they had been fishing in an old Dutch print."

THE ROYAL SPORT NAUTIQUE

5. Explain the following: "We are all employed in commerce during the day; but in the evening, *voyez-vous, nous sommes sérieux.*"
6. "Neither of us had the least desire to drive the course of the sun against Apollo." Explain the point and the allusion.

AT MAUBEUGE

7. "To pass the frontier in a train is a difficult matter for the *Arethusa.*" Why?
8. "One person in *Maubeuge,* however, showed me something more than his outside." Explain this.

ON THE SAMBRE CANALISED: TO QUARTES

9. How does Stevenson describe the river when the sun was right ahead? And what is his simile for the black cow with the white head?
10. Explain (1) "I hate cynicism"; (2) "a great amphora of hammered brass."

WE ARE PEDLARS

11. What was the supper provided for the two "hinds"? And
what did the writer and his friend have? What are Stevenson's
reflections on the contrast?

PONT-SUR-SAMBRE

12. Explain (1) flibbertigibbet; (2) képi; (3) galette.
13. Describe Monsieur Hector Gilliard and his family.

TO LANDRECIES

14. Think of another smell as characteristic and delightful as
the smell of trees, and describe it in the manner of R. L. S.

15. "Heine wished to lie like Merlin under the oaks." Who
was Heine? Find out what you can about him; and look up
Merlin.

AT LANDRECIES

16. Compare what Stevenson says about donkeys here with
"The Green Donkey Driver" in Travels with a Donkey.
17. Who entertained the travellers at Landrecies, and how?

CANAL BOATS

18. What is "the better part of religion," and "the better part
of manliness"?
19. Describe the ideal canal barge.

THE OISE IN FLOOD

20. What do you notice about the following:—"the river ran
flush and fleet"—"the sun poured its clear and catholic looks"—
"the shadows lay as solid on the swift surface of the stream as on
the stable meadows"—"the reeds stood shivering from top to
toe"?
21. How does Stevenson work out his little homily on the
stream and death?

A BY-DAY

22. What was the contents of "the hawker's little book"?

ORIGNY SAINTE-BENOÎTE

23. "Why was the lymphatic bagman martyred?" Answer the question.

TO MOY

24. Explain "we sacrificed a hecatomb of minutes to the gods of tobacco and digestion." "He was quite feverish at the end, and pleaded demoniacal possession."

LA FÈRE OF CURSED MEMORY

25. Why "of cursed memory"? Explain, with a quotation, exactly what happened.

NOYON CATHEDRAL

26. Describe all the people R. L. S. saw in the Cathedral.

AT COMPIÈGNE

27. What was there peculiar and interesting about the Town Hall?

CHANGED TIMES

28. "I take it, I was about as near Nirvana as would be convenient in practical life; and if this is so, I make the Buddhists my sincere compliments." Explain what this means, and how R. L. S. got so near.

PRÉCY AND THE MARIONETTES

29. "Monsieur will understand the vanity of an artist!" Who says this—and what does he refer to?

EPILOGUE

30. Why was the *Arethusa* arrested, and how was he eventually restored to freedom?

TRAVELS WITH A DONKEY
IN THE CEVENNES

My Dear Sidney Colvin,

The journey which this little book is to describe was very agreeable and fortunate for me. After an uncouth beginning, I had the best of luck to the end. But we are all travellers in what John Bunyan calls the wilderness of this world—all, too, travellers with a donkey; and the best that we find in our travels is an honest friend. He is a fortunate voyager who finds many. We travel, indeed, to find them. They are the end and the reward of life. They keep us worthy of ourselves; and, when we are alone, we are only nearer to the absent.

Every book is, in an intimate sense, a circular letter to the friends of him who writes it. They alone take his meaning; they find private messages, assurances of love, and expressions of gratitude dropped for them in every corner. The public is but a generous patron who defrays the postage. Yet though the letter is directed to all, we have an old and kindly custom of addressing it on the outside to one. Of what shall a man be proud, if he is not proud of his friends? And so, my dear Sidney Colvin, it is with pride that I sign myself affectionately yours,

R. L. S.

CONTENTS

VELAY

UPPER GÉVAUDAN

OUR LADY OF THE SNOWS

UPPER GÉVAUDAN (continued)

THE COUNTRY OF THE CAMISARDS

CONTENTS

VELAY

Many are the mighty things, and naught is more mighty than man. . . . He masters by his devices the tenant of the fields.—SOPHOCLES.

Who hath loosed the bands of the wild ass?—JOB.

THE DONKEY, THE PACK, AND THE PACK-SADDLE

IN a little place called Le Monastier, in a pleasant highland valley fifteen miles from Le Puy, I spent about a month of fine days. Monastier is notable for the making of lace, for drunkenness, for freedom of language, and for unparalleled political dissension. There are adherents of each of the four French parties—Legitimists, Orleanists, Imperialists, and Republicans—in this little mountain-town; and they all hate, loathe, decry, and calumniate each other. Except for business purposes, or to give each other the lie in a tavern brawl, they have laid aside even the civility of speech. 'Tis a mere mountain Poland. In the midst of this Babylon I found myself a rallying point; everyone was anxious to be kind and helpful to the stranger. This was not merely from the natural hospitality of mountain people, nor even from the surprise with which I was regarded as a man living of his own free will in Le Monastier, when he might just as well have lived anywhere else in this big world; it arose a good deal from my projected excursion southward through the Cevennes. A traveller of my sort was a thing hitherto unheard of in that district. I was looked upon with contempt, like a man who should project a journey to the moon, but yet with a respectful interest, like one setting forth for the inclement Pole. All were ready to help in my preparations; a crowd of sympathisers supported me at the critical moment of a bargain; not a step was taken but was heralded by glasses round and celebrated by a dinner or a breakfast.

It was already hard upon October before I was ready to set forth, and at the high altitudes over which my road lay there was no Indian summer to be looked for. I was determined, if not to camp out, at least to have the means of camping out in my possession; for there is nothing more harassing to an easy mind than the necessity of reaching shelter by dusk, and the hospitality of a village inn is not always to be reckoned sure by those who trudge on foot. A tent, above all for a solitary traveller, is troublesome to pitch, and troublesome to strike again; and even on the march it forms a conspicuous feature in your baggage. A sleeping-sack, on the other hand, is always ready—you have only to get into it; it serves a double purpose—a bed by night, a portmanteau by day; and it does not advertise your intention of camping out to every curious passer-by. This is a huge point. If the camp is not secret, it is but a troubled resting-place; you become a public character; the convivial rustic visits your bedside after an early supper; and you must sleep with one eye open, and be up before the day. I decided on a sleeping-sack; and after repeated visits to Le Puy, and a deal of high living for myself and my advisers, a sleeping-sack was designed, constructed, and triumphantly brought home.

This child of my invention was nearly six feet square, exclusive of two triangular flaps to serve as a pillow by night and as the top and bottom of the sack by day. I call it "the sack," but it was never a sack by more than courtesy; only a sort of long roll or sausage, green waterproof cart-cloth without and blue sheep's fur within. It was commodious as a valise, warm and dry for a bed. There was luxurious turning room for one; and at a pinch the thing might serve for two. I could bury myself in it up to the neck; for my head I trusted to a fur cap, with a hood to fold down over my ears and a band to pass under my nose like a respirator; and in case of heavy rain I proposed to make myself a little tent, or tentlet, with my waterproof coat, three stones, and a bent branch.

It will readily be conceived that I could not carry this huge package on my own, merely human, shoulders. It remained to choose a beast of burden. Now, a horse is a fine lady among animals, flighty, timid, delicate in eating, of tender health; he is too valuable and too restive to be left alone, so that you are chained to your brute as to a fellow galley-slave; a dangerous road puts him out of his wits; in short, he's an uncertain and exacting ally, and adds thirty-fold to the troubles of the voyager. What I required was something cheap and small and hardy, and of a stolid and peaceful temper; and all these requisites pointed to a donkey.

There dwelt an old man in Monastier, of rather unsound intellect according to some, much followed by streetboys, and known to fame as Father Adam. Father Adam had a cart, and to draw the cart a diminutive she-ass, not much bigger than a dog, the colour of a mouse, with a kindly eye and a determined under-jaw. There was something neat and high-bred, a quakerish elegance, about the rogue that hit my fancy on the spot. Our first interview was in Monastier market-place. To prove her good temper, one child after another was set upon her back to ride and one after another went head over heels into the air; until a want of confidence began to reign in youthful bosoms, and the experiment was discontinued from a dearth of subjects. I was already backed by a deputation of my friends; but as if this were not enough, all the buyers and sellers came round and helped me in the bargain; and the ass and I and Father Adam were the centre of a hubbub for near half an hour. At length she passed into my service for the consideration of sixty-five francs and a glass of brandy. The sack had already cost eighty francs and two glasses of beer; so that Modestine, as I instantly baptised her, was upon all accounts the cheaper article. Indeed, that was as it should be; for she was only an appurtenance of my mattress, or self-acting bedstead on four castors.

I had a last interview with Father Adam in a billiard-room at the witching hour of dawn, when I administered the brandy. He professed himself greatly touched by the separation, and declared he had often bought white bread for the donkey when he had been content with black bread for himself; but this, according to the best authorities, must have been a flight of fancy. He had a name in the village for brutally misusing the ass; yet it is certain that he shed a tear, and the tear made a clean mark down one cheek.

By the advice of a fallacious local saddler, a leather pad was made for me with rings to fasten on my bundle; and I thoughtfully completed my kit and arranged my toilette. By way of armoury and utensils, I took a revolver, a little spirit-lamp and pan, a lantern and some half-penny candles, a jack-knife and a large leather flask. The main cargo consisted of two entire changes of warm clothing—besides my travelling wear of country velveteen, pilot-coat, and knitted spencer—some books, and my railway-rug, which, being also in the form of a bag, made me a double castle for cold nights. The permanent larder was represented by cakes of chocolate and tins of Bologna sausage. All this, except what I carried about my person, was easily stowed into the sheepskin bag; and by good fortune I threw in my empty knapsack, rather for convenience of carriage than from any thought that I should want it on my journey. For more immediate needs I took a leg of cold mutton, a bottle of Beaujolais, an empty bottle to carry milk, an egg-beater, and a considerable quantity of black bread and white, like Father Adam, for myself and donkey, only in my scheme of things the destinations were reversed.

Monastrians, of all shades of thought in politics, had agreed in threatening me with many ludicrous misadventures, and with sudden death in many surprising forms. Cold, wolves, robbers, above all the nocturnal practical joker, were daily and eloquently forced on my attention. Yet in these vaticinations, the true, patent danger was left out. Like Christian, it was from my pack I suffered by the way. Before telling my own mishaps, let me in two words relate the lesson of my experience. If the pack is well strapped at the ends, and hung at full length—not doubled, for your life—across the pack-saddle, the traveller is safe. The saddle will certainly not fit, such is the imperfection of our transitory life; it will assuredly topple and tend to overset; but there are stones on every roadside, and a man soon learns the art of correcting any tendency to overbalance with a well-adjusted stone.

On the day of my departure I was up a little after

five; by six, we began to load the donkey; and ten
minutes after, my hopes were in the dust. The pad
would not stay on Modestine's back for half a moment.
I returned it to its maker, with whom I had so contume-
lious a passage that the street outside was crowded
from wall to wall with gossips looking on and listening.
The pad changed hands with much vivacity; perhaps
it would be more descriptive to say that we threw it
at each other's heads; and, at any rate, we were very
warm and unfriendly, and spoke with a deal of freedom.

I had a common donkey pack-saddle—a *barde*, as
they call it—fitted upon Modestine; and once more
loaded her with my effects. The doubled sack, my
pilot-coat (for it was warm, and I was to walk in my
waistcoat), a great bar of black bread, and an open
basket containing the white bread, the mutton, and the
bottles, were all corded together in a very elaborate
system of knots, and I looked on the result with fatuous
content. In such a monstrous deck-cargo, all poised
above the donkey's shoulders, with nothing below to
balance, on a brand-new pack-saddle that had not yet
been worn to fit the animal, and fastened with brand-new
girths that might be expected to stretch and slacken by
the way, even a very careless traveller should have
seen disaster brewing. That elaborate system of knots,
again, was the work of too many sympathisers to be
very artfully designed. It is true they tightened the
cords with a will; as many as three at a time would
have a foot against Modestine's quarters, and be hauling
with clenched teeth; but I learned afterwards that one
thoughtful person, without any exercise of force, can
make a more solid job than half-a-dozen heated and
enthusiastic grooms. I was then but a novice; even
after the misadventure of the pad nothing could disturb

my security, and I went forth from the stable-door as
an ox goeth to the slaughter.

THE GREEN DONKEY-DRIVER

THE bell of Monastier was just striking nine as I got quit
of these preliminary troubles and descended the hill
through the common. As long as I was within sight of
the windows, a secret shame and the fear of some
laughable defeat withheld me from tampering with
Modestine. She tripped along upon her four small
hoofs with a sober daintiness of gait; from time to time
she shook her ears or her tail; and she looked so small
under the bundle that my mind misgave me. We got
across the ford without difficulty—there was no doubt
about the matter, she was docility itself—and once
on the other bank, where the road begins to mount
through pine-woods, I took in my right hand the unhal-
lowed staff, and with a quaking spirit applied it to the
donkey. Modestine brisked up her pace for perhaps
three steps, and then relapsed into her former minuet.
Another application had the same effect, and so with
the third. I am worthy the name of an Englishman,
and it goes against my conscience to lay my hand
rudely on a female. I desisted, and looked her all over
from head to foot; the poor brute's knees were trembling
and her breathing was distressed; it was plain that she
could go no faster on a hill. God forbid, thought I,
that I should brutalise this innocent creature; let her
go at her own pace, and let me patiently follow.

What that pace was, there is no word mean enough
to describe; it was something as much slower than a
walk as a walk is slower than a run; it kept me hanging

on each foot for an incredible length of time; in five
minutes it exhausted the spirit and set up a fever in all
the muscles of the leg. And yet I had to keep close at
hand and measure my advance exactly upon hers;
for if I dropped a few yards into the rear, or went on
a few yards ahead, Modestine came instantly to a halt
and began to browse. The thought that this was to
last from here to Alais nearly broke my heart. Of all
conceivable journeys, this promised to be the most
tedious. I tried to tell myself it was a lovely day;
I tried to charm my foreboding spirit with tobacco;
but I had a vision ever present to me of the long, long
roads, up hill and down dale, and a pair of figures ever
infinitesimally moving, foot by foot, a yard to the minute,
and, like things enchanted in a nightmare, approaching
no nearer to the goal.

In the meantime there came up behind us a tall
peasant, perhaps forty years of age, of an ironical snuffy
countenance, and arrayed in the green tail-coat of the
country. He overtook us hand over hand, and stopped
to consider our pitiful advance.

"Your donkey," says he, "is very old?"

I told him, I believed not.

Then, he supposed, we had come far.

I told him, we had but newly left Monastier.

"*Et vous marchez comme ça!*" cried he; and, throwing
back his head, he laughed long and heartily. I watched
him, half prepared to feel offended, until he had satisfied
his mirth; and then, "You must have no pity on these
animals," said he; and, plucking a switch out of a
thicket, he began to lace Modestine about the stern-
works, uttering a cry. The rogue pricked up her ears
and broke into a good round pace, which she kept up
without flagging, and without exhibiting the least

symptom of distress, as long as the peasant kept beside us. Her former panting and shaking had been, I regret to say, a piece of comedy.

My *deus ex machina*, before he left me, supplied some excellent, if inhumane, advice; presented me with the switch, which he declared she would feel more tenderly than my cane; and finally taught me the true cry or masonic word of donkey-drivers, "Proot!" All the time, he regarded me with a comical, incredulous air, which was embarrassing to confront; and smiled over my donkey-driving, as I might have smiled over his orthography, or his green tail-coat. But it was not my turn for the moment.

I was proud of my new lore, and thought I had learned the art to perfection. And certainly Modestine did wonders for the rest of the forenoon, and I had a breathing space to look about me. It was Sabbath; the mountain fields were all vacant in the sunshine; and as we came down through St. Martin de Frugères, the church was crowded to the door, there were people kneeling without upon the steps, and the sound of the priest's chanting came forth out of the dim interior. It gave me a home feeling on the spot; for I am a countryman of the Sabbath, so to speak, and all Sabbath observances, like a Scottish accent, strike in me mixed feelings, grateful and the reverse. It is only a traveller, hurrying by like a person from another planet, who can rightly enjoy the peace and beauty of the great ascetic feast. The sight of the resting country does his spirit good. There is something better than music in the wide unusual silence; and it disposes him to amiable thoughts, like the sound of a little river or the warmth of sunlight.

In this pleasant humour I came down the hill to where Goudet stands in a green end of a valley, with

Château Beaufort opposite upon a rocky steep, and the stream, as clear as crystal, lying in a deep pool between them. Above and below, you may hear it wimpling over the stones, an amiable stripling of a river, which it seems absurd to call the Loire. On all sides, Goudet is shut in by mountains; rocky footpaths, practicable at best for donkeys, join it to the outer world of France; and the men and women drink and swear, in their green corner, or look up at the snow-clad peaks in winter from the threshold of their homes, in an isolation, you would think, like that of Homer's Cyclops. But it is not so; the postman reaches Goudet with the letter-bag; the aspiring youth of Goudet are within a day's walk of the railway at Le Puy; and here in the inn you may find an engraved portrait of the host's nephew, Régis Senac, "Professor of Fencing and Champion of the two Americas," a distinction gained by him, along with the sum of five hundred dollars, at Tammany Hall, New York, on the 10th April, 1876.

I hurried over my mid-day meal, and was early forth again. But, alas, as we climbed the interminable hill upon the other side, "Proot!" seemed to have lost its virtue. I prooted like a lion, I prooted mellifluously like a sucking-dove; but Modestine would be neither softened nor intimidated. She held doggedly to her pace; nothing but a blow would move her, and that only for a second. I must follow at her heels, incessantly belabouring. A moment's pause in this ignoble toil, and she relapsed into her own private gait. I think I never heard of anyone in as mean a situation. I must reach the lake of Bouchet, where I meant to camp, before sun-down, and, to have even a hope of this, I must instantly maltreat this uncomplaining animal. The sound of my own blows sickened me.

Once, when I looked at her, she had a faint resemblance to a lady of my acquaintance who formerly loaded me with kindness; and this increased my horror of my cruelty.

To make matters worse, we encountered another donkey, ranging at will upon the roadside; and this other donkey chanced to be a gentleman. He and Modestine met nickering for joy, and I had to separate the pair and beat down their young romance with a renewed and feverish bastinado. If the other donkey had had the heart of a male under his hide, he would have fallen upon me tooth and hoof; and this was a kind of consolation—he was plainly unworthy of Modestine's affection. But the incident saddened me, as did everything that spoke of my donkey's sex.

It was blazing hot up the valley, windless, with vehement sun upon my shoulders; and I had to labour so consistently with my stick that the sweat ran into my eyes. Every five minutes, too, the pack, the basket, and the pilot-coat would take an ugly slew to one side or the other; and I had to stop Modestine, just when I had got her to a tolerable pace of about two miles an hour, to tug, push, shoulder, and readjust the load. And at last, in the villaage of Ussel, saddle and all, the whole hypothec turned round and grovelled in the dust below the donkey's belly. She, none better pleased, incontinently drew up and seemed to smile; and a party of one man, two women, and two children came up, and, standing round me in a half-circle, encouraged her by their example.

I had the devil's own trouble to get the thing righted; and the instant I had done so, without hesitation, it toppled and fell down upon the other side. Judge if I was hot! And yet not a hand was offered to assist

me. The man, indeed, told me I ought to have a
package of a different shape. I suggested, if he knew
nothing better to the point in my predicament, he might
hold his tongue. And the good-natured dog agreed
with me smilingly. It was the most despicable fix. I
must plainly content myself with the pack for Modestine,
and take the following items for my own share of the
portage: a cane, a quart flask, a pilot-jacket heavily
weighted in the pockets, two pounds of black bread,
and an open basket full of meats and bottles. I believe
I may say I am not devoid of greatness of soul; for I did
not recoil from this infamous burden. I disposed it,
Heaven knows how, so as to be mildly portable, and
then proceeded to steer Modestine through the village.
She tried, as was indeed her invariable habit, to enter
every house and every courtyard in the whole length;
and, encumbered as I was, without a hand to help
myself, no words can render an idea of my difficulties.
A priest, with six or seven others, was examining a
church in process of repair, and he and his acolytes
laughed loudly as they saw my plight. I remembered
having laughed myself when I had seen good men
struggling with adversity in the person of a jackass, and
the recollection filled me with penitence. That was in
my old light days, before this trouble came upon me.
God knows at least that I shall never laugh again,
thought I. But oh, what a cruel thing is a farce to
those engaged in it!

A little out of the village, Modestine, filled with the
demon, set her heart upon a by-road, and positively
refused to leave it. I dropped all my bundles, and, I
am ashamed to say, struck the poor sinner twice across
the face. It was pitiful to see her lift up her head with
shut eyes, as if waiting for another blow. I came

very near crying; but I did a wiser thing than that, and sat squarely down by the roadside to consider my situation under the cheerful influence of tobacco and a nip of brandy. Modestine, in the meanwhile, munched some black bread with a contrite hypocritical air. It was plain that I must make a sacrifice to the gods of shipwreck. I threw away the empty bottle destined to carry milk; I threw away my own white bread, and, disdaining to act by general average, kept the black bread for Modestine; lastly, I threw away the cold leg of mutton and the egg-whisk, although this last was dear to my heart. Thus I found room for everything in the basket, and even stowed the boating-coat on the top. By means of an end of cord I slung it under one arm; and although the cord cut my shoulder, and the jacket hung almost to the ground, it was with a heart greatly lightened that I set forth again.

I had now an arm free to thrash Modestine, and cruelly I chastised her. If I were to reach the lakeside before dark, she must bestir her little shanks to some tune. Already the sun had gone down into a windy-looking mist; and although there were still a few streaks of gold far off to the east on the hills and the black fir-woods, all was cold and grey about our onward path. An infinity of little country by-roads led hither and thither among the fields. It was the most pointless labyrinth. I could see my destination overhead, or rather the peak that dominates it; but choose as I pleased, the roads always ended by turning away from it, and sneaking back towards the valley, or northward along the margin of the hills. The failing light, the waning colour, the naked, unhomely, stony country through which I was travelling, threw me into some despondency. I promise you, the stick was not idle; I think every decent step that Modestine took must have cost me at least two emphatic blows. There was not another sound in the neighbourhood but that of my unwearying bastinado.

Suddenly, in the midst of my toils, the load once more bit the dust, and, as by enchantment, all the cords were simultaneously loosened, and the road scattered with my dear possessions. The packing was to begin again from the beginning; and as I had to invent a new and better system, I do not doubt but I lost half an hour. It began to be dusk in earnest as I reached a wilderness of turf and stones. It had the air of being a road which should lead everywhere at the same time; and I was falling into something not unlike despair when I saw two figures stalking towards me over the stones. They walked one behind the other like tramps, but their pace was remarkable. The son led the way, a tall, ill-made, sombre, Scottish-looking man; the mother followed, all in her Sunday's best, with an elegantly embroidered ribbon to her cap, and a new felt hat atop, and proffering, as she strode along with kilted petticoats, a string of obscene and blasphemous oaths.

I hailed the son, and asked him my direction. He pointed loosely west and north-west, muttered an inaudible comment, and, without slackening his pace for an instant, stalked on, as he was going, right athwart my path. The mother followed without so much as raising her head. I shouted and shouted after them, but they continued to scale the hillside, and turned a deaf ear to my outcries. At last, leaving Modestine by herself, I was constrained to run after them, hailing the while. They stopped as I drew near, the mother still cursing; and I could see she was a handsome, motherly, respectable-looking woman. The son once more answered me roughly and inaudibly, and was for setting out again. But this time I simply collared the mother, who was nearest me, and, apologising for my violence, declared that I could not let them go until they had put me on my road. They were neither of them offended —rather mollified than otherwise; told me I had only to follow them; and then the mother asked me what I wanted by the lake at such an hour. I replied, in the Scottish manner, by inquiring if she had far to go herself. She told me, with another oath, that she had an hour and a half's road before her. And then, without salutation, the pair strode forward again up the hillside in the gathering dusk.

I returned for Modestine, pushed her briskly forward, and, after a sharp ascent of twenty minutes, reached the edge of a plateau. The view, looking back on my day's journey, was both wild and sad. Mount Mézenc and the peaks beyond St. Julien stood out in trenchant gloom against a cold glitter in the east; and the intervening field of hills had fallen together into one broad wash of shadow, except here and there the outline of a wooded sugar-loaf in black, here and there a white irregular patch to represent a cultivated farm; and here and there a blot where the Loire, the Gazeille, or the Laussonne wandered in a gorge.

Soon we were on a high-road, and surprise seized on my mind as I beheld a village of some magnitude close at hand; for I had been told that the neighbourhood of the lake was uninhabited except by trout. The road smoked in the twilight with children driving home cattle from the fields; and a pair of mounted stride-legged women, hat and cap and all, dashed past me at a hammering trot from the canton where they had been to church and market. I asked one of the children where I was. At Bouchet St. Nicolas, he told me.

Thither, about a mile south of my destination, and on the other side of a respectable summit, had these confused roads and treacherous peasantry conducted me. My shoulder was cut, so that it hurt sharply; my arm ached like toothache from perpetual beating; I gave up the lake and my design to camp, and asked for the *auberge*.

I HAVE A GOAD

THE *auberge* of Bouchet St. Nicolas was among the least pretentious I have ever visited; but I saw many more of the like upon my journey. Indeed, it was typical of these French highlands. Imagine a cottage of two stories, with a bench before the door; the stable and kitchen in a suite, so that Modestine and I could hear each other dining; furniture of the plainest, earthen floors, a single bedchamber for travellers, and that without any convenience but beds. In the kitchen cooking and eating go forward side by side, and the family sleep at night. Anyone who has a fancy to wash must do so in public at the common table. The food is sometimes spare; hard fish and omelette have been my portion more than once; the wine is of the smallest, the brandy abominable to man; and the visit of a fat sow, grouting under the table and rubbing against your legs, is no impossible accompaniment to dinner.

But the people of the inn, in nine cases out of ten, show themselves friendly and considerate. As soon as you cross the doors you cease to be a stranger; and although these peasantry are rude and forbidding on the highway, they show a tincture of kind breeding when you share their hearth. At Bouchet, for instance,

I uncorked my bottle of Beaujolais, and asked the host to join me. He would take but little.

" I am an <u>amateur</u> of such wine, do you see? " he said, *lover.* "and I am capable of leaving you not enough."

In these <u>hedge-inns</u> the traveller is expected to eat *small country inn* with his own knife; unless he ask, no other will be supplied: with a glass, a <u>whang</u> of bread, and an iron *slice* fork, the table is completely laid. My knife was cordially admired by the landlord of Bouchet, and the spring filled him with wonder.

"I should never have guessed that," he said. "I would bet," he added, weighing it in his hand, "that this cost you not less than five francs."

When I told him it had cost me twenty, his jaw dropped.

He was a mild, handsome, sensible, friendly old man, astonishingly ignorant. His wife, who was not so pleasant in her manners, knew how to read, although I do not suppose she ever did so. She had a share of brains and spoke with a cutting emphasis, like one who ruled the roast.

" My man knows nothing," she said, with an angry nod; "he is like the beasts."

And the old gentleman <u>signified acquiescence</u> with his *nodded in agreement* head. There was no contempt on her part, and no shame on his; the facts were accepted loyally, and no more about the matter.

I was tightly cross-examined about my journey; and the lady understood in a moment, and sketched out what I should put into my book when I got home. "<u>Whether people harvest or not in such or such a place; if there were forests; studies of manners; what, for example, I and the master of the house say to you; the beauties of Nature, and all that</u>." And she interrogated me with a look.

"It is just that," said I.

"You see," she added to her husband, "I understood that."

They were both much interested by the story of my misadventures.

"In the morning," said the husband, "I will make you something better than your cane. Such a beast as that feels nothing; it is in the proverb—*dur comme un âne*; you might beat her insensible with a cudgel, and yet you would arrive nowhere."

Something better! I little knew what he was offering. The sleeping-room was furnished with two beds. I had one; and I will own I was a little abashed to find a young man and his wife and child in the act of mounting into the other. This was my first experience of the sort; and, if I am always to feel equally silly and extraneous, I pray God it be my last as well. I kept my eyes to myself, and know nothing of the woman except that she had beautiful arms, and seemed no whit embarrassed by my appearance. As a matter of fact, the situation was more trying to me than to the pair. A pair keep each other in countenance; it is the single gentleman who has to blush. But I could not help attributing my sentiments to the husband, and sought to conciliate his tolerance with a cup of brandy from my flask. He told me that he was a cooper of Alais travelling to St. Etienne in search of work, and that in his spare moments he followed the fatal calling of a maker of matches. Me he readily enough divined to be a brandy merchant.

I was up first in the morning (Monday, September 23rd), and hastened my toilette guiltily, so as to leave a clear field for madam, the cooper's wife. I drank a bowl of milk, and set off to explore the neighbourhood of Bouchet. It was perishing cold, a grey, windy, wintry morning; misty clouds flew fast and low; the wind piped over the naked platform; and the only speck of colour was away behind Mount Mézenc and the eastern hills, where the sky still wore the orange of the dawn.

It was five in the morning, and four thousand feet above the sea; and I had to bury my hands in my pockets and trot. People were trooping out to the labours of the field by twos and threes, and all turned round to stare upon the stranger. I had seen them coming back last night, I saw them going afield again; and there was the life of Bouchet in a nutshell.

When I came back to the inn for a bit of breakfast, the landlady was in the kitchen combing out her daughter's hair; and I made her my compliments upon its beauty.

"Oh no," said the mother; "it is not so beautiful as it ought to be. Look, it is too fine."

Thus does a wise peasantry console itself under adverse physical circumstances, and by a startling democratic process, the defects of the majority decide the type of beauty.

"And where," said I, "is monsieur?"

"The master of the house is upstairs," she answered, "making you a goad."

Blessed be the man who invented goads! Blessed the innkeeper of Bouchet St. Nicolas, who introduced me to their use! This plain wand, with an eighth of an inch of pin, was indeed a sceptre when he put it in my hands. Thenceforward Modestine was my slave. A prick, and she passed the most inviting stable door. A prick, and she broke forth into a gallant little trotlet that devoured the miles. It was not a remarkable speed, when all was said; and we took four hours to cover ten miles at the best of it. But what a heavenly change since yesterday! No more wielding of the ugly cudgel; no more flailing with an aching arm; no more broadsword exercise, but a discreet and gentlemanly fence. And what although now and then a drop of blood should appear on Modestine's mouse-coloured wedge-like rump? I should have preferred it otherwise, indeed; but yesterday's exploits had purged my heart of all humanity. The perverse little devil, since she would not be taken with kindness, must even go with pricking.

It was bleak and bitter cold, and, except a cavalcade of stride-legged ladies and a pair of post-runners, the road was dead solitary all the way to Pradelles. I scarce remember an incident but one. A handsome foal with a bell about his neck came charging up to us upon a stretch of common, sniffed the air martially as one about to do great deeds, and suddenly thinking otherwise in his green young heart, put about and galloped off as he had come, the bell tinkling in the wind. For a long while afterwards I saw his noble attitude as he drew up, and heard the note of his bell; and when I struck the high-road, the song of the telegraph-wires seemed to continue the same music.

Pradelles stands on a hillside, high above the Allier, surrounded by rich meadows. They were cutting aftermath on all sides, which gave the neighbourhood, this gusty autumn morning, an untimely smell of hay. On the opposite bank of the Allier the land kept mounting for miles to the horizon: a tanned and sallow autumn landscape, with black blots of fir-wood and white roads wandering through the hills. Over all this the clouds shed a uniform and purplish shadow, sad and somewhat menacing, exaggerating height and distance, and throwing into still higher relief the twisted ribbons of the highway. It was a cheerless prospect, but one stimulating to a traveller. For I was now upon the limit of Velay, and all that I beheld lay in another county— wild Gévaudan, mountainous, uncultivated, and but recently disforested from terror of the wolves.

Wolves, alas, like bandits, seem to flee the traveller's advance; and you may trudge through all our comfortable Europe, and not meet with an adventure worth the name. But here, if anywhere, a man was on the frontiers of hope. For this was the land of the ever-memorable BEAST, the Napoleon Bonaparte of wolves. What a career was his! He lived ten months at free quarters in Gévaudan and Vivarais; he ate women and children and "shepherdesses celebrated for their beauty"; he pursued armed horsemen; he had been seen at broad noonday chasing a post-chaise and outrider along the king's high-road, and chaise and outrider fleeing before him at the gallop. He was placarded like a political offender, and ten thousand francs were offered for his head. And yet, when he was shot and sent to Versailles, behold! a common wolf, and even small for that. "Though I could reach from pole to pole," sang Alexander Pope; the Little Corporal shook Europe; and if all wolves had been as this wolf, they would have changed the history of man. M. Élie Berthet has made him the hero of a novel, which I have read, and do not wish to read again.

I hurried over my lunch, and was proof against the landlady's desire that I should visit our Lady of Pradelles, "who performed many miracles, although she was of wood"; and before three-quarters of an hour I was goading Modestine down the steep descent that leads to Langogne on the Allier. On both sides of the road, in

F

big dusty fields, farmers were preparing for next spring.
Every fifty yards a yoke of great-necked stolid oxen
were patiently haling at the plough. I saw one of these
mild formidable servants of the glebe, who took a sudden
interest in Modestine and me. The furrow down which
he was journeying lay at an angle to the road, and his
head was solidly fixed to the yoke like those of carya-
tides below a ponderous cornice; but he screwed round
his big honest eyes and followed us with a ruminating
look, until his master bade him turn the plough and
proceed to reascend the field. From all these furrowing
ploughshares, from the feet of oxen, from a labourer
here and there who was breaking the dry clods with a
hoe, the wind carried away a thin dust like so much
smoke. It was a fine, busy, breathing, rustic landscape;
and as I continued to descend, the highlands of Gévaudan
kept mounting in front of me against the sky.

I had crossed the Loire the day before; now I was
to cross the Allier; so near are these two confluents in
their youth. Just at the bridge of Langogne, as the
long-promised rain was beginning to fall, a lassie of some
seven or eight addressed me in the sacramental phrase,
"*D'où'st-ce-que vous venez?*" She did it with so high
an air that she set me laughing; and this cut her to the
quick. She was evidently one who reckoned on respect,
and stood looking after me in silent <u>dudgeon</u>, as I crossed
the bridge and entered the county of Gévaudan.

Annoyance

UPPER GÉVAUDAN

The way also here was very wearisome through dirt and slab-
biness; nor was there on all this ground so much as one inn or
victualling-house wherein to refresh the feebler sort.—*Pilgrim's
Progress*.

A CAMP IN THE DARK

THE next day (Tuesday, September 24th), it was two
o'clock in the afternoon before I got my journal written
up and my knapsack repaired, for I was determined to
carry my knapsack in the future and have no more
ado with baskets; and half an hour afterwards I set
out for Le Cheylard l'Évêque, a place on the borders
of the forest of Mercoire. A man, I was told, should
walk there in an hour and a half; and I thought it scarce
too ambitious to suppose that a man encumbered with
a donkey might cover the same distance in four hours.

All the way up the long hill from Langogne it rained
and hailed alternately; the wind kept freshening steadily,
although slowly; plentiful hurrying clouds—some drag-
ging veils of straight rain-shower, others massed and
luminous as though promising snow—careered out of
the north and followed me along my way. I was soon
out of the cultivated basin of the Allier, and away
from the ploughing oxen, and such-like sights of the
country. Moor, heathery marsh, tracts of rock and
pines, woods of birch all jewelled with the autumn
yellow, here and there a few naked cottages and bleak
fields,—these were the characters of the country. Hill

and valley followed valley and hill; the little green and stony cattle-tracks wandered in and out of one another, split into three or four, died away in marshy hollows, and began again sporadically on hillsides or at the borders of a wood.

There was no direct road to Cheylard, and it was no easy affair to make a passage in this uneven country and through this intermittent labyrinth of tracks. It must have been about four when I struck Sagnerousse, and went on my way rejoicing in a sure point of departure. Two hours afterwards, the dusk rapidly falling, in a lull of the wind, I issued from a fir-wood where I had long been wandering, and found, not the looked-for village, but another marish bottom among rough-and-tumble hills. For some time past I had heard the ringing of cattle-bells ahead; and now, as I came out of the skirts of the wood, I saw near upon a dozen cows and perhaps as many more black figures, which I conjectured to be children, although the mist had almost unrecognisably exaggerated their forms. These were all silently following each other round and round in a circle, now taking hands, now breaking up with chains and reverences. A dance of children appeals to very innocent and lively thoughts; but, at nightfall on the marshes, the thing was eerie and fantastic to behold. Even I, who am well enough read in Herbert Spencer, felt a sort of silence fall for an instant on my mind. The next I was pricking Modestine forward, and guiding her like an unruly ship through the open. In a path, she went doggedly ahead of her own accord, as before a fair wind; but once on the turf or among heather, and the brute became demented. The tendency of lost travellers to go round in a circle was developed in her to the degree of passion, and it took all the steering I had in me to keep even a decently straight course through a single field.

While I was thus desperately tacking through the bog, children and cattle began to disperse, until only a pair of girls remained behind. From these I sought direction on my path. The peasantry in general were but little disposed to counsel a wayfarer. One old devil simply retired into his house, and barricaded the door on my approach; and I might beat and shout myself hoarse, he turned a deaf ear. Another, having given me a direction which, as I found afterwards, I had misunderstood, complacently watched me going wrong without adding a sign. He did not care a stalk of parsley if I wandered all night upon the hills! As for these two girls, they were a pair of impudent sly sluts, with not a thought but mischief. One put out her tongue at me, the other bade me follow the cows, and they both giggled and jogged each other's elbows. The Beast of Gévaudan ate about a hundred children of this district; I began to think of him with sympathy.

Leaving the girls, I pushed on through the bog, and got into another wood and upon a well marked road. It grew darker and darker. Modestine, suddenly beginning to smell mischief, bettered the pace of her own accord, and from that time forward gave me no trouble. It was the first sign of intelligence I had occasion to remark in her. At the same time, the wind freshened into half a gale, and another heavy discharge of rain came flying up out of the north. At the other side of the wood I sighted some red windows in the dusk. This was the hamlet of Fouzilhic; three houses on a hillside, near a wood of birches. Here I found a delightful old man, who came a little way with me in the rain to put me safely on the road for Cheylard. He would hear of no reward, but shook his hands above his head almost as if in menace, and refused volubly and shrilly, in unmitigated *patois*.

All seemed right at last. My thoughts began to turn upon dinner and a fireside, and my heart was agreeably softened in my bosom. Alas, and I was on the brink of new and greater miseries! Suddenly, at a single swoop, the night fell. I have been abroad in many a black night, but never in a blacker. A glimmer of rocks, a glimmer of the track where it was well beaten, a certain fleecy density, or night within night, for a tree,—this was all that I could discriminate. The sky was simply darkness overhead; even the flying clouds pursued their way invisibly to human eyesight. I could not distinguish my hand at arm's-length from the track, nor my goad, at the same distance, from the meadows or the sky.

Soon the road that I was following split, after the fashion of the country, into three or four in a piece of rocky meadow. Since Modestine had shown such a fancy for beaten roads, I tried her instinct in this predicament. But the instinct of an ass is what might be expected from the name; in half a minute she was clambering round and round among some boulders, as lost a donkey as you would wish to see. I should have camped long before had I been properly provided; but as this was to be so short a stage, I had brought no wine, no bread for myself, and little over a pound for my lady friend. Add to this, that I and Modestine were both handsomely wetted by the showers. But now, if I could have found some water, I should have camped at once in spite of all. Water, however, being entirely absent, except in the form of rain, I determined to return to Fouzilhic, and ask a guide a little farther on my way—"a little farther lend thy guiding hand."

The thing was easy to decide, hard to accomplish. In this sensible roaring blackness I was sure of nothing but the direction of the wind. To this I set my face. The road had disappeared, and I went across country, now in marshy opens, now baffled by walls unscalable to Modestine, until I came once more in sight of some red windows. This time they were differently disposed. It was not Fouzilhic, but Fouzilhac, a hamlet little distant from the other in space, but worlds away in the spirit of its inhabitants. I tied Modestine to a gate, and groped forward, stumbling among rocks, plunging mid-leg in bog, until I gained the entrance of the village. In the first lighted house there was a woman who would not open to me. She could do nothing, she cried to me through the door, being alone and lame; but if I would apply at the next house, there was a man who could help me if he had a mind.

They came to the next door in force, a man, two women, and a girl, and brought a pair of lanterns to examine the wayfarer. The man was not ill-looking, but had a shifty smile. He leaned against the doorpost, and heard me state my case. All I asked was a guide as far as Cheylard.

"*C'est que, voyez-vous, il fait noir*," said he.

I told him that was just my reason for requiring help.

"I understand that," said he, looking uncomfortable; "*mais—c'est—de la peine.*"

I was willing to pay, I said. He shook his head. I rose as high as ten francs; but he continued to shake his head.

"Name your own price, then," said I.

"*Ce n'est pas ça*," he said at length, and with evident difficulty; "but I am not going to cross the door—*mais je ne sortirai pas de la porte.*"

I grew a little warm, and asked him what he proposed that I should do.

"Where are you going beyond Cheylard?" he asked by way of answer.

"That is no affair of yours," I returned, for I was not going to indulge his bestial curiosity; "it changes nothing in my present predicament."

"*C'est vrai, ça,*" he acknowledged, with a laugh; "*oui, c'est vrai. Et d'où venez-vous?*"

A better man than I might have felt nettled.

"Oh," said I, "I am not going to answer any of your questions, so you may spare yourself the trouble of putting them. I am late enough already; I want help. If you will not guide me yourself, at least help me to find someone else who will."

"Hold on," he cried suddenly. "Was it not you who passed in the meadow while it was still day?"

"Yes, yes," said the girl, whom I had not hitherto recognised; "it was monsieur; I told him to follow the cows."

"As for you, mademoiselle," said I, "you are a *farceuse.*"

"And," added the man, "what the devil have you done to be still here?"

What the devil, indeed! But there I was.

"The great thing," said I, "is to make an end of it"; and once more proposed that he should help me to find a guide.

"*C'est que,*" he said again, "*c'est que—il fait noir.*"

"Very well," said I; "take one of your lanterns."

"No," he cried, drawing a thought backward, and again intrenching himself behind one of his former phrases; "I will not cross the door."

I looked at him. I saw unaffected terror struggling

on his face with unaffected shame; he was smiling pitifully and wetting his lip with his tongue, like a detected
schoolboy. I drew a brief picture of my state, and
asked him what I was to do.

"I don't know," he said; "I will not cross the door."

Here was the Beast of Gévaudan, and no mistake.

"Sir," said I, with my most commanding manners,
"you are a coward."

And with that I turned my back upon the family
party, who hastened to retire within their fortifications;
and the famous door was closed again, but not till I
had overheard the sound of laughter. *Filia barbara pater
barbarior*. Let me say it in the plural: the Beasts of
Gévaudan.

The lanterns had somewhat dazzled me, and I ploughed
distressfully among stones and rubbish-heaps. All the
other houses in the village were both dark and silent; and
though I knocked at here and there a door, my knocking
was unanswered. It was a bad business; I gave up
Fouzilhac with my curses. The rain had stopped, and
the wind, which still kept rising, began to dry my coat
and trousers. "Very well," thought I, "water or no
water, I must camp." But the first thing was to
return to Modestine. I am pretty sure I was twenty
minutes groping for my lady in the dark; and if it had
not been for the unkindly services of the bog, into which
I once more stumbled, I might have still been groping
for her at the dawn. My next business was to gain the
shelter of a wood, for the wind was cold as well as bois-
terous. How, in this well-wooded district, I should
have been so long in finding one, is another of the insoluble mysteries of this day's adventures; but I will
take my oath that I put near an hour to the discovery.

At last black trees began to show upon my left, and,

suddenly crossing the road, made a cave of unmitigated blackness right in front. I call it a cave without exaggeration; to pass below that arch of leaves was like entering a dungeon. I felt about until my hand encountered a stout branch, and to this I tied Modestine, a haggard, drenched, desponding donkey. Then I lowered my pack, laid it along the wall on the margin of the road, and unbuckled the straps. I knew well enough where the lantern was; but where were the candles? I groped and groped among the tumbled articles, and, while I was thus groping, suddenly I touched the spirit-lamp. Salvation! This would serve my turn as well. The wind roared unwearyingly among the trees; I could hear the boughs tossing and the leaves churning through half a mile of forest; yet the scene of my encampment was not only as black as the pit, but admirably sheltered. At the second match the wick caught flame. The light was both livid and shifting; but it cut me off from the universe, and doubled the darkness of the surrounding night.

I tied Modestine more conveniently for herself, and broke up half the black bread for her supper, reserving the other half against the morning. Then I gathered what I should want within reach, took off my wet boots and gaiters, which I wrapped in my waterproof, arranged my knapsack for a pillow under the flap of my sleeping-bag, insinuated my limbs into the interior, and buckled myself in like a *bambino*. I opened a tin of Bologna sausage and broke a cake of chocolate, and that was all I had to eat. It may sound offensive, but I ate them together, bit by bite, by way of bread and meat. All I had to wash down this revolting mixture was neat brandy; a revolting beverage in itself. But I was rare and hungry; ate well, and smoked one of the best cigarettes in my experience. Then I put a stone in my straw hat, pulled the flap of my fur cap over my neck and eyes, put my revolver ready to my hand, and snuggled well down among the sheepskins.

I questioned at first if I were sleepy, for I felt my heart beating faster than usual, as if with an agreeable excitement to which my mind remained a stranger. But as soon as my eyelids touched, that subtle glue leaped between them, and they would no more come separate. The wind among the trees was my lullaby. Sometimes it sounded for minutes together with a steady, even rush, not rising nor abating; and again it would swell and burst like a great crashing breaker, and the trees would patter me all over with big drops from the rain of the afternoon. Night after night, in my own bedroom in the country, I have given ear to this perturbing concert of the wind among the woods; but whether it was a difference in the trees, or the lie of the ground, or because I was myself outside and in the midst of it, the fact remains that the wind sang to a different tune among these woods of Gévaudan. I hearkened and hearkened: and meanwhile sleep took gradual possession of my body and subdued my thoughts and senses; but still my last waking effort was to listen and distinguish, and my last conscious state was one of wonder at the foreign clamour in my ears.

Twice in the course of the dark hours—once when a stone galled me underneath the sack, and again when the poor patient Modestine, growing angry, pawed and stamped upon the road—I was recalled for a brief while to consciousness, and saw a star or two overhead, and the lace-like edge of the foliage against the sky. When I awoke for the third time (Wednesday, September 25th), the world was flooded with a blue light, the mother of the dawn. I saw the leaves labouring in the wind and the ribbon of the road; and, on turning my head, there was Modestine tied to a beech, and standing half across the path in an attitude of inimitable patience. I closed my eyes again, and set to thinking over the experience of the night. I was surprised to find how easy and pleasant it had been, even in this tempestuous weather. The stone which annoyed me would not have been there, had I not been forced to camp blindfold in the opaque night; and I had felt no other inconvenience, except when my feet encountered the lantern or the second volume of Peyrat's *Pastors of the Desert* among the mixed contents of my sleeping-bag; nay, more, I had felt not a touch of cold, and awakened with unusually lightsome and clear sensations.

With that, I shook myself, got once more into my boots and gaiters, and, breaking up the rest of the bread for Modestine, strolled about to see in what part of the world I had awakened. Ulysses, left on Ithaca, and with a mind unsettled by the goddess, was not more pleasantly astray. I have been after an adventure all my life, a pure dispassionate adventure, such as befell early and heroic voyagers; and thus to be found by morning in a random woodside nook in Gévaudan—not knowing north from south, as strange to my surroundings as the first man upon the earth, an inland castaway —was to find a fraction of my day-dreams realised. I was on the skirts of a little wood of birch, sprinkled with a few beeches; behind, it adjoined another wood of fir; and in front, it broke up and went down in open order into a shallow and meadowy dale. All around there were bare hilltops, some near, some far away, as the perspective closed or opened, but none apparently much higher than the rest. The wind huddled the trees. The

golden specks of autumn in the birches tossed shiveringly.
Overhead the sky was full of strings and shreds of vapour,
flying, vanishing, reappearing, and turning about an
axis like tumblers, as the wind hounded them through *PIGEONS*
heaven. It was wild weather and famishing cold. I
ate some chocolate, swallowed a mouthful of brandy,
and smoked a cigarette before the cold should have
time to disable my fingers. And by the time I had got
all this done, and had made my pack and bound it on
the pack-saddle, the day was tiptoe on the threshold of
the east. We had not gone many steps along the lane
before the sun, still invisible to me, sent a glow of gold
over some cloud mountains that lay ranged along the
eastern sky.

The wind had us on the stern, and hurried us bitingly
forward. I buttoned myself into my coat, and walked
on in a pleasant frame of mind with all men, when
suddenly, at a corner, there was Fouzilhic once more in
front of me. Nor only that, but there was the old
gentleman who had escorted me so far the night before,
running out of his house at sight of me, with hands
upraised in horror.

"My poor boy!" he cried, "what does this mean?"

I told him what had happened. He beat his old
hands like clappers in a mill, to think how lightly he
had let me go; but when he heard of the man of Fouzilhac, anger and depression seized upon his mind.

"This time, at least," said he, "there shall be no
mistake."

And he limped along, for he was very rheumatic, for
about half a mile, and until I was almost within sight
of Cheylard, the destination I had hunted for so long.

CHEYLARD AND LUC

CANDIDLY, it seemed little worthy of all this searching. A few broken ends of village, with no particular street, but a succession of open places heaped with logs and faggots; a couple of tilted crosses, a shrine to Our Lady of all Graces on the summit of a little hill; and all this, upon a rattling highland river, in the corner of a naked valley. What went ye out for to see? thought I to myself. But the place had a life of its own. I found a board, commemorating the liberalities of Cheylard for the past year, hung up, like a banner, in the diminutive and tottering church. In 1877, it appeared, the inhabitants subscribed forty-eight francs ten centimes for the "Work of the Propagation of the Faith." Some of this, I could not help hoping, would be applied to my native land. Cheylard scrapes together halfpence for the darkened souls in Edinburgh; while Balquhidder and Dunrossness bemoan the ignorance of Rome. Thus, to the high entertainment of the angels, do we pelt each other with evangelists, like schoolboys bickering in the snow.

The inn was again singularly unpretentious. The whole furniture of a not ill-to-do family was in the kitchen: the beds, the cradle, the clothes, the plate-rack, the meal-chest, and the photograph of the parish priest. There were five children, one of whom was set to its morning prayers at the stair-foot soon after my arrival, and a sixth would ere long be forthcoming. I was kindly received by these good folk. They were much interested in my misadventure. The wood in which I had slept belonged to them; the man of Fouzilhac they thought a monster of iniquity, and counselled me warmly

to summon him at law—"because I might have died."
The good wife was horror-stricken to see me drink over
a pint of uncreamed milk.

"You will do yourself an evil," she said. "Permit
me to boil it for you."

After I had begun the morning on this delightful
liquor, she having an infinity of things to arrange, I
was permitted, nay requested, to make a bowl of chocolate for myself. My boots and gaiters were hung up
to dry, and seeing me trying to write my journal on
my knee, the eldest daughter let down a hinged table
in the chimney-corner for my convenience. Here I
wrote, drank my chocolate, and finally ate an omelette
before I left. The table was thick with dust; for, as
they explained, it was not used except in winter weather.
I had a clear look up the vent, through brown agglomer-
ations of soot and blue vapour, to the sky; and whenever
a handful of twigs was thrown on to the fire, my legs
were scorched by the blaze.

The husband had begun life as a muleteer, and when
I came to charge Modestine showed himself full of the
prudence of his art. "You will have to change this
package," said he; "it ought to be in two parts, and then
you might have double the weight."

I explained that I wanted no more weight; and for
no donkey hitherto created would I cut my sleeping-bag
in two.

"It fatigues her, however," said the innkeeper; "it
fatigues her greatly on the march. Look."

Alas, there were her two forelegs no better than raw beef
on the inside, and blood was running from under her
tail. They told me when I started, and I was ready to
believe it, that before a few days I should come to love
Modestine like a dog. Three days had passed, we had

shared some misadventures, and my heart was still as cold as a potato towards my beast of burden. She was pretty enough to look at; but then she had given proof of dead stupidity, redeemed indeed by patience, but aggravated by flashes of sorry and ill-judged light-heartedness. And I own this new discovery seemed another point against her. What the devil was the good of a she-ass if she could not carry a sleeping-bag and a few necessaries? I saw the end of the fable rapidly approaching, when I should have to carry Modestine. Æsop was the man to know the world! I assure you I set out with heavy thoughts upon my short day's march.

It was not only heavy thoughts about Modestine that weighted me upon the way; it was a leaden business altogether. For first, the wind blew so rudely that I had to hold on the pack with one hand from Cheylard to Luc; and second, my road lay through one of the most beggarly countries in the world. It was like the worst of the Scottish Highlands, only worse; cold, naked, and ignoble, scant of wood, scant of heather, scant of life. A road and some fences broke the unvarying waste, and the line of the road was marked by upright pillars, to serve in time of snow.

Why anyone should desire to visit either Luc or Cheylard is more than my much-inventing spirit can suppose. For my part, I travel not to go anywhere, but to go. I travel for travel's sake. The great affair is to move; to feel the needs and hitches of our life more nearly; to come down off this feather-bed of civilisation, and find the globe granite underfoot and strewn with cutting flints. Alas, as we get up in life, and are more preoccupied with our affairs, even a holiday is a thing that must be worked for. To hold a pack upon a pack-saddle against a gale out of the freezing north is no high industry, but it is one that serves to occupy and compose the mind. And when the present is so exacting, who can annoy himself about the future?

I came out at length above the Allier. A more unsightly prospect at this season of the year it would be hard to fancy. Shelving hills rose round it on all sides, here dabbled with wood and fields, there rising to peaks alternately naked and hairy with pines. The colour throughout was black or ashen, and came to a point in the ruins of the castle of Luc, which pricked up impudently from below my feet, carrying on a pinnacle a tall white statue of Our Lady, which, I heard with interest, weighed fifty quintals, and was to be dedicated on the 6th of October. Through this sorry landscape trickled the Allier and a tributary of nearly equal size, which came down to join it through a broad nude valley in Vivarais. The weather had somewhat lightened, and the clouds massed in squadron; but the fierce wind still hunted them through heaven, and cast great ungainly splashes of shadow and sunlight over the scene.

Luc itself was a straggling double file of houses wedged between hill and river. It had no beauty, nor was there any notable feature, save the old castle overhead with its fifty quintals of brand-new Madonna. But the inn was clean and large. The kitchen, with its two box-beds hung with clean check curtains, with its wide stone chimney, its chimney-shelf four yards long and garnished with lanterns and religious statuettes, its array of chests and pair of ticking clocks, was the very model of what a kitchen ought to be—a melodrama kitchen, suitable for bandits or noblemen in disguise. Nor was the scene disgraced by the landlady, a handsome, silent, dark old woman, clothed and hooded in black like a nun.

Even the public bedroom had a character of its own, with the long deal tables and benches, where fifty might have dined, set out as for a harvest-home, and the three box-beds along the wall. In one of these, lying on straw and covered with a pair of table-napkins, did I do penance all night long in goose-flesh and chattering teeth, and sigh, from time to time as I awakened, for my sheepskin sack and the lee of some great wood.

OUR LADY OF THE SNOWS

I behold
The House, the Brotherhood austere—
And what am I, that I am here?

MATTHEW ARNOLD.

FATHER APOLLINARIS

NEXT morning (Thursday, 20th September) I took the road in a new order. The sack was no longer doubled, but hung at full length across the saddle, a green sausage six feet long with a tuft of blue wool hanging out of either end. It was more picturesque, it spared the donkey, and, as I began to see, it would insure stability, blow high, blow low. But it was not without a pang that I had so decided. For although I had purchased a new cord, and made all as fast as I was able, I was yet jealously uneasy lest the flaps should tumble out and scatter my effects along the line of march.

My way lay up the bald valley of the river, along the march of Vivarais and Gévaudan. The hills of Gévaudan on the right were a little more naked, if anything, than those of Vivarais upon the left, and the former had a monopoly of a low dotty underwood that grew thickly in the gorges and died out in solitary burrs upon the shoulders and the summits. Black bricks of fir-wood were plastered here and there upon both sides, and here and there were cultivated fields. A railway ran beside the river; the only bit of railway in Gévaudan,

although there are many proposals afoot and surveys
being made, and even, as they tell me, a station standing
ready built in Mende. A year or two hence and this
may be another world. The desert is beleaguered. Now
may some Languedocian Wordsworth turn the sonnet
into *patois*: "Mountains and vales and floods, heard
YE that whistle?"

At a place called La Bastide I was directed to leave
the river, and follow a road that mounted on the left
among the hills of Vivarais, the modern Ardèche; for
I was now come within a little way of my strange
destination, the Trappist monastery of Our Lady of
the Snows. The sun came out as I left the shelter of a
pine-wood, and I beheld suddenly a fine wild landscape
to the south. High rocky hills, as blue as sapphire,
closed the view, and between these lay ridge upon ridge,
heathery, craggy, the sun glittering on veins of rock,
the underwood clambering in the hollows, as rude as
God made them at the first. There was not a sign of
man's hand in all the prospect; and, indeed, not a trace
of his passage, save where generation after generation
had walked in twisted footpaths, in and out among the
beeches, and up and down upon the channelled slopes.
The mists, which had hitherto beset me, were now
broken into clouds, and fled swiftly and shone brightly
in the sun. I drew a long breath. It was grateful
to come, after so long, upon a scene of some attraction
for the human heart. I own I like definite form in
what my eyes are to rest upon; and if landscapes were
sold, like the sheets of characters of my boyhood, one
penny plain and twopence coloured, I should go the
length of twopence every day of my life.

But if things had grown better to the south, it was
still desolate and inclement near at hand. A spidery

cross on every hilltop marked the neighbourhood of a religious house; and a quarter of a mile beyond, the outlook southward opening out and growing bolder with every step, a white statue of the Virgin at the corner of a young plantation directed the traveller to Our Lady of the Snows. Here, then, I struck leftward, and pursued my way, driving my secular donkey before me, and creaking in my secular boots and gaiters, towards the asylum of silence.

I had not gone very far ere the wind brought to me the clanging of a bell, and somehow, I can scarce tell why, my heart sank within me at the sound. I have rarely approached anything with more unaffected terror than the monastery of Our Lady of the Snows. This it is to have had a Protestant education. And suddenly, on turning a corner, fear took hold on me from head to foot—slavish, superstitious fear; and though I did not stop in my advance, yet I went on slowly, like a man who should have passed a bourne unnoticed, and strayed into the country of the dead. For there, upon the narrow new-made road, between the stripling pines, was a mediæval friar, fighting with a barrowful of turfs. Every Sunday of my childhood I used to study the Hermits of Marco Sadeler—enchanting prints, full of wood and field and mediæval landscapes, as large as a county, for the imagination to go a-travelling in; and here, sure enough, was one of Marco Sadeler's heroes. He was robed in white like any spectre, and the hood falling back, in the instancy of his contention with the barrow, disclosed a pate as bald and yellow as a skull. He might have been buried any time these thousand years, and all the lively parts of him resolved into earth and broken up with the farmer's harrow.

I was troubled besides in my mind as to etiquette.

Durst I address a person who was under a vow of silence?
Clearly not. But drawing near, I doffed my cap to
him with a far-away superstitious reverence. He nodded
back, and cheerfully addressed me. Was I going to
the monastery? Who was I? An Englishman? Ah,
an Irishman, then?

"No," I said, "a Scotsman."

A Scotsman? Ah, he had never seen a Scotsman
before. And he looked me all over, his good, honest,
brawny countenance shining with interest, as a boy might
look upon a lion or an alligator. From him I learned
with disgust that I could not be received at Our Lady
of the Snows; I might get a meal, perhaps, but that
was all. And then, as our talk ran on, and it turned
out that I was not a pedlar, but a literary man, who
drew landscapes and was going to write a book, he
changed his manner of thinking as to my reception (for I
fear they respect persons even in a Trappist monastery),
and told me I must be sure to ask for the Father Prior,
and state my case to him in full. On second thoughts
he determined to go down with me himself; he thought
he could manage for me better. Might he say that
I was a geographer?

No; I thought, in the interests of truth, he positively
might not.

"Very well, then" (with disappointment), "an
author."

It appeared he had been in a seminary with six young
Irishmen, all priests long since, who had received news-
papers and kept him informed of the state of ecclesiastical
affairs in England. And he asked me eagerly after
Dr. Pusey, for whose conversion the good man had continued ever since to pray night and morning.

"I thought he was very near the truth," he said;

"and he will reach it yet; there is so much virtue in prayer."

He must be a stiff, ungodly Protestant who can take anything but pleasure in this kind and hopeful story. While he was thus near the subject, the good father asked me if I were a Christian; and when he found I was not, or not after his way, he glossed it over with great good-will.

The road which we were following, and which this stalwart father had made with his own two hands within the space of a year, came to a corner, and showed us some white buildings a little farther on beyond the wood. At the same time the bell once more sounded abroad. We were hard upon the monastery. Father Apollinaris (for that was my companion's name) stopped me.

"I must not speak to you down there," he said. "Ask for the Brother Porter, and all will be well. But try to see me as you go out again through the wood, where I may speak to you. I am charmed to have made your acquaintance."

And then suddenly raising his arms, flapping his fingers, and crying out twice, "I must not speak, I must not speak!" he ran away in front of me, and disappeared into the monastery door.

I own this somewhat ghastly eccentricity went a good way to revive my terrors. But where one was so good and simple, why should not all be alike? I took heart of grace, and went forward to the gate as fast as Modestine, who seemed to have a disaffection for monasteries, would permit. It was the first door, in my acquaintance of her, which she had not shown an indecent haste to enter. I summoned the place in form, though with a quaking heart. Father Michael, the Father-Hospitaller, and a pair of brown-robed brothers came to the gate and spoke with me a while. I think my sack was the great attraction; it had already beguiled the heart of poor Apollinaris, who had charged me on my life to show it to the Father Prior. But whether it was my address, or the sack, or the idea speedily published among that part of the brotherhood who attend on strangers that I was not a pedlar after all, I found no difficulty as to my reception. Modestine was led away by a layman to the stables, and I and my pack were received into Our Lady of the Snows.

THE MONKS

FATHER MICHAEL, a pleasant, fresh-faced, smiling man, perhaps of thirty-five, took me to the pantry, and gave me a glass of liqueur to stay me until dinner. We had some talk, or rather I should say he listened to my prattle indulgently enough, but with an abstracted air, like a spirit with a thing of clay. And truly, when I remember that I descanted principally on my appetite, and that it must have been by that time more than eighteen hours since Father Michael had so much as broken bread, I can well understand that he would find an earthly savour in my conversation. But his manner, though superior, was exquisitely gracious; and I find I have a lurking curiosity as to Father Michael's past.

The whet administered, I was left alone for a little in the monastery garden. This is no more than the main court, laid out in sandy paths and beds of parti-coloured dahlias, and with a fountain and a black statue of the Virgin in the centre. The buildings stand around

it four-square, bleak, as yet unseasoned by the years
and weather, and with no other features than a belfry
and a pair of slated gables. Brothers in white, brothers
in brown, passed silently along the sanded alleys; and
when I first came out, three hooded monks were kneeling
on the terrace at their prayers. A naked hill commands
the monastery upon one side, and the wood commands
it on the other. It lies exposed to wind; the snow falls
off and on from October to May, and sometimes lies
six weeks on end; but if they stood in Eden, with a
climate like heaven's, the buildings themselves would
offer the same wintry and cheerless aspect; and for my
part, on this wild September day, before I was called
to dinner, I felt chilly in and out.

When I had eaten well and heartily, Brother Ambrose,
a hearty conversable Frenchman (for all those who wait
on strangers have the liberty to speak), led me to a little
room in that part of the building which is set apart for
MM. les retraitants. It was clean and whitewashed,
and furnished with strict necessaries, a crucifix, a bust
of the late Pope, the *Imitation* in French, a book of
religious meditations, and the *Life of Elizabeth Seton*,
evangelist, it would appear, of North America and of
New England in particular. As far as my experience
goes, there is a fair field for some more evangelisation
in these quarters; but think of Cotton Mather! I should
like to give him a reading of this little work in heaven,
where I hope he dwells; but perhaps he knows all that
already, and much more; and perhaps he and Mrs.
Seton are the dearest friends, and gladly unite their
voices in the everlasting psalm. Over the table, to
conclude the inventory of the room, hung a set of
regulations for *MM. les retraitants*: what services they
should attend, when they were to tell their beads or

meditate, and when they were to rise and go to rest. At the foot was a notable N.B.: "*Le temps libre est employé à l'examen de conscience, à la confession, à faire de bonnes résolutions,*" etc. To make good resolutions, indeed! You might talk as fruitfully of making the hair grow on your head.

I had scarce explored my niche when Brother Ambrose returned. An English boarder, it appeared, would like to speak with me. I professed my willingness, and the friar ushered in a fresh, young, little Irishman of fifty, a deacon of the Church, arrayed in strict canonicals, and wearing on his head what, in default of knowledge, I can only call the ecclesiastical shako. He had lived seven years in retreat at a convent of nuns in Belgium, and now five at Our Lady of the Snows; he never saw an English newspaper; he spoke French imperfectly, and had he spoken it like a native, there was not much chance of conversation where he dwelt. With this, he was a man eminently sociable, greedy of news, and simple-minded like a child. If I was pleased to have a guide about the monastery, he was no less delighted to see an English face and hear an English tongue.

He showed me his own room, where he passed his time among breviaries, Hebrew Bibles, and the Waverley Novels. Thence he led me to the cloisters, into the chapter-house, through the vestry, where the brothers' gowns and broad straw hats were hanging up, each with his religious name upon a board—names full of legendary suavity and interest, such as Basil, Hilarion, Raphael, or Pacifique; into the library, where were all the works of Veuillot and Chateaubriand, and the *Odes et Ballades*, if you please, and even Molière, to say nothing of innumerable fathers and a great variety of local and general historians. Thence my good Irishman took me round the workshops, where brothers bake bread, and make cartwheels, and take photographs; where one superintends a collection of curiosities, and another a gallery of rabbits. For in a Trappist monastery each monk has an occupation of his own choice, apart from his religious duties and the general labours of the house. Each must sing in the choir, if he has a voice and ear, and join in the hay-making if he has a hand to stir; but in his private hours, although he must be occupied, he may be occupied on what he likes. Thus I was told that one brother was engaged with literature; while Father Apollinaris busies himself in making roads, and the Abbot employs himself in binding books. It is not so long since this Abbot was consecrated, by the way; and on that occasion, by a special grace, his mother was permitted to enter the chapel and witness the ceremony of consecration. A proud day for her to have a son a mitred abbot; it makes you glad to think they let her in.

In all these journeyings to and fro, many silent fathers and brethren fell in our way. Usually they paid no more regard to our passage than if we had been a cloud; but sometimes the good deacon had a permission to ask of them, and it was granted by a peculiar movement of the hands, almost like that of a dog's paws in swimming, or refused by the usual negative signs, and in either case with lowered eyelids and a certain air of contrition, as of a man who was steering very close to evil.

The monks, by special grace of their Abbot, were still taking two meals a day; but it was already time for their grand fast, which begins somewhere in September and lasts till Easter, and during which they eat but once in the twenty-four hours, and that at two in the afternoon, twelve hours after they have begun the toil and vigil of the day. Their meals are scanty, but even of these they eat sparingly; and though each is allowed a small carafe of wine, many refrain from this indulgence. Without doubt, the most of mankind grossly overeat themselves; our meals serve not only for support, but as a hearty and natural diversion from the labour of life. Yet, though excess may be hurtful, I should have thought this Trappist regimen defective. And I am astonished, as I look back, at the freshness of face and cheerfulness of manner of all whom I beheld. A happier nor a healthier company I should scarce suppose that I have ever seen. As a matter of fact, on this bleak upland, and with the incessant occupation of the monks, life is of an uncertain tenure, and death no infrequent visitor, at Our Lady of the Snows. This, at least, was what was told me. But if they die easily, they must live healthily in the meantime, for they seemed all firm of flesh and high in colour; and the only morbid sign that I could observe, an unusual brilliancy of eye, was one that served rather to increase the general impression of vivacity and strength.

Those with whom I spoke were singularly sweet-tempered, with what I can only call a holy cheerfulness in air and conversation. There is a note, in the direction to visitors, telling them not to be offended at the curt speech of those who wait upon them, since it is proper to monks to speak little. The note might have been spared; to a man the hospitallers were all brimming with innocent talk, and, in my experience of the monastery, it was easier to begin than to break off a conversation. With the exception of Father Michael, who was a man of the world, they showed themselves full of kind and healthy interest in all sorts of subjects—in politics, in voyages, in my sleeping-sack—and not without a certain pleasure in the sound of their own voices.

As for those who are restricted to silence, I can only wonder how they bear their solemn and cheerless isolation. And yet, apart from any view of mortification, I can see a certain policy, not only in the exclusion of women, but in this vow of silence. I have had some experience of lay phalansteries, of an artistic, not to say a bacchanalian, character; and seen more than one association easily formed and yet more easily dispersed. With a Cistercian rule, perhaps they might have lasted longer. In the neighbourhood of women it is but a touch-and-go association that can be formed among defenceless men; the stronger electricity is sure to triumph; the dreams of boyhood, the schemes of youth, are abandoned after an interview of ten minutes, and the arts and sciences, and professional male jollity, deserted at once for two sweet eyes and a caressing accent. And next after this, the tongue is the great divider.

I am almost ashamed to pursue this worldly criticism of a religious rule; but there is yet another point in which the Trappist order appeals to me as a model of wisdom. By two in the morning the clapper goes upon the bell, and so on, hour by hour, and sometimes quarter by quarter, till eight, the hour of rest; so infinitesimally is the day divided among different occupations. The man who keeps rabbits, for example, hurries from his hutches to the chapel, the chapter-room, or the refectory, all day long: every hour he has an office to sing, a duty to perform; from two, when he rises in the dark, till eight, when he returns to receive the comfortable gift of sleep, he is upon his feet and occupied with manifold and changing business. I know many persons, worth several thousands in the year, who are not so fortunate in the disposal of their lives. Into how many houses would not the note of the monastery bell, dividing the day into manageable portions, bring peace of mind and healthful activity of body! We speak of hardships, but the true hardship is to be a dull fool, and permitted to mismanage life in our own dull and foolish manner.

From this point of view, we may perhaps better understand the monk's existence. A long novitiate and every proof of constancy of mind and strength of body is required before admission to the order; but I could not find that many were discouraged. In the photographer's studio, which figures so strangely among the outbuildings, my eye was attracted by the portrait of a young fellow in the uniform of a private of foot. This was one of the novices, who came of age for service, and marched and drilled and mounted guard for the proper time among the garrison of Algiers. Here was a man who had surely seen both sides of life before deciding; yet as soon as he was set free from service he returned to finish his novitiate.

This austere rule entitles a man to heaven as by right. When the Trappist sickens, he quits not his habit; he lies in the bed of death as he has prayed and laboured in his frugal and silent existence; and when the Liberator comes, at the very moment, even before they have carried him in his robe to lie his little last in the chapel among continual chantings, joy-bells break forth, as if for a marriage, from the slated belfry, and proclaim throughout the neighbourhood that another soul has gone to God.

At night, under the conduct of my kind Irishman, I took my place in the gallery to hear compline and *Salve Regina*, with which the Cistercians bring every day to a conclusion. There were none of those circumstances which strike the Protestant as childish or as tawdry in the public offices of Rome. A stern simplicity, height-

ened by the romance of the surroundings, spoke directly
to the heart. I recall the whitewashed chapel, the
hooded figures in the choir, the lights alternately
occluded and revealed, the strong manly singing, the
silence that ensued, the sight of cowled heads bowed in
prayer, and then the clear trenchant beating of the bell,
breaking in to show that the last office was over and the
hour of sleep had come; and when I remember, I am not
surprised that I made my escape into the court, with
somewhat whirling fancies, and stood like a man be-
wildered in the windy starry night.

But I was weary; and when I had quieted my spirits
with Elizabeth Seton's memoirs—a dull work—the cold
and the raving of the wind among the pines (for my room
was on that side of the monastery which adjoins the
woods) disposed me readily to slumber. I was wakened
at black midnight, as it seemed, though it was really two
in the morning, by the first stroke upon the bell. All
the brothers were then hurrying to the chapel; the dead
in life, at this untimely hour, were already beginning the
uncomforted labours of their day. The dead in life—
there was a chill reflection. And the words of a French
song came back into my memory, telling of the best of
our mixed existence:

> Que t'as de belles filles,
> Giroflé!
> Girofla!
> Que t'as de belles filles,
> L'Amour les comptera!

And I blessed God that I was free to wander, free to
hope, and free to love.

THE BOARDERS

ʀ there was another side to my residence at Our Lady
of the Snows. At this late season there were not many
boarders; and yet I was not alone in the public part of
the monastery. This itself is hard by the gate, with a
small dining-room on the ground-floor and a whole cor-
ridor of cells similar to mine upstairs. I have stupidly
forgotten the board for a regular *retraitant*; but it was
somewhere between three and five francs a day, and I
think most probably the first. Chance visitors like myself might give what they chose as a free-will offering,
but nothing was demanded. I may mention that when
I was going away, Father Michael refused twenty francs
as excessive. I explained the reasoning which led me to
offer him so much; but even then, from a curious point
of honour, he would not accept it with his own hand.
"I have no right to refuse for the monastery," he explained, "but I should prefer if you would give it to one
of the brothers."

I had dined alone, because I arrived late; but at supper
I found two other guests. One was a country parish
priest, who had walked over that morning from the seat
of his cure near Mende to enjoy four days of solitude and
prayer. He was a grenadier in person, with the hale
colour and circular wrinkles of a peasant; and as he complained much of how he had been impeded by his skirts
upon the march, I have a vivid fancy portrait of him,
striding along, upright, big-boned, with kilted cassock,
through the bleak hills of Gévaudan. The other was a
short, grizzling, thick-set man, from forty-five to fifty,
dressed in tweed with a knitted spencer, and the red
ribbon of a decoration in his button-hole. This last was

a hard person to classify. He was an old soldier, who had seen service and risen to the rank of commandant ; and he retained some of the brisk decisive manners of the camp. On the other hand, as soon as his resignation was accepted, he had come to Our Lady of the Snows as a boarder, and, after a brief experience of its ways, had decided to remain as a novice. Already the new life was beginning to modify his appearance ; already he had acquired somewhat of the quiet and smiling air of the brethren; and he was yet neither an officer nor a Trappist, but partook of the character of each. And certainly here was a man in an interesting nick of life. Out of the noise of cannon and trumpets, he was in the act of passing into this still country bordering on the grave, where men sleep nightly in their grave-clothes, and, like phantoms, communicate by signs.

At supper we talked politics. I make it my business, when I am in France, to preach political good-will and moderation, and to dwell on the example of Poland, much as some alarmists in England dwell on the example of Carthage. The priest and the commandant assured me of their sympathy with all I said, and made a heavy sighing over the bitterness of contemporary feeling.

"Why, you cannot say anything to a man with which he does not absolutely agree," said I, "but he flies up at you in a temper."

They both declared that such a state of things was anti-christian.

While we were thus agreeing, what should my tongue stumble upon but a word in praise of Gambetta's moderation. The old soldier's countenance was instantly suffused with blood ; with the palms of his hands he beat the table like a naughty child.

" *Comment, monsieur ?* " he shouted. " *Comment ?*
G

Gambetta moderate? Will you dare to justify these words?"

But the priest had not forgotten the tenor of our talk. And suddenly, in the height of his fury, the old soldier found a warning look directed on his face; the absurdity of his behaviour was brought home to him in a flash; and the storm came to an abrupt end, without another word.

It was only in the morning, over our coffee (Friday, 27th September), that this couple found out I was a heretic. I suppose I had misled them by some admiring expressions as to the monastic life around us; and it was only by a point-blank question that the truth came out. I had been tolerantly used both by simple Father Apollinaris and astute Father Michael; and the good Irish deacon, when he heard of my religious weakness, had only patted me upon the shoulder and said, "You must be a Catholic and come to heaven." But I was now among a different sect of orthodox. These two men were bitter and upright and narrow, like the worst of Scotsmen, and indeed, upon my heart, I fancy they were worse. The priest snorted aloud like a battle-horse.

"*Et vous prétendez mourir dans cette espèce de croyance?*" he demanded; and there is no type used by mortal printers large enough to qualify his accent.

I humbly indicated that I had no design of changing

But he could not away with such a monstrous attitude. "No, no," he cried; "you must change. You have come here, God has led you here, and you must embrace the opportunity."

I made a slip in policy; I appealed to the family affections, though I was speaking to a priest and a soldier, two classes of men circumstantially divorced from the kind and homely ties of life.

"Your father and mother?" cried the priest. "Very

well; you will convert them in their turn when you go home.''

I think I see my father's face! I would rather tackle the Gætulian lion in his den than embark on such an enterprise against the family theologian.

But now the hunt was up; priest and soldier were in full cry for my conversion; and the Work of the Propagation of the Faith, for which the people of Cheylard subscribed forty-eight francs ten centimes during 1877, was being gallantly pursued against myself. It was an odd but most effective proselytising. They never sought to convince me in argument, where I might have attempted some defence; but took it for granted that I was both ashamed and terrified at my position, and urged me solely on the point of time. Now, they said, when God had led me to Our Lady of the Snows, now was the appointed hour.

"Do not be withheld by false shame," observed the priest, for my encouragement.

For one who feels very similarly to all sects of religion, and who has never been able, even for a moment, to weigh seriously the merit of this or that creed on the eternal side of things, however much he may see to praise or blame upon the secular and temporal side, the situation thus created was both unfair and painful. I committed my second fault in tact, and tried to plead that it was all the same thing in the end, and we were all drawing near by different sides to the same kind and undiscriminating Friend and Father. That, as it seems to lay spirits, would be the only gospel worthy of the name. But different men think differently; and this revolutionary aspiration brought down the priest with all the terrors of the law. He launched into harrowing details of hell. The damned, he said—on the authority of a little book which he had read not a week before, and which, to add conviction to conviction, he had fully intended to bring along with him in his pocket—were to occupy the same attitude through all eternity in the midst of dismal tortures. And as he thus expatiated, he grew in nobility of aspect with his enthusiasm.

As a result the pair concluded that I should seek out the Prior, since the Abbot was from home, and lay my case immediately before him.

"*C'est mon conseil comme ancien militaire,*" observed the commandant; "*et celui de monsieur comme prêtre.*"

"*Oui,*" added the *curé*, sententiously nodding; "*comme ancien militaire—et comme prêtre.*"

At this moment, whilst I was somewhat embarrassed how to answer, in came one of the monks, a little brown fellow, as lively as a grig, and with an Italian accent, who threw himself at once into the contention, but in a milder and more persuasive vein, as befitted one of these pleasant brethren. Look at *him*, he said. The rule was very hard; he would have dearly liked to stay in his own country, Italy—it was well known how beautiful it was, the beautiful Italy; but then there were no Trappists in Italy; and he had a soul to save; and here he was.

I am afraid I must be at bottom, what a cheerful Indian critic has dubbed me, "a faddling hedonist," for this description of the brother's motives gave me somewhat of a shock. I should have preferred to think he had chosen the life for its own sake, and not for ulterior purposes; and this shows how profoundly I was out of sympathy with these good Trappists, even when I was doing my best to sympathise. But to the *curé* the argument seemed decisive.

"Hear that!" he cried. "And I have seen a marquis here, a marquis, a marquis"—he repeated the holy word

three times over—"and other persons high in society;
and generals. And here, at your side, is this gentleman,
who has been so many years in armies—decorated, an old
warrior. And here he is, ready to dedicate himself to
God."

I was by this time so thoroughly embarrassed that I
pleaded cold feet, and made my escape from the apartment. It was a furious windy morning, with a sky much
cleared, and long and potent intervals of sunshine; and I
wandered until dinner in the wild country towards the
east, sorely staggered and beaten upon by the gale, but
rewarded with some striking views.

At dinner the Work of the Propagation of the Faith
was recommenced, and on this occasion still more dis-
tastefully to me. The priest asked me many questions
as to the contemptible faith of my fathers, and received
my replies with a kind of ecclesiastical titter.

"Your sect," he said once; "for I think you will
admit it would be doing it too much honour to call it a
religion."

"As you please, monsieur," said I. *"La parole est à
vous."*

At length I grew annoyed beyond endurance; and
although he was on his own ground and, what is more to
the purpose, an old man, and so holding a claim upon my
toleration, I could not avoid a protest against this uncivil
usage. He was sadly discountenanced.

"I assure you," he said, "I have no inclination to
laugh in my heart. I have no other feeling but interest
in your soul."

And there ended my conversion. Honest man! he
was no dangerous deceiver; but a country parson, full of
zeal and faith. Long may he tread Gévaudan with his
kilted skirts—a man strong to walk and strong to com-

fort his parishioners in death! I daresay he would beat bravely through a snowstorm where his duty called him; and it is not always the most faithful believer who makes the cunningest apostle.

UPPER GÉVAUDAN (*continued*)

The bed was made, the room was fit,
By punctual eve the stars were lit;
The air was still, the water ran;
No need there was for maid or man,
When we put up, my ass and I,
At God's green caravanserai.

—Old Play.

ACROSS THE GOULET

THE wind fell during dinner, and the sky remained clear; so it was under better auspices that I loaded Modestine before the monastery gate. My Irish friend accompanied me so far on the way. As we came through the wood, there was Père Apollinaris hauling his barrow; and he too quitted his labours to go with me for perhaps a hundred yards, holding my hand between both of his in front of him. I parted first from one and then from the other with unfeigned regret, but yet with the glee of the traveller who shakes off the dust of one stage before hurrying forth upon another. Then Modestine and I mounted the course of the Allier, which here led us back into Gévaudan towards its sources in the forest of Mercoire. It was but an inconsiderable burn before we left its guidance. Thence, over a hill, our way lay through a naked plateau, until we reached Chasseradès at sundown.

The company in the inn kitchen that night were all men employed in survey for one of the projected railways.

They were intelligent and conversable, and we decided
the future of France over hot wine, until the state of the
clock frightened us to rest.   There were four beds in the
little upstairs room; and we slept six.   But I had a bed
to myself, and persuaded them to leave the window open.

"Hé, bourgeois; il est cinq heures!" was the cry that
wakened me in the morning (Saturday, 28th September).
The room was full of a transparent darkness, which dimly
showed me the other three beds and the five different
nightcaps on the pillows.   But out of the window the
dawn was growing ruddy in a long belt over the hill-tops,
and day was about to flood the plateau.   The hour was
inspiriting; and there seemed a promise of calm weather,
which was perfectly fulfilled.   I was soon under way
with Modestine.   The road lay for a while over the
plateau, and then descended through a precipitous village
into the valley of the Chassezac.   This stream ran among
green meadows, well hidden from the world by its steep
banks; the broom was in flower, and here and there was
a hamlet sending up its smoke.

At last the path crossed the Chassezac upon a bridge,
and, forsaking this deep hollow, set itself to cross the
mountain of La Goulet.   It wound up through Lestampes
by upland fields and woods of beech and birch, and with
every corner brought me into an acquaintance with some
new interest.   Even in the gully of the Chassezac my
ear had been struck by a noise like that of a great bass
bell ringing at the distance of many miles; but this, as I
continued to mount and draw nearer to it, seemed to
change in character, and I found at length that it came
from someone leading flocks afield to the note of a rural
horn.   The narrow street of Lestampes stood full of
sheep, from wall to wall—black sheep and white, bleat-
ing with one accord like the birds in spring, and each one

accompanying himself upon the sheep-bell round his
neck. It made a pathetic concert, all in treble. A little
higher, and I passed a pair of men in a tree with pruning-
hooks, and one of them was singing the music of a
bourrée. Still further, and when I was already threading
the birches, the crowing of cocks came cheerfully up to
my ears, and along with that the voice of a flute discours-
ing a deliberate and plaintive air from one of the upland
villages. I pictured to myself some grizzled, apple-
cheeked, country schoolmaster fluting in his bit of a
garden in the clear autumn sunshine. All these beautiful and interesting sounds filled my heart with an
unwonted expectation; and it appeared to me that, once
past this range which I was mounting, I should descend
into the garden of the world. Nor was I deceived, for I
was now done with rains and winds and a bleak country.
The first part of my journey ended here; and this was
like an induction of sweet sounds into the other and more
beautiful.

There are other degrees of *feyness*, as of punishment,
besides the capital; and I was now led by my good spirits
into an adventure which I relate in the interest of future
donkey-drivers. The road zigzagged so widely on the
hillside, that I chose a short cut by map and compass,
and struck through the dwarf woods to catch the road
again upon a higher level. It was my one serious con-
flict with Modestine. She would none of my short cut;
she turned in my face; she backed, she reared; she,
whom I had hitherto imagined to be dumb, actually
brayed with a loud hoarse flourish, like a cock crowing
for the dawn. I plied the goad with one hand; with the
other, so steep was the ascent, I had to hold on the pack-
saddle. Half a dozen times she was nearly over back-
wards on the top of me; half a dozen times, from sheer

weariness of spirit, I was nearly giving it up, and leading
her down again to follow the road.   But I took the thing
as a wager, and fought it through.   I was surprised, as I
went on my way again, by what appeared to be chill
rain-drops falling on my hand, and more than once
looked up in wonder at the cloudless sky.   But it was
only sweat which came dropping from my brow.

Over the summit of the Goulet there was no marked
road—only upright stones posted from space to space to
guide the drovers.   The turf underfoot was springy and
well scented.   I had no company but a lark or two, and
met but one bullock-cart between Lestampes and Bleymard.   In front of me I saw a shallow valley, and beyond
that the range of the Lozère, sparsely wooded and well
enough modelled in the flanks, but straight and dull in
outline.   There was scarce a sign of culture; only about
Bleymard, the white high-road from Villefort to Mende
traversed a range of meadows, set with spiry poplars,
and sounding from side to side with the bells of flocks and
herds.

A NIGHT AMONG THE PINES

From Bleymard after dinner, although it was already
late, I set out to scale a portion of the Lozère.   An ill-
marked stony drove-road guided me forward; and I met
nearly half a dozen bullock-carts descending from the
woods, each laden with a whole pine-tree for the winter's
firing.   At the top of the woods, which do not climb very
high upon this cold ridge, I struck leftward by a path
among the pines, until I hit on a dell of green turf, where
a streamlet made a little spout over some stones to serve
me for a water-tap.   "In a more sacred or sequestered

bower . . . nor nymph nor faunus haunted." The trees
were not old, but they grew thickly round the glade:
there was no outlook, except north-eastward upon distant
hill-tops, or straight upward to the sky; and the encampment felt secure and private like a room.   By the time
I had made my arrangements and fed Modestine, the day
was already beginning to decline. I buckled myself to
the knees into my sack and made a hearty meal; and as
soon as the sun went down, I pulled my cap over my
eyes and fell asleep.

  Night is a dead monotonous period under a roof; but
in the open world it passes lightly, with its stars and dews
and perfumes, and the hours are marked by changes in
the face of Nature. What seems a kind of temporal
death to people choked between walls and curtains, is
only a light and living slumber to the man who sleeps
afield. All night long he can hear Nature breathing
deeply and freely; even as she takes her rest, she turns
and smiles; and there is one stirring hour unknown to
those who dwell in houses, when a wakeful influence goes
abroad over the sleeping hemisphere, and all the outdoor
world are on their feet. It is then that the cock first
crows, not this time to announce the dawn, but like a
cheerful watchman speeding the course of night. Cattle
awake on the meadows; sheep break their fast on dewy
hillsides, and change to a new lair among the ferns; and
houseless men, who have lain down with the fowls, open
their dim eyes and behold the beauty of the night.

  At what inaudible summons, at what gentle touch of
Nature, are all these sleepers thus recalled in the same
hour to life? Do the stars rain down an influence, or do
we share some thrill of mother earth below our resting
bodies? Even shepherds and old country-folk, who are
the deepest read in these arcana, have not a guess as

to the means or purpose of this nightly resurrection.
Towards two in the morning they declare the thing takes
place; and neither know nor inquire further. And at
least it is a pleasant incident. We are disturbed in our
slumber only, like the luxurious Montaigne, "that we
may the better and more sensibly relish it." We have a
moment to look upon the stars. And there is a special
pleasure for some minds in the reflection that we share
the impulse with all outdoor creatures in our neighbourhood, that we have escaped out of the Bastille of civilisation, and are become, for the time being, a mere kindly
animal and a sheep of Nature's flock.

When that hour came to me among the pines, I
wakened thirsty. My tin was standing by me half full
of water. I emptied it at a draught; and feeling broad
awake after this internal cold aspersion, sat upright to
make a cigarette. The stars were clear, coloured, and
jewel-like, but not frosty. A faint silvery vapour stood
for the Milky Way. All around me the black fir-points
stood upright and stock-still. By the whiteness of the
pack-saddle, I could see Modestine walking round and
round at the length of her tether; I could hear her steadily
munching at the sward; but there was not another sound,
save the indescribable quiet talk of the runnel over the
stones. I lay lazily smoking and studying the colour
of the sky, as we call the void of space, from where
it showed a reddish grey behind the pines to where it
showed a glossy blue-black between the stars. As if to
be more like a pedlar, I wear a silver ring. This I could
see faintly shining as I raised or lowered the cigarette;
and at each whiff the inside of my hand was illuminated,
and became for a second the highest light in the landscape.

A faint wind, more like a moving coolness than a

stream of air, passed down the glade from time to time;
so that even in my great chamber the air was being
renewed all night long. I thought with horror of the
inn at Chasseradès and the congregated nightcaps; with
horror of the nocturnal prowesses of clerks and students,
of hot theatres and pass-keys and close rooms. I have
not often enjoyed a more serene possession of myself,
nor felt more independent of material aids. The outer
world, from which we cower into our houses, seemed after
all a gentle habitable place; and night after night a man's
bed, it seemed, was laid and waiting for him in the fields,
where God keeps an open house. I thought I had redis-
covered one of those truths which are revealed to savages
and hid from political economists: at the least, I had
discovered a new pleasure for myself. And yet even
while I was exulting in my solitude I became aware of a
strange luck. I wished a companion to lie near me in
the starlight, silent and not moving, but ever within
touch. For there is a fellowship more quiet even than
solitude, and which, rightly understood, is solitude made
perfect. And to live out of doors with the woman a man
loves is of all lives the most complete and free.

As I thus lay, between content and longing, a faint
noise stole towards me through the pines. I thought, at
first, it was the crowing of cocks or the barking of dogs at
some very distant farm; but steadily and gradually it
took articulate shape in my ears, until I became aware
that a passenger was going by upon the high-road in the
valley, and singing loudly as he went. There was more
of good-will than grace in his performance; but he trolled
with ample lungs; and the sound of his voice took hold
upon the hillside, and set the air shaking in the leafy
glens. I have heard people passing by night in sleeping
cities; some of them sang; one, I remember, played

loudly on the bagpipes. I have heard the rattle of a cart or carriage spring up suddenly after hours of stillness, and pass, for some minutes, within the range of my hearing as I lay abed. There is a romance about all who are abroad in the black hours, and with something of a thrill we try to guess their business. But here the romance was double: first, this glad passenger, lit internally with wine, who sent up his voice in music through the night; and then I, on the other hand, buckled into my sack, and smoking alone in the pine-woods betweeen four and five thousand feet towards the stars.

When I awoke again (Sunday, 29th September), many of the stars had disappeared; only the stronger companions of the night still burned visibly overhead; and away towards the east I saw a faint haze of light upon the horizon, such as had been the Milky Way when I was last awake. Day was at hand. I lit my lantern, and by its glow-worm light put on my boots and gaiters; then I broke up some bread for Modestine, filled my can at the water-tap, and lit my spirit-lamp to boil myself some chocolate. The blue darkness lay long in the glade where I had so sweetly slumbered; but soon there was a broad streak of orange melting into gold along the mountain-tops of Vivarais. A solemn glee possessed my mind at this gradual and lovely coming in of day. I heard the runnel with delight; I looked round me for something beautiful and unexpected; but the still black pine-trees, the hollow glade, the munching ass, remained unchanged in figure. Nothing had altered but the light, and that, indeed, shed over all a spirit of life and of breathing peace, and moved me to a strange exhilaration.

I drank my water-chocolate, which was hot if it was not rich, and strolled here and there, and up and down about the glade. While I was thus delaying, a gush of steady wind, as long as a heavy sigh, poured direct out of the quarter of the morning. It was cold, and set me sneezing. The trees near at hand tossed their black plumes in its passage; and I could see the thin distant spires of pine along the edge of the hill rock slightly to and fro against the golden east. Ten minutes after, the sunlight spread at a gallop along the hillside, scattering shadows and sparkles, and the day had come completely.

I hastened to prepare my pack, and tackle the steep ascent that lay before me, but I had something on my mind. It was only a fancy; yet a fancy will sometimes be <u>importunate</u>. I had been most hospitably received and punctually served in my green <u>caravanserai</u>. The room was airy, the water excellent, and the dawn had called me to a moment. I say nothing of the tapestries or the <u>inimitable</u> ceiling, nor yet of the view which I commanded from the windows; but I felt I was in someone's debt for all this liberal entertainment. And so it pleased me, in a half-laughing way, to leave pieces of money on the turf as I went along, until I had left enough for my night's lodging. I trust they did not fall to some rich and <u>churlish</u> drover.

THE COUNTRY OF THE CAMISARDS

We travelled in the print of olden wars;
  Yet all the land was green;
  And love we found, and peace,
  Where fire and war had been.
They pass and smile, the children of the sword—
  No more the sword they wield;
  And O, how deep the corn
  Along the battlefield!
W. P. BANNATYNE.

THE COUNTRY OF THE CAMISARDS:

ACROSS THE LOZÈRE

THE track that I had followed in the evening soon died out, and I continued to follow over a bald turf ascent a row of stone pillars, such as had conducted me across the Goulet. It was already warm, I tied my jacket on the pack, and walked in my knitted waistcoat. Modestine herself was in high spirits, and broke of her own accord, for the first time in my experience, into a jolting trot that sent the oats swashing in the pocket of my coat. The view, back upon the northern Gévaudan, extended with every step; scarce a tree, scarce a house, appeared upon the fields of wild hill that ran north, east, and west, all blue and gold in the haze and sunlight of the morning. A multitude of little birds kept sweeping and twittering about my path; they perched on the stone pillars, they pecked and strutted on the turf, and I saw them circle in volleys in the blue air, and show, from time to

time, translucent flickering wings between the sun and
me.

Almost from the first moment of my march, a faint
large noise, like a distant surf, had filled my ears.   Sometimes I was tempted to think it the voice of a neighbouring waterfall, and sometimes a subjective result of the
utter stillness of the hill.   But as I continued to advance,
the noise increased, and became like the hissing of an
enormous tea-urn, and at the same time breaths of cool
air began to reach me from the direction of the summit.
At length I understood.   It was blowing stiffly from the
south upon the other slope of the Lozère, and every step
that I took I was drawing nearer to the wind.

Although it had been long desired, it was quite unex-
pectedly at last that my eyes rose above the summit.   A
step that seemed no way more decisive than many other
steps that had preceded it—and, "like stout Cortez
when, with eagle eyes, he stared on the Pacific," I took
possession, in my own name, of a new quarter of the
world.   For behold, instead of the gross turf rampart
I had been mounting for so long, a view into the hazy
air of heaven, and a land of intricate blue hills below my
feet.

The Lozère lies nearly east and west, cutting Gévaudan
into two unequal parts; its highest point, this Pic de
Finiels, on which I was then standing, rises upwards of
five thousand six hundred feet above the sea, and in clear
weather commands a view over all lower Languedoc to
the Mediterranean Sea.   I have spoken with people who
either pretended or believed that they had seen, from the
Pic de Finiels, white ships sailing by Montpellier and
Cette.   Behind was the upland northern country through
which my way had lain, peopled by a dull race, without
wood, without much grandeur of hill-form, and famous

in the past for little beside wolves. But in front of me, half veiled in sunny haze, lay a new Gévaudan, rich, picturesque, illustrious for stirring events. Speaking largely, I was in the Cevennes at Monastier, and during all my journey; but there is a strict and local sense in which only this confused and shaggy country at my feet has any title to the name, and in this sense the peasantry employ the word. These are the Cevennes with an emphasis: the Cevennes of the Cevennes. In that undecipherable labyrinth of hills, a war of bandits, a war of wild beasts, raged for two years between the Grand Monarch with all his troops and marshals on the one hand, and a few thousand Protestant mountaineers upon the other. A hundred and eighty years ago, the Camisards held a station even on the Lozère, where I stood; they had an organisation, arsenals, a military and religious hierarchy; their affairs were "the discourse of every coffee-house" in London; England sent fleets in their support; their leaders prophesied and murdered; with colours and drums, and the singing of old French psalms, their bands sometimes affronted daylight, marched before walled cities, and dispersed the generals of the king; and sometimes at night, or in masquerade, possessed themselves of strong castles, and avenged treachery upon their allies and cruelty upon their foes. There, a hundred and eighty years ago, was the chivalrous Roland, "Count and Lord Roland, generalissimo of the Protestants in France," grave, silent, imperious, pock-marked ex-dragoon, whom a lady followed in his wanderings out of love. There was Cavalier, a baker's apprentice with a genius for war, elected brigadier of Camisards at seventeen, to die at fifty-five the English governor of Jersey. There again was Castanet, a partisan leader in a voluminous peruke and with a taste for controversial divinity.

Strange generals, who moved apart to take counsel with the God of Hosts, and fled or offered battle, set sentinels or slept in an unguarded camp, as the Spirit whispered to their hearts! And there, to follow these and other leaders, was the rank and file of prophets and disciples, bold, patient, indefatigable, hardy to run upon the mountains, cheering their rough life with psalms, eager to fight, eager to pray, listening devoutly to the oracles of brain-sick children, and mystically putting a grain of wheat among the pewter balls with which they charged their muskets.

I had travelled hitherto through a dull district, and in the track of nothing more notable than the child-eating beast of Gévaudan, the Napoleon Bonaparte of wolves, But now I was to go down into the scene of a romantic chapter—or, better, a romantic footnote—in the history of the world. What was left of all this bygone dust and heroism? I was told that Protestantism still survived in this head seat of Protestant resistance; so much the priest himself had told me in the monastery parlour. But I had yet to learn if it were a bare survival, or a lively and generous tradition. Again, if in the northern Cevennes the people are narrow in religious judgments, and more filled with zeal than charity, what was I to look for in this land of persecution and reprisal—in a land where the tyranny of the Church produced the Camisard rebellion, and the terror of the Camisards threw the Catholic peasantry into legalised revolt upon the other side, so that Camisard and Florentin skulked for each other's lives among the mountains?

Just on the brow of the hill, where I paused to look before me, the series of stone pillars came abruptly to an end; and only a little below, a sort of track appeared and began to go down a breakneck slope, turning like a cork-

screw as it went. It led into a valley between falling
hills, stubbly with rocks like a reaped field of corn, and
floored farther down with green meadows. I followed
the track with <u>precipitation</u>; the steepness of the slope,
the continual agile turning of the line of the descent, and
the old unwearied hope of finding something new in a
new country, all conspired to lend me wings. Yet a little
lower and a stream began, collecting itself together out
of many fountains, and soon making a glad noise among
the hills. Sometimes it would cross the track in a bit
of waterfall, with a pool, in which Modestine refreshed
her feet.

The whole descent is like a dream to me, so rapidly
was it accomplished. I had scarcely left the summit
ere the valley had closed round my path, and the sun
beat upon me, walking in a stagnant lowland atmosphere.
The track became a road, and went up and down in easy
undulations. I passed cabin after cabin, but all seemed
deserted; and I saw not a human creature, nor heard any
sound except that of the stream. I was, however, in a
different country from the day before. The stony skele-
ton of the world was here vigorously displayed to sun
and air. The slopes were steep and changeful. Oak-
trees clung along the hills, well grown, wealthy in leaf,
and touched by the autumn with strong and luminous
colours. Here and there another stream would fall in
from the right or the left, down a gorge of snowwhite and
<u>tumultuary</u> boulders. The river in the bottom (for it
was rapidly growing a river, collecting on all hands as it
trotted on its way) here foamed a while in desperate
rapids, and there lay in pools of the most enchanting sea-
green shot with watery browns. As far as I have gone,
I have never seen a river of so changeful and delicate a
hue; crystal was not more clear, the meadows were not

by half so green; and at every pool I saw I felt a thrill
of longing to be out of these hot, dusty, and material
garments, and bathe my naked body in the mountain air
and water. All the time as I went on I never forgot it
was the Sabbath; the stillness was a perpetual reminder,
and I heard in spirit the church-bells clamouring all over
Europe, and the psalms of a thousand churches.

At length a human sound struck upon my ear—a cry
strangely modulated between _pathos_ and derision; and
looking across the valley, I saw a little urchin sitting in
a meadow, with his hands about his knees, and dwarfed
to almost comical smallness by the distance. But the
rogue had picked me out as I went down the road, from
oak wood on to oak wood, driving Modestine; and he
made me the compliments of the new country in this
tremulous high-pitched salutation. And as all noises
are lovely and natural at a sufficient distance, this also,
coming through so much clean hill air and crossing all the
green valley, sounded pleasant to my ear, and seemed a
thing rustic, like the oaks or the river.

A little after, the stream that I was following fell into
the Tarn at Pont de Montvert of bloody memory.

PONT DE MONTVERT

ONE of the first things I encountered in Pont de Montvert
was, if I remember rightly, the Protestant temple; but this
was but the type of other novelties. A _subtle_ atmosphere distinguishes a town in England from a town in
France, or even in Scotland. At Carlisle you can see
you are in one country; at Dumfries, thirty miles away,
you are as sure that you are in the other. I should find
it difficult to tell in what particulars Pont de Montvert

differed from Monastier or Langogne, or even Bleymard;
but the difference existed, and spoke eloquently to the
eyes. The place, with its houses, its lanes, its glaring
river-bed, wore an indescribable air of the South.

All was Sunday bustle in the streets and in the public-
house, as all had been Sabbath peace among the mountains. There must have been near a score of us at dinner
by eleven before noon; and after I had eaten and
drunken, and sat writing up my journal, I suppose as
many more came dropping in one after another, or by
twos and threes. In crossing the Lozère I had not only
come among new natural features, but moved into the
territory of a different race. These people, as they hurriedly despatched their viands in an intricate sword-
play of knives, questioned and answered me with a degree
of intelligence which excelled all that I had met, except
among the railway folk at Chasseradès. They had open
telling faces, and were lively both in speech and manner.
They not only entered thoroughly into the spirit of my
little trip, but more than one declared, if he were rich
enough, he would like to set forth on such another.

Even physically there was a pleasant change. I had
not seen a pretty woman since I left Monastier, and there
but one. Now of the three who sat down with me to
dinner, one was certainly not beautiful—a poor timid
thing of forty, quite troubled at this roaring *table d'hôte*,
whom I squired and helped to wine, and pledged and
tried generally to encourage, with quite a contrary effect;
but the other two, both married, were both more handsome than the average of women. And Clarisse? What
shall I say of Clarisse? She waited the table with a
heavy placable nonchalance, like a performing cow; her
great grey eyes were steeped in amorous languor; her
features, although fleshy, were of an original and accurate

design; her mouth had a curl; her nostrils spoke of dainty pride; her cheek fell into strange and interesting lines. It was a face capable of strong emotion, and, with training, it offered the promise of delicate sentiment. It seemed pitiful to see so good a model left to country admirers and a country way of thought. Beauty should at least have touched society; then, in a moment, it throws off a weight that lay upon it, it becomes conscious of itself, it puts on an elegance, learns a gait and a carriage of the head, and, in a moment, *patet dea*. Before I left I assured Clarisse of my hearty admiration. She took it like milk, without embarrassment or wonder, merely looking at me steadily with her great eyes; and I own the result upon myself was some confusion. If Clarisse could read English, I should not dare to add that her figure was unworthy of her face. Hers was a case for stays; but that may perhaps grow better as she gets up in years.

Pont de Montvert, or Greenhill Bridge, as we might say at home, is a place memorable in the story of the Camisards. It was here that the war broke out; here that those southern Covenanters slew their Archbishop Sharpe. The persecution on the one hand, the febrile enthusiasm on the other, are almost equally difficult to understand in these quiet modern days, and with our easy modern beliefs and disbeliefs. The Protestants were one and all beside their right minds with zeal and sorrow. They were all prophets and prophetesses. Children at the breast would exhort their parents to good works. "A child of fifteen months at Quissac spoke from its mother's arms, agitated and sobbing, distinctly and with a loud voice." Marshal Villars has seen a town where all the women "seemed possessed by the devil," and had trembling fits, and uttered prophecies publicly upon the streets. A prophetess of Vivarais was hanged at Montpellier because blood flowed from her eyes and nose, and she declared that she was weeping tears of blood for the misfortunes of the Protestants. And it was not only women and children. Stalwart dangerous fellows, used to swing the sickle or to wield the forest axe, were likewise shaken with strange paroxysms, and spoke oracles with sobs and streaming tears. A persecution unsurpassed in violence had lasted near a score of years, and this was the result upon the persecuted; hanging, burning, breaking on the wheel, had been in vain; the dragoons had left their hoof-marks over all the country-side; there were men rowing in the galleys, and women pining in the prisons of the Church; and not a thought was changed in the heart of any upright Protestant.

Now the head and forefront of the persecution—after Lamoignon de Bâvile—François de Langlade du Chayla (pronounce Chéïla), Archpriest of the Cevennes and Inspector of Missions in the same country, had a house in which he sometimes dwelt in the town of Pont de Montvert. He was a conscientious person, who seems to have been intended by nature for a pirate, and now fifty-five, an age by which a man has learned all the moderation of which he is capable. A missionary in his youth in China, he there suffered martyrdom, was left for dead, and only succoured and brought back to life by the charity of a pariah. We must suppose the pariah devoid of second-sight, and not purposely malicious in this act. Such an experience, it might be thought, would have cured a man of the desire to persecute; but the human spirit is a thing strangely put together; and, having been a Christian martyr, Du Chayla became a Christian persecutor. The Work of the Propagation of the Faith went roundly forward in his hands. His house

in Pont de Montvert served him as a prison. There he
closed the hands of his prisoners upon live coal, and
plucked out the hairs of their beard, to convince them
that they were deceived in their opinions. And yet had
not he himself tried and proved the inefficacy of these
carnal arguments among the Buddhists in China?

Not only was life made intolerable in Languedoc, but
flight was rigidly forbidden. One Massip, a muleteer,
and well acquainted with the mountain-paths, had
already guided several troops of fugitives in safety to
Geneva; and on him, with another convoy, consisting
mostly of women dressed as men, Du Chayla, in an evil
hour for himself, laid his hands. The Sunday following
there was a conventicle of Protestants in the woods of
Altefage upon Mount Bougès; where there stood up one
Séguier—Spirit Séguier, as his companions called him—
a wool-carder, tall, black-faced, and toothless, but a man
full of prophecy. He declared, in the name of God, that
the time for submission had gone by, and they must
betake themselves to arms for the deliverance of their
brethren and the destruction of the priests.

The next night, 24th July, 1702, a sound disturbed
the Inspector of Missions as he sat in his prison-house at
Pont de Montvert: the voices of many men upraised in
psalmody drew nearer and nearer through the town. It
was ten at night; he had his court about him, priests,
soldiers, and servants, to the number of twelve or
fifteen; and now dreading the insolence of a conventicle
below his very windows, he ordered forth his soldiers to
report. But the psalm-singers were already at his door,
fifty strong, led by the inspired Séguier, and breathing
death. To their summons, the archpriest made answer
like a stout old persecutor, and bade his garrison fire
upon the mob. One Camisard (for, according to some,

it was in this night's work that they came by the name)
fell at this discharge: his comrades burst in the door with
hatchets and a beam of wood, overran the lower story of
the house, set free the prisoners, and finding one of them
in the *vine*, a sort of Scavenger's Daughter of the place
and period, redoubled in fury against Du Chayla, and
sought by repeated assaults to carry the upper floors.
But he, on his side, had given absolution to his men, and
they bravely held the staircase.

"Children of God," cried the prophet, "hold your
hands.   Let us burn the house, with the priest and the
satellites of Baal."

The fire caught readily.   Out of an upper window Du
Chayla and his men lowered themselves into the garden
by means of knotted sheets; some escaped across the
river under the bullets of the insurgents; but the archpriest himself fell, broke his thigh, and could only crawl
into the hedge.   What were his reflections as this second
martyrdom drew near?   A poor, brave, besotted, hate-
ful man, who had done his duty resolutely according to
his light both in the Cevennes and China.   He found at
least one telling word to say in his defence; for when the
roof fell in and the upbursting flames discovered his
retreat, and they came and dragged him to the public
place of the town, raging and calling him damned—"If
I be damned," said he, "why should you also damn
yourselves?"

Here was a good reason for the last; but in the course
of his inspectorship he had given many stronger which
all told in a contrary direction; and these he was now to
hear.   One by one, Séguier first, the Camisards drew
near and stabbed him.   "This," they said, "is for my
father broken on the wheel.   This for my brother in the
galleys.   That for my mother or my sister imprisoned

in your cursed convents." Each gave his blow and his reason; and then all kneeled and sang psalms around the body till the dawn. With the dawn, still singing, they defiled away towards Frugères, farther up the Tarn, to pursue the work of vengeance, leaving Du Chayla's prison-house in ruins, and his body pierced with two-and-fifty wounds upon the public place.

'Tis a wild night's work, with its accompaniment of psalms; and it seems as if a psalm must always have a sound of threatening in that town upon the Tarn. But the story does not end, even so far as concerns Pont de Montvert, with the departure of the Camisards. The career of Séguier was brief and bloody. Two more priests and a whole family at Ladevèze, from the father to the servants, fell by his hand or by his orders; and yet he was but a day or two at large, and restrained all the time by the presence of the soldiery. Taken at length by a famous soldier of fortune, Captain Poul, he appeared unmoved before his judges.

"Your name?" they asked.

"Pierre Séguier."

"Why are you called Spirit?"

"Because the Spirit of the Lord is with me."

"Your domicile?"

"Lately in the desert, and soon in heaven."

"Have you no remorse for your crimes?"

"I have committed none. *My soul is like a garden full of shelter and of fountains.*"

At Pont de Montvert, on the 12th of August, he had his right hand stricken from his body, and was burned alive. And his soul was like a garden? So perhaps was the soul of Du Chayla, the Christian martyr. And perhaps if you could read in my soul, or I could read in yours, our own composure might seem little less surprising.

Du Chayla's house still stands, with a new roof, beside one of the bridges of the town; and if you are curious you may see the terrace-garden into which he dropped.

IN THE VALLEY OF THE TARN

A NEW road leads from Pont de Montvert to Florac by the valley of the Tarn; a smooth sandy ledge, it runs about half-way between the summit of the cliffs and the river in the bottom of the valley; and I went in and out, as I followed it, from bays of shadow into promontories of afternoon sun. This was a pass like that of Killie-crankie; a deep turning gully in the hills, with the Tarn making a wonderful hoarse uproar far below, and craggy summits standing in the sunshine high above. A thin fringe of ash-trees ran about the hill-tops, like ivy on a ruin; but on the lower slopes, and far up every glen, the Spanish chestnut-trees stood each four-square to heaven under its tented foliage. Some were planted, each on its own terrace no larger than a bed; some, trusting in their roots, found strength to grow and prosper and be straight and large upon the rapid slopes of the valley; others, where there was a margin to the river, stood marshalled in a line and mighty like cedars of Lebanon. Yet even where they grew most thickly they were not to be thought of as a wood, but as a herd of stalwart individuals; and the dome of each tree stood forth separate and large, and as it were a little hill, from among the domes of its companions. They gave forth a faint sweet perfume which pervaded the air of the afternoon; autumn had put tints of gold and tarnish in the green; and the sun so shone through and kindled the broad foliage, that each chestnut was relieved against

another, not in shadow, but in light.   A humble sketcher
here laid down his pencil in despair.

I wish I could convey a notion of the growth of these
noble trees; of how they strike out boughs like the oak,
and trail sprays of drooping foliage like the willow; of
how they stand on upright fluted columns like the pillars
of a church; or like the olive, from the most shattered
bole can put out smooth and youthful shoots, and begin
a new life upon the ruins of the old.   Thus they partake
of the nature of many different trees; and even their
prickly top-knots, seen near at hand against the sky,
have a certain palm-like air that impresses the imagination.   But their individuality, although compounded of
so many elements, is but the richer and the more original.
And to look down upon a level filled with these knolls of
foliage, or to see a clan of old unconquerable chestnuts
cluster "like herded elephants" upon the spur of a
mountain, is to rise to higher thoughts of the powers that
are in Nature.

Between Modestine's laggard humour and the beauty
of the scene, we made little progress all that afternoon;
and at last finding the sun, although still far from setting,
was already beginning to desert the narrow valley of
the Tarn, I began to cast about for a place to camp in.
This was not easy to find; the terraces were too narrow,
and the ground, where it was unterraced, was usually
too steep for a man to lie upon.   I should have slipped
all night, and awakened towards morning with my feet
or my head in the river.

After perhaps a mile, I saw, some sixty feet above the
road, a little plateau large enough to hold my sack, and
securely parapeted by the trunk of an aged and enormous
chestnut.   Thither, with infinite trouble, I goaded and
kicked the reluctant Modestine, and there I hastened

to unload her. There was only room for myself upon the plateau, and I had to go nearly as high again before I found so much as standing room for the ass. It was on a heap of rolling stones, on an artificial terrace, certainly not five feet square in all. Here I tied her to a chestnut, and having given her corn and bread and made a pile of chestnut-leaves, of which I found her greedy, I descended once more to my own encampment.

The position was unpleasantly exposed. One or two carts went by upon the road; and as long as daylight lasted I concealed myself, for all the world like a hunted Camisard, behind my fortification of vast chestnut trunk; for I was passionately afraid of discovery and the visit of jocular persons in the night. Moreover, I saw that I must be early awake; for these chestnut gardens had been the scene of industry no further gone than on the day before. The slope was strewn with lopped branches, and here and there a great package of leaves was propped against a trunk; for even the leaves are serviceable, and the peasants use them in winter by way of fodder for their animals. I picked a meal in fear and trembling, half lying down to hide myself from the road; and I daresay I was as much concerned as if I had been a scout from Joani's band above upon the Lozère, or from Salomon's across the Tarn, in the old times of psalm-singing and blood. Or, indeed, perhaps more; for the Camisards had a remarkable confidence in God; and a tale comes back into my memory of how the Count of Gévaudan, riding with a party of dragoons and a notary at his saddlebow to enforce the oath of fidelity in all the country hamlets, entered a valley in the woods, and found Cavalier and his men at dinner, gaily seated on the grass, and their hats crowned with box-tree garlands, while fifteen women washed their linen in the stream. Such was a field festival in 1703; at that date Antony Watteau would be painting similar subjects.

This was a very different camp from that of the night before in the cool and silent pine-woods. It was warm and even stifling in the valley. The shrill song of frogs, like the tremolo note of a whistle with a pea in it, rang up from the riverside before the sun was down. In the growing dusk, faint rustlings began to run to and fro among the fallen leaves; from time to time a faint chirping or cheeping noise would fall upon my ear; and from time to time I thought I could see the movement of something swift and indistinct between the chestnuts. A profusion of large ants swarmed upon the ground; bats whisked by, and mosquitoes droned overhead. The long boughs with their bunches of leaves hung against the sky like garlands; and those immediately above and around me had somewhat the air of a trellis which should have been wrecked and half overthrown in a gale of wind.

Sleep for a long time fled my eyelids; and just as I was beginning to feel quiet stealing over my limbs, and settling densely on my mind, a noise at my head startled me broad awake again, and, I will frankly confess it, brought my heart into my mouth. It was such a noise as a person would make scratching loudly with a finger-nail; it came from under the knapsack which served me for a pillow, and it was thrice repeated before I had time to sit up and turn about. Nothing was to be seen, nothing more was to be heard, but a few of these mysterious rustlings far and near, and the ceaseless accompaniment of the river and the frogs. I learned next day that the chestnut gardens are infested by rats; rustling, chirping, and scraping were probably all due to these; but the puzzle, for the moment, was insoluble, and I had to compose myself for sleep, as best I could, in wondering uncertainty about my neighbours.

I was awakened in the grey of the morning (Monday, 30th September) by the sound of footsteps not far off upon the stones, and opening my eyes, I beheld a peasant going by among the chestnuts by a footpath that I had not hitherto observed. He turned his head neither to the right nor to the left, and disappeared in a few strides among the foliage. Here was an escape! But it was plainly more than time to be moving. The peasantry were abroad; scarce less terrible to me in my nondescript position than the soldiers of Captain Poul to an undaunted Camisard. I fed Modestine with what haste I could; but as I was returning to my sack, I saw a man and a boy come down the hillside in a direction crossing mine. They unintelligibly hailed me, and I replied with inarticulate but cheerful sounds, and hurried forward to get into my gaiters.

The pair, who seemed to be father and son, came slowly up to the plateau, and stood close beside me for some time in silence. The bed was open, and I saw with regret my revolver lying patently disclosed on the blue wool. At last, after they had looked me all over, and the silence had grown laughably embarrassing, the man demanded in what seemed unfriendly tones:

"You have slept here?"

"Yes," said I. "As you see."

"Why?" he asked.

"My faith," I answered lightly, "I was tired."

He next inquired where I was going and what I had had for dinner; and then, without the least transition, *"C'est bien,"* he added, "come along." And he and his son, without another word, turned off to the next chestnut-tree but one, which they set to pruning. The thing had passed off more simply than I hoped. He was a grave, respectable man; and his unfriendly voice did not imply that he thought he was speaking to a criminal, but merely to an <u>inferior</u>.

I was soon on the road, nibbling a cake of chocolate and seriously occupied with a case of conscience. Was I to pay for my night's lodging? I had slept ill, the bed was full of fleas in the shape of ants, there was no water in the room, the very dawn had neglected to call me in the morning. I might have missed a train, had there been any in the neighbourhood to catch. Clearly, I was dissatisfied with my entertainment; and I decided I should not pay unless I met a beggar.

The valley looked even lovelier by morning; and soon the road descended to the level of the river. Here, in a place where many straight and prosperous chestnuts stood together, making an isle upon a <u>swarded</u> terrace, I made my morning toilette in the water of the Tarn. It was marvellously clear, thrillingly cool; the soap-suds disappeared as if by magic in the swift current, and the white boulders gave one a model for cleanliness. To wash in one of God's rivers in the open air seems to me a sort of cheerful solemnity or semi-pagan act of worship. To dabble among dishes in a bedroom may perhaps make clean the body; but the imagination takes no share in such a cleansing. I went on with a light and peaceful heart, and sang psalms to the spiritual ear as I advanced.

Suddenly up came an old woman, who point-blank demanded alms.

"Good," thought I; "here comes the waiter with the bill."

And I paid for my night's lodging on the spot.   Take

H

it how you please, but this was the first and the last beggar that I met with during all my tour.

A step or two farther I was overtaken by an old man in a brown nightcap, clear-eyes, weather-beaten, with a faint excited smile. A little girl followed him, driving two sheep and a goat; but she kept in our wake, while the old man walked beside me and talked about the morning and the valley. It was not much past six; and for healthy people who have slept enough, that is an hour of expansion and of open and trustful talk.

"Connaissez-vous le Seigneur?" he said at length.

I asked him what Seigneur he meant; but he only repeated the question with more emphasis and a look in his eyes denoting hope and interest.

"Ah," said I, pointing upwards, "I understand you now. Yes, I know Him; He is the best of acquaintances."

The old man said he was delighted. "Hold," he added, striking his bosom; "it makes me happy here." There were a few who know the Lord in these valleys, he went on to tell me; not many, but a few. "Many are called," he quoted, "and few chosen."

"My father," said I, "it is not easy to say who know the Lord; and it is none of our business. Protestants and Catholics, and even those who worship stones, may know Him and be known by Him; for He has made all."

I did not know I was so good a preacher.

The old man assured me he thought as I did, and repeated his expressions of pleasure at meeting me. "We are so few," he said. "They call us Moravians here; but down in the Department of Gard, where there are also a good number, they are called Derbists, after an English pastor."

I began to understand that I was figuring, in questionable taste, as a member of some sect to me unknown; but I was more pleased with the pleasure of my companion than embarrassed by my own equivocal position. Indeed, I can see no dishonesty in not avowing a difference; and especially in these high matters, where we have all a sufficient assurance that, whoever may be in the wrong, we ourselves are not completely in the right. The truth is much talked about; but this old man in a brown nightcap showed himself so simple, sweet, and friendly, that I am not unwilling to profess myself his convert. He was, as a matter of fact, a Plymouth Brother. Of what that involves in the way of doctrine I have no idea nor the time to inform myself; but I know right well that we are all embarked upon a troublesome world, the children of one Father, striving in many essential points to do and to become the same. And although it was somewhat in a mistake that he shook hands with me so often and showed himself so ready to receive my words, that was a mistake of the truth-finding sort. For charity begins blindfold; and only through a series of similar misapprehensions rises at length into a settled principle of love and patience, and a firm belief in all our fellow-men. If I deceived this good old man, in the like manner I would willingly go on to deceive others. And if ever at length, out of our separate and sad ways, we should all come together into one common house, I have a hope, to which I cling dearly, that my mountain Plymouth Brother will hasten to shake hands with me again.

Thus, talking like Christian and Faithful by the way, he and I came down upon a hamlet by the Tarn. It was but a humble place, called La Vernède, with less than a dozen houses, and a Protestant chapel on a knoll. Here he dwelt; and here, at the inn, I ordered my breakfast. The inn was kept by an agreeable young man, a stone-breaker on the road, and his sister, a pretty and engaging girl. The village schoolmaster dropped in to speak with the stranger. And these were all Protestants—a fact which pleased me more than I should have expected; and, what pleased me still more, they seemed all upright and simple people. The Plymouth Brother hung round me with a sort of yearning interest, and returned at least thrice to make sure I was enjoying my meal. His behaviour touched me deeply at the time, and even now moves me in recollection. He feared to intrude, but he would not willingly forgo one moment of my society; and he seemed never weary of shaking me by the hand.

When all the rest had drifted off to their day's work, I sat for near half an hour with the young mistress of the house, who talked pleasantly over her seam of the chestnut harvest, and the beauties of the Tarn, and old family affections, broken up when young folk go from home, yet still subsisting. Hers, I am sure, was a sweet nature, with a country plainness and much delicacy underneath; and he who takes her to his heart will doubtless be a fortunate young man.

The valley below La Vernède pleased me more and more as I went forward. Now the hills approached from either hand, naked and crumbling, and walled in the river between cliffs; and now the valley widened and became green. The road led me past the old castle of Miral on a steep; past a battlemented monastery, long since broken up and turned into a church and parsonage; and past a cluster of black roofs, the village of Cocurès, sitting among vineyards, and meadows, and orchards thick with red apples, and where, along the highway, they were knocking down walnuts from the roadside trees, and gathering them in sacks and baskets. The hills, however much the vale might open, were still tall and bare, with cliffy battlements and 'here and there a pointed summit; and the Tarn still rattled through the stones with a mountain noise. I had been led, by bagmen of a picturesque turn of mind, to expect a horrific country after the heart of Byron; but to my Scottish eyes it seemed smiling and plentiful, as the weather still gave an impression of high summer to my Scottish body; although the chestnuts were already picked out by the autumn, and the poplars, that here began to mingle with them, had turned into pale gold against the approach of winter.

There was something in this landscape, smiling although wild, that explained to me the spirit of the Southern Covenanters. Those who took to the hills for conscience' sake in Scotland had all gloomy and bedevilled thoughts; for once that they received God's comfort they would be twice engaged with Satan; but the Camisards had only bright and supporting visions. They dealt much more in blood, both given and taken; yet I find no obsession of the Evil One in their records. With a light conscience, they pursued their life in these rough times and circumstances. The soul of Séguier, let us not forget, was like a garden. They knew they were on God's side, with a knowledge that has no parallel among the Scots; for the Scots, although they might be certain of the cause, could never rest confident of the person.

"We flew," says one old Camisard, "when we heard the sound of psalm-singing, we flew as if with wings. We felt within us an animating ardour, a transporting desire. The feeling cannot be expressed in words. It is a thing that must have been experienced to be under-

stood. However weary we might be, we thought no
more of our weariness, and grew light so soon as the
psalms fell upon our ears.''

The valley of the Tarn and the people whom I met
at La Vernède not only explain to me this passage, but
the twenty years of suffering which those, who were so
stiff and so bloody when once they betook themselves
to war, endured with the meekness of children and the
constancy of saints and peasants.

FLORAC

On a branch of the Tarn stands Florac, the seat of a
sub-prefecture, with an old castle, an alley of planes,
many quaint street-corners, and a live fountain welling
from the hill. It is notable, besides, for handsome
women, and as one of the two capitals, Alais being the
other, of the country of the Camisards.

The landlord of the inn took me, after I had eaten,
to an adjoining *café*, where I, or rather my journey,
became the topic of the afternoon. Everyone had some
suggestion for my guidance; and the sub-prefectorial
map was fetched from the sub-prefecture itself, and
much thumbed among coffee-cups and glasses of liqueur.
Most of these kind advisers were Protestant, though I
observed that Protestant and Catholic intermingled in
a very easy manner; and it surprised me to see what a
lively memory still subsisted of the religious war.
Among the hills of the south-west, by Mauchline, Cum-
nock, or Carsphairn, in isolated farms or in the manse,
serious Presbyterian people still recall the days of the
great persecution, and the graves of local martyrs are
still piously regarded. But in towns and among the

so-called better classes, I fear that these old doings have
become an idle tale. If you met a mixed company in
the King's Arms at Wigtown, it is not likely that the
talk would run on Covenanters. Nay, at Muirkirk of
Glenluce, I found the beadle's wife had not so much
as heard of Prophet Peden. But these Cévenols were
proud of their ancestors in quite another sense; the war
was their chosen topic; its exploits were their own
patent of nobility; and where a man or a race has had
but one adventure, and that heroic, we must expect
and pardon some prolixity of reference. They told me
the country was still full of legends hitherto uncollected;
I heard from them about Cavalier's descendants—not
direct descendants, be it understood, but only cousins
or nephews—who were still prosperous people in the
scene of the boy-general's exploits; and one farmer had
seen the bones of old combatants dug up into the air
of an afternoon in the nineteenth century, in a field
where the ancestors had fought, and the great-grand-
children were peaceably ditching.

Later in the day one of the Protestant pastors was
so good as to visit me: a young man, intelligent and
polite, with whom I passed an hour or two in talk.
Florac, he told me, is part Protestant, part Catholic;
and the difference in religion is usually doubled by a
difference in politics. You may judge of my surprise,
coming as I did from such a babbling purgatorial Poland
of a place as Monastier, when I learned that the population lived together on very quiet terms; and there was
even an exchange of hospitalities between households
thus doubly separated. Black Camisard and White
Camisard, militiaman and Miquelet and dragoon,
Protestant prophet and Catholic cadet of the White
Cross, they had all been sabring and shooting, burning,

pillaging, and murdering, their hearts hot with indignant passion; and here, after a hundred and seventy years, Protestant is still Protestant, Catholic still Catholic, in mutual toleration and mild amity of life. But the race of man, like that indomitable nature whence it sprang, has medicating virtues of its own; the years and seasons bring various harvests; the sun returns after the rain; and mankind outlives secular animosities, as a single man awakens from the passions of a day. We judge our ancestors from a more divine position; and the dust being a little laid with several centuries, we can see both sides adorned with human virtues and fighting with a show of right.

I have never thought it easy to be just, and find it daily even harder than I thought. I own I met these Protestants with delight and a sense of coming home. I was accustomed to speak their language, in another and deeper sense of the word than that which distinguishes between French and English; for the true Babel is a divergence upon morals. And hence I could hold more free communication with the Protestants, and judge them more justly, than the Catholics. Father Apollinaris may pair off with my mountain Plymouth Brother as two guileless and devout old men; yet I ask myself if I had as ready a feeling for the virtues of the Trappist; or, had I been a Catholic, if I should have felt so warmly to the dissenter of La Vernède. With the first I was on terms of mere forbearance; but, with the other, although only on a misunderstanding and by keeping on selected points, it was still possible to hold converse and exchange some honest thoughts. In this world of imperfection we gladly welcome even partial intimacies. And if we find but one to whom we can speak out of our heart freely, with whom we can walk in love and simplicity without dissimulation, we have no ground of quarrel with the world or God.

IN THE VALLEY OF THE MIMENTE

On Tuesday, 1st October, we left Florac late in the afternoon, a tired donkey and tired donkey-driver. A little way up the Tarnon, a covered bridge of wood introduced us into the valley of the Mimente. Steep rocky red mountains overhung the stream; great oaks and chestnuts grew upon the slopes or in stony terraces; here and there was a red field of millet or a few apple-trees studded with red apples; and the road passed hard by two black hamlets, one with an old castle atop to please the heart of the tourist.

It was difficult here again to find a spot fit for my encampment. Even under the oaks and chestnuts the ground had not only a very rapid slope, but was heaped with loose stones; and where there was no timber the hills descended to the stream in a red precipice tufted with heather. The sun had left the highest peak in front of me, and the valley was full of the lowing sound of herdsmen's horns as they recalled the flocks into the stable, when I spied a bight of meadow some way below the roadway in an angle of the river. Thither I descended, and, tying Modestine provisionally to a tree, proceeded to investigate the neighbourhood. A grey pearly evening shadow filled the glen; objects at a little distance grew indistinct and melted bafflingly into each other; and the darkness was rising steadily like an exhalation. I approached a great oak which grew in the meadow, hard by the river's brink; when to my disgust the voices of children fell upon my ear, and I beheld a house round the angle on the other bank. I had half a mind to pack and be gone again, but the growing darkness moved me to remain. I had only to make no noise until the night was fairly come, and trust to the dawn to call me early in the morning. But it was hard to be annoyed by neighbours in such a great hotel.

A hollow underneath the oak was my bed. Before I had fed Modestine and arranged my sack, three stars were already brightly shining, and the others were beginning dimly to appear. I slipped down to the river, which looked very black among its rocks, to fill my can; and dined with a good appetite in the dark, for I scrupled to light a lantern while so near a house. The moon, which I had seen a pallid crescent all afternoon, faintly illuminated the summit of the hills, but not a ray fell into the bottom of the glen where I was lying. The oak rose before me like a pillar of darkness; and overhead the heartsome stars were set in the face of the night. No one knows the stars who has not slept, as the French happily put it, *à la belle étoile*. He may know all their names and distances and magnitudes, and yet be ignorant of what alone concerns mankind—their serene and gladsome influence on the mind. The greater part of poetry is about the stars; and very justly, for they are themselves the most classical of poets. These same far-away worlds, sprinkled like tapers or shaken together like a diamond dust upon the sky, had looked not otherwise to Roland or Cavalier, when, in the words of the latter, they had "no other tent but the sky, and no other bed than my mother earth."

All night a strong wind blew up the valley, and the acorns fell pattering over me from the oak. Yet, on this first night of October, the air was as mild as May, and I slept with the fur thrown back.

I was much disturbed by the barking of a dog, an animal that I fear more than any wolf. A dog is vastly braver, and is besides supported by the sense of duty. If you kill a wolf, you meet with encouragement and praise; but if you kill a dog, the sacred rights of property and the domestic affections come clamouring round you for redress. At the end of a fagging day, the sharp cruel note of a dog's bark is in itself a keen annoyance; and to a tramp like myself, he represents the sedentary and respectable world in its most hostile form. There is something of the clergyman or the lawyer about this engaging animal; and if he were not amenable to stones, the boldest man would shrink from travelling afoot. I respect dogs much in the domestic circle; but on the highway, or sleeping afield, I both detest and fear them.

I was awakened next morning (Wednesday, 2nd October) by the same dog—for I knew his bark—making a charge down the bank, and then, seeing me sit up, retreating again with great alacrity. The stars were not yet quite extinguished. The heaven was of that enchanting mild grey-blue of the early morn. A still clear light began to fall, and the trees on the hillside were outlined sharply against the sky. The wind had veered more to the north, and no longer reached me in the glen; but as I was going on with my preparations, it drove a white cloud very swiftly over the hill-top; and looking up, I was surprised to see the cloud dyed with gold. In these high regions of the air, the sun was already shining as at noon. If only the clouds travelled high enough, we should see the same thing all night long. For it is always daylight in the fields of space.

As I began to go up the valley, a draught of wind

came down it out of the seat of sunrise, although the
clouds continued to run overhead in an almost contrary
direction. A few steps farther, and I saw a whole
hillside gilded wit the sun; and still a little beyond,
between two peaks a centre of dazzling brilliancy
appeared floating in the sky, and I was once more face
to face with the big bonfire that occupies the kernel
of our system.

I met but one human being that forenoon, a dark
military-looking wayfarer, who carried a game-bag on
a baldric; but he made a remark that seems worthy
of record. For when I asked him if he were Protestant
or Catholic—

"Oh," said he. "I make no shame of my religion. I
am a Catholic."

He made no shame of it! The phrase is a piece of
natural statistics; for it is the language of one in a
minority. I thought with a smile of Bavile and his
dragoons, and how you may ride rough-shod over a
religion for a century, and leave it only the more lively
for the friction. Ireland is still Catholic; the Cevennes
still Protestant. It is not a basketful of law-papers,
nor the hoofs and pistol-butts of a regiment of horse,
that can change one tittle of a ploughman's thoughts.
Outdoor rustic people have not many ideas, but such
as they have are hardy plants, and thrive flourishingly
in persecution. One who has grown a long while in
the sweat of laborious noons, and under the stars at
night, a frequenter of hills and forests, an old honest
countryman, has, in the end, a sense of communion
with the powers of the universe, and amicable relations
towards his God. Like my mountain Plymouth Brother,
he knows the Lord. His religion does not repose upon
a choice of logic; it is the poetry of the man's experience,

the philosophy of the history of his life. God, a
great power, like a great shining sun, has appeared
this simple fellow in the course of years, and become
the ground and essence of his least reflections; and you
may change creeds and dogmas by authority, or proclaim
a new religion with the sound of trumpets, if you will;
but here is a man who has his own thoughts, and will
stubbornly adhere to them in good and evil. He is a
Catholic, a Protestant, or a Plymouth Brother, in the
same indefeasible sense that a man is not a woman, or a
woman not a man. For he could not vary from his
faith, unless he could eradicate all memory of the past,
and, in a strict and not a conventional meaning, change
his mind.

THE HEART OF THE COUNTRY

I was now drawing near to Cassagnas, a cluster of black
roofs upon the hillside, in this wild valley, among chestnut gardens, and looked upon in the clear air by many
rocky peaks. The road along the Mimente is yet new,
nor have the mountaineers recovered their surprise
when the first cart arrived at Cassagnas. But although
it lay thus apart from the current of men's business,
this hamlet had already made a figure in the history of
France. Hard by, in caverns of the mountain, was one
of the five arsenals of the Camisards; where they laid
up clothes and corn and arms against necessity, forged
bayonets and sabres, and made themselves gunpowder
with willow charcoal and saltpetre boiled in kettles.
To the same caves, amid this multifarious industry,
the sick and wounded were brought up to heal; and
there they were visited by the two surgeons, Chabrier

and Tavan, and secretly nursed by women of the neighbourhood.

Of the five legions into which the Camisards were divided, it was the oldest and the most obscure that had its magazines by Cassagnas. This was the band of Spirit Séguier; men who had joined their voices with his in the 68th Psalm as they marched down by night on the Archpriest of the Cevennes. Séguier, promoted to heaven, was succeeded by Salomon Couderc, whom Cavalier treats in his memoirs as chaplain-general to the whole army of the Camisards. He was a prophet; a great reader of the heart, who admitted people to the sacrament or refused them, by "intentively viewing every man" between the eyes; and had the most of the Scriptures off by rote. And this was surely happy; since in a surprise in August, 1703, he lost his mule, his portfolios, and his Bible. It is only strange that they were not surprised more often and more effectually; for this legion of Cassagnas was truly patriarchal in its theory of war, and camped without sentries, leaving that duty to the angels of the God for whom they fought. This is a token, not only of their faith, but of the trackless country where they harboured. M. de Caladon, taking a stroll one fine day, walked without warning into their midst, as he might have walked into "a flock of sheep in a plain," and found some asleep and some awake and psalm-singing. A traitor had need of no recommendation to insinuate himself among their ranks, beyond "his faculty of singing psalms"; and even the prophet Salomon "took him into a particular friendship." Thus, among their intricate hills, the rustic troop subsisted; and history can attribute few exploits to them but sacraments and ecstasies.

People of this tough and simple stock will not, as I

have just been saying, prove variable in religion; nor
will they get nearer to apostasy than a mere external
conformity like that of Naaman in the house of Rimmon.
When Louis XVI, in the words of the edict, "convinced
by the uselessness of a century of persecutions, and
rather from necessity than sympathy," granted at last a
royal grace of toleration, Cassagnas was still Protestant;
and to a man, it is so to this day. There is, indeed,
one family that is not Protestant, but neither is it
Catholic. It is that of a Catholic *curé* in revolt, who has
taken to his bosom a schoolmistress. And his conduct,
it is worth noting, is disapproved by the Protestant
villagers.

"It is a bad idea for a man," said one, "to go back
from his engagements."

The villagers whom I saw seemed intelligent after a
countrified fashion, and were all plain and dignified in
manner. As a Protestant myself, I was well looked
upon, and my acquaintance with history gained me
further respect. For we had something not unlike a
religious controversy at table, a gendarme and a merchant with whom I dined being both strangers to the
place, and Catholics. The young men of the house
stood round and supported me; and the whole discussion
was tolerantly conducted, and surprised a man brought
up among the infinitesimal and contentious differences
of Scotland. The merchant, indeed, grew a little warm,
and was far less pleased than some others with my
historical acquirements. But the gendarme was mighty
easy over it all.

"It's a bad idea for a man to change," said he; and
the remark was generally applauded.

That was not the opinion of the priest and soldier at
Our Lady of the Snows. But this is a different race;

and perhaps the same great-heartedness that upheld them to resist, now enables them to differ in a kind spirit. For courage respects courage; but where a faith has been trodden out, we may look for a mean and narrow population. The true work of Bruce and Wallace was the union of the nations; not that they should stand apart a while longer, skirmishing upon their borders; but that, when the time came, they might unite with self-respect.

The merchant was much interested in my journey, and thought it dangerous to sleep afield.

"There are the wolves," said he; "and then it is known you are an Englishman. The English have always long purses, and it might very well enter into someone's head to deal you an ill blow some night."

I told him I was not much afraid of such accidents; and at any rate judged it unwise to dwell upon alarms or consider small perils in the arrangement of life. Life itself, I submitted, was a far too risky business as a whole to make each additional particular of danger worth regard. "Something," said I, "might burst in your inside any day of the week, and there would be an end of you, if you were locked into your room with three turns of the key."

"*Cependant,*" said he, "*coucher dehors!*"

"God," said I, "is everywhere."

"*Cependant, coucher dehors!*" he repeated, and his voice was eloquent of terror.

He was the only person, in all my voyage, who saw anything hardy in so simple a proceeding; although many considered it superfluous. Only one, on the other hand, professed much delight in the idea; and that was my Plymouth Brother, who cried out, when I told him I sometimes preferred sleeping under the stars to a close and noisy alehouse, "Now I see that you know the Lord!"

The merchant asked me for one of my cards as I was leaving, for he said I should be something to talk of in the future, and desired me to make a note of his request and reason; a desire with which I have thus complied.

A little after two I struck across the Mimente, and took a rugged path southward up a hillside covered with loose stones and tufts of heather. At the top, as is the habit of the country, the path disappeared; and I left my she-ass munching heather, and went forward alone to seek a road.

I was now on the separation of two vast watersheds; behind me all the streams were bound for the Garonne and the Western Ocean; before me was the basin of the Rhone. Hence, as from the Lozère, you can see in clear weather the shining of the Gulf of Lyons; and perhaps from here the soldiers of Salomon may have watched for the topsails of Sir Cloudesley Shovel, and the long-promised aid from England. You may take this ridge as lying in the heart of the country of the Camisards; four of the five legions camped all round it and almost within view—Salomon and Joani to the north, Castanet and Roland to the south; and when Julien had finished his famous work, the devastation of the High Cevennes, which lasted all through October and November, 1703, and during which four hundred and sixty villages and hamlets were, with fire and pickaxe, utterly subverted, a man standing on this eminence would have looked forth upon a silent, smokeless, and dispeopled land. Time and man's activity have now repaired these ruins; Cassagnas is once more roofed and sending up domestic smoke; and in the chestnut gardens, in low and leafy corners, many a prosperous farmer returns, when the day's work is done, to his children and bright hearth. And still it was perhaps the wildest view of all my journey. Peak upon peak, chain upon chain of hills ran surging southward, channelled and sculptured by the winter streams, feathered from head to foot with chestnuts, and here and there breaking out into a coronal of cliffs. The sun, which was still far from setting, sent a drift of misty gold across the hill-tops, but the valleys were already plunged in a profound and quiet shadow.

A very old shepherd, hobbling on a pair of sticks, and wearing a black cap of liberty, as if in honour of his nearness to the grave, directed me to the road for St. Germain de Calberte. There was something solemn in the isolation of this infirm and ancient creature. Where he dwelt, how he got upon this high ridge, or how he proposed to get down again, were more than I could fancy. Not far off upon my right was the famous Plan de Font Morte, where Poul with his Armenian sabre slashed down the Camisards of Séguier. This, methought, might be some Rip Van Winkle of the war, who had lost his comrades, fleeing before Poul, and wandered ever since upon the mountains. It might be news to him that Cavalier had surrendered, or Roland had fallen fighting with his back against an olive. And while I was thus working on my fancy, I heard him hailing in broken tones, and saw him waving me to come back with one of his two sticks. I had already got some way past him; but, leaving Modestine once more, retraced my steps.

Alas, it was a very commonplace affair. The old gentleman had forgot to ask the pedlar what he sold, and wished to remedy this neglect.

I told him sternly, "Nothing."

"Nothing?" cried he.

I repeated "Nothing," and made off.

It's odd to think of, but perhaps I thus became as inexplicable to the old man as he had been to me.

The road lay under chestnuts, and though I saw a hamlet or two below me in the vale, and many lone houses of the chestnut farmers, it was a very solitary march all afternoon; and the evening began early underneath the trees. But I heard the voice of a woman singing some sad, old, endless ballad not far off. It seemed to be about love and a *bel amoureux*, her handsome sweetheart; and I wished I could have taken up the strain and answered her, as I went on upon my invisible woodland way, weaving, like Pippa in the poem, my own thoughts with hers. What could I have told her? Little enough; and yet all the heart requires. How the world gives and takes away, and brings sweethearts near only to separate them again into distant and strange lands; but to love is the great amulet which makes the world a garden; and "hope, which comes to all," outwears the accidents of life, and reaches with tremulous hand beyond the grave and death. Easy to say: yea, but also, by God's mercy, both easy and grateful to believe!

We struck at last into a wide white high-road carpeted with noiseless dust. The night had come; the moon had been shining for a long while upon the opposite mountain; when on turning a corner my donkey and I issued ourselves into her light. I had emptied out my brandy at Florac, for I could bear the stuff no longer, and replaced it with some generous and scented Volnay; and now I drank to the moon's sacred majesty upon the road. It was but a couple of mouthfuls; yet I became thenceforth unconscious of my limbs, and my blood flowed with luxury. Even Módestine was inspired by this purified nocturnal sunshine, and bestirred her little hoofs as to a livelier measure. The road wound and descended swiftly among masses of chestnuts. Hot dust rose from our feet and flowed away. Our two shadows—mine deformed with the knapsack, hers comically bestridden by the pack—now lay before us clearly outlined on the road, and now, as we turned a corner, went off into the ghostly distance, and sailed along the mountain like clouds. From time to time a warm wind rustled down the valley, and set all the chestnuts dangling their bunches of foliage and fruit; the ear was filled with whispering music, and the shadows danced in tune. And next moment the breeze had gone by, and in all the valley nothing moved except our travelling feet. On the opposite slope, the monstrous ribs and gullies of the mountain were faintly designed in the moonshine; and high overhead, in some lone house, there burned one lighted window, one square spark of red in the huge field of sad nocturnal colouring.

At a certain point, as I went downward, turning many acute angles, the moon disappeared behind the hill; and I pursued my way in great darkness, until another turning shot me without preparation into St. Germain de Calberte. The place was asleep and silent, and buried in opaque night. Only from a single open door, some lamplight escaped upon the road to show me that I was come among men's habitations. The two last gossips of the evening, still talking by a garden wall, directed me to the inn. The landlady was getting her chicks to bed; the fire was already out, and had, not without grumbling, to be rekindled; half an hour later, and I must have gone supperless to roost.

THE LAST DAY

WHEN I awoke (Thursday, 3rd October), and, hearing a
great flourishing of cocks and chuckling of contented
hens, betook me to the window of the clean and comfortable room where I had slept the night, I looked forth on
a sunshiny morning in a deep vale of chestnut gardens.
It was still early, and the cockcrows, and the slanting
lights, and the long shadows, encouraged me to be out
and look round me.

St. Germain de Calberte is a great parish nine leagues
round about. At the period of the wars, and immediately before the devastation, it was inhabited by two
hundred and seventy-five families, of which only nine
were Catholic; and it took the *curé* seventeen September
days to go from house to house on horseback for a
census. But the place itself, although capital of a canton, is scarce larger than a hamlet. It lies terraced across
a steep slope in the midst of mighty chestnuts. The
Protestant chapel stands below upon a shoulder; in the
midst of the town is the quaint old Catholic church.

It was here that poor Du Chayla, the Christian martyr,
kept his library and held a court of missionaries; here he
had built his tomb, thinking to lie among a grateful
population whom he had redeemed from error; and
hither on the morrow of his death they brought the body,
pierced with two-and-fifty wounds, to be interred. Clad
in his priestly robes, he was laid out in state in the church.
The *curé*, taking his text from Second Samuel, twentieth
chapter and twelfth verse, "And Amasa wallowed in his
blood in the highway," preached a rousing sermon, and
exhorted his brethren to die each at his post, like their
unhappy and illustrious superior. In the midst of this
eloquence there came a breeze that Spirit Séguier was

near at hand; and behold! all the assembly took to their
horses' heels, some east, some west, and the *curé* himself
as far as Alais.

Strange was the position of this little Catholic metro-
polis, a thimbleful of Rome, in such a wild and contrary
neighbourhood.   On the one hand, the legion of Salomon overlooked it from Cassagnas; on the other it was
cut off from assistance by the legion of Roland at Mialet.
The *curé* Louvrelenil, although he took a panic at the
archpriest's funeral, and so hurriedly decamped to Alais,
stood well by his isolated pulpit, and thence uttered
fulminations against the crimes of the Protestants.
Salomon besieged the village for an hour and a half, but
was beaten back.   The militiamen, on guard before the
curé's door, could be heard, in the black hours, singing
Protestant psalms and holding friendly talk with the
insurgents.   And in the morning, although not a shot
had been fired, there would not be a round of powder in
their flasks.   Where was it gone?   All handed over to
the Camisards for a consideration.   Untrusty guardians
for an isolated priest!

That these continual stirs were once busy in St.
Germain de Calberte, the imagination with difficulty
receives; all is now so quiet, the pulse of human life now
beats so low and still in this hamlet of the mountains.
Boys followed me a great way off, like a timid sort of
lion-hunters; and people turned round to have a second
look, or came out of their houses, as I went by.   My
passage was the first event, you would have fancied,
since the Camisards.   There was nothing rude or forward in this observation; it was but a pleased and wondering scrutiny, like that of oxen or the human infant;
yet it wearied my spirits, and soon drove me from the
street.

I took refuge on the terraces, which are here greenly carpeted with sward, and tried to imitate with a pencil the inimitable attitudes of the chestnuts as they bear up their canopy of leaves. Ever and again a little wind went by, and the nuts dropped all around me, with a light and dull sound, upon the sward. The noise was as of a thin fall of great hailstones; but there went with it a cheerful human sentiment of an approaching harvest and farmers rejoicing in their gains. Looking up, I could see the brown nut peering through the husk, which was already gaping; and between the stems the eye embraced an amphitheatre of hill, sunlit and green with leaves.

I have not often enjoyed a place more deeply. I moved in an atmosphere of pleasure, and felt light and quiet and content. But perhaps it was not the place alone that so disposed my spirit. Perhaps someone was thinking of me in another country; or perhaps some thought of my own had come and gone unnoticed, and yet done me good. For some thoughts, which sure would be the most beautiful, vanish before we can rightly scan their features; as though a god, travelling by our green highways, should but ope the door, give one smiling look into the house, and go again for ever. Was it Apollo, or Mercury, or Love with folded wings? Who shall say? But we go the lighter about our business, and feel peace and pleasure in our hearts.

I dined with a pair of Catholics. They agreed in the condemnation of a young man, a Catholic, who had married a Protestant girl and gone over to the religion of his wife. A Protestant born they could understand and respect; indeed, they seemed to be of the mind of an old Catholic woman, who told me that same day there was no difference between the two sects, save that "wrong was more wrong for the Catholic," who had more light and guidance; but this of a man's desertion filled them with contempt.

"It is a bad idea for a man to change," said one.

It may have been accidental, but you see how this phrase pursued me; and for myself, I believe it is the current philosophy in these parts. I have some difficulty in imagining a better. It's not only a great flight of confidence for a man to change his creed and go out of his family for heaven's sake; but the odds are—nay, and the hope is—that, with all this great transition in the eyes of man, he has not changed himself a hairbreadth to the eyes of God. Honour to those who do so, for the wrench is sore. But it argues something narrow, whether of strength or weakness, whether of the prophet or the fool, in those who can take a sufficient interest in such infinitesimal and human operations, or who can quit a friendship for a doubtful process of the mind. And I think I should not leave my old creed for another, changing only words for other words; but by some brave reading, embrace it in spirit and truth, and find wrong as wrong for me as for the best of other communions.

The phylloxera was in the neighbourhood; and instead of wine we drank at dinner a more economical juice of the grape—La Parisienne, they call it. It is made by putting the fruit whole into a cask with water; one by one the berries ferment and burst; what is drunk during the day is supplied at night in water: so, with ever another pitcher from the well, and ever another grape exploding and giving out its strength, one cask of Parisienne may last a family till spring. It is, as the reader will anticipate, a feeble beverage, but very pleasant to the taste.

What with dinner and coffee, it was long past three before I left St. Germain de Calberte. I went down beside the Gardon of Mialet, a great glaring watercourse devoid of water, and through St. Etienne de Vallée Française, or Val Francesque, as they used to call it; and towards evening began to ascend the hill of St. Pierre. It was a long and steep ascent. Behind me an empty carriage returning to St. Jean du Gard kept hard upon my tracks, and near the summit overtook me. The driver, like the rest of the world, was sure I was a pedlar; but, unlike others, he was sure of what I had to sell. He had noticed the blue wool which hung out of my pack at either end; and from this he had decided, beyond my power to alter his decision, that I dealt in blue-wool collars, such as decorate the neck of the French draught-horse.

I had hurried to the topmost powers of Modestine, for I dearly desired to see the view upon the other side before the day had faded. But it was night when I reached the summit; the moon was riding high and clear; and only a few grey streaks of twilight lingered in the west. A yawning valley, gulfed in blackness, lay like a hole in created nature at my feet; but the outline of the hills was sharp against the sky. There was Mount Aigoal, the stronghold of Castanet. And Castanet, not only as an active undertaking leader, deserves some mention among Camisards; for there is a spray of rose among his laurel; and he showed how, even in a public tragedy, love will have its way. In the high tide of war he married, in his mountain citadel, a young and pretty lass called Mariette. There were great rejoicings; and the bride-groom released five-and-twenty prisoners in honour of the glad event. Seven months afterwards, Mariette, the Princess of the Cevennes, as they called her in derision, fell into the hands of the authorities, where it was like to have gone hard with her. But Castanet was a man of execution, and loved his wife. He fell on Valleraugue, and got a lady there for a hostage; and for the first and last time in that war there was an exchange of prisoners. Their daughter, pledge of some starry night upon Mount Aigoal, has left descendants to this day.

Modestine and I—it was our last meal together—had a snack upon the top of St. Pierre, I on a heap of stones, she standing by me in the moonlight and decorously eating bread out of my hand. The poor brute would eat more heartily in this manner; for she had a sort of affection for me, which I was soon to betray.

It was a long descent upon St. Jean du Gard, and we met no one but a carter, visible afar off by the glint of the moon on his extinguished lantern.

Before ten o'clock we had got in and were at supper: fifteen miles and a stiff hill in little beyond six hours!

FAREWELL, MODESTINE!

ON examination, on the morning of 4th October, Modestine was pronounced unfit for travel. She would need at least two days' repose, according to the ostler; but I was now eager to reach Alais for my letters; and, being in a civilised country of stage-coaches, I determined to sell my lady friend and be off by the diligence that afternoon. Our yesterday's march, with the testimony of the driver who had pursued us up the long hill of St. Pierre, spread a favourable notion of my donkey's capabilities. Intending purchasers were aware of an unrivalled opportunity. Before ten I had an offer of twenty-five francs; and before noon, after a desperate engagement, I sold her, saddle and all, for five-and-thirty. The pecuniary gain is not obvious, but I had bought freedom into the bargain.

St. Jean du Gard is a large place, and largely Protestant. The maire, a Protestant, asked me to help him in a small matter which is itself characteristic of the country. The young women of the Cevennes profit by the common religion and the difference of the language to go largely as governesses into England; and here was one, a native of Mialet, struggling with English circulars from two different agencies in London. I gave what help I could; and volunteered some advice, which struck me as being excellent.

One thing more I note. The phylloxera has ravaged the vineyards in this neighbourhood; and in the early morning, under some chestnuts by the river, I found a party of men working with a cider-press. I could not at first make out what they were after, and asked one fellow to explain.

"Making cider," he said. *"Oui, c'est comme ça. Comme dans le nord!"*

There was a ring of sarcasm in his voice: the country was going to the devil.

It was not until I was fairly seated by the driver, and rattling through a rocky valley with dwarf olives, that I became aware of my bereavement. I had lost Modestine. Up to that moment I had thought I hated her; but now she was gone,

And oh!
The difference to me!

For twelve days we had been fast companions; we had travelled upwards of a hundred and twenty miles, crossed several respectable ridges, and jogged along with our six legs by many a rocky and many a boggy by-road. After the first day, although sometimes I was hurt and distant in manner, I still kept my patience; and as for her, poor soul! she had come to regard me as a god. She loved to eat out of my hand. She was patient, elegant in form, the colour of an ideal mouse, and inimitably small. Her faults were those of her race and sex; her virtues were her own. Farewell, and if for ever——

Father Adam wept when he sold her to me; after I had sold her in my turn, I was tempted to follow his example; and being alone with a stage-driver and four or five agreeable young men, I did not hesitate to yield to my emotion.

LITERARY ALLUSIONS IN "TRAVELS WITH A DONKEY"

ÆSOP: A Greek writer of fables—a Thracian or Phrygian slave who lived in the sixth century B.C.

ARNOLD, MATTHEW:

> "I behold
> The House, the brotherhood austere."

This is from Stanzas from the Grande Chartreuse.

CHATEAUBRIAND: A writer and politician opposed to the French Revolution.

CHRISTIAN: From Bunyan's *Pilgrim's Progress*. His "pack" was the burden of his sins. See also Christian and Faithful in the section *The Valley of the Tarn*.

CORTEZ: "like stout Cortez . . ." From Keats' sonnet "On first looking into Chapman's Homer."

COTTON, MATHER: Puritan. Wrote a history of New England from the religious angle.

THE IMITATION OF CHRIST: The great devotional book written by Thomas à Kempis in the fifteenth century.

MILTON. "A little further lend thy guiding hand." This is a misquotation from *Samson Agonistes*—"further" should be "onward."

MOLIÈRE: The great French writer of Comedy. 1622–73.

MONTAIGNE: French writer who invented the Essay. 1533–92.

NAAMAN IN THE HOUSE OF RIMMON: See 2 Kings v. 18.

ODES AND BALLADES: By Victor Hugo.

PIPPA: From Browning's poem *Pippa Passes*—about the effect of a happy girl's song on everyone who heard her.

POPE, ALEXANDER: The line "Though I could reach from pole to pole" is not by Pope. R. L. S. may have been thinking of Watts.

PSALM LXVIII.: "Let God arise and let His enemies be scattered."

RIP VAN WINKLE: From Washington Irving's *Sketch Book*—about a man who returned to his village after a sleep of twenty years.

SPENCER, HERBERT: A nineteenth-century English philosopher
—a materialist.

ULYSSES (*Greek*—Odysseus): Was left on his island ‚home of
Ithaca in his sleep, by the Phœnicians. Athene was the
goddess.

WAVERLEY NOVELS: The novels of Sir Walter Scott.

WORDSWORTH: (*a*) "Mountains and vales and floods." Quotation formed from the sonnet beginning "Proud were ye,
mountains . . ."

(*b*)   ". . . And oh!
The difference to me!"

This is from the Lucy poem, beginning "She dwelt among the
untrodden ways."

QUESTIONS ON "TRAVELS WITH A DONKEY"

THE DONKEY, THE PACK, AND THE PACK-SADDLE

1. Describe a sleeping-sack as devised and used by R. L. S.
2. "Like Christian, it was from my pack I suffered on the way." Explain the allusion.

THE GREEN DONKEY-DRIVER

3. Look up *Deus ex machina*, and find out what it means.
4. "I prooted mellifluously like a sucking dove." What is the allusion?

I HAVE A GOAD

5. "Blessed be the man who invented goads!" Explain what happened.

A CAMP IN THE DARK

6. Why did R. L. S. and Modestine spend the night in the open?

CHEYLARD AND LUC

7. "A melodrama kitchen." Why does he thus describe the kitchen at Luc? What was the landlady like?

FATHER APOLLINARIS

8. "Penny plain and twopence coloured." Look up the essay by R. L. S. on this very subject. You will find it in *Memories and Portraits*, No. 13.
9. "Father Michael, the Father Hospitaller." What does this mean? Look it up.

THE MONKS

10. What does R. L. S. tell us of the monks' hobbies, and their reading?

THE BOARDERS

11. Look out "Trappists" in the encyclopædia.

ACROSS THE GOULET and A NIGHT AMONG THE PINES

12. What sounds are mentioned in these two chapters?

ACROSS THE LOZÈRE and PONT DE MONTVERT

13. Who were the Camisards?　Write a brief note or précis of this story.

14. "And Clarisse?　What shall I say of Clarisse?"　Briefly, what does he say of Clarisse?

IN THE VALLEY OF THE TARN

15. R. L. S. says "At that date (1703) Anthony Watteau would be painting similar subjects."　Find out all you can about Anthony Watteau and his pictures.

FLORAC

16. "You may judge of my surprise when I learned that the population lived together on very quiet terms."　Explain this in your own words.

IN THE VALLEY OF THE MIMENTE

17. Write a note about the stars and what you yourself have thought about them.

THE HEART OF THE COUNTRY

18. Look up the story of Naaman and the house of Rimmon.

THE LAST DAY

19. "The phylloxera was in the neighbourhood."　What was this?

FAREWELL, MODESTINE!

20. "—but now she was gone,
　　　　　　'And oh!
　　　The difference to me!' "
Who wrote this? and what is he referring to?　See Literary Allusions, and then look it up.